Metropolitan Anthony of Sourozh

Metropolitan Anthony in the Cathedral gallery, where he dealt with correspondence. Portrait by Kirill Sokolov, 1980. Oil, collage, plywood.

Metropolitan Anthony of Sourozh
A Life

Avril Pyman

The Lutterworth Press

The Lutterworth Press
P.O. Box 60
Cambridge
CB1 2NT
United Kingdom

www.lutterworth.com
publishing@lutterworth.com

ISBN: 978 0 7188 9449 8

British Library Cataloguing in Publication Data
A record is available from the British Library

Copyright © Avril Pyman, 2016

First Published, 2016

All rights reserved. No part of this edition may be reproduced, stored electronically or in any retrieval system, or transmitted in any form or by any means, electronic, mechanical, photocopying, recording, or otherwise, without prior written permission from the Publisher (permissions@lutterworth.com).

Contents

List of Illustrations		vii
Foreword		ix
Acknowledgements		xiii
CHAPTER ONE.	From Prince to Pauper: Origins and Childhood, 1914-1922	1
CHAPTER TWO.	Alienation and Revelation: Growing up in Exile, 1922-1929	8
CHAPTER THREE.	Conflicting Vocations: The Formation of a Monk "in the World", 1928-1937	16
CHAPTER FOUR.	Surgeon in the French Army and Monk in the Surgery, 1937-1949	32
CHAPTER FIVE.	Priesthood, Move to London, Ministry in the Russian Orthodox Church in Great Britain, 1949-1957	45
CHAPTER SIX.	Fame in a Divided World, 1957-1963	68
CHAPTER SEVEN.	The International Arena, 1963-1974	89
CHAPTER EIGHT.	The Consolidation of the Second Diocese of Sourozh, 1974-1989	121
CHAPTER NINE.	Mission to Russia and New Problems in England, 1983-2003	156
CHAPTER TEN.	Agony	184
Endnotes		199
Glossary of Proper Names		230
Index of Proper Names		273

List of Illustrations

Note: All images are used with permission of the MASF Archive in Moscow.

Metropolitan Anthony in the gallery of the Cathedral where he dealt with correspondence, portrait by Kirill Sokolov, 1980. Oil, collage, plywood.	ii
Andrei Bloom with his mother and grandmother, June 1914	3
Andrei as a toddler with his father, Boris Eduardovich Bloom	5
Andrei as a child in Persia	6
Andrei as a schoolboy with mother and grandmother, France	10
Andrei as a boy with other *Vitiazi* and Father Georgii Shumkin at summer camp in France	11
Archimandrite Afanasii (Nechaev), Anthony's spiritual father	19
Camp leader in France with ACER	21
Passport photograph, 1939	33
In uniform with mother and grandmother before leaving for the front, 1939	35
Surgeon, 1943	39
At the Fellowship of St Alban and St Sergius (FSASS) conference, 1948, with Father Georgii Florovsky and Vladimir Lossky	43
Anthony as a young priest in London, 1949	49
At the conference of the FSASS, 1952	51

Consecration as Bishop, 30 November 1957	71
Summer camp, July 1979	77
The Blessing of the Waters of the Thames, 1960	78
The Holy Mountain, Athos, 1963	93
With Patriarch Aleksii I, 1964	99
London, 1966. Archbishop Vasilii Krivoshein, Archbishop Michael Ramsey, Metropolitan Anthony, Bishop Vladimir Sabodan, Archpriest Vitalii Borovoi	105
Addressing the Moscow Theological Academy, December 1966	107
Blessing the congregation in the Church of St Nicholas in Khamovniki, Moscow, 1969	113
Metropolitan Anthony answering questions at an informal private meeting in Moscow, 1971 or 1972	117
In Finland, 1974	122
Report of Browning Award for Lifetime Achievement, 1974	123
Break in talks with a Methodist group in Kemble, 2 June 1984	129
Interior of the Cathedral in Ennismore Gardens	135
Icon of the saints of Great Britain and Ireland	147
Anthony's seventieth birthday celebration, June 1984	153
Celebration of 400 years of Moscow Patriarchate, October 1989	163
In the Cathedral bookshop, August 1995	169
Committal, 13 August 2003, Deacon Peter Scorer	198

Foreword

The story of Metropolitan Anthony (Bloom) is many-sided. Born in Lausanne, the son of a diplomat and member of the "serving aristocracy" of Tsarist Russia, he spent his childhood in Persia, his father's last diplomatic posting, and then, after the Revolution, ended up, as so many Russians did, in Paris. There he trained as a doctor and became (in secret) a monk. After the war he was ordained priest and soon given the rather odd appointment of Chaplain to the Fellowship of St Alban and St Sergius in England – odd, because though he was linguistically talented, English was not one of his languages. In England he became priest to one of the Russian Orthodox parishes in London, eventually at the Russian Orthodox Cathedral in Ennismore Gardens in Kensington, becoming Bishop, Archbishop, and finally Metropolitan of Sourozh, as well as for a time Patriarchal Exarch to Western Europe. During the 1960s and 1970s he became well-known outside Orthodox circles, and was for many a beacon of an assured, and intelligent, faith in a period of much questioning and doubt among Christians in the West, not least in England. This witness to traditional orthodox Christianity was, in a way, symbolised in the television debate he engaged in with the famous atheist intellectual, Marghanita Laski, in 1970 – "traditional, orthodox", but still surprising and challenging: in response to Laski's puzzlement at his belief in God, Metropolitan Anthony replied, " . . . it seems to me that the word 'belief' is misleading. It gives the impression of something optional. . . . I believe because I know that God exists, and I'm puzzled how you manage not to know."

He remained in England, leading the Russian Orthodox Church until his death in 2003, seeing his church develop from a congregation of Russian émigrés to a mixed congregation of Orthodox of all backgrounds, including many English converts – a living witness to, and embodiment of, the universality of Orthodoxy. This is, however, only part of the story. During the 1960s and 1970s especially, he became well-known in the Soviet Union through his broadcast sermons, which – along with the sermons by the

Russian Orthodox theologian and exile, Fr Alexander Schmemann, then living in the United States – kept alive the flame of the faith in the midst of an atheist regime intent on exterminating any trace of Christianity. Many owed their faith to these sermons, which presented Orthodoxy not as a relic from the past, but as a living, and intelligent, faith.

Metropolitan Anthony's presentation of Orthodoxy was in many ways unique, for all its faithfulness to tradition. He himself had rediscovered his ancestral faith by reading – in order to expose once and for all to his rebellious mind its falsity – St Mark's Gospel. As he read, he became convinced of the presence of the risen Christ, and found a faith that never thereafter deserted him. He had little time for academic theology, little time for a human confection of concepts, however clever (or especially if clever). Faith grew from experience and that experience was something to be found, and nourished, in prayer. Metropolitan Anthony would have been surprised to be thought of as a theologian, but such he was: speaking from his heart, from his experience, of what he knew (think of his remark to Marghanita Laski at the beginning of the aforementioned interview). He spoke, too, of prayer. But above all, he communicated: there were no treatises, but an abundance of sermons and talks, and perhaps even more important the communication that took place in conversation. He would also have disdained the sobriquet "intellectual", but his understanding was based on a profound intellectual commitment, and a willingness to question ideas that made little sense to him, however traditional. He could listen, too. Not infrequently one can detect in his way of putting things ideas and images drawn from poets, not just Russians, but Germans, too. It was thought that lived on his breath, not tired ideas remembered.

There are few well placed to give an account of the many sides of Metropolitan Anthony's life, but one of them is Avril Pyman (Sokolova). She is a distinguished scholar of Russian literature, who specialises in the "Silver Age" that led up to the Bolshevik Revolution and continued to flourish during the earlier years of communist Russia – the culture into which the then Andrei Bloom was born (the composer Aleksandr Scriabin was an step-uncle). Furthermore, she learnt her Russian from the émigré Russians in Paris in the 1940s and 1950s – the very émigré circles from which Metropolitan Anthony came. In the early 1960s, Avril Pyman married the Russian artist, Kirill Sokolov, and went to live in Moscow, whence they returned in 1974. A devout Christian, she decided to embrace Russian Orthodoxy, since living in Moscow and worshipping in the embassy church would have attracted unwelcome attention. The then Father Anthony Bloom received her into the Orthodox Church. Avril Pyman thus knew Metropolitan Anthony from early days, and has experience of the encouragement he gave, not least to the intellectuals of Moscow, through his broadcast sermons. We in the UK know about the impact that he made, among the Orthodox and beyond, in our own country; Avril can help us to understand, as an eye-witness, what he came to mean in Russia during the dark days of the Soviet Union.

She is therefore uniquely qualified to write this biography of Metropolitan Anthony, able to speak from firsthand knowledge of what he meant both in Russia and in England. Her profound knowledge of Russian literary culture enables her to discern the intellectual roots of a complex man and priest who was such a vivid and compelling witness to the depths of Orthodoxy for his contemporaries.

The Very Revd Archpriest Andrew Louth FBA,
Professor Emeritus of Patristic and Byzantine Studies,
Durham University

Acknowledgements

Work on this book originated from a request from Elena Iurevna Sadovnikova, immunologist and biologist, but here in her capacity as archivist of the Metropolitan Anthony of Sourozh Foundation (MASF) and translator of his "Last Talks",[1] to write a biographical afterword to her Russian version. She swept aside my protests that, being a specialist on Russian symbolism rather than on the Russian Church and already in my late seventies, I would be incapable of the necessary research. Over the course of several years thereafter, Elena trundled hefty folders of archive material in a wheely-bag across Moscow and up to my daughter's third-storey flat for me to read at my leisure. The MASF, as she had promised, had already done a great deal of research and, indeed, she herself had laboured tirelessly, harvesting material from British and Russian archives which, most generously, she now put at my disposal. From this grew the wider project for a full-length biography – a genre that has long fascinated me on the principle of gathering mosaic chips of evidence and moving them around until they tell a story and form a portrait. My only qualifications were experience of the genre and love of my subject – Anthony stood godfather when he accepted me into the Orthodox Church in 1963 and remained a lifelong friend and spiritual counsellor to me and my Russian husband, the artist Kirill Sokolov, who he allowed to paint his portrait. It helped that I remember World War Two, studied Russian with émigrés in Paris (on and off from 1949 to 1957), am English by birth and upbringing but lived in the Soviet Union from 1963 to 1974, and had friends among the Metropolitan's devoted Russian admirers. My daughter and two granddaughters resident in Moscow provided me with space to work there after my husband's death in 2004, and have been supportive in every possible way.

* * *

In the actual process of writing and revising the manuscript, I have been helped more than I can say by my friends, the late Tatiana and her sister

Elena Maidanovich, ex-President of the Metropolitan Anthony of Sourozh Foundation in Moscow. Tatiana read the first drafts and made invaluable suggestions on further reading, on where it would be more effective to tell the story in Vladyka Anthony's own words, on episodes that could give more colour and relevance and, occasionally, on deleting guess-work. Elena also read and corrected the typescript and served as an untiring source of accurate information about the Church in Russia and Paris and on a number of peripheral characters. Both sisters provided photo materials and personal reminiscences, Tatiana having lived in Paris and London since 1973 while Elena remained basically resident in Moscow. I am grateful to the MASF for permission to reproduce the photographs in this book.

I also have to thank three research assistants: Clementine Rehbinder, who conducted interviews for me in Paris, obtained a copy of Andrei Bloom's (as he was then) doctoral thesis from the Sorbonne and identified his teachers, and Anisa Jameson and Natalia Rumiantseva, who helped me with the Glossary of Proper Names – not to mention all those who kindly replied to letters of enquiry about their own or their family's dates of birth and death, including Metropolitan Anthony's niece Roxana, who replied politely: "Unfortunately I do not yet know the date and place of my demise."

I am grateful to Father Andrew Louth, an old and dear friend since before his ordination as an Orthodox priest, colleague at the University of Durham and Vicar of my own much-loved Orthodox parish of St Cuthbert and St Bede, for unfailing support and encouragement, for lending me invaluable reference books, for vetting the complex typescript before recommending it for publication and for agreeing to write a foreword.

Christine Jameson-Gates has, in spite of illness, been tremendously patient in word-processing and correcting this book, as she was with my earlier books, *A History of Russian Symbolism* (1994) and *Pavel Florensky* (2010). There are so many people over the years I just couldn't have done without – and she, for the last forty of them, has been among the foremost.

Over the years, members of the MASF have done sterling work to locate and document scattered publications of talks, sermons and interviews. They have also compiled a list of recently published books by and about him available to purchase on the internet.[2]

Avril Pyman

Chapter One

From Prince to Pauper: Origins and Childhood, 1914-1922

"The child is the only part of a person that is truly eternal."[1]

Tragic and cataclysmic – such was the background to the life of the child who was to become known by the somewhat forbidding title of Metropolitan Anthony of Sourozh. Sourozh itself – the courtesy title of an archdiocese that in fact comprised Great Britain and Ireland – has long since vanished from the map. Some traces of the ancient city, visited, according to legend, by St Andrew the First Called at the dawn of Christianity, are still to be found amongst archaeological digs in the pleasant resort town of Sudak in Crimea, Cymeraria, the Shadowland, home through the centuries to Greeks, Jews, Tartars, Ukrainians and Russians – and for many years a "virtual" see of the Russian Orthodox Church with no resident hierarch. The title, however, remained in the gift of the Moscow Patriarchate, together with that of the equally non-existent diocese of Sergievo, and they were conferred successively on Anthony, upon his consecration and upon his being raised to the rank of Archbishop. With hindsight, these ancient Russian sees were, by virtue of their phantom nature, peculiarly fitted to convey the dignity of a homeless monk in a world the history of which he once compared to "a transparent ribbon of film" projected against the solid background of the Cross, the Resurrection and the Ascension, events that "are always current, as it were, at the very centre of history, always events not of the past but of the present day".[2]

The future Metropolitan Archbishop was born into this transient and transparent world on 19 June 1914 in the home of his maternal grandfather, Nikolai Scriabin, a retired diplomat from a predominantly military family who had taken up residence in Lausanne with his Italian wife, whose Orthodox name was Ol'ga. Their daughter Ksenia's husband, Boris Eduardovich Bloom, whom she had originally met as one of her father's aides, a fellow Orientalist and representative of the Russian "serving nobility" of mixed Scottish, Dutch and Russian ancestry, was between postings, and the young couple were on a visit to the Scriabins at the time of the birth. Their son was baptised Andrew, Andrei[i] in Russian, by the resident Greek Orthodox priest.[ii] Within a couple of months, however, the outbreak of World War One precipitated Bloom's recall to Moscow, where the family took up residence with Scriabin relatives on Bol'shoi Nikolopeskovskii Pereulok in a house occupied by Nikolai's son by his first marriage, the composer Aleksandr Scriabin.[iii]

The child could not have been fully aware of the depletion of his immediate family that set in almost immediately, with the death of his grandfather Nikolai in 1914. Ksenia Nikolaevna's older full brother, and later both younger brothers, were killed in action during World War One and the ensuing civil war. Her half-brother, Aleksandr, died in the spring of 1915 at the age of forty-three. Thus it came about that when Boris Eduardovich Bloom received his next posting to Persia, he took with him not only his wife and infant son, but also his widowed mother-in-law Ol'ga Il'inichna, in her early fifties at the time, who was to remain an inalienable part of Andrei's life until her death in London in 1957.

Bloom's service as representative of Imperial Russia with the title of Consul-in-Chief in Persia required frequent changes of residence. Andrei's memories of the time were correspondingly kaleidoscopic. As children do, he remembered things in close-up: a ram with "an odd habit of coming into the drawing room, and pulling all the flowers out of the vases with his teeth and then, rather than eating them, laying them on the table next to the vases, after which he lay down in the armchair";[3] a favourite dog; how he proudly informed his mother that he *knew* all fruit must be washed before eating and had carefully rinsed the piece of pineapple he had been caught with in a little ditch by the roadside.[4] Not surprisingly, he suffered from almost chronic dysentery. When he was confined to the house, his grandmother would read to him most beautifully old tales and fairy stories in French and so, he recalled, he saw no particular reason to make the effort to learn to read to himself. There was an indulgent Russian nanny to take care of him

---

i. I prefer this spelling to the French "André", which entails a different pronunciation of the "a" to the Russian, which is more like that of the English Andrew.

ii. Many years later, Metropolitan Anthony recalled, "I met the priest who had baptized me. It was a very amusing meeting, because I arrived there [in Lausanne, 1961] as a young bishop (young in consecration), met him and said, 'Father Constantine, I am so glad to see you again!' He looked at me and said, 'Forgive me, you must be mistaken, for I do not think that we have ever met.' I replied, 'Father Constantine, you should be ashamed of yourself. We have known each other for years, and you do not recognise me?' 'No, forgive me, I do not recognise you. . . .' 'But you baptised me!'" (Metropolitan Anthony of Sourozh, "Without Notes" in *Encounter*, trans. from the Russian by Tatiana Wolff, Darton, Longman and Todd, 2005. Further "Without Notes", p.170.)

iii. The street has been renamed Ulitsa Vakhtangova.

Chapter One

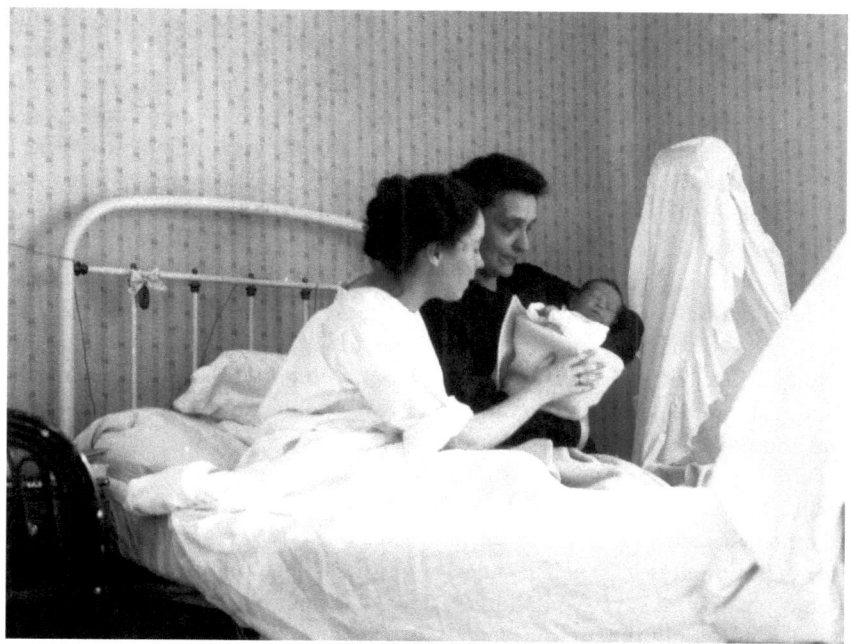

Andrei Bloom with his mother and grandmother, June 1914

for the first three or four years,[5] Persian servants, flowering gardens and cool, enclosed courtyards, which gave him a lasting image for the cloistered life. Beyond these, in contrast, lay the bustling activity of eastern cities with mules, camels and donkeys laden with colourful merchandise, great desolate expanses of arid plain and mountain, wild beasts and a series of domestic pets always at risk from the predators without. Ksenia Nikolaevna was a splendid horsewoman who loved hunting, an authority to whom Andrei could only look up as a very small boy just learning to master a recalcitrant donkey, all the more so as riding was an essential skill. Andrei would be seven years old before he saw a car![6] Boris Eduardovich was even then a quiet, retiring figure, but the child could not have been unaware of his father's status, not just within the household but amongst all they met.

The Revolution in Russia did not at first impinge on the family's way of life, though the nanny departed to her home village in the nascent Soviet Union in 1918. Andrei then came more constantly under the care of his mother and grandmother, who spoke and read to him in French and Russian, which was not, of course, the grandmother's first language anyway. He was later to recount how she had acquired it largely through reading Turgenev and spoke fluently but quaintly in the idiom of the nineteenth-century novel. Both women kindled the child's creative imagination, encouraging him to draw the stories read to him. His father introduced him to adventure stories and heroic tales read in

Russian, and imbued him with his own sense of duty and an ethic of self-sacrifice, service and vocation. "What is important," he was to say later, when Andrei was old enough to understand, "is not whether you live or die. What is important is what you are living for and for what you are prepared to die."[7] For now, he simply learned from his parents' example and imbibed from them a beautiful, spontaneous and quite ineradicable old-world courtesy, which was constantly to astonish his contemporaries and win him many friends.

For instance, in answer to a question about "righteous wrath", he was to tell his audience how once "I had invited a clergyman of a different denomination to speak to a group of Russian pupils. He gave a talk in which he reviled our faith from end to end, and I burned with rage and indignation, but, *being the host, I could do nothing about it.*"[8] The words in italics are quite peripheral to the story he was telling, intended to show how we should bear one another's burdens rather than call down the vengeance of the Lord on our enemies as in the Old Testament, but they express very well the absolute requirements of his early upbringing. Other instances of Anthony's courtesy as guest rather than host I remember from personal contact: how this least self-indulgent and most abstemious of men, who, as far as possible, always avoided invitations to dinner before or after speaking, would – in a family environment – invariably praise the hostess's cooking and partake enthusiastically of second helpings. After his mother's death, he would graciously accept gifts of food from parishioners who felt he did not look after himself properly, but surreptitiously pass them on to even poorer members of his parish or take non-perishables as gifts to Russia. When I was living there from 1963 to 1974, he would almost always produce a very English bar of milk chocolate as to a god-daughter still considered as part-child. One Russian visitor to his hide-out in the Cathedral in Ennismore Gardens recalled with astonishment how, when he took his leave, the elderly Archbishop insisted on helping him into his overcoat.[9] A priest recounts how, in the 1960s, his mother, "just another unknown old woman in a headscarf", rushed up to the black limousine in which the Bishop had just taken his seat after a long and exhausting service, to ask a blessing, and how thrilled she had been when he opened the door and jumped out of the car to bestow it.[10] When another young priest showed him the way to a quasi-clandestine venue in an eighth-floor Moscow flat to meet parishioners of Father Aleksandr Men', only to discover that the lift was out of order, the 75-year-old Metropolitan, seeing the young man quite at a loss how to deal with the situation, assured him that the climb would do him good as he was missing his morning exercise – and set off cheerfully up the stairs.[11] "It is really high time you *civilised* him," he reproached me in laughing protest as my late husband Kirill – tears in his eyes after a *panikhida* for his mother – thrust money into the Metropolitan's hands instead of slipping it, as etiquette demanded, into the collection box for the Cathedral.

Andrei as a toddler with his father, Boris Eduardovich Bloom

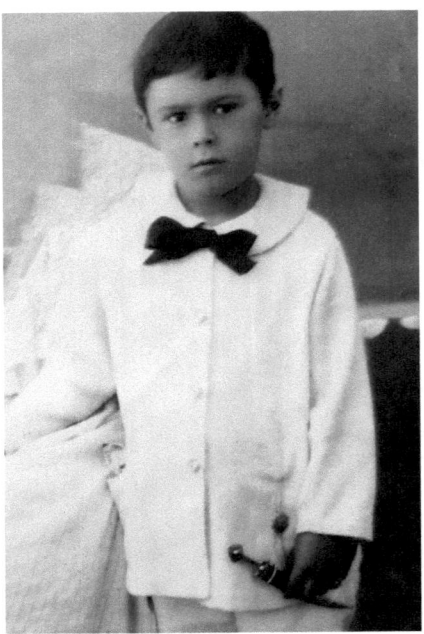
Andrei as a child in Persia

That the boy Andrei grew up so truly "civilised" is certainly the result of early environment, but the environment was burning up all around him like a morning mist. The Empire his father represented was crumbling and his parents' extended family and material possessions were disappearing into the vortex of revolution. By 1920, Tsar and Empire were no longer there to represent, and turmoil and civil war threatened to destabilise life in Persia itself. The family was forced to split up, Boris Eduardovich remaining behind to oversee the evacuation of the consulate before leaving for Europe, and the women and Andrei going on ahead by carriage and on horseback across the mountains in a bid to reach the Blooms' ancestral Scotland, initially travelling under the protection of "honest" bandits, who, Andrei recalled not without humour, his parents deemed more reliable than the Persian army of the time.

There could be no question of going back to Russia – all family possessions there had been confiscated and Bloom would not have considered putting his professional skills at the service of the Bolshevik government, which did not, at the time, enjoy much in the way of diplomatic recognition. His family owned only what they could take with them.

Having jolted their way across the mountains of north Persia and Kurdistan, grandmother, mother and the six-year-old Andrei changed onto barges to continue their journey down the Tigris and Euphrates. Andrei was struck by the wonder of their confluence but disillusioned by a glimpse of the scruffy tree in a parched enclosure said to be the site of the Garden of Eden:

> It is a wonderful sight: the Euphrates is wide and blue and the Tigris is fast-flowing and its water is red, and it flows into the Euphrates and for several hundred metres it is possible to see the red water of the Tigris in the midst of the blue water of the Euphrates. In the forest there is a large meadow and in the middle of it, surrounded by a fence, is a little dried up tree. It was covered all over with little bits of rag. . . .[12]

Chapter One

In later life, he always insisted he had absolutely no desire to go on pilgrimage to experience the Holy Land at first hand.

From Basra the only safe route by sea was towards India, where they were delayed for a further month in a stifling but gloriously colourful Bombay before obtaining a passage to Southampton on a decrepit ship. The little boy hoped ardently for shipwreck on a desert island, but the vessel made it as far as Gibraltar, where the passengers, for their own safety, were put ashore with their baggage. One trunk, however, went on without them to Southampton, the one containing most of their favourite things, and was not retrieved until fourteen years later (shortly followed, in 1935, by a residue of personal effects from the Scriabin home in Lausanne).

> This was a huge event, because this was one of those chests, into which everything which one *could* not leave was thrown at the last minute. First we had reasonably packed all that was *necessary*, and left that which we could not *possibly* take, and at the last minute – for the heart is not made of stone – into this chest were, of course, put all the most precious things, which I as a boy was a thousand times more interested in than in warm underwear or sensible shoes. . . .[13]

CHAPTER TWO

Alienation and Revelation: Growing Up in Exile, 1922-1929

*"God helps us when there is no-one else to help.
God is there at the point of greatest tension,
at the breaking point, at the centre of the storm."*[1]

The family's first destination was Paris, but here Ksenia Nikolaevna failed to find any means of support and they travelled on to her mother's sister, who had married an Austrian. That summer Ksenia Nikolaevna and Andrei, now seven years old, found seasonal work on a farm over the border in Yugoslavia where, as "dirty Russian refugees", they underwent their first experience of xenophobic hostility, but returned in the autumn to Vienna to the kindly great-aunt with whom they were able to stay for the next eighteen months.

Here, a reluctant Andrei, unimpressed by his Austrian great-uncle's argument that it was the only way to learn to support a family, was put to school, where he acquired a lifelong native-speaker proficiency in the German language but suffered considerable culture shock. As an Orthodox, he was rejected for religious instruction, first by the Jewish rabbi as a Christian and then by the Roman Catholic priest as a heretic, a rejection that – no believer in cramming children with second-hand piety – he was inclined to regard then and later as an unmitigated boon, yet still a clear indication of his otherness. More painful was the class mistress's reaction to his first attempt at an essay on the subject of "What I want to be when I grow up". A recent visit to the Vienna zoo had inspired the lively boy with the notion that nothing could be more desirable than to become a monkey, leaping and frisking among green branches, and he produced an inspired illustrated composition on the subject. Used to praise and encouragement for his imaginative drawings and conscious that to write an essay in German was quite an achievement for a bilingual Franco-Russian eight-year-old brought up in Persia, Andrei rose with confidence when requested to stand. Venomously, the class mistress proceeded to hold him up to ridicule before the whole class. They beheld before them, she said, a retrogressive Russian barbarian who, far from dreaming of serving home and fatherland in some useful occupation, had shamelessly declared his ambition to revert to the feckless life of a mindless beast. Andrei's toy monkey had a cheeky face and sad, clever eyes, and he always nurtured a concept of paradise very similar to the state of buoyant innocence and oneness with the natural world he had endeavoured to depict in his essay.[2] He was hurt not only in his pride as a Russian and a bright schoolboy, but in his heart, his innermost imaginings.

Whether it was the arrival of Boris Eduardovich in Paris via Istanbul or the awkwardness of trespassing further on the generous hospitality of the Viennese-Italian family of her aunt remains unclear, but Ksenia Nikolaevna moved her son and mother to the French capital in 1923. They did not, however, rejoin her husband, and the marriage did not withstand the catastrophic collapse of their whole way of life. Boris Eduardovich appears to have felt personally guilty for the fall of the regime he had served and withdrew from family and friends into penitential seclusion. His specialist knowledge of the Middle East and oriental languages might have ensured him a teaching job at least, but he made no effort to re-establish himself in this way, took whatever manual work presented itself as a kind of expiation for his former privileged existence, and elected to live alone. He and Ksenia Nikolaevna divorced and, though neither remarried, she reverted to her maiden name. She never, however, broke off relations with Andrei's father, and, as the boy became more independent, he would continue to visit him, though on occasion he would be met by a notice pinned to the door: "Don't bother knocking. I will not answer even if I am in."

From her arrival in Paris, therefore, Ksenia Nikolaevna was on her own with an elderly mother quite unqualified to contribute in any way to the family budget and a high-spirited nine-year-old boy, inwardly seething at their pariah status as part of a flood of Russian émigrés, resented by the French at a time of rising unemployment and threatening financial crisis, and comforted only by the remarkable mutual solidarity of an exiled community united by culture in the most all-embracing sense of the word: religion, tradition, language – and nostalgia. It was this solidarity – "hardly anyone had money to share, but they would all share food and roof and fellow-feeling with you just because you, too, were Russian"[3] – that infected this polyglot lad of mixed ancestry and cosmopolitan background with a lifelong patriotism, a steadfast devotion to the land and people of which he can have had no conscious memory but to which, in this furnace of want and deprivation, he now forged an irrevocable loyalty.

As a family they did not even have a home of their own, but took separate temporary lodgings wherever a foothold could be found. Ksenia Nikolaevna attempted to establish Andrei on one of the scholarships offered by the Roman Catholic Church to select Russian émigré children at their

Andrei as a schoolboy with mother and grandmother, France

privileged boarding schools. An interview appeared to go well and a place was duly offered but, it transpired, on condition the boy should be raised a Roman Catholic. Indignantly, Andrei, at that time a strictly non-observant Orthodox, marched his mother out of the institution: "I'm not for sale!"

Clearly, the child felt threatened and diminished. Possibly he also did not fully understand, and resented the fact that neither parent could find room for him in their lives. Both were desperate to lodge him elsewhere, somewhere, anywhere. Certainly the immediate consequence of this flash of hubris was dour in the extreme. Andrei's parents had no choice but to opt for the cheapest possible boarding school and their son became a weekly boarder in a deprived quarter of Paris with a high rate of criminality. The school was bleak and rough. The dormitory had seventy beds, which the boys were not allowed to leave at night even to relieve themselves. Corporal punishment – never by law inflicted on members of the nobility (*dvorianstvo*) in Russia and so outside family lore as well as personal experience and, in Andrei's book, inconceivably degrading – was here the norm. Bullying was unremitting. Some boys carried knives. At first, Andrei had no idea how to stand up for himself, but soon, at the instigation of unsympathetic teachers, he was to learn to fight back and become proficient with his fists. Even as an elderly bishop he recounted with some glee how he had seen off a tramp who came to the Cathedral demanding money with menaces by threatening to break a tooth or two for him before succumbing to any rough stuff![4]

Andrei never found solace in the doctrine of the survival of the fittest, however. Indeed, so miserable did he become that he did his ten-year-old

Chapter Two

Andrei (far right) as a boy with other Vitiazi *and Father Georgii Shumkin at summer camp in France ("some sense of dignity, community and self-respect")*

best to get himself run over in the street, habitually shutting his eyes before crossing the road, until a near success earned him yet another thrashing at the hands of a furious French cabby.

"Never," he was to recall, "in the whole of my life have I endured so much fear and pain, both physical and emotional. And the things I learned then, apart from endurance, were things I had to spend a long time unlearning later on: first, that every human being of either sex, of whatever age and size, is a danger to you; second, that you can survive only if you become strong, absolutely devoid of emotion and third, that you can survive only by learning the law of the jungle."[5]

Aware that his mother would have been unutterably distressed by her inability to relieve her son's misery, Andrei told her nothing. At weekends Ksenia Nikolaevna put him up in the room she had from the hotel where she worked as a receptionist, which carried an absolute taboo on overnight visitors. She would bid him goodnight in front of the manager and smuggle him back in on all fours behind the reception desk – and out in the mornings by the same route. In 1925 all this humiliation was compounded by the Soviet decree stripping émigrés of their nationality. The Nansen passports, which gave them right of residence but not necessarily of travel, were an inadequate substitute, and only membership of a Russian scout movement, the *Vitiazi* (or "Warriors"), who organised camps in the country during the summer holidays, gave the boy back some sense of dignity, community and self-respect – albeit a somewhat harsh one. The ethos of the *Vitiazi* was militaristic Russian patriotism and strongly anti-Soviet, but here at least Andrei found some joy in comradeship and physical achievement. Here, also, as a natural leader and a true knight by nature and nurture, he was much valued.

The boarding school where the young Bloom was to remain until the age of twelve, however, was still a joyless struggle to survive; only the immediate goal of transferring to a *lycée* motivated him to turn in a constantly acceptable standard of work. Thus, aged twelve, he duly transferred to the Lycée Condorcet, where he covered the increased expenses his parents were unable to meet by giving private tuition to other pupils in mathematics or any other subject in which he was – albeit slightly – more advanced, including Latin, to which he was addicted, and German, which he knew anyway.

In 1927 Andrei joined the ACER (Association chrétienne des étudiants russes) camps run by the Russian Student Christian Movement attached to the YMCA – to the dismay of the organisers of the *Vitiazi*, who regarded him as a model activist.[6] Although still indifferent to religion, Andrei did, here in the ACER camps, experience disinterested Christian love, as it seemed to him, for the first time, from their pastor, the gawky Father Georgii Shumkin, to whom he was to write almost thirty years later that he would always consider himself "one of batiushka's boys", invoking upon the old man the Grace of God "for your love for Him and for us lesser brethren". In Shumkin's memory, he wrote: "Many children's prayers will burn like candles unto ages of ages before the Throne of the Lord, alight for ever with a child's gratitude and love."[7] Indeed, the personal benevolence of the "little father" (*batiushka*) towards his young charges was something beyond Andrei's experience at the time and was stored away to be fully understood and appreciated at a later date as his "first deep spiritual experience",[8] although it did not immediately impinge on his passive resistance to church parade at camp or to his parents' occasional attempts to introduce him to religious practice at the Russian Cathedral in Rue Daru on special days such as his name day or Good Friday. The technique the boy had developed to avoid this was entirely successful. He would inhale the first cloud of incense to be wafted his way, and faint – a troublesome experience for his keepers which, after several repetitions, neither father nor mother were willing to undergo.

By 1928, Ksenia Nikolaevna had established herself as an eminently employable multilingual typist and could afford to rent a modest flat in the outskirts of Paris in Bois-Colombes for herself, her mother and Andrei. For the first time since being precipitated into the appalling boarding school, Andrei had a place to call his own and to share with those he loved. He was doing well, too, at the Lycée. Yet suddenly there was nothing left to aspire to, no immediate aims. Parental separation had hardened into divorce and Andrei's father's insistence on a "cause" to live for compounded a strong negative reaction to the curious state of weightlessness often brought about by a sudden release from pressure. Andrei now had all he required, all he had yearned for, but neither he nor his life appeared to have any further goal, any true meaning; and so at fourteen he made the shocking decision to put an end to this meaningless if contented existence should he not, over the next year, discover "for what he was alive and for what he was prepared to die". Like Ivan Karamazov, he was prepared to "return his ticket" to an unjust or non-existent Creator.

That he did not do so was either entirely fortuitous or, as he himself believed, thanks to a divine intervention, his reception of which was made possible by a gesture of elementary solidarity with the friends he had made in the ACER camps and at their centre in Paris. One fine day, Andrei arrived at the centre for a game of volleyball, only to be told by his "leader" that sport was cancelled and his presence required at a lecture by Father Sergii Bulgakov, whom they themselves had invited. In the face of Andrei's vigorous objections the leader begged him to preserve face by constituting at least a physical presence at the lecture: "You don't have to listen to what he says."

Father Sergii, however, spoke loudly and distinctly – and Andrei could not help but listen. He described himself at the time as a young barbarian. Certainly he was, not unlike Camus' "Stranger", profoundly alienated and full of undirected energy. Though life was – for the moment – going smoothly enough, he belonged nowhere and was going nowhere in a world he had now learned from experience was at best indifferent, more often perilously hostile. It was, therefore, an offence to be told by this scholarly old priest that he, and all the other tough and disaffected émigré youngsters who made up the audience, were bound in love to a gentle but clearly ineffective God who bade them be humble and meek and turn the other cheek. By the end of the talk, Andrei was seething, and set straight off for home to check with his mother's New Testament whether this was really what his native Russian Church was all about. If so, he thought, it was time to stop merely avoiding being bored by religion and to reject belief in God once and for all openly and honestly, in the upright manner inculcated into him by his early upbringing.

What followed Andrei kept for many years in his heart of hearts, and only told the story when directly challenged by a young man not unlike the self he recalled having been at the time: "*Why* do you believe in God?" Afterwards, he retold it many times in various languages,[9] but, as it happened, the first telling was in English and can be set down here in his own words:

> I expected nothing good from my reading, so I counted the chapters of the four Gospels to be sure I read the shortest, not to waste time unnecessarily. I started to read St Mark's Gospel.

While I was reading the beginning of St Mark's Gospel, before I reached the third chapter, I suddenly became aware that on the other side of my desk there was a presence. And the certainty was so strong that it was Christ standing there that it never left me. This was the real turning point. Because Christ was alive and I had been in His presence I could say with certainty that what the Gospel said about the crucifixion of the prophet of Gallilee was true, and the centurion was right when he said: "Truly He is the son of God". It was in the light of the Resurrection that I could read with certainty the story of the Gospel, knowing that everything was true in it because the impossible event of the Resurrection was to me more certain than any event in history. History I had to believe, the Resurrection I knew for a fact. I did not discover, as you see, the Gospel beginning with its first message of the Annunciation and it did not unfold for me as a story which one can believe or disbelieve. It began as an event that left all problems of disbelief behind because it was a direct and personal experience.

T.W. [Timothy Wilson]: And the conviction has stayed with you all your life? There have been no times when you doubted your faith?

Bloom: I became absolutely certain within myself that Christ is alive and that certain things existed. I didn't have all the answers, but had touched that experience. I was certain that ahead of me there were answers, visions, possibilities. That is what I mean by faith – not doubting in the sense of being in confusion and perplexity, but doubting in order to discover the reality of life, the kind of doubt that makes you want to question and discover more, that makes you want to explore.[10]

One of the wisest of Anthony's Russian admirers, Sergei Averintsev, was later to comment on how this baptism by fire was to make Metropolitan Anthony's faith equally acceptable to English hippies and to Russians brought up without benefit of clergy in the Soviet period: "[I]n no sense metaphorically, he truly saw the Living Christ. And how! From the depths of pain, protest, bitterness, which rendered all pious outdated phrases intolerable. From such depths at which man is unable to accept anything but God."[11]

The first discovery was made as Andrei explored further beyond the breakneck rush of St Mark, whose gospel begins with John the Baptist and reads like an action-packed and muscular precis of a mission on which Jesus and his summarily selected disciples, crowded and questioned and beset by the sick, the hostile and the possessed, have no time to "so much as eat bread" (Mark 3:30). He went on to the other gospels and discovered in Matthew, to his genuine surprise, that Christ had not just come into the world to save sinners and heal the sick but out of love for the just and the unjust, like Father Georgii Shumkin. If you wanted to follow Him – and the boy was already irrevocably committed – you must learn to do the same. Hitherto, Andrei had loved his family and a few friends, but had armoured himself with stoic indifference and wary distrust against the all too many unlovable characters who had encroached on his youthful awareness.

Suddenly, it came over him that this marvellous explosion of energy that was Jesus Christ, this tragic young man who had set aside His divinity and conquered death itself, had done it all "out of solidarity"[i] for human beings who were without exception his own creatures who He had "loved into existence". Having realised this, there was no time to be lost. At one stroke, Andrei had found a reason for living and something eminently worth dying for, ineffable joy and a tragic challenge that was to test him to the uttermost for the rest of his life. He had found a creed that appealed to his innate virtues: chivalry, loyalty and a passionate need for devotion "unto death", as he was to say frequently in the occasionally quaint English he acquired from reading the Authorised Version of the Bible. He had to tell everybody about this miraculous discovery – but first he had to learn how, for, as he recalled later, "my first efforts were unworthy".

---

i. "Why do you use that political word 'solidarity'?" the Bishop was occasionally asked. "I use it because people understand what it means," he replied.

CHAPTER THREE

Conflicting Vocations: The Formation of a Monk "in the World", 1928-1937

"My life has been very different from the life of a student in our days – hard, hungry and harsh at times and I could not preach a smooth and warm sermon."[1]

From that time Andrei Bloom sought increasing responsibility in the summer camps and stopped fainting at church. On the contrary, he became a regular attender, assisted the priest as altar-boy and, in 1931, was consecrated server by the burly, charismatic and very Russian Metropolitan Evlogii who, after the Synod of Karlovy Sremtsy of 1927-28 chose to break all ties with the Soviet Union, had elected to remain loyal to the persecuted Mother Church in Russia and the Patriarchal *locum tenens* Sergii and, at the time, had retained the allegiance of the majority of his Paris flock and of the Theological Institute of St Sergius.[2] That same year, however, Sergii was pressured into making a formal declaration of loyalty to the Soviet government. Although he tried, Evlogii could not continue to represent his essentially anti-Bolshevik diocese and conform to Moscow's embargo on criticism of the Soviets. In 1931 he joined the Archbishop of Canterbury in an ecumenical service of prayer for persecuted Christians in the USSR and was relieved of his role as representative of the Patriarch and administrator of the Russian Orthodox parishes of Western Europe. Evlogii betook himself and a large section of his outraged flock under the temporary protection of the Patriarch of Constantinople, the senior "Ecumenical" Patriarch of the Orthodox Church.

A stubborn remnant, however, remained faithful, under Bishops Elevferii and Veniamin, to the Moscow Patriarchate, among them the newly consecrated server Andrei, Vladimir Lossky, the brothers Kovalevsky, Leonid Ouspensky and a number of intellectuals who belonged to a society calling itself the Brotherhood of St Photius. Paradoxically, the brotherhood perceived fidelity to the suffering Church in Russia as not incompatible with the mission to bring the light of a materially disinherited orthodoxy to illumine and restore the Church in the West to what it had been in the Age of Faith before the schisms, not by proselytising, but by penetrating Roman Catholicism and Protestantism of all shades with the renewed radiance of a Christianity which, purified by suffering and persecutions, had come to resemble the Church before Constantine gave it imperial sanction. Like the young Andrei, the Brotherhood of St Photius saw no reason to break away from their Mother Church, but rather felt themselves called upon to sustain her spiritual presence in the free world outside the Soviet Union. Metropolitan Anthony was to recall this attitude, from which he never wavered, in a BBC interview in 1996:

> I was sure that under wise leadership the Russian emigration could remain loyal to our native Church and never submit to any pressure from the Soviet Authorities. And this was something I actually experienced a short time afterwards, when the Patriarchal parishes received a letter from Moscow ordering them to refrain from all political activity. And our clergy wrote to the Patriarchate that we are political émigrés and have the right to combat the Soviet regime and Communism, but that the clergy were prepared to promise not to turn the pulpit into a platform for preaching politics.[3]

The idea of abandoning the Church in Russia seemed to the ardent youth comparable to fleeing the field of battle; indeed, at the time, to hold fast to this filial bond signified no less than to be "the free voice and the free body of the Russian Church and of our Russian motherland", a role that he was later to fulfil most faithfully in holy orders.

The remnant of Russians who felt the same way naturally required a church – and they established themselves in the basement of an old garage on Rue Pétel. The new Church of the Three Holy Hierarchs was soon sympathetically embellished by two remarkable émigré icon painters, Leonid Ouspensky and Grigorii Krug, and acquired a warm catacomb ambience.

Bishop Veniamin departed for America in 1933 and it was striding up the steps from this basement church that Andrei, arriving late, first encountered his successor as Vicar of the parish, Archimandrite Afanasii (Nechaev),[4] the light of Christ radiant in a face still concentrated on the service he had been celebrating. "You cannot truly believe in God unless you have seen this light illumine the face of another human being," he was to say afterwards.[5] Impulsively, the tardy schoolboy planted himself in the way of the unknown monk, who had but recently returned from a parish in southern France, and asked him to be his spiritual guide. Andrei, at that time, wanted nothing more than to become a monk himself, to devote his whole life to Christ, to go out into the desert and fight demons

– as some of his more ambitious reading had suggested was only fitting for a "spiritual athlete". Shipwreck on a desert island and the free life of monkeys in the canopy were never altogether absent from his dreams.

However, there were drawbacks. It was beyond his means to travel even to the nearest desert and, given the Nansen passport, he would scarcely have been in a position to obtain permission to reside there. Worse, there were his mother and grandmother to think of, who would surely look to him for support as he grew up. There was no Russian Orthodox monastery in France and even the seminary at the Institute of St Sergius seemed to think Andrei was too young to enrol for the necessary training, telling him to come back in twenty years' time – rather more years, indeed, than he had lived through up to that moment. Afanasii agreed to become his father confessor but this opened no doors to a monastic future.

When Andrei confided his ambition to his father, who, notwithstanding his penchant for seclusion, loved his son dearly,[i] Boris Eduardovich agreed he was duty-bound to discharge his earthly obligations to his family before embarking on the religious life, but scotched the idea of going straight from school into manual labour. His son, he said, should not follow his example in this respect, but should study to realise his full potential and learn to be useful to his fellow man before concentrating on his own salvation. Why should he not study medicine and at least face up to a period of healing bodies rather than souls?

There were, in fact, excellent reasons why not. The subjects Andrei most enjoyed at the Lycée were Latin and architecture and, if he thought of himself as a scholar at all, it was as a classicist. He was duly awarded his baccalauréat in Philosophy in 1931. Nevertheless, Boris Eduardovich's advice resonated with both himself and his spiritual mentor. With the

---

i. Boris Eduardovich Bloom's love for his son and residual feeling for his family comes across very clearly from two 1935 letters preserved in the MASF Archive. The first, dated 2 September 1935, is addressed to Andrei in one of the ACER camps and tells of the arrival of a trunk full of treasures from his grandfather's home (icons, an old photograph album, linen, tripods) in Lausanne, which had delighted his mother and grandmother when he delivered it to them: "We had coffee on the balcony then at six o'clock I went on to the Three Hierarchs. Now here is a categorical order: you will receive a postal order for 100 francs. Get your teeth seen to at once. You know yourself how rotten teeth affect people physically and mentally. . . . I kiss you hard, hard, my dear, my beloved. How good it is that you write regularly. Mama and *babushka* await your letters like manna from heaven, read them, re-read them and send them on to me. Your Papa." The second of 20 October, using the diminutive of a pet name, "Dodinka", is evidently sent to cheer him in a moment of discouragement: "Don't be downhearted. The Lord alone knows what is for the best, live well, do conscientiously what you have to do, and hope in the Lord God for all the rest. . . . If I can I'll come and see you all for lunch on Saturday instead of Thursday. I kiss you all."

latter's blessing, Andrei decided to requalify in 1934, after a special preparatory science course at the Sorbonne, before entering the medical faculty at the same university, thus committing himself to eight more years of study with no funding.

This ambitious but sensible programme did not in any way diminish the young aspirant's firm intention to train himself up in devotion to Christ and to eschew the further responsibilities which would inevitably result in setting up a family of his own. He understood this not as a retreat from the world and the human condition, but as a way of devoting all his energies to learning and prayer, the better to play his part in the establishment of the Kingdom of God on Earth as in Heaven, and to perfect the art of sharing his wonder and gratitude and love for the Redeemer with his fellows. In the words of a prayer disseminated among young Russians in 1917:

Archimandrite Afanasii (Nechaev), Anthony's spiritual father

> In full awareness and at every hour I wish to play my part in the redemption of the world, to remain a light among all shattering events, to be one of Thy lighthouses.
>
> I go, Lord, into the world to fulfil Thy will, with the one wish to stand a true servant at the post to which Thou has appointed me, to be ready to meet Thee as is fitting.[6]

Andrei was fully aware that such service, like any strenuous achievement in sport or the arts, required years of training. The decision to put himself under obedience to Father Afanasii was clearly one made in Heaven. Having heard the young man's first confession, Afanasii told him to pick away patiently at his multitudinous sins, eliminating them one by one, rather than – as the boy had rather expected – to renounce the world then and there, once and for all. Faced with this gradualist approach to ascetic endeavour, he took as his models a simple Russian peasant-soldier Athonite monk, Saint Silouan, whose vocation was to pray for the world, and an obscure lay brother at Father Afanasii's monastery of Valaam, who had felt himself unworthy to become a full monk until he had mastered this most strenuous monastic discipline.

So much we know from various interviews given and stories told by Bishop Anthony as examples from his own experience in later life. How, though, did others see him at the time, this curious, dedicated youth with his passion for volleyball, for arguing, for going out on a limb, his innate good manners, sparkling gift of mimicry and distinctly French wit? Of those in his own household he himself recounts how, one day when he was deep in prayer, his grandmother asked him to help clean the carrots. "Not now, Granny. I'm praying." "Well, I don't think much of your religion if it stops you helping about the house," the old lady replied bracingly.[7] Neither were his nearest and dearest impressed by his aspirations to keep the monastic fasts! Their fare was Spartan enough as it was, and now – for weeks on end – nothing but boiled vegetables, not so much as a sprinkling of cheese on the macaroni. A monk, moreover, should not touch women, even close relations, and this unfamiliar taboo was at one time a source of genuine distress to mother and grandmother. Andrei, however, long past this stage by the time he became a priest, was later to stress the importance of touch in pastoral work and was always ready with an affectionate hug or a firm hand on the shoulder of his spiritual children – male or female. As a young doctor he sat all night holding the hand of a dying soldier and he nursed his mother most lovingly during her last illness, carrying her out into the fresh air and caring for her physical needs. When his grandmother, as a very old lady, burst into tears over some broken crockery, declaring she was no longer of any use to anyone, even to do the washing up, he took her in his arms and assured her that she still fulfilled a function for which absolutely no one else was qualified. "What's that?" she demanded sceptically. "Being my granny." "And strange as it may seem," he concluded, "that really cheered her up."[8]

But people of his own age? "He was always very intense, very serious and very likeable. His brown eyes burned. I saw him at several thés dansants," recalls Vera Bouteneff.[9] "He did not like to dance and told me he prayed hard in such circumstances."

"I remember him particularly in the ACER," recalled Father Nikolai Lossky. "More than anything he taught us to play volleyball, he was very *sportif*."[10] Anna Garret, another witness to his energy and enthusiasm as a leader in the camps, recalled the almost military discipline he would impose, combining cleanliness, order and prompt obedience with "joy", and cited as typical an occasion when forest fires were raging near the camps and a watch was set; Andrei, roused to take his turn as sentry, sprang to attention and saluted, still in his sleep.[11]

Tatisha Behr remembered their passionate arguments both at these same camps and as the beneficiary of private tuition in maths when studying for her baccalauréat: "He had the most crazy ideas and was stubborn as a mule. Sometimes we actually physically came to blows. But as a confessor he was unique. Absolute concentration. There was no-one there but you, him and God."[12]

Chapter Three

Camp leader in France with ACER ("some kind of a star")

Marina Fennel recalls that, when she first met Andrei in 1939, she was twelve years old. He was not yet fully qualified but enthusiastically doctored the youngsters in the camps. "Apart from that he would make us do gym in the mornings. He was very *sportif*, very agreeable and very witty. The young women adored him (*étaient en adoration*), he was very good-looking, right to the end." In his talks, Andrei would, even then, always give examples to make people laugh: "he was very gay,[i] he had enormous charm, charisma."[13]

---

i. Of course the word "gay" is used here in the sense of gallant, lively and amusing.

Of his own accounts of his work as leader in the ACER camps, two stand out. One was the occasion when some of his charges discovered that he spent much of the night in solitary prayer and asked if they might join him. The camp was in the mountains in the south and he took them out on the hillside, where they prayed set prayers and improvisations until dawn, feeling no fatigue. Another was more mundane. He was trudging barefoot up a mountain path when a local farmer suddenly yelled at him that he must be mad – there was broken glass almost under his feet. Andrei replied readily enough: "I've only got the one pair of shoes, you see, and I keep them for the town." The farmer marched him off to his home, and presented him with an enormous pair of boots – which he wore with real gratitude for the rest of the summer.[14]

Indeed, Andrei and his family were not just hard up – they were extremely poor. During his last years at school and throughout university, he would teach in the evenings and do his homework over the weekend, often working straight through the night until eight o'clock in the morning and then collapsing for four or five hours' sleep. Even so, he would frequently forego his lunch or save the bus fare by walking in order to afford books, and recalled sometimes feeling quite dizzy with hunger and exhaustion by the time he reached home.[15] The sustained effort made this young man (*si gai, si sportif, si spirituel*) as tough as a trained soldier, capable of leading an exceptionally active life on short commons and little sleep. True, he never grew beyond five feet eight inches in height, but the Scriabins were not tall as a family and he considered himself "of middle height".[16] Certainly, his erect bearing and high Orthodox hat never allowed him to be dwarfed on camera, either by Russian Orthodox or Anglican colleagues. Although the brown eyes were early shadowed by rings of weariness, the face of the young Andrei Bloom appears healthy in his photographs.

Together with "praying hard" when faced with the seduction of the *thés dansants* and, indeed, the ascesis he practised at all times, the harsh regime necessitated by poverty most probably spared him the worst of the inevitable temptations of the flesh that the autobiographical divagations in his teaching (those personal "examples to make people laugh") chastely ignore. His later take on love and marriage was both joyous and tragic, a commitment one to another of two immortal souls which reaches beyond the grave. Attraction without such commitment could and should be combatted, because it not only belittles the other person but is the desecration of a mystery. Love is both idealistic and realistic. It comes as the perception of the other as an icon, a revelation of spiritual beauty, maintained in faith and not excluding an equally clear perception of the ways in which this icon may have been spoilt and besmirched, felt not as criticism but as a burning desire to help, to restore, to cherish.[17] "When he was young he was very much loved by children and even more by young women," a friend recalls. "He was very handsome when he was young. I asked him once why he didn't pay attention to any of the women and he said he did not want to offend any of them. So he remained a monk. He is a very remarkable person."[18] "Any opinion I may have on that subject is entirely academic," he would say deprecatingly when married people came to him with sexual problems. As a doctor, however, he was not mealy-mouthed and, when asked if man and wife who knew one of them to be a carrier of disease should abstain from intercourse, replied: "Ideally, probably, yes. But it is quite unrealistic to demand this of young people in love and cohabitating."[i] For such cases, he said, he would advocate sterilisation of one or both partners. God gave man minds and skills to resolve such dilemmas and, though opposed to abortion unless for strictly medical reasons and, albeit in a compassionate fashion, to euthanasia, he was open to argument and consistently refrained from condemning enlightened scientific intervention in the biological process.

The study of the natural sciences, then medicine, to which Andrei had committed himself at the Sorbonne, interested and inspired him. The more he found out about God's world – and he was studying at a most exciting time in mathematics and physics and was fortunate enough to be taught the latter in the department of Maurice Curie – the more it filled him with wonder, and the more profoundly he understood the potential stature of the human creature whose brain was capable of unravelling the laws of nature and what the German poet Hesse called "the falling of far stars". Yet his purpose remained divided. Many years later he told Father Sergei Hackel:

> When I had just embarked on the study of medicine my father said to me: "how splendid to be a Christian doctor", – and I answered him, sore at heart: "That's as may be, but I would rather be the least of lay brothers in the most obscure of monasteries." I can't say I ever fulfilled that ambition, so many years have gone by since then, more than sixty, but the feeling has remained that I would like to end my life alone in a monastery; not so much in order to take part in great long services, but to have a cell and long periods of silence and solitude.[19]

It was well for him, therefore, that throughout his double apprenticeship to medicine and the monastic life the young man was guided, protected from excess but kept firm of purpose by the altogether remarkable Archimandrite Afanasii. Born in 1886, Anatolii Nechaev was the son of a priest,[20] but one who had rebelled, together with his elder brother, against

---

i. His open-minded attitude as expressed in an interview with Sergei Hackel for the BBC Russian service indeed provoked a virulent attack online in Russia in which he was accused of a fascist attitude to mentally or physically defective children and of disregarding the fact that all human beings have immortal souls and are born into the world by the will of God. (See http://antimodern.ru/abort-sourozh/. Copy in MASF Archive.)

the brutality and boredom of the provincial seminary to which he was sent to be educated. Declaring agnosticism, the brothers refused to enter the priesthood and involved themselves heart and soul in the great movement "to sow enlightenment on the field of Russia", acquiring and dispensing secular education. To this end they organised evening classes, workers' libraries and so on, although lack of funds was a serious impediment, and they took on manual jobs on the land and the railway during the day to support their widowed mother and numerous younger siblings. In spite of their rebellion against the Church, the brothers were imbued with a gentle Christian morality and did not become involved in revolutionary activity, although they did seek funding from the co-operative movement – not much less suspicious from the point of view of the authorities. It was a way of life that seemed good to Afanasii even after he became aware, in part surprisingly, through contact with the Salvation Army, that learning without faith was sterile. In the chaos of war, revolution, civil war and the establishment of the dictatorship of the proletariat, he had continued as odd-job man and itinerant hedge-teacher in the disputed Russo-Finnish lands of Karelia but, in 1923, gravitated just over the new Finnish border, learned Swedish and continued to teach the poor and needy, no longer as an agnostic but as a lay missionary. In "quarantine" on the border, he made friends with some Russian monks from the island monastery of Valaam, who invited him to visit their island. At the time, the very thought of the passive way shut off from the suffering world seemed quite alien to him and it was not until two and a half years later that he made his way to the port of Serdobol on Lake Ladoga, took the steamer to Valaam, and understood that he had come home. "Nationality is a sacred thing and unhappy is he who is uprooted from it and cannot put down roots elsewhere."[21] He had been seeking refreshment of spirit to enhance his missionary work but stayed on as long as he could as a labourer at the monastery, then returned as soon as possible to become a novice. Here, in this isolated Russian monastery, in physical work in the woods and on the waters and in singing with the choir, Anatolii Nechaev discovered an imponderable awareness of the presence of God and of His care for the created world, a feeling of joy and belonging. He was at ease, too, with the unsentimental benevolence and serenity of the monks. It was not an easy regime: eight hours of communal prayers, eight of labour and eight for eating, conversing and sleeping, but this, he found, gave him strength and endurance beyond anything he had experienced in his energetic life in the world. Although the future Father Afanasii had come to accept the possibility of belief through the example of his Salvation Army friend[i] and through his reading of William James' *A Pluralistic Universe*,

---

i. Afanasii does not mention this influence in his memoirs but he must have told both his spiritual children – Metropolitan Anthony and the nun Genofeva – about it, as they both do so, the nun adding that he broke off ties with the

which convinced him a man could be both a critically thinking intellectual and a believing Christian, he was still, at first, suspicious of the "consolations" of religion and felt that there was no hope of achieving communion with the Divine until one had oneself attained a high degree of perfection. Now, on Valaam, he found the humility to take his preliminary vows and to entrust his sins immediately to the grace of God rather than struggle for self-improvement before confronting his Maker "not as a sinner but as one of the righteous. Of course, I did not think so clearly, had no such clear picture of my position, as I write it now, but basically that was exactly how it was. And of course, on that basis, I had not been able to come close to God."[22]

Nevertheless, Anatolii did not settle on Valaam. His newfound serenity was disturbed by the monastery's break with the Moscow Patriarchate and the introduction of the new calendar, which became a cause for bitter dissension amongst the hitherto peaceful brethren. Also, his active mind felt somewhat under-exercised, something of which his superiors in the monastery were evidently well aware, for in 1926 they sent him to train as a theologian in Paris. They were not, however, in a position to allot him more money than was essential for the fare for his journey and, had it not been for the charity of the crew on the Baltic steamer and the friendly interest of fellow passengers, the gaunt but cheerful novice-monk would have starved *en route*. Anatolii was never to have the opportunity to return to his beloved monastery. The Russian emigration in France was in need of priests and Metropolitan Evlogii received him as a fully-professed monk with the name of Afanasii shortly after he enrolled at the Institute of St Sergius, reclaiming him for the Moscow Patriarchate, to which he was to remain faithful until his death, and directing him to minister to a Russian parish in the south. After Evlogii, in his turn, sought the protection of Constantinople in 1931 and Bishop Veniamin departed for the United States two years later, Father Afanasii was recalled to Paris as Vicar of the new Church of the Three Holy Hierarchs – and took on the spiritual directorship of Andrei Bloom.

It was a happy meeting. Afanasii, a Christian first and a monk afterwards, a man of simple country priestly stock yet of wide-ranging experience and venturesome spirit, a lifelong seeker after truth and enlightenment, who carried in his heart the memory of the excellent loneliness, gentleness and simplicity of the Valaam monastery, was well-qualified to guide the ardent aspirations of a stateless youth who could not afford to become a monk. In

---

Salvation Army after he became aware that its presence in the Soviet Union was not without political motivation. To Anthony, the story of his recovery of a faith lost in the grind of Russian Orthodox officialdom in Tsarist Russia through contact with the active philanthropy of the protestant organisation and the intellectual questioning of William James, before he came to the revelation of Valaamo, made Afanasii someone to whom he himself could relate with absolute empathy and trust, "a man of our times".

a sense, Afanasii was a Martha who knew that Mary had indeed chosen the better part, but who was clearly aware, from his own experience, that all human beings have to find and tread the path God intends for them, to serve where they are sent. He was, most probably, as his disciple later said of him, "not a saint, but simply a man of our times"[23] – but a man who had chosen to consecrate his time to the service of God and his fellows.

Having taken Andrei on, Afanasii worked steadily to set him free: from himself, from fear, from passions, prejudices and the trammels of imagined virtue as of real evil, and ultimately even from dependence on his spiritual father. He taught the young man to acquire this freedom gradually, gently, with the odd flash of humour, as when Andrei came to him with the awful confession that he had spoilt his Lenten fast by eating chicken on Good Friday.[i] "You have so many sins on your conscience," his confessor commented amiably, "that I really don't see that a bite or two of chicken is here or there."[24] In the same way, although a great advocate of the spiritual strength monks can achieve by keeping all the offices, Afanasii was aware that his penitent was exhausting himself in the struggle to fulfil the eight hours of prayer rule at home and university. "So, you're praying a lot, are you?" he enquired; "You enjoy praying?" He imposed a six-month period during which his penitent was to confine himself to five prostrations and the humblest and briefest of supplications – "Through the prayers of those who love me, Lord have mercy" – then go about his daily tasks with a light heart. "The devil," Afanasii writes in his reminiscences of Valaam, "is particularly dangerous when he approaches us in the guise of our good genius with good advice. He particularly likes to suggest to monks that they attempt feats beyond their strength."[25] True, he insisted that the way of the monk is the way of the Cross – only not in his own strength but in Christ's:

> [N]o-one knows how much bloody struggle, spiritual and corporal, is concealed behind the stone walls of the monastery, what cross every monk bears on his shoulders, what price he pays for this openheartedness to his neighbour, this gentleness, this strength of spirit he knows how to impart to the souls of those who are overburdened, weary and exhausted. Those are all secrets of the monastic life known only to the monk himself and to Christ – He is the One who perfects the secret life of a monk, his Renewer, his strength and his joy.[26]

Andrei continued under obedience to this spiritual father until Afanasii's death shortly after professing him a full monk under the name of Antonii, after the founder of the Kievo-Pechersky Monastery, in 1943. It was a very special form of training designed to accustom the individual to seek not

---

i. For the best of good reasons: Andrei had been invited to dine by a very poor family. As a guest, he had been unable to refuse the scraggy bird which his hosts could ill afford.

his own but God's will, not to relieve him of responsibility for himself and others but, through the spiritual guide, to entrust all to God. As a priest, Anthony was always to insist that such a relationship should be entered into only voluntarily and with total commitment to a spiritually experienced guide or *starets*, deploring the tendency among comparatively inexperienced priests in late-twentieth-century Russia to encourage their penitents to accept direction on every aspect of daily life, something he considered spiritually perilous for both pastor and penitent.[27] The task of a spiritual director, he said, is to lead his pupil into the presence of God and then efface himself. When Father Afanasii died, Anthony did wonder whether he should seek a replacement, but was profoundly comforted by a dream in which the *starets* appeared to him to say that there was no reason why the relationship should be broken off by death and that he would continue to watch over him in prayer.

That is not to say that the youth Andrei always found obedience easy. There was an incident when he asked for Afanasii's blessing to try for a competitive examination that promised much-needed prize money and kudos. Scenting vanity, the monk bade him sit the exam but not win the prize. Andrei obeyed and achieved – according to his own account without perceptible spiritual benefit – a mediocre result. Another test of his humility was Afanasii's suggestion that, since he seemed to be becoming "some kind of a star" in the young people's summer camps, he should refrain from this work for a while. This he did, pleading pressure of work at the university. Still harder was Afanasii's insistence that, before taking vows as a monk, Andrei must be ready to renounce the world, including his family. Afanasii himself had "abandoned" a beloved, widowed mother in Russia when he entered the monastery in Valaam and felt that Andrei must be prepared to make the same sacrifices, even though there was no monastery for him to enter, before pronouncing his initial vows. It was a terrible decision and when in 1939 the young man eventually made it, expecting to be retained in the church to sleep on the floor of his mentor's cell, he was totally overthrown at first and more angry than grateful to be sent off home and put "under obedience" to his own mother and anyone else who might be put in authority over him. Of course, he had warned his mother of his intention and their relationship was never quite the same again, although it remained exceptionally alive, close and loving.

Still, the discipline of obedience, though not always easy, was not imposed from without, but freely accepted because Andrei wanted to become like his mentor: strong, free and unafraid, a clean window onto the "gentle light" of Christ, and a purveyor of that light to his fellow men. And it worked. Afanasii had been a missionary first then, finding something lacking, had become a monk, then a priest. Andrei, under his guidance, became first a doctor, then a monk, then a priest, then a missionary, and drew all his life on the spiritual strength and inner freedom he had learned during his long novitiate without benefit of monastery.

The second powerful influence on Andrei Bloom during his student years also, albeit indirectly, stemmed from Afanasii, who, in 1936, sent him to serve in the francophone Orthodox parish of the Mother of God, Joy of all who Sorrow, and of Ste Geneviève of Paris.

> And that was the beginning of a whole renaissance. Until then there had been resistance to everything non-Russian and non-Orthodox, but here we blossomed out. . . . How sore at heart and unwilling I was to commit myself! But then I began to see how the gift of Orthodoxy could change the lives of people who were not Russians, how their souls opened out, how their minds became receptive, the birth of a new attitude to our motherland and to our Church.[28]

The vicar at the time was Protopriest Mikhail Iudin-Bel'sky, but the original inspiration behind the church came from the Brotherhood of St Photius and the Russophile French monk Father Lev Gillet. The idea of celebrating in French had been originally approved by Metropolitan Evlogii. He had intended the initiative to serve the needs of young second-generation émigrés no longer fluent in their native Russian and unable to follow the services in Church Slavonic, but it also came to meet the spiritual requirements of an increasing congregation of French Orthodox who came from both the Roman Catholic and Protestant Churches, often through marriage but also attracted by the stability of ancient forms and the charismatic witness of the poverty-stricken but intellectually vibrant Russian community. The growing emphasis on outreach beyond Russian émigré circles stemmed largely from the Brotherhood of St Photius, who dreamed of a revitalisation of Western Christianity that would grow naturally from contact between their dispossessed Russian Church and the countries where its adherents had settled. Untrammelled by the ethnic limitations and oppressive historical experience of the Eastern Church would spring an Orthodox revival close in spirit to the original impulse of the spread of Christianity, able to draw freely upon the rich heritage of the undivided Church. The Brotherhood was founded on 11 February 1925 by "a group of students, all fiercely Orthodox, all open to European culture and modern thought"[29] (Vladimir and Madeleine Lossky, Pavel Evdokimov, Nadezhda Gorodetskaia, Nicholas and Militza Zernov and Maksim and Evgraf Kovalevsky, all highly articulate young intellectuals), who met up with Father Lev Gillet, a French Benedictine monk whom Evlogii had received from the Roman Catholic Church into communion with the Orthodox Church "without abjuration" at an ACER conference in 1928. Father Lev was enchanted by the Russians' enthusiasm and readiness for sacrifice: "The great attraction of this religious movement," he wrote to his brother at the time, "is that there is nothing formal or conventional about it, everything there is fresh and spontaneous, like sap rising. Russian young people in Paris help me to understand the birth of the Church in Jerusalem as described in Acts."[30]

Encouraged by Evlogii, whose plan was originally merely to "save the Orthodox youth among those Russians, who had lost their national identity",[31] a commission was set up headed by the Kovalevsky brothers to translate the Liturgy into French. In this way, the ethos of the Brotherhood came to imbue the whole parish – but it was Father Lev who nurtured their feeling for the catholicity, the universality of Orthodoxy. Without in any way encouraging proselytism, he worked towards a Western expression of Orthodoxy that would, by its very nature, reach out in witness and mission, all the more because it was not triumphalist, not intended to confound other denominations, but rather to raise "from indigenous springs" the tradition of the undivided Church. When the ex-Benedictine took over the infant "French parish" he refined and nourished this line of thought, working out in practice over the late 1920s and early 1930s a concept of Orthodox Christianity that was supra-national, universal and evangelical. Evlogii's blessing and the goodwill of such luminaries as Lev Zander and Sergii Bulgakov ensured the benevolent interest of the Institute of St Sergius and it was here, in November 1927, that the first Liturgy was celebrated in French, followed by the first "parish meeting". In the January 1929 issue of the new parish magazine, *La Voie*, Lev Gillet formulated their aims:

> At the beginning our community planned to provide for the spiritual needs of a number of Russian refugees who had become French in language and nationality. We need, moreover, to provide for the spiritual needs of a few French people who profess the Orthodox faith, whether as a result of family ties with Russia or through free choice. Thus our parish was founded. It is not part of the framework of the Russian Church. It is true that we are currently under the jurisdiction of the Metropolitan of the Russian Orthodox Church in western Europe, and that canonically we depend on him. However, if we depend upon His Eminence Metropolitan Evlogii, it is not because he is the head of the Russian Orthodox Church in western Europe, but (following the census) because he is the closest bishop to our infant community. It is possible, even natural, that French Orthodoxy, when it has reached a certain stage of development, might become autonomous. And, as Orthodoxy is neither Byzantine nor Slav, but universal, it is up to western Orthodox to create a type of Orthodoxy which belongs to the west and which, by returning to traditional local roots, could have marked differences from the Eastern sort.

We do not practise proselytism. We respect and love our brothers in Christ. Far from dreaming of a battle or competition, we pray for collaboration wherever possible. We deplore the fact that Christian unity has been broken and we ask God that it may soon be re-established.

We have ties with the ancient "orthodox" tradition in France, with that "most Christian" France of the centuries when East and West were not separated. Saint Irenaeus (who was the bridge between East and West), the martyrs of Lyons and Vienne, Saint Denis, Saint Martin de Tours, Sainte Geneviève: these are some of the great names with whom we wish to associate ourselves.[32]

It was this little parish, inspired by Father Lev's lucid search for unity via a return to common roots, fired by the enthusiasm of dispossessed young Russians who had found a new calling in the propagation of the one treasure left to them – a treasure "where their hearts were also", their Orthodox Christianity – that, from 1936, was to provide the French-educated Russian patriot Andrei Bloom with his apprenticeship to active service in the Church. Nikolai Lossky says that Andrei was not a member of the St Photius Brotherhood – presumably he was simply too young at the time he first became interested in the Church. However, at the bidding of Father Afanasii, who felt his disciple's youth and French schooling would make him useful to the French parishioners, he joined them in serving in and around the Church of the Mother of God, Joy of all who Sorrow and Ste Geneviève, which, like every Russian Orthodox church in Paris, was chronically short-handed and dependent on the enthusiasm of its parishioners for singers, readers and servers. By the time Andrei was directed to offer his services to the struggling community, Father Lev was no longer full-time resident, but, though often absent and of no fixed abode in Paris, he still celebrated the Divine Liturgy there whenever he was able and, when he did so, delivered a brief extempore sermon on the Gospel of the day, sharing with the congregation his own social, evangelical and mystic Orthodox faith, an experiential faith rooted in a sacramental, eschatological vision of the world.

Andrei's association with the charismatic French priest-monk, therefore, pre-dated not only his own ordination but even his qualification as a doctor of medicine and his first profession of monastic vows. Indeed, the very idea of a monastic vocation in the world was already being lived out by the itinerant, endemically homeless Frenchman, as it was by his friend Mother Maria (Skobtsova), at whose hostel for destitute compatriots Gillet served as visiting chaplain from 1935 to 1938. It was a concept of monasticism dear to the heart of Sergii Bulgakov, Pavel Evdokimov, Father Aleksandr Elchaninov and other Russians whose thought reached back to Vladimir

Solov'ev's mission to convey the essence of Christianity to the secular world through secular culture rather than against the trend of modern thought. Although Andrei loved the sobriety and silence of his mentor's memory of Valaam and his own dream of desert monasticism and was somewhat disturbed by the sight of Mother Maria smoking and chatting over a glass of beer like any lay intellectual,[33] and although his fierce traditionalism meant he admired Georgii Florovsky's uncompromisingly patristic stance above the somewhat amorphous platonicism of the Solovievian school, he served his apprenticeship as an ecclesiastic in the extraordinarily free and modern French Orthodox parish engendered by Father Lev Gillet. It was Gillet and Bulgakov who invited the young Dr Bloom to address the Fellowship of St Albans and St Sergius in London; it was Gillet who then suggested to Anthony that he become a priest; it was Father Lev and the priest Mikhail Bel'sky he asked to sponsor him at his consecration as bishop, and, at the French priest's funeral in the Greek Cathedral in London, he acknowledged a very real debt both to the man himself and to his kenotic understanding of monasticism:

> One day, we shall all stand before the face of the Lord. Father Lev, who from childhood gave his heart to poverty, will stand in silence, his hands empty before God. His hands will be empty because he has given everything, conscious only of being a sinner whose only hope rests in the unconditional love of God.
>
> Will it not be marvellous, then, for those who have not heard his voice in vain and who have loved him actively, to present the fruit of their lives to the Lord and to say to him "I was only a field, Father Lev was the sower, his word the seed. Let my whole life now be to his glory."[34]

Now, re-examining the time between the spiritual experience which made the future Metropolitan Anthony aware of his own calling and the time he launched into adult life as a doctor, these two formative sources emerge very clearly: the robust spirituality and wise counsel of the country priest's son from the Monastery of Valaam, Afanasii, and the inspired ecumenical vision of the Catholic Orthodox monk of the Eastern Church, Lev Gillet. It was a combination that could only have come about in the melting pot of the Russian emigration in Paris in the 1930s. Metropolitan Anthony acknowledged several other intellectual influences, notably those of the Orthodox theologian Vladimir Lossky, the icon painter Leonid Ouspensky and the theologian Georgii Florovsky. Nevertheless, it was surely Lev and Afanasii, those two strikingly dissimilar "monks without a monastery", who influenced his growth, moulded his understanding of the Church of Christ in the world, and, more than any other human agency, shaped his future.

Chapter Four

Surgeon in the French Army and Monk in the Surgery, 1937-1949

As soldiers of Christ let us go forth into life with new hope and with new strength, let us bring into this cold world our own fiery, victorious joy, so that every soul might rejoice, so that all fear might be dispersed, so that the light of Christ might shine forth upon all people, upon all without exception, and cry aloud: "Glory be to God in the highest and on Earth peace, good will towards man." Amen.[1]

In 1937, Boris Eduardovich Bloom fell ill. He came to visit his family for the Easter feast. Father and son spent some time alone together, during which they talked, opening their hearts and minds to one another as never before "with a deep communion of silence at the root of our meeting". When Andrei returned from his hospital practice, his father was dead. "I was not even upset I hadn't said goodbye to him," he recalled many years later. "We had said everything that needed to be said to one another during that last talk."[2]

In that same year Andrei and his mother became naturalised French citizens. This ensured that, when war finally broke out in 1939, he was subject to call-up and drafted into the medical corps of the French army, having completed his medical studies at the Sorbonne but not yet submitted his doctoral thesis. Before departing for the army, he took his preliminary vows in secret as a monk. During training, Afanasii's having put him "under obedience" to anyone set in authority over him took on an almost ludicrous aspect, "going to the limits of perfect absurdity" under the hail of orders from the corporal in charge of new recruits.[3] Much later, Bishop Anthony was to describe ideal obedience, whether to the promptings of God or to a spiritual director, as the attitude of a dog in training, all eager attention and wagging tail. Possibly Afanasii's injunction helped him to pass easily from the training camp to a commission as field surgeon. He never, though, depicted his soldier self as an example of disciplined humility or conformism, but told rather how he got into trouble for exhorting a pompous young superior officer not to make a fool of himself before his men by constantly puffing up his own authority and, on a later occasion, after he himself was commissioned, how he was subjected to boycott by his own mess for letting down their dignity as officers by wading in to clean out a filthy surgery with his own hands – obviously a task for other ranks. Anti-communist by conviction the young surgeon certainly was, but also, by nature, a true egalitarian and a free spirit.

We know very little about Andrei's brief war record, except that he was awarded the *médaille d'honneur* for active devotion in tending the wounded as leader of

Passport photograph, 1939

a mobile unit under enemy bombardment and that his fluent German brought him into immediate contact with hospitalised prisoners: the man with the broken hand whose shattered finger he managed to save from the quick and easy option of amputation on learning he was by trade a watchmaker; the bewildered farmer's boy afraid to die alone whose hand he held through the night when off duty; and the young Nazi whom he could not help admiring for his defiance in the face of death: "I am not at all sorry to die because we are beating you all along the line."[4]

They were indeed! Andrei, no pacifist, was as fiercely opposed to National Socialism and the ambitions of the Third Reich as he was to communism and always maintained he would have volunteered for the army had he not been called up. What he did volunteer for as the German army swept into Paris and the French demobilised was to stay on and accompany the military hospital in which he was serving to help them evacuate to unoccupied territory, for which we have the evidence of a friend with whom he met up on the way, who needed to return to Paris and to whom he unhesitatingly gave "all the money he had" to help him on his way, having first extracted a painful bee-sting.[5] Here too we have some evidence from loving women and children, such as the daughter of a nurse who served under him in one of the hospitals where he worked, who wrote years later on reading one of his books to tell him that her mother had often told her she would have died had young Dr Bloom not taken time off from his wounded soldiers to heal her of some virulent childish sickness.[6]

When finally demobilised in the environments of Pau, Dr Bloom discovered that his mother and grandmother had been evacuated to the Limoges region, where he eventually found them in a little village:

Mother was ill, Grandmother was old, and I decided we would return to Paris and see what we could do there. My first idea was to join France Libre. However, this proved impossible because by this time the Pyrenees were blockaded. Possibly somebody with more initiative would have managed it, but I did not.

We reached a village near the demarcation line of the Occupied Zone, and I went to the town hall. I was then in full army uniform, apart from my jacket, which I had bought in order to hide as much of my uniform as possible, and I went to the Mayor to explain that I needed a pass. He said to me, "You know that this is impossible. I am afraid that I would be shot for it." Nobody was allowed to cross the demarcation line without a German pass. I went on and on persuading him, and finally he said to me, "You know what we shall do: I will put a piece of paper here on the table, which has to be filled in, and here is the mayor's stamp. You will take it and stamp the paper – and then you will steal it. If you are arrested, I will say that you stole them from me." That was all I needed. I needed papers, and if I had been arrested they would not have started asking him, they would in any case imprison me. I filled in the papers and we crossed the line, which was also very amusing. My mother, grandmother and I were in different carriages, not for conspiratorial reasons but simply because there were no other seats available. In my compartment there were four old French ladies, who were trembling with fear because they were convinced the Germans would tear them to bits, and a totally drunk French soldier who shouted the whole time that if a German should appear he would kill him at once: boom, boom, boom. And the old ladies believed it: a German inspector would come in, the solider would shout, and we would all be shot for it. I was travelling in a certain state of apprehension because under my jacket I was in full army uniform and army personnel were not allowed to enter – or rather they were allowed to but they would be immediately taken to prisoner of war camps. I decided that I needed to stand up in such a way that the inspector would not look at me below the shoulders, and therefore suggested to my travelling companions that as I could speak German they should give me their passports and I would deal with the inspector. When the German officer came in, I jumped up, stood right against him, almost pressing myself against him so that he would see nothing except my jacket, gave him the papers, explained everything, and he even thanked me for it. . . .[7]

On their return to Paris, Andrei continued at least loosely attached to service in military hospitals and, throughout the occupation, contrived to subsidise the family budget by taking on supplementary replacement

*In uniform with mother and grandmother
before leaving for the front, 1939*

teaching in a variety of subjects at the Russian school. At a time when the Lossky family were fully engaged with the Resistance, when Mother Maria and her associates were doing all in their power to save Jews and others directly threatened by the Nazi regime and Father Afanasii was – without qualm of conscience – issuing false certificates of baptism to any who came to him for help, Andrei Bloom was recruited by an elderly French doctor he had known before the war to the French medical Resistance. He and his medical friends falsified x-rays when young people conscripted to work for the Germans behind the lines were sent in for examination. The one thing the occupying authorities were really careful about, he recorded, was infection, and tuberculosis ruled you out for working in Germany. Soon, he was leading a double life, moving men and weapons under cover in medical vehicles, treating the wounded, circulating literature. He and his mother took a solemn oath not to betray anyone else involved in these activities, even should one be tortured in front of the other – the Gestapo's methods had very soon become notorious. Indeed, Mother Maria (Skobtsova), her son Iurii, Father Dmitrii Klepinin and their friend Bunakov Fondaminsky, a convert from Judaism, were arrested early in 1943 and perished in concentration camps. Father Afanasii, twice detained but on each occasion released, was subjected to constant harassment by the occupying authorities, particularly after the invasion of

Russia.[i] Andrei himself was rounded up only once, by chance for being out after curfew, and subjected to a hair-raising interrogation by a suspicious French policeman who, convinced the name Bloom was English, refused to believe he was a Russian-born citizen of France: "The Russians all have heavy cheekbones and slitty eyes – we have been told so," he kept repeating, glaring at his captive's neat features and burning brown eyes. "You've got us mixed up with the Chinese," Andrei assured him. His interrogator decided to try another, ideological tack, and asked his opinion of Hitler and the Third Reich. Convinced he had been detected and the man was playing with him, Andrei decided on a last fling and told him – in no uncertain terms. To his utter amazement, the officer's face lit up in response. He was ordered to get out of the guardroom before worse befell him. "I did nothing very heroic in the Resistance," was his own assessment in interviews.[8]

Bloom's teaching at the Russian school is better documented and was recalled with enthusiasm. One pupil, Veronica Lossky, recalls:

> He was much loved, particularly because he was quite different in manner from the others [the other teachers], he was not authoritarian, indeed it was as though he were our equal (not all that much different in age, he must have been about 20 [in fact, by that time, he was nearer 30, but that is how she remembers him] and we between 10 and 12). There was a spirit of camaraderie, but that didn't mean a free-for-all. He was fair without the constraint or outward discipline that everyone else imposed on us, which irked us and made us giggle. If he asked anything of us we wanted to do it because he would explain and it was reasonable. He was simply intelligent in his way of maintaining discipline and he was not, as a result, strict. He was just fair, requiring what was really essential.[9]

At the same time, Andrei continued steadfastly to pursue his double vocation. In 1943, Afanasii finally received him as a full monk under the name Anthony in honour of the founder of the Kievo-Pechersky Monastery. There was a last barrier: Andrei had asked to be professed "in secret" so that he might continue to practise as a doctor and support his family, but Afanasii, at this final stage, demanded that he make a total commitment. You could not, he said, strike a bargain with God and "have it both ways". However, when the young man, finally broken in spirit, agreed even to put his new hard-won profession and his beloved dependants in the hands of

---

i. The Germans were originally inclined to go easy on White Russian émigrés, seeing them as potential allies against communism, but after the invasion of the Soviet Union in 1941, when Stalin allowed the Patriarch to speak unscripted on air and he appealed to all Orthodox to defend their country, they became suspicious and hostile, particularly towards the Moscow Patriarchal Church.

God, his spiritual guide gave his blessing to his taking them back upon his own shoulders and continuing as a "secret" monk. As the Metropolitan said in his deeply affectionate memoir of Afanasii, it was for God to provide the ram for sacrifice – Abraham did not slip off to market beforehand to purchase a substitute for his only son. It would not have been the same thing at all. In fact, though, the "secret" was a pretty open one. According to Anthony's friend Nikolai Lossky, "everybody knew" and one of his pupils at the Russian School, Marina Fennel, remembers: "He defended his thesis the day I was sitting my baccalauréat and we bumped into each other in the corridor of the Sorbonne. He was in tearing spirits. I think it was very soon after that that he was professed monk, in secret because he wanted to go on supporting his family."[10]

The thesis, rather surprisingly for a monk who has been working as an army surgeon, is an elegant and strictly clinical defence of a non-invasive operation technique perfected by Dr Picot, to remove via the "vagino-perinal route" fistulas situated far up the vagina on the wall of the bladder, often the result of a hysterectomy. It gives a description of four alternative methods, detailed case histories of various operations, and due consideration to the critique of Picot's method by other surgeons who tended to ascribe his remarkable success rate to his skill in operating rather than to his chosen way of entry which, they felt, constituted an operation in itself before the fistula is reached and might lead to interior damage to either bladder or vagina. Bloom's thesis concludes with a rebuttal of these criticisms which draws on the support of an eminent oncologist, Dr R. Couvelaire, to prove that Picot's preferred method of carefully negotiated anatomical separation rather than cutting is less likely to cause bilateral damage than other means. The thesis, presented on 28 July 1943 for Bloom's doctorate in Medicine, is dedicated to Professor M. Couvelaire, honorary Professor at the Faculty of Medicine, Commander of the Legion of Honour, Croix de Guerre, "who has been so kind as to do us the honour of accepting the direction of this thesis: in token of my profound gratitude"; to Dr G. Picot, surgeon of the hospitals, "who has done us the single honour of entrusting to us the exposition and the defence of the beautiful technique of which he is author"; and to Dr Roger Couvelaire, hospital surgeon and professor of the faculty, "who inspired this thesis and in whom we have always found a most reliable guide and constant support". There is also an "in memoriam" for Professors R. Gregorie, A. Havelacque and F. Ratlevy, "who have been our unforgettable teachers", for Monsieur Joyet-Lavergne, Inspector of the Academy, and for Jacques Millet and Raoul Combes, Professors of the Faculty of Science at Paris, "who taught me to love and know the natural sciences"; and, no doubt lest anyone who had helped him in any way might feel slighted or forgotten, a dedication to "my teachers at the faculty and in the hospitals". On the front page, there are two more, less formal dedications:

Aux miens.
A mes amis.[11]

That the now fully qualified Dr Bloom did not take advantage of the freedom from monastic rule essential to active life in the world is clear from many small fragments of recollection.

Indeed, it was amidst the dangers, the utter vulnerability of life under the occupation that he experienced an extraordinarily intense epiphany:

> I was walking across Paris without the permit to see a patient. I was crossing a bridge, the moon was full, I was in full view and the order for German patrols was to shoot to kill anyone who was to be seen in the streets after a certain time. And of a sudden I became aware of the divine presence in such overwhelming manner that right in the middle of this bridge I knelt down and bowed to the ground, and said to the Lord, "Lord, if for Your victory on earth and in Heaven You must claim my utter destruction let it be and glory be to You!" A phrase which is absurd perhaps in itself but which expresses what I felt of the greatness, the beauty of a God to whom one can give oneself unreservedly.[12]

Once, walking with Father Afanasii in a neglected Russian graveyard, he became quite carried away by the old priest's suggestion that he camp out in the grounds to care for the graves and pray for the souls of the departed, a kind of modern "desert" which immediately appealed to the newly consecrated monk Anthony's romantic heart. The two monastics "in the world" spent some time seriously discussing the practical possibilities of such a course of action, and it was Afanasii who first burst out laughing, clapped Anthony on the shoulder and exclaimed: "You know, all this is quite impossible! You have to work."[13]

Again, coming across Father Afanasii waiting at a bus stop, Anthony hurried up to him gladly: "Father Afanasii, now you've made a monk of me, but you never gave me any rule of prayer." "Whatever do you want a rule for?" Afanasii replied. "You're a monk now – pray all the time!"[14] He had not been taught to keep the rules. He had been taught boundless trust in God and love for his fellows – a more exacting, because never perfectly fulfillable, discipline.

One "rule", however, Anthony himself invented there and then, taking as his criterion of poverty the minimum diet recommended as compatible with keeping up health and strength to a wartime French population in the grip of austerity. He made an agreement with his mother that this was to be the touchstone of their housekeeping, even should they live on into a time of plenty. To give pleasure to guests this rule may well have been more honoured in the breach than in the observance. Ksenia Nikolaevna and her

Surgeon, 1943

son were no killjoys and, according to Nikolai Lossky, neither professional nor monastic conscience stood in the way of Dr Bloom's prescribing surgical spirit when his friends could not obtain vodka to celebrate Pancake Day![15] Nevertheless, there is ample evidence that Anthony, throughout his long life, lived at well below what is now considered "poverty-level" and ate very sparingly; also, however splendidly robed he may have appeared in church, the shabby black cassock, occasionally held together by a visible safety-pin, which he wore every day, became positively legendary in his London diocese. The St Petersburg lady, who made several films of the Russian

Church in London and of Anthony preaching, catching a glimpse of him as an old man out in the street carrying his weekly shopping and described his appearance as an old man coming home to the Cathedral from the nearby Knightsbridge shops as that of a *bomzh* – one of those displaced people *bez opredellenogo mesta zhitel'stva*[i] who lived in the underground heating systems of post-Soviet Russian cities and scavenged through other people's rubbish for scraps.

It was not until finally demobilised after the end of the war that Bloom, who had been reluctant to go through the formalities of registration under the occupation, set up his own practice as a doctor. When De Gaulle led the Free French into Paris, indeed, the remobilised Dr Bloom was in some way, as medic and bodyguard, attached to his suite. He always remembered with admiration the immensely tall General stalking on up the aisle of Notre-Dame after a sudden burst of gunfire from the shadows had sent his escort diving for the shelter of the pews! The liberation also left less uplifting memories. Anthony was sickened by the public humiliation of collaborators. One revenge attack he witnessed at first hand was a man he knew to have betrayed fellow Resistance workers, a very bad man, being marched shaven-headed, beaten, bloodied and pelted with filth to execution. As the procession passed him by, he realised Christ must have looked like that, staggering under His cross. In the hospitals, he would use all his authority to protect threatened patients, whatever their nationality or past record.

Ksenia Nikolaevna, Ol'ga Il'inichna and Anthony had, by the time he opened his first surgery, been living some ten years at 3 Rue, Île Saint-Louis on the Seine river in Paris. He acquired a bicycle, on which he hurtled around the comparatively empty, post-war streets to visit his patients. Some paid, but it was said that the surgery was always full of elderly émigrés who could not. When not with his patients, Anthony would encourage young people, many of them his ex-pupils from the Russian school, to foregather at his house in an informal Bible study group. Veronica Lossky remembers how eagerly they would assemble at the family flat in the early evening. Anthony would ask each adolescent member of the group to prepare their own commentary on a passage or on two apparently contradictory passages of scripture. She recalls being allotted "not peace but a sword" and "love one another", still deeply gratified by the commendation that her presentation was "très bien réflechi" (very well thought-through). Sometimes, he would expand on passages himself, which was "even more interesting".[16]

It was still under the name of André Bloom that he attended the Fifth International Conference on Religious Psychology which took place at the Maison d'Avon in Fontainebleau on 19 September 1948 and gave a paper on

---

i. Hence the acronym "bomzh": of no fixed abode.

"Contemplation and Ascesis", published in the resultant proceedings. This begins, in his elegant native speaker's French:

> Contemplation is neither something people do nor yet a transitory state.
> It should be the whole of one's being, for it is the one and only foundation: "and this is life eternal, that they should know Thee the only true God." (John 17:3).
> It is the one and only vocation. The way, the reason for being.[17]

In the parlance of the Eastern Church, he explains, the individual is the human being accessible to our senses and knowledge, Adam, who has become "as one of us". As such, the individual is opposed to the community. The *person*, on the other hand, is as non-confrontational as the touch of a pianist, the tone of a voice. The "person" is defined by that name written on a stone and prepared for each one of the saved according to the Book of Revelations. The "person" does not oppose others but is *with* (the French is in fact *towards*) them and *with* God (John 1:1). Moving from the contemplative to the active life, Dr Bloom continues:

> Action, for a contemplative, that is to say for all Christians inclusively, has no value in itself: it either bears witness to or teaches the spiritual life, which is not to say pious thoughts and emotions, but the putting into practice of the life desired by God, which forges – through tragedy – the human soul.[18]

The brief bibliography at the end of this paper refers the reader to Vladimir Lossky's *Essai sur la Théologie mystique de l'Eglise d'Orient* (Aubier, 1943) and Lev Gillet's *Orthodox Spirituality: An Outline of the Orthodox Ascetical and Mystical Tradition by a Monk of the Eastern Church* (London, SPCK, 1945).

The emphasis on "tragedy" suggests, beyond the influence of these two older friends, the whole intellectual and spiritual climate engendered by the journal *Put'* ("The Way") founded in 1925 by Nikolai Berdiaev and Lev Shestov (the author of *The Philosophy of Tragedy* based on the works of Tolstoy, Dostoevsky and Nietzsche). *Put'* had come out regularly as *La Voie: organe de la pensée religieuse russe* until 1940 and served to unite and express the free interaction of divergent currents of Russian twentieth-century religious thought. Its authors included, among others and besides the founders, Georgii Florovsky; Vasilii Zenkovsky, author of a history of Russian philosophy; Boris Vysheslavtsev; Semen Frank; Vladimir Il'in; Sergii Bulgakov; Georgii Fedotov; Nikolai Onufrievich Lossky, father of Anthony's "older friend" the theologian Vladimir, and grandfather of his "younger friend" Nikolai Lossky; and Nicholas Zernov. Antoine Arjakovsky, in his monumental study of the journal and its contributors, describes *Put'* as "a space circumscribed in time and place in whose womb matured the consciousness of an intellectual generation united by the common trauma of revolution and exile as well as by the cultural memory of Russia's past".[19]

The monk Anthony matured too late and was too busy with his medical studies to be a contributor to *Put'*, but he was certainly a reader, inspired among other things by Berdiaev's dictum "that we are not in exile but on a mission" (*"ne v izgnanii a v poslanii"*) and by the broad tolerance of an editorial policy that allowed readers to acknowledge the true and the beautiful beyond the borders of the Judeo-Greek tradition of Christian culture and to argue out their own inter-Orthodox differences on its pages. Anthony, indeed, always had respect for other revelations of the Divine Nature, albeit partial, not yet containing the "Fullness of Truth". He teased his mentor Vladimir Lossky, who tended to discount other creeds wholesale as "paganism", by presenting him with a bouquet of quotations from the Upanishads and asking his help to trace their patristic provenance. The good theologian came back to him with all the required attributions to sayings of various Fathers of the Church and, when shown the actual source, admitted good-naturedly that he must indeed rethink his attitude.

It is clear from the evening classes, from the active role he played at the YMCA Conference of 1947 and from this first venture into print that Dr Bloom's medical practice did not divert him altogether from the "angelic way". Indeed, he was inclining more and more towards the priesthood, constantly anxious about the amount of time and energy he nevertheless had to devote to medicine.

One day, as he sat in his surgery waiting for a patient, he opened his Bible at random and found himself reading in the twenty-eighth chapter of Isaiah:

> "And if thou draw out thy soul to the hungry and the afflicted soul; then shall the light rise in obscurity, and thy darkness be as the noonday." (v.10) I baulked; because all my life I had been very reticent, and my spiritual father brought me up never to tell anybody about my inner life. At that time I was being pressurised to become a priest: "We need priests," but that would mean opening out. You can never supress every spark of your own inner life if you are trying to help someone else. I thought: Surely God isn't telling me: yes, go on and lay your inner life out like a stall at market, open up, let people take what they want? . . . I read the same verse three times, three times the meaning came through quite clearly. . . . What it says is: feed the souls of the hungry. And in the context that boils down to: feed the one who has no food. And as I understood it, it decided my fate. I decided: yes, I'll become a priest. Possibly it was a temptation and I ought not to have succumbed to it, but that's another question.[20]

It is not surprising, at this stage, that Lev Gillet and Sergii Bulgakov, who had become deeply involved with the Orthodox-Anglican Fellowship of St Alban and St Sergius, should have invited Dr Bloom to join them in explaining the Orthodox approach at a conference in London in 1948.

The still youthful-looking 34-year-old doctor of medicine, clean-shaven and with a distinct spring in his step, was not what the Fellowship really expected of an Orthodox theologian, but they found his presence among them inspiring and, when it became clear that the Russian Orthodox Church in Paris had ordained him priest, invited him to come to London as their chaplain.

This next step in Bloom's career

At the Fellowship of St Alban and St Sergius (FSASS) conference, 1948, with Father Georgii Florovsky and Vladimir Lossky

was, however, no easier than his switch from philosophy to medicine or his renunciation of the world before becoming a monk. Ksenia Nikolaevna was so overcome that she retreated alone to the country before writing to their Bishop the Exarch Metropolitan Seraphim (Lukianov), from whom she believed she had obtained a promise that the Church would not dissuade her son from the medical practice at which he was proving such a success unless she as well as he were reconciled to the prospect: "Yet it is enough for me to think of the possibility of Andrei's being ordained for everything to go dark before my eyes, my heart to hurt and my mind to mist over." Quite apart from her own personal reactions, she went on, "there is another reason, and that is my sincere conviction that Andrei does much more moral and spiritual good in his calling as a doctor than he would as a priest, to whom those of no or little faith, or simply the French, will involuntarily react with some degree of suspicion or prejudice."[21]

In the face of the Metropolitan's persuasions, his insistence on the need for educated younger priests, and her son's need to serve with undivided heart and mind, she eventually capitulated gracefully, merely extracting a promise from Anthony that he would refrain from further estranging his fellow human beings by growing a beard – at least during her lifetime. This promise he kept.

On 22 October 1948, he was ordained deacon by Metropolitan Seraphim, then priest on 14 November. After brief service in Paris and Geneva, he was appointed, as requested, Chaplain to the Fellowship of St Alban and

St Sergius in London. The Metropolitan reported to His Holiness Aleksii Patriarch of all Russia: "Doctor Bloom is a remarkable personality. He is 34 years old. For the last six years he has been a monk in secret, professed by the Vicar of the Church of the Three Holy Hierarchs in Paris Archimandrite Afanasii under the name of Anthony. He is a sober and devout monk, a sound self-taught theologian, without specific academic education in this field, a good doctor, very kind-hearted, much loved and respected in Paris, Russian by nationality, a French citizen. He will conduct a fine Orthodox mission among the English without it being in any way an overt official mission, discretely, calmly, but correctly and conscientiously. In the future, I believe, priestmonk Anthony will be a luminary of our Church."[22]

Chapter Five

Priesthood, Move to London, Ministry in the Russian Orthodox Church in Great Britain, 1949-1957

[A] priest is one who makes all his life a living sacrifice to God, who sanctifies himself in the image of Christ and who hallows everyone and everything around him; Peter asked Christ: "Who then can be saved?" The Lord replied, "To men it is not possible but all things are possible to God," no human strength, no human power can unite us to God and cleanse us of all impurity, but the Lord has said to Paul "My grace sufficeth unto thee; my strength deploys itself in weakness" – as the wind fills a sail, the frailest part of a boat, and carries the heavy ship together with all its passengers towards its goal. . . .[1]

"I think I enjoyed being a parish priest in London more than being an archbishop," Anthony was to recall in 1973. "Being a parish priest meant visiting the old, the sick and the lonely – that's the true essence of Christianity."[2] Indeed, it was his involvement with the small parish of the Moscow Patriarchate in London, between 250 and 300 families when he first arrived there, at the Church of St Philip on Buckingham Palace Road, that was to determine Anthony's future, although his initial employer was the Fellowship of St Alban's and St Sergius, who found him and his family temporary lodgings in the Shepherd's Bush/Notting Hill Gate area and for whom he officiated at their house-church of St Basil the Great at St Basil's House. Here, he learned to give talks in English – proclaiming the Gospel and telling people about the Russian Church and Eastern Orthodoxy. Uncertain of the language, he began by asking his mother, who spoke it well, to translate a written text, and by reading this out, but was afterwards buttonholed by Father Lev Gillet, who told him always to speak to his audience, not read from a piece of paper. Father Anthony protested that his English was inadequate. "Never mind," snapped the famously irascible Father Lev, his eyes alight with mischief. "At least we'll have a good laugh and not die of boredom." "I never wanted my son to become a priest," Ksenia

Nikolaevna commented in mock despair, "but I really never expected that it would entail your becoming an itinerant stand-up comic." And, indeed, the Fellowship arranged for their new chaplain to spread his message far and wide. He acquitted himself with honour, attending a conference at Eastbourne in 1948 and the dedication of St Basil's Church in 1949 in his capacity as chaplain,[3] gaining golden opinions from the Vicar of St Paul and St Mark in Dock Street, where he talked about "The Christian Church in Russia" and "brought with him an atmosphere of sanctity and charm which filled us all with respect and admiration for that great Christian Church of the East".[4] He also delighted the Scots in Dundee, Aberdeen, Perth, Glasgow and St Andrews with talks on the same subject in "excellent", if still laboured, English, talks that left them "thrilled and inspired",[5] and with amusing interviews with references to his own Scottish origins and the formidable highland "aunt" (whom the Blooms never, in fact, managed to trace) who had once chopped off a cat-burglar's fingers with an axe as he tried to climb into her window and then "gone back to bed". Whatever else, the new chaplain of the Fellowship of St Albans and St Sergius had his wits about him and was far from boring. His early service as a "comisvoyageur orthodoxe",[i] under the auspices of the Fellowship, brought him into demand as speaker and preacher in non-Orthodox churches throughout Great Britain and ensured good relations with the Anglican Communion – in spite of his somewhat suspect attachment to Russia and what members of the Synodal Church (ROCOR) referred to as Moscow's "Soviet Church".

It was, however, the tiny patriarchal parish that shared the Church of St Philip's with this same inimical "Synodal Church" which, from the outset, engaged his heart. Their resident vicar, Protopriest Vladimir Theokritoff, had recently, in December 1946, acquired a parish house at 34 Upper Addison Gardens and, by 1947, under the Exarch Metropolitan Seraphim and together with Father Lev Gillet and Father Vasilii Timofeev, had consecrated the ground floor as the "little church" of St Sergius. Father Vladimir was old and in poor health, so was grateful for the help of an energetic young priest, though to begin with he did not entrust him with the cure of souls but only with preaching and celebrating the Liturgy. Neither was he immediately accepted by Father Vladimir's old established parishioners. While still attached primarily to the Fellowship of St Alban and St Sergius, Anthony was called upon at the last minute to replace Vladimir Lossky as speaker at the parish house:

> And so here was Father Vladimir Theokritoff leading me down the stairs and I hear the resonant voice of a certain lady, one of our boldest, firmest and most convinced parishioners: "It's a scandal! We invited a

---

i. Metropolitan Anthony of Sourozh introduced himself as a commercial traveller for "Orthodoxy" ("*Commis voyageur orthodoxe*") to a conference in Lausanne (*La Suisse*, 23 July 1964).

great theologian, a man of standing, and now we're palmed off with some little medic no-one has ever heard of. I think we should all go now so that he realises we do not want him here!" By then I was on the last tread, there was nowhere to run, nor did I feel like running. I entered the room and said: "I heard what was said just now. Of course, I shall not keep anyone here. I shall turn away and whoever wants to can go home" – and turned my face to the wall. A few minutes later the same bold lady said: "all right then, we've decided to stay and hear what you have to say." That was the beginning of our parish talks for grown-ups, the beginning of our classes for children. And of course in parallel there was choir practice with Mikhail Ivanovich Theokritoff, the brother of Father Vladimir and the father of our present Father Michael's wife[i].[6]

In an undated letter written to Metropolitan Seraphim in 1949, Father Anthony asks forgiveness for not having sent in a report of progress earlier "since a degree of disorientation from the newness of the conditions of life here and, indeed, its contents cannot excuse my guilt towards you".[7] It is a humble letter, thanking the Metropolitan for the confidence placed in him by the Church and asking his Bishop's prayers "as I see more clearly all the time that I am far from the necessary spiritual maturity". He had, he writes, been very busy learning English, putting his flat in order, which he and his women-folk did with their own hands,[ii] and helping Father Vladimir, who was being very kind and with whom he concelebrated twice a week at St Basil's, an early service on Wednesday mornings at 7:30 in English and on Saturday in either Church Slavonic or English, other week-day services being in Slavonic. When in London he assisted Father Vladimir at St Philip's in any way he required and was also organising a youth group.

For St Albans and St Sergius he gave talks, travelled around, and organised a discussion group. Sometimes he celebrated outside London – for instance, for the week beginning Lazarus Saturday he celebrated all services in full with Father Nicholas Gibbes in Oxford, where he had a beautiful chapel sparsely attended by between three and seven people on weekdays and twenty to thirty on Sundays – a mixed congregation of British, Greeks and Bulgarians as well as Russians of high intellectual calibre, people such as Lampert, Bolshakov, Konovalov, Gorodetskaia and Nicholas and Militza Zernov. Father Nicholas badly needed an educated priest to help him cope with this lively group of Orthodox. In Cambridge, Anthony had celebrated an Orthodox service in English in an Anglican church with a well-rehearsed

---
i. Father Michael Fortounatto's wife was the icon painter Marianna.
ii. At a MASF conference in the Serbian Church in London, Irina Kirillova read the delightful reminiscences of how she first met the young priest Father Anthony as a next door neighbour, looking round in some confusion as to how to cope with the rubbish disposal.

choir of English students, attended by about eighty undergraduates and dons, and spent two days talking about various aspects of "Russian Orthodoxy today" in Ridley House. On the first day of Easter, he celebrated at the home of Professor Frank, who was housebound, and he took several special services (*treby*) in Cambridge, a service of intercession (*moleben*) and prayers for the repose of the soul (*panikhida*) in the houses of scattered Orthodox.

His Oxbridge visits had resulted in bookings for six lectures on mediaeval Holy Russia in Oxford and, in Cambridge, on liturgical and dogmatic differences between the Eastern Orthodox and other confessions, and on the Russian Church during the Revolution.

For all this, of course, as well as for a number of lectures at various London venues which ranged from working-class audiences to student societies, he needed to prepare, and he tells Metropolitan Seraphim in the letter that he devoted three to six hours a day to study of his own and other confessions in various languages. His special interest, however, remained people. He writes of a regular group of Anglo-Russian young people of no particular church, some of them unchristened, who met with him regularly for two or three hours' discussion. He would introduce a subject and they asked questions. For these youngsters, for whom he had high hopes, he asked the Metropolitan's prayers. There were, he writes, three particular Orthodox whom he had been coaching in German throughout Lent to prepare them for their first confession and communion and was now continuing to teach, at their own request, scripture and Liturgy. They were soon to be joined by two Englishmen who had for some years been hoping to become Orthodox.

These young people were his only spiritual children (by tacit agreement with Father Vladimir, though in Oxford Father Nicholas occasionally asked him to take confessions, which he did to the best of his ability).

A problem, however, arose with Father Vladimir's failing health and Anthony was asked to take over the parish. This he declined to do as it was a full-time job and he was, at that moment, still in the employment of the Fellowship, and had promised to speak at various "strategically" important venues. With the exception of certain days he was able to take over the services, Vigil and Liturgy on Sundays at St Philip's and the services for Ascension, Whitsun and the Feast of St Peter and St Paul. He could not, however, undertake to celebrate there regularly on weekdays and wanted to be officially freed of obligation to celebrate requested services (*treby*), although he would respond to requests when free to do so. Nevertheless, he asked to be released from all such duties to the parish from 27 July onwards, from which date he had committed himself to twenty days of conducting daily seminaries at the Fellowship. He trusted that Metropolitan Seraphim would approve of his not taking on more than he could accomplish and would agree to his accepting the limited responsibility suggested, although he felt the best thing would be for someone to come to England to replace Father Vladimir.

Anthony as a young priest in London, 1949

Evidently there was no one suitable available, as the Exarch responded with an order of 20 May 1949 that Anthony should take responsibility for the parish during the Vicar's illness. Later that year Seraphim retired from the Exarchate and was replaced, briefly, by Metropolitan Photii, Archbishop of Finland and Lithuania, whom Anthony "loved and respected".[8] Next was Father Nikolai (Eremin), soon to become

Bishop then Archbishop of Clichy and then Metropolitan of Korsun, who became the young priest's regular mentor and correspondent. When Father Vladimir died, Father Anthony was appointed as a temporary replacement, to be assisted, from July 1950, by Father Aleksandr Turintsev to help him carry out his duties to parish and fellowship during the busy summer months. On 9 September of the same year, Father Anthony was confirmed as permanent vicar of the Russian Patriarchal parish in London. Less than two years later, the Exarch was reporting to Patriarch Aleksei that in this capacity he had "earned great popularity in Russian circles as among the English".[9]

The work was all new to him and the situation delicate. Anthony consulted Bishop Nikolai (Eremin), who had been kind and compassionate at Father Afanasii's funeral in 1943 and was an old and trusted friend, on a variety of questions arising from problems quite outside his experience as doctor, monk and lecturer: might he, for instance, or might he not remarry a convert to Orthodoxy who had divorced his previous wife by a civic marriage "without a church divorce"? An Anglican convert, Geoffrey Taylor, whom he and Father Lev had sent to study at the St Sergius Institute in Paris, wished to become a hieromonk with the name of Kirill and help in the parish. He could actually afford to do so without a stipend: might Anthony take advantage of this as it would so help the English members of his flock to have a priest of their own language and culture, or might such a step offend the Anglicans? Was he right to recommend the Swiss Orthodox woman,[i] a great admirer of Mother Maria (Skobtsova), who had taken the veil under his guidance, to an English Benedictine monastery where he had an excellent rapport with the Mother Abbess?

Clearly, one of the great difficulties with which the new priest had to contend from the very beginning was his relationship with the Synodal Russian Church, with whom his own parish shared the Church of St Philip's and who considered it necessary to re-sanctify the altar after the "Soviet" church had celebrated there. His first effort as peacemaker was a complete

---

i. This was Mother Maria (Gysi) who did eventually found her own tiny Orthodox convent with two other nuns, Sister Thekla and Sister Katherine, and wrote and published a number of books, notably *The Fool and Other Writings* (Library of Orthodox Thinking, 1980). See also *Mother Maria: Her Life in Letters*, edited by Sister Thekla, Darton, Longman and Todd, 1979, and for Father Anthony's role the Introduction to this book by Sister Thekla, pp. xxiii, xxv, xxvii. Mother Maria was happy and fulfilled in the Benedictine Abbey and Bishop Anthony professed her in their chapel as an Orthodox nun in 1958, although she did not leave the Benedictines until 1965, when they generously allotted her a house for her own Orthodox enclave, still under the guidance of Bishop Anthony until 1970 when, with the death of the Russian Patriarch Aleksii, the nuns chose to transfer their allegiance to the Ecumenical Patriarchate which, they felt, would give more scope to the development of an ethnically neutral monastic life.

Chapter Five

At the conference of the FSASS, 1952

failure. Characteristically, he decided on a direct, personal approach and went to beard their vicar, Father Vitalii, in his home. The door was opened by a long-skirted, long-haired, smooth-faced individual whom he greeted politely as *Matushka* – "little mother", the normal, respectfully affectionate address in Russian for a priest's wife. In tones worthy of Shaliapin, the door ward replied, with a distinctly minatory glare, "I am *not* Matushka, I'm the deacon." Anthony was still struggling to regain his aplomb when confronted with Father Vitalii. He trotted out his carefully considered speech: how their parishes were divided only by political, not religious considerations – both were Orthodox, both émigré, both Russian – so surely they could share the church the Anglicans had so kindly allotted them without the entrenched mutual hostility that had so far prevailed? His opposite number heard him out patiently then delivered his verdict: he had nothing against Anthony personally, except that he not only did not consider him a priest, but – far worse – knew him to be in the service of Antichrist. There seemed, at this juncture, nothing more to be said, and the younger man departed discomforted, though in later years, after the fall of communism, he was to speak up strenuously in favour of the reunion of all scattered factions of the Russian Church.

For the present, all he could do was to build on the inevitable overlap of personal relationships in the émigré community and to concentrate on the problem shared by all the Orthodox churches in Great Britain: the problem of a new, almost entirely anglophone and culturally disorientated generation who no longer felt at home in their parents' churches, and to work hard to establish good relations with those organisations where the Orthodox met Christians of other denominations on neutral ground. Attitudes between individual Russians were softening; after all, the Russian Church was the Russian Church, to whichever patriarchate or synod they owed allegiance, and there was a general feeling that their divisions, originating as they did in the turbulent post-revolutionary period, were purely temporal and, therefore, essentially temporary. Father Anthony's growing reputation as a compassionate and energetic pastor who knew the world and understood the problems of the twentieth century brought him many individuals and some influential friends from the Synodal congregation who just happened to "go to church" on a day he was celebrating in St Philip's. On the other hand, his modern appearance (he had kept the promise not to grow a beard) and personal charm made some distrust him all the more and it took years to live down his reputation as a "Red", a possible KGB plant, perhaps a "sleeper", who was also a consummate actor – something in the nature of a spiritual honey-trap![i]

It was the death of Stalin in 1953 that brought about a major shift in attitudes everywhere, though of course this did not happen overnight. In Russia, the Patriarch celebrated a *panikhida* for the repose of his soul which Father Anthony, who did not, explained as consistent with the Church always praying for the head of state, as Orthodox people in England of whatever origin pray for the Queen and the royal family. However, feeling no such local obligation in the case of the Soviet dictator, he went on record publicly that he did not see "how we can pray for a professed atheist"[10] and that, since he and his congregation were no longer Russian citizens, it would be a political demonstration were they to sing a public *panikhida*. Privately, to those genuinely concerned that any church should refuse to pray for the soul of a sinner, Father Anthony replied that, while a formal service of intercession would clearly be inappropriate, the church in fact regularly prayed for "those who persecute us" and there was no taboo on private prayer.

Still, it took a long time to hammer home the point of the Patriarchal parish's independence of the Soviet state. As late as 1956 *The Evening News* reported that, in answer to a public challenge on his allegiance emanating from the Synodal Church, Anthony Bloom had replied: "Any such suggestion is quite untrue. The allegiance which my Parish owes to the Patriarch is purely ecclesiastical and no allegiance is owed to the Soviet government. All my parishioners – and not only the 85-90% of them who are British citizens – give their allegiance in all temporal matters to the Queen and offer prayers on her behalf at every service."[11] However, he and

---

i. I myself recall conversations in this vein between Russian émigré friends in the late 1940s/early 1950s.

his parish inevitably came in for renewed criticism from the rival Russian Church when, as the situation in Russia itself began to change during the Thaw, representatives of the Orthodox Church in Russia were permitted to visit the UK to discuss ecumenical matters with the Church of England and to join the World Council of Churches.

This situation, however, did not arise immediately after Stalin's death. Meanwhile, the service Father Anthony rendered to his parishioners was one of devoted pastoral care. After the death of Father Vladimir he had moved with his mother and grandmother to the parish house at 34 Upper Addison Gardens, and their door was open to all comers. Ksenia Nikolaevna's flawless good manners, the grandmother's increasingly vague and frail homeliness, and Anthony's loving attention to every person of whatever age or sex who had need of him made a true sanctuary of their home, which incorporated the ground-floor church and a large basement assembly room. It was known in the community that if your silver spoons were found to have disappeared after a visit from a certain alcoholic but well-loved member of the parish, one only had to ring Father Anthony, who would persuade him to give them back. It was also known that he would always answer the phone and talk, comfort and advise – whether on matters spiritual or practical – and that he had friends in medicine and law to whom he would direct parishioners with problems he could not solve for them. His care for the young people was unremitting, however busy he might be about other matters. His first spontaneous efforts to organise study groups culminated in 1956 with a rallying call to all parents in the form of a Christmas letter.

Was it not a matter for tears, he demanded, that, when all the Christian world was turning to Orthodoxy with such lively interest, when people of all confessions were studying it and finding in it the fullness of truth and of life in Christ, "that those to whom God has confided this priceless treasure should set no value on it, should embrace other creeds or remain Orthodox in name only?"[12]

On the back of the letter is a questionnaire, asking:

1. For any children's names and surnames.
2. Do the children receive any religious instruction at home and, if not, would they, the parents, like the church to provide it?
3. Do they know about the Saturday school already up and running? Is there any reason it is difficult for their children to attend?
4. Do their children speak Russian?
5. What languages are spoken in the home?
6. Would they, the parents, agree to co-operate with the church by either arranging for their children to attend school or for a priest or helper to instruct them at home?
7. For the address of the parents.

The questionnaire came with a request to childless parishioners to pass it on to anyone who might be interested. This hands-on approach entailed involving others in parish work and infecting them with his own enthusiasm, bringing out dormant talent and accepting as well as giving help.

The difficulty of running these instruction courses was that children came in different age groups, so eventually the juniors were taken one week and the seniors the next, reducing the "Saturday school" to a fortnightly event for each child!

At the same time he did not neglect the more stable adult audience who faithfully attended and enjoyed weekday *besedy* (talks), at which the priest would speak extempore for forty to forty-five minutes, then take questions. For these, though there was always a "theme", he would not prepare but trust to the Spirit to prompt him to speak in a way relevant to this or that particular audience at this or that particular time, thus reaching hearts and minds with utmost immediacy. Again, the talks were conducted in separate groups for English-speakers and those more at home in their native Russian. The "theme" was usually sacral, intended to lead them deeper into the actual service: the Liturgy; the Lord's Prayer; the Creed.

Above all, Father Anthony was known and venerated as a confessor, one who could convey the infinite and healing forgiveness of God to the truly penitent, but who could also demand of an old woman on her deathbed that she be reconciled with her son-in-law before he would give her absolution. On one occasion he denied an old friend and eminently virtuous parishioner absolution because she always came to him "with the same sins" and didn't appear to be doing anything about them. On another, he shocked and startled an old lady, who had thought to get away with a formal acknowledgement that she was guilty of "all mortal sins", with the earnest question, "But surely you, N.N., who are so generally respected, are not a *thief*? Or an *adulteress*?"[i]

Old friends like Nikolai and Veronica Lossky would come all the way from Paris to make their confession to him. He listened, drew you in ever deeper, often by his silence, cleared you out, cleaned you up and sent you on your way not chastened, not comforted, but encouraged and reintegrated into the mysterious and tragic work of salvation. His approach to his penitents was always individual, never unctuous or conciliating but loving and discriminatory, and as with the children at the Russian school in Paris, he combined authority with solidarity – solidarity with the most unlikely people.

---

i. Some of these stories Metropolitan Anthony told himself, others I heard from those involved. They are in part the reason why he always refused to attempt autobiography, saying his life was made up of other people's troubles which he had no right to retell. In view of this, it would seem intrusive to source them in separate detail, yet they are eminently worth retelling from the point of view of human interest.

During the times of British difficulties with Archbishop Makarios in Cyprus, Father Anthony was encouraged to attend Greek detainees in HM prisons, because – thought the British authorities – the Greek clergy were not to be trusted. Aside from the political prisoners, he also came across and made friends with a good few common thieves. "How do I know I won't come home some fine day and find you've stripped my house and church of all its valuables?" he asked one, to whom he had given his address in case of need. "How can you say so, Father?" the thief had replied indignantly; "We never rob our own sort."

He had fathomless sympathy for the agonies of the rebellious young and often, where there was real conflict, sided with the child against the parents, with the scapegrace against the righteous. He always wore his cassock, even on public transport, saying that it was a good way to advertise his calling, and fellow passengers would take him into their confidence. They thought, he would say, that he looked so peculiar he could not possibly be in league with anyone who might challenge the legality or propriety of their private concerns.

Yet for all his approachability he had, as the Irish say, "the power": he could calm fears, exorcise ghosts and banish household pests; one of his favourite stories involved reading the riot act to a mouse who sat rigidly to attention as he donned his stole and read the prayer against infestations over it – then obediently vacated the premises together with friends and relations. "Where did they go?" I asked him, after he had deprecatingly told me how he would never have attempted such a thing had his mother not insisted exorcism was more humane than traps or poison and, since he had insisted on becoming a priest, they might as well put the power conferred upon him into practice in their daily lives. He had told her that he would recite the prayers but, on this occasion, she, together with the saint who had composed them, must do the believing. To my question he replied with a look at once rueful and amused: "I very much fear that they must have gone to the neighbours."

This capacity for seeing the funny side was immensely endearing in one so serious. "Father Anthony," I asked on another occasion when struggling with my Cambridge PhD in the late 1950s, "how do you translate '*preosviashchennyi*'?" "Literally, I'm afraid, as 'super-sanctified'," he replied, "but I dare say you could get away with 'the most reverend'!" Similarly, much later, when asked the correct style of address for an Orthodox bishop, which by that time he was, he answered: "My Lord, your Grace, your Reverence – but not your Honour or your Worship or your Highness and certainly not, as I was once introduced, as 'the sainted ex-Patriarch of the Russian Church in Western Europe'."[13] He really enjoyed such absurdities and his humour and gift of mimicry made him an entertaining companion, yet there was about him a passionate vulnerability which attracted young and old alike.

It was this mixture of spontaneous humanity and tireless dedication to the service of God and man that, more even than intelligence and diplomatic skills, allayed the initial suspicions with which the new Russian priest was surrounded and attracted more and more people to the Russian Patriarchal Church he represented.

When Anthony Bloom arrived in London, the position of that church in the Orthodox community there was, at best, marginal; he was not even accepted as a member of the Union of Orthodox Priests in Great Britain under the presidency of the Archbishop of Thyateira, the senior Orthodox cleric in London. In 1954, Father Anthony submitted a detailed report to his friend the Exarch, Archbishop Nikolai (Eremin) of Clichy,[i] on the state of inter-Orthodox relations in London.[14] The Archbishop of Thyateira, as representative of the Greek Orthodox Church and the Ecumenical Patriarch of Constantinople, Anthony reported, occupied the position of *primus inter pares* and senior Orthodox hierarch in London both from the Orthodox and the Anglican point of view, though whether or how much this depended on the personality of the incumbent, who had recently been replaced, it was hard to say. With the Serbian Church both he and his predecessor Father Vladimir Theokritoff had long had excellent relations, and he admired the way clergy managed to maintain links with their mother church in Tito's communist Yugoslavia without offending the political sensibilities of their émigré flock. The attitude of the "autocephalous" Polish Church (in fact consisting mainly of ethnic Russians, Galatians and others) was conditioned by their desire to preserve independence from both the Synodal and the Patriarchal Russian churches. Other Orthodox local churches tended to represent tiny minorities, but all, apart from his own parish, were members of the Union of Orthodox Priests. He had applied to join this body but, in spite of the backing of the Serbs, had not been accepted because his church's ties with the Moscow Patriarchate were considered "unacceptable to the new emigration".[ii] All that could be done to amend this situation was to build on the inevitable overlap in personal relationships between the two "Russian" parishes, to concentrate on the problem shared by all Eastern Orthodox churches in Great Britain of how to deal with an almost entirely anglophone and culturally disorientated second and third generation, and to work hard for good relationships with those organisations where Orthodox, Anglicans and those of other denominations met on common ground and the Orthodox felt it incumbent on them to preserve a measure of mutual courtesy and tolerance. The Fellowship of St Albans and St Sergius, for

---

i. The French, not having an established Church, did not object to foreign bishops taking local titles.

ii. i.e. the so-called "second emigration" from the Soviet Union who, finding themselves in the West by fortune of war, had chosen not to return to almost certain arrest and imprisonment in their native land.

instance, was shunned by the "other parish" as already thoroughly infiltrated by the non-Synodal clergy, but was frequented by Greek and Serbian Orthodox, with whom he could meet there on equal terms. The Anglican and Eastern Churches Association provided an enclave where all Orthodox sunk their differences, as they tended to do at theological conferences with other churches arranged by the Union of Foreign Clergy in London.

As to the problem of culturally and linguistically disaffected Orthodox youth, it was one that Father Anthony, with the experience of the Church of Ste Geneviève and the Mother of God Joy of all who Sorrow behind him, worked at hard and enthusiastically within his own parish, both from the angle of organising Russian language and culture study groups and of introducing more English into the actual service. On this, he co-operated with Serbs and to some extent with Greeks whose young people were also reaching out towards an anglophone Orthodoxy that would resonate with their British cultural heritage. Indeed, Father Anthony, like Lev Gillet in his time, was sensitive to a growing requirement for a Western European Orthodoxy, in his case an autocephalous British Church which would meet the requirements of his now overwhelmingly naturalised British and increasingly native-English-speaking parish. One of his most enthusiastic co-operators was Father Vladimir Rodzyanko of the Serbian Church who aimed, as he did, to help the young who wanted to free Orthodoxy in Great Britain of its ethnic and political divisions: "he takes all those who are frightened of me and sends me those who can be included in our small English community," he wrote to Archbishop Nikolai in this same extensive report.

There was ample scope in the situation he described for any diplomatic talent Anthony Bloom might have inherited from his father and grandfather, and the percipience and lucidity of his analysis, as well as his subsequent success in establishing the suspect Russian Patriarchal Church as a much respected and, indeed, highly valued member of ecclesiastical society in Great Britain, suggests this was considerable.

It was put to the test that very year by the Anglican Church's decision to sell St Philip's Church for demolition. Two redundant Anglican churches were on offer: All Saints in Ennismore Gardens was to go to the Synodal Church as the senior Russian Orthodox parish in London; St Anne's and St Agnes in Gresham Street in the City of London was to go to the Patriarchal. To the recently promoted Hegumen Anthony it seemed that the city church was too remote for his ageing but steadily increasing congregation, who lived mostly in west London, and, indeed, that the offer was something of an affront to the Mother Church he represented. All Saints was not only better situated but much larger. Anthony held out for an alternative offer and persuaded Archbishop Nikolai to write to H.M. Waddams asking him whether an alternative or reversed offer could not be made, as the remote city church would entail a decline in the number of attendees and might have "a negative effect" on "the real importance and prestige of our church, which might have regrettable consequences for relations between the Church of England and the Russian Orthodox Church".[15] Waddams, as Secretary of the Department for Relations with Foreign Churches in Lambeth Palace, could, as he explained to Anthony, do no more than make this known to the London Diocesan Fund in whose gift the churches were, and Anthony, who could be stiff-necked where his dignity as representative of the Mother Church was concerned, was upset to receive a somewhat patronising letter from the Secretary of the Fund, the Archdeacon of Hackney M.A. Hodgins, impressing on him the desirability of "a Wren Church of interesting architecture", which "being fairly small should not be expensive to maintain, to heat and to light". "I think," Hodgins continued, "that a congregation should be glad to have, and, indeed, think it a privilege to be able to use, a Wren Church, and I cannot help feeling that your people are inclined to exaggerate the difficulty of getting to the church. The city of London is very well served by public transport . . . with regard to All Saints, Ennismore Gardens, it must be remembered that this is a big church, expensive from the point of view of maintenance, and a little difficult to find. . . . It is not, of course, easy for us to find churches to spare in exactly the desired position. If it should happen in future that a church in the western part of London should become available, I would certainly let you know, but I cannot, I am afraid, see any immediate prospect of it."[16]

Whether or not the words were actually addressed to him in a face-to-face interview, Anthony subsequently reduced the Archdeacon's well-rounded admonitions to the pithy: "I was told: Beggars can't be choosers." He roughed out but wisely discarded a first response making the point that to Russian émigrés ("our congregation and our Archbishop"), if not to the English, it was an obvious fact that a city church was of considerably lower standing than one in the residential parts of London and they were surprised the Anglican Church "seemingly gives its preference and support to a congregation which is in schism with the main body of the Russian Church".[17] Wisely, however, this combative reply was discarded in favour of a polite acknowledgement that, although to serve in a Wren church might certainly be considered a privilege, he as vicar and his congregation felt "quite confident about their ability to maintain and heat a larger church, but were concerned about the implications of steadily increasing fares on public transport" for their poorer brethren. The new letter, which was actually sent, ended with restrained insistence: "I beg to submit these different points for your kind attention and I remain Yours very sincerely, Hegumen Anthony Bloom."[18]

The Archdeacon replied with an urbane ultimatum. It had, he wrote, been decided after due consultation that "in view of your unwillingness to accept a church in the city for the use of your congregation, we should have no option but to allow the present arrangement to continue, whereby the two Russian congregations share the use of one building". In the meantime, the Church of St Philip must be vacated by both congregations. A letter from Hodgin's secretary added that the Diocesan Fund was prepared to assist with transfer to and installation of church property in All Saints.

Anthony welcomed the decision. It would, he explained to Archbishop Nikolai, give people who were already wavering more time to decide which parish they really wished to belong to and spare both parties the onerous division of shared property. He neither wanted nor needed an absolute victory achieved by worldly means because "morally we here in England are gaining ground by the day both in English society and among the Russians".[19] Count Kleinmichel, however, for the Synodal Church, refused outright to consider a continuation of the sharing arrangement and the Anglicans, now committed to their offer of a shared church, found themselves in cordial contact with an eminently reasonable and amenable Moscow Patriarchal Church and flouted and spurned by the Synodal whom they had, indeed, formerly favoured. "The situation has got out of hand," exclaimed Hodgins over the telephone to Anthony in a last-minute attempt to rescind the offer of All Saints to either or both parishes on condition of willingness to share, but the whole thing was now in the public domain and Anthony ready and willing to sign up to a clause that would allow the Synodal parish to change its mind.[20]

To the hard core of the Synodal Church, it seemed as though Anthony Bloom had outsmarted them, and their Archbishop Afanasii confirmed Kleinmichel's refusal to share. It also seemed to them by this time that the Anglicans, blind to the Moscow Patriarchate's dependence on the Soviet government, now wrongly considered it to represent the true Russian Church and were all too ready to receive delegations, such as the visit of Metropolitan Pitirim of Belarus, whose arrival in London in July 1955 to discuss an impending Anglo-Orthodox conference confirmed their worst fears. "Unfortunately," wrote a correspondent of the Russian language organ of the Russian National Association in Great Britain, "there are people in Russian émigré and it would have seemed anti-communist circles, who now belong to the congregation of the Patriarchal Church. Why they allow themselves to be deceived and lend their names to give respectability to Soviet trickery is past understanding. . . . Surely it should be clear to our people by now that the Church in the USSR is the servant of the State and its preaching an off-shoot of the propaganda of Soviet Communism!"[21]

In the previous number, a different correspondent had deplored the welcome given by émigrés to representatives of the Russian Church in even stronger terms: "And is it not obvious that the task of the Patriarchal parishes in Europe is to cultivate pro-Soviet moods among the Russian emigration which will eventually completely undermine morale and lead them to submit to Communist domination."[22]

The position of the Church in Moscow as a potential force for the emancipation of the Russian people from imposed Marxist doctrine was defended by an ex-member of the same Russian National Association in a letter of resignation, which deplored the mish-mash of politics and religion in the pieces quoted above and suggested they amounted to an insult to the Christian Church as a whole and an infringement on his own freedom of conscience as a Russian Orthodox.[23]

Times, though, were changing, and the very virulence of these polemics appears to have arisen as a reaction against a new spirit of tolerance and a growing émigré sympathy for the martyred Mother Church in the country for which many still felt an acute nostalgia. Not least Hegumen Anthony, who, in the summer of 1956, received his first invitation to visit the long forbidden land of his origins, an invitation that, to his intense chagrin, he felt bound to refuse – in order not to fuel the hostility of those who had not yet learned, as he himself put it, to distinguish God from Caesar:

> Having considered the situation from all angles, [he wrote to the Exarch,] and discussed it with the Parish Council, I feel bound to refuse the longed for invitation now offered me. This is the unanimous opinion and wish of all members of the Parish Council without exception and of all but one of the delegates to our half-yearly General Council Meeting. All are convinced, as (to my intense grief) I am myself, that such a trip would put an end to the very existence of the Parish: very many would leave, the wafflers would fade away, and our ill-wishers would exploit our own disintegration as ammunition against the Patriarchal Church in general, using it as apparent evidence that we are on friendly terms with the Soviet State and in receipt of money from them.

He is well aware, Anthony continues in the same letter, that such attitudes may seem very odd to people living in France, but that is the way things are here in England:

> I do hope you will credit the need for such caution and that I have reached this decision with great sadness and only because I am conscious of my responsibility for human souls with whom you, my Lord, and in your person the whole Russian Church have entrusted me, not only for the faithful and true but for Her wavering, timorous and erring children. And do I need to say that I am forgoing the most cherished dream of my life?[24]

In spite or in part because of his apparent success, the Vicar of the Russian Patriarchal parish had good reason to fear disintegration from within. Apart from the imposing matriarchs of his congregation who, like the widows of the philosopher Semen Frank and the composer Nikolai

Medtner, regarded him as an inexperienced young man and a theological ignoramus and constantly called him to order for infringing tradition, or the obstreperous old nun in charge of minding the church who one day "took the bit between her teeth" and refused to recognise his authority, then wanted her job back when he relieved her of her duties, there was Mr Allan, the *starosta* or church warden elected under Father Vladimir, who was emerging as a serious opponent of Father Anthony's missionary outreach and of the introduction of the English language in some church services. The former, Allan was convinced, was an offence to the established Church of England and the latter to the sensibilities of the Russian congregation. As Anthony had explained to his Exarch, he had indeed, besides the English-speaking naturalised British Russians, their spouses, and their children, who were now returning to reinvigorate a parish that had dwindled to the elderly and the very young, acquired a number of English converts, mostly university graduates but also some quite simple people, who had asked to be admitted to the Orthodox Church and whom he had gladly received, normally after a probationary period of at least eighteen months and a recommendation to discuss the matter with a priest of their own denomination. Without sidelining the Russian core congregation, he wanted these people to feel at home in what was now their church also, and he repeated his wish to ordain as hieromonk his and Lev Gillet's protégé Geoffrey Taylor (Father Kirill). This was a special case and did not mean he intended to open wide the doors to Anglican priests dissatisfied with the policies of their own Church. Dissatisfaction, he considered, was an insufficient reason for wishing to become Orthodox and, in any case, the Russian Patriarchal Church was in no position to provide all those troubled by such issues as women's place in the Church with stipends and parishes. Nevertheless, Anthony's success and his evident desire for outreach beyond the bounds of ethnicity was causing some anxiety in Anglican circles and H.M. Waddams had, in the presence of the *starosta*, advised him that he should be careful to keep the priesting of Father Kirill a low-profile event lest he be seen to be deliberately proselytising. Mr Allan had understood this as an official warning and taken fright, addressing an urgent letter to the Exarch on 21 October 1954[25] asking him to come to England himself, regulate the activities of his vicar and settle the differences to which these had given rise within the parish and in their relationship with the Anglican Church. It was, in Allan's view, unethical for a guest church in a foreign country and detrimental to the welfare of the parish that Father Anthony spent so much time preaching away, and the idea of appointing an ex-Anglican English priest was controversial in itself. "The parish has always been Russian, is supported by Russian money and cannot be anything other than a Russian Orthodox parish. Our language and our church are the only links which join us to our Motherland and Mother Church, we do not want to lose that last link."[26]

Neither, of course, did Father Anthony, but he nurtured the dream of Russians rekindling a Western form of Orthodox Christianity in the countries where they found themselves living as exiles – and it was a dream shared not only by friends in the Fellowship of St Alban and St Sergius, such as the now ageing Father Lev, but also by friends in Paris, including the Exarch, whose unqualified support he won on a visit to the Church of the Three Holy Hierarchs in the following year. In February 1955 he was able to report back to Archbishop Nikolai that he had told a general meeting of parishioners "that you unreservedly bless my work – Russian and English, and my efforts to deepen and widen the knowledge of Orthodoxy in England in a spirit of peace and brotherly communion in Christ, and that those questions which have ignited controversy among us are not a matter for the flock to debate but are the responsibility of the Archbishop and his appointed vicar and a question for their conscience".[27] Somewhat authoritarian, perhaps, but Anthony and the Exarch, by now deeply involved in the "tense struggle" as to where their church was to go after the evacuation of St Philips, commanded the loyalty of the majority and, precisely one year later, at another general meeting of parishioners which Mr Allan did not even attend, Anthony was able to report to them that they now had a firm promise that the Church of All Saints would be theirs if the "*Karlovchane*" (the Synodal Church) persisted in their refusal to share. A new *starosta* was elected, Professor Korenchevsky ("honest, a good churchman, cultivated and with experience of social work"), and the parish, in full awareness of the financial burden it was shouldering, agreed to take on responsibility for maintenance of the new church and for the expenses involved in adapting it to Orthodox usage. The Anglicans, by July of that year, hammered out an agreement with the Russian Patriarchal Church that they would take on (to the tune of £2000) repairs to roof and fabric of All Saints if the Orthodox accepted responsibility for redecoration and further maintenance. In this Anthony was ably assisted by Korenchevsky, who worked out the small print with Hodgin's secretary and the builders and who had soon proved himself, as Anthony confided to Archbishop Nikolai, "a veritable treasure, capable of pulling me up and averting mistakes: it is such a comfort to have a *starosta* who genuinely cares for the parish, tries to rally everybody and gets them to 'pull together'. Since we separated from the *Karlovchane* the congregation has grown considerably. At Easter, which we celebrated in the Serbian Church, there were about 500 people at Matins and during Passion Week about 300 came to confession and took communion."[28]

True, not even Father Anthony was altogether sanguine about the financial potential of his still tiny and far from wealthy parish. Madame Frank told him that he had taken leave of his senses and the Anglicans had been sufficiently doubtful to listen with some sympathy to a proposal, made mid-negotiation by Mr Allan to the secretary of the Archbishop of Canterbury over a good dinner at Prunier's, that the Russian Church in England should appeal directly to Moscow for funding, bypassing the indigent émigré exarchate in Paris. The secretary, although he agreed there was "a good deal to be said" for persuading the Patriarch to fund his London church, was sufficiently astute to perceive the hidden agenda that the move might lead to Anthony Bloom, with whom the *starosta* appeared to be "at variance", being replaced as vicar by Father Sophronii from France. "I do not," he reported cannily, "agree with the ideas which lie behind it in Mr Allan's mind."[29] Clearly, Anthony's standing with the Church of England was higher than his *starosta* had feared. As for Anthony himself, he was categorically opposed to compromising the financial independence of his impecunious parish, which, he felt, "should live absolutely independently by its own labour and its own sacrifices".[30]

Stressing that it was the inestimable God-given privilege of the Patriarchal Church abroad to represent the courage and steadfast sanctity of the persecuted Mother Church, he issued an eloquent appeal for funds for the upkeep and makeover of the new church and encouraged the organisation of a special church bazaar involving the sale of some precious Russian antiques and treasured possessions, as well as artefacts made by the parishioners and home-made refreshments. Both brought in surprising sums of money. Finally, Russian dancers and musicians rallied to the appeal and a "Bakst" concert with the pianist Moisevitch, the ballerina Svetlana Beriozova, the harpist Korchinska, and several well-known English dancers was organised as a benefit for the church at the Royal Opera House. Though Church rules prohibited Anthony from attending this event, he wrote the artists involved glowing individual thank-you letters, wishing them "strength of soul and body and increasing joy and insight into Beauty and Art".[31]

The publicity engendered by these colourful events did the Russian Patriarchal Church no harm at all in British society and the effort to raise the cash gave impetus to the already growing solidarity between Russian and English parishioners. They needed one another and the very boldness of the undertaking created a slightly crazy team spirit, a glorious feeling of having successfully defied common sense. Anthony's "people", or "set", as the Anglicans called them, rose to the challenge. Their beloved pastor had led them well, defending the prestige of their parish; it was exciting to be in possession of a beautiful, spacious church in an accessible part of London and they had not been made to look grasping or unreasonable or to approach any authority cap-in-hand.

In August the Patriarchate, delighted at how much their London vicar had accomplished without making any demands on their scant supply of foreign currency, raised Anthony to the rank of Archimandrite, and Archbishop Nikolai agreed to come to England for the consecration of the new church, which was to be known as the Church of the Dormition of the

Mother of God and All Saints, combining the Anglican dedication with that of the chapel attached to the old Tsarist consulate. Anthony asked him to bring everything necessary for the celebration of an episcopal Liturgy, as the London church had none of the required sacred objects and vestments, not even a spare antimins to permit him and Father Kirill, now ordained, to celebrate the Liturgy in different places on the same day.

Invitations went out to Anglicans and non-Russian Orthodox as well as to Orthodox Russian émigrés in London and Western Europe to attend the ceremony at Ennismore Gardens on 16 December 1956. There were not a few refusals. Some Anglican prelates felt it was inappropriate to reconsecrate the church at all, and said so. The Archbishop of Canterbury let it be known through Waddams that for him to be present would increase the number of occasions he would be obliged to attend, but sent a representative and agreed readily to receive the Exarch of the Russian Patriarchal Church at Lambeth Palace on the day after he conducted the service of dedication. Waddams himself was present, as was the Right Reverend James Vievo, Bishop of Kensington, to whose diocese the Church of All Saints, closed down in July 1954 by order of the Church commissioners for lack of attendance, had originally belonged. A new Armenian bishop, the Right Reverend Bessak Toumanian, attended the service, as did the head of the Greek Orthodox Church in London and Pastor Reverdin of the Swiss Reformed, French-speaking Church.[32]

Success breeds success and, by August 1957, some nine months after the opening for worship of the new church, Archimandite Anthony was extending "a very pressing invitation (at the suggestion of Patriarch Alexis)" to Canon Waddams and the Bishop of Fulham to be present at his consecration as Bishop at a date after the end of September to suit themselves "in view of the fact that my appointment is intended to strengthen the ties between the Anglican and the Russian Orthodox Church".[33] Moscow had, understandably, thought to appoint him Bishop of London, but this, Anthony was warned by both Waddams and the Greek Bishop of Thyateira, who had been involved in a similar awkwardness when Constantinople had suggested *he* be Greek Orthodox Bishop of England or, more romantically, of Thule, would not have strengthened ties but rather put a strain on relations between the Russian Orthodox and a distinctly territorial established Church of England. Anthony wrote off urgently to ask both Exarch and Patriarchate that he be dignified with a Russian title since there was already an Anglican Bishop of London (not to mention of Fulham and of Kensington and it would be rather undignified to go for Shepherd's Bush or Knightsbridge!), and it was agreed he would be Bishop of Sergievo, particularly satisfactory as the small house-church in Upper Addison Gardens was dedicated to St Sergius. His exact title, however, was a comparatively small matter of Church politics.

Chapter Five

Anthony Bloom, personal friend of several English bishops, leader of a vibrant, growing and (miraculously) solvent Russian Patriarchal Church, and Vicar of the Church of the Dormition and All Saints, Ennismore Gardens, was more than a newly mitred figure on the chessboard of foreign Church relations in London – he was an ally to be reckoned with, a widely recognised voice, a well-known face, and a charismatic Christian presence in a confused and fearful world.

He was also a man in process of losing the one human being to whom he was not a "Father" but a child, to be cherished and chastened and laughed at and with. Ksenia Nikolaevna, in the years of their life together in London, had come to accept her son's new calling. On her arrival in England, which entailed a first experience of flying, she had decreed that she would never be downcast by the weather, as now she knew that above the clouds the sun shone and the sky was always blue. "My joy," she wrote to him in a letter of 15 June 1953; "My boy, light of my eyes, I love you. Always remember that I have always been happy and am happy now, but that my greatest happiness is in you, my own son. May God keep you, Your Mama."[34] The tender love between mother and son, formerly tinged with a bracing irony and a certain toughness on both sides, grew deeper and more open as it became clear that there was a limit to the time allotted them. In the winter of 1955-56 Ksenia Nikolaevna was admitted to hospital, where she was retained for almost four months but released without diagnosis.[35] She was readmitted at the end of May for the removal of a kidney. A large tumour was discovered and, while awaiting the results of the biopsy, Anthony asked Archbishop Nikolai to send a replacement priest so that he could take her to convalesce in the country from 23 June to 14 July. Things were not made easier by Ol'ga Il'inichna's advancing dementia, but here Tatisha Behr came to the rescue, inviting her to stay for long periods in her roomy south London home, already bursting at the seams to accommodate her own children and the unmarried mothers who, as Father Anthony teased her, were sent her to be cared for directly by God because she was "too stupid" to comprehend His Word as such, in the abstract. This great kindness on the part of Anthony's parishioner and ex-pupil gave mother and son the chance to profit from the time afforded them by Father Aleksandr Turintsev, whom Archbishop Nikolai dispatched from Paris to relieve Anthony, in peace and companionship in a rural retreat provided by another parishioner.

Anthony was not well himself. Slipped discs were causing him acute pain and he was unable to sit for any length of time ("Thank God I can stand endlessly," he reported to his exarch). That summer he was fitted with a surgical corset, something he had long resisted as it would hinder him from bowing before the altar.

Ksenia Nikolaevna felt better for her brief holiday in the company of her son but in April of the following year she was found to have a new growth on the duodenum. Anthony was shown the x-rays before she was again admitted to hospital for an exploratory operation. The doctors, however, decided against operating. Ksenia Nikolaevna was sent home with painkillers and sleeping pills but nothing to combat nausea and feeling extremely weak. Barbara Morshead, an English convert devoted to both Ksenia Nikolaevna and her son who was acting as housekeeper, told Archbishop Nikolai of this situation in a letter of 4 May 1957, stressing the courage of both and confiding gratefully that Ksenia Nikolaevna allowed her to care for her when Anthony had to be elsewhere.

> [He] is terribly tired and looks so suffering, though he says nothing at all hardly of what he is feeling. He says that he has faced up to everything that may come. But I know that he dreads the possibility of a long illness with great suffering for her. He finds it very hard to see her suffer even now, when it is not anything like as hard as it could become later. I think it would help both to have letters from you.[36]

Her letter was followed by a confidential report from Anthony that his mother had inoperable cancer of the lining of the stomach. He did not want to tell her just yet but, if she proved fit to stand the journey, would love to give her the last joy of another countryside holiday when he would prepare her for what was to come in peace.[37] Nikolai sent Father Aleksandr again with letters of sympathy and Anthony's next, evidently written from their country retreat, tells how his mother, though very weak, could still walk a little and was happy to lie out in the garden. The letters also carry news of a busy parish: the Grand Prince who required a "church divorce"; the Orthodox monk who had gone and got married in an Anglican church; his perennial struggles with the obstreperous caretaker; and the problems of two new postulants – a whole plethora of distracting human relationships which made him particularly grateful for the chance to be alone with his dying mother.[38]

What he did not know at the time was that, two days after he wrote this letter from the country, Moscow was preparing to heap still more responsibility on his shoulders. It was on 7 July 1957 that Metropolitan Nikolai of Krutitsy and Kolomna wrote appointing him "Bishop of London" and Vicar to the Exarch, who had long been complaining of overwork, and saw Anthony as a particularly useful assistant, not only for his human and spiritual qualities but because of his linguistic ability and the fact that French citizenship made it easy for him to travel. Anthony himself would ruefully recount how, when he protested his unworthiness of the honours heaped upon him to his Russian colleagues, he got the not particularly reassuring reply: "But you are such an excellent organiser and financial manager."[39] He was in no danger of seeing himself as "super-sanctified". Naturally, though, Metropolitan Nikolai's letter plunged him into a plethora of correspondence and diplomatic activity at the very time when he was most needed at home.

On 16 October his grandmother passed away quietly of old age. Though he felt she had in fact been lost to him for some time, it had to be dealt with. She had changed, he had written distressfully to the Exarch in April of that year, from a flowing river "into a quickmire, and instead of a clean river bed sparkling up for all to see there is mud, rotting vegetation, writhing monsters and the stink of decay"; he added wistfully what a grace it is when old age comes like a second childhood, the child being the only part of a person that is truly eternal.[40] Ksenia Nikolaevna had rallied again after their brief holiday and was, he wrote to the Exarch a few days after Ol'ga Il'inichna's death, bearing up well: "She is alert in spirit and shows great endurance and calm in the face of slowly approaching death. We talk about it often and quite simply, we are able to share all the illumination and shoulder together all the heaviness."[41]

On November 29/30, with considerable pomp and circumstance which we shall consider in more detail in the next chapter, Archimandrite Anthony was named and consecrated Bishop of Sergievo. On 16-17 December he left his mother briefly for a pastoral gathering in Paris where, deeply moved and surrounded by old friends and mentors, he told them: "I stand on the threshold of a new road as a man from whom the past has fallen away and who has no future. I stand in total ignorance, as I am setting out at the call of God, and He is my Lord and I shall go to whatsoever country he calls me."[42] By February 1958, Ksenia Nikolaevna "first felt strongly and in all reality that she is dying. The dying may be slow, but death is surely coming, and I am trying to make the most of every minute so that death should not take Mama unawares."[43] It is possible, Father Anthony says in one of his books, to express so much in the smallest acts of care for the dying – bringing them a cup of tea, straightening a pillow. . . .

Death finally came on Good Friday, 11 April 1958, while Anthony was celebrating the bearing forth of the Shroud. His Easter telegram to the Exarch reads: "Christ is risen and there are no dead in the Grave", and this, the joy of Easter, was the message he managed to convey to his flock and to Soviet listeners to the service over the radio.

> And when Easter was over, and a few days later the funeral was over, I returned home alone. Inwardly it was as though I'd been turned to stone, I could not weep, I didn't know what to do with myself. And you know what happened? A girl came, who, every year, used to bring my mother a single shoot of some spring flower. She rang the bell and I opened the door and all she said to me was: "I always brought your mother a plant like this one. Now she has died, I thought I would give it to you." And I burst out sobbing over that plant. It played the part professional mourners used to play, it opened up my soul, it made tears and recovery possible, a new life, because that kind of constraint, of paralysis has to be lifted with the help of other people.[44]

Chapter Six

Fame in a Divided World, 1957-1963

> *The Orthodox Church believes that it contains the fullness of Truth and the fullness of Life. But it knows how rich in faith, devotion to God and living Spirit, the Holy Spirit, are all those who worship Christ in singleness of heart. And for this reason, together with them, united by the same hope and the same joy and expectation, we pray the Lord to break down all the barriers which divide us from one another and to make us one loving, grateful family, resplendent with the gifts of the Holy Spirit. When, such a short time ago, I found myself in the churches of Moscow, Leningrad, Pskov, in the Pskov Monastery of the Caves and the Trinity St Sergius Monastery, in the Cathedral at Vladimir, I told everyone that in the West and all over the face of the earth Russian people are scattered who have kept their love and loyalty to their native Church and their native land. And I brought with me to everyone I met the love of our diaspora and the love of all those Westerners who, having no human ties with our Church and native land, have found a way to Christ in the Orthodox Church thanks to our diaspora and the love of the Russian Church.*[1]

To understand the interaction between the Patriarchate and its Exarchate for Western Europe it helps to look more closely at the correspondence between London, Paris and Moscow at the time Anthony Bloom was consecrated Bishop and appointed Suffragan to Exarch Nikolai (Eremin). Indeed, there is no other way we can begin to understand his meteoric course or the dedicated balancing act between loyalty to the Russian Church and unblemished prestige in the rest of the world that he was to sustain for the next forty years.

As early as 26 February 1955, Archbishop Nikolai had put in a request to the Patriarchate to promote two suffragan bishops to help him with his work at the Exarchate: Archimandrite Sergii (Shevich), a longstanding member of the Committee at the Exarchate in Paris and due for promotion, and Hegumen Anthony (Bloom).

There were, he wrote, as many as 60,000 Orthodox in Great Britain who needed a vicar bishop. Bloom was on good terms with the Anglicans, who had always inclined favourably towards the Orthodox Church. For both these reasons, he wrote, "our Church" has, in the person of Hegumen Anthony, a representative it would be hard to better. Thanks to his work among young people, his involvement with various ecclesiastical organisations and his ministry as Vicar of "our Church", he has earned general love and respect. His conduct as monk, his devotion to pastoral work, his observance of canon law, and his administrative, organisational and missionary talents have elevated him to first place (after the Greek Archbishop Exarch) among the Orthodox in England. To ensure that the Russian Patriarchal Church continues to occupy this place is highly desirable. Hegumen Anthony, moreover, is French by passport, a doctor by education, fluent in languages: Russian, English, French and German; he was professed monk in 1943. There is no hindrance to his carrying out tasks for the Church in any country.[2]

There was, as the Patriarchate was to discover before it came to discuss this letter in July 1957, no objection to Anthony Bloom's appointment as Bishop Suffragan to the Exarch from the point of view of the Soviet Foreign Office, or to his being included once more in an invitation to visit the Soviet Union. An edict was duly issued in July 1957 to inform Archimandrite (as he had by then become) Anthony of his new appointment as Bishop of London, which, as we have seen, on 15 August 1957 was amended to Bishop of Sergievo at the recipient's request. On 12 September 1957, the Patriarchate approved the expense of his solemn consecration at Ennismore Gardens. Not only was the occasion one entailing considerable splendour and the widest possible hospitality, but it would be necessary to fit out the Archimandrite and his humble parish with the vestments and regalia required to perform an episcopal Liturgy. Archbishop Nikolai was also given the go-ahead to discuss Anthony's salary, but Anthony himself appears to have balked at this and chosen to get by on the very modest stipend he already received from the parish, plus only reimbursement for travel and other unavoidable expenses incurred by his new duties. In fact, Archbishop Nikolai found managing the finances of a demanding Exarchate a heavy burden, and was very much hoping that Anthony, who must have appeared possessed of a positively uncanny ability to require nothing for himself yet to conjure money from thin air when it was needed by his church, would, at least partially, shoulder it for him. This hope was shared by the Exarchate Committee, who found their current leader sadly lacking in fiscal ability.[3]

Preparation for the enthronement went forward in a flurry of good will. The Russian Church approved their candidate Bishop's desire to include as many representatives of the Church of England hierarchy as would accept invitations and also clergy from other national churches in Great Britain.

At the Exarch's request, the ceremony was to take place in London and he would officiate in person, assisted by the Greek Bishop Iakovos (Virvos) of Apamea, to whom Anthony had written a personal letter, hoping that his health would permit him "to take part in my consecration as Bishop as in that way I shall also receive the blessing of a Church which is Mother to all us young Slavonic Churches". The Greek dignitary, who was at the time acting representative of the Ecumenical Patriarch, replied that he was genuinely delighted at Anthony's appointment and shared his ideal of unity and co-operation.[4] Geoffrey Fisher, Archbishop of Canterbury, wrote to Exarch Nikolai on 23 September that he too was happy with the appointment and that Anthony's continued ministry in the UK "would contribute to the cordial relations which already appertain between our two churches".[5]

At Archimandrite Anthony's own request, the beloved pastor of the camps of his youth, Protopriest Georgii Shumkin, and his constant ally and supporter from the Serbian Church in London, Father Vladimir Rodzianko, led him into the ceremony of consecration. Also present, and associated with Anthony's service with the French-speaking parish of Ste Geneviève and the Mother of God, Joy of all who Sorrow, were Fathers Mikhail Bel'sky and Lev Gillet, who, again at his request, acted as sponsors.[i] Father Nicholas Gibbes and Archimandrite Vasilii Krivoshein, who was having difficulty obtaining a *permis de séjour* from the French and was temporarily attached to the Oxford parish, were present, as were the Hieromonk Kirill (Taylor), the French Father Dionisii (Denis Chambault) from the Paris Exarchate, and representatives of the Serbian Church – an assembly that, as Bel'sky says in his account of the proceedings, bore witness to the unity of the various national Orthodox Churches "in faith, in the sacraments, in the outpouring of Divine Love".[6] From the Anglican Church, the Bishop of Fulham represented the Archbishop of Canterbury, and H.M. Waddams was present in his capacity as Secretary to the Lambeth Palace Council of Foreign Affairs. The Bishop of Kensington, representing the Bishop of London, stressed he was also present as a personal friend.

"From my youth up I have made it a rule to seek for nothing and to refuse nothing," Anthony had written in the letter to the Patriarchate in which he accepted his new appointment, adding that he was, nevertheless, overawed to be chosen to enter the ranks of the Apostles and to be entrusted, should the occasion arise, to lay down his life for his flock.[7] Curiously, his friend and advocate the Exarch was disturbed by the new Bishop's speech at the

---

i. On 11 September 1957, Anthony wrote to the Exarch asking "for Father Lev Gillet to conduct me to my consecration as Bishop; I am bound to him by more than 20 years of friendship and owe him a great deal for the formation of my inner life. Would you permit that at both the naming and the consecration ceremonies I should be brought in by Father Mikhail (Bel'sky) and Father Lev?" (letter in MASF Archive).

*Consecration as Bishop, 30 November 1957. Between
Father Michael Bel'sky (right) and Father Lev Gillet (left)*

"naming" ceremony, which referred to Constantinople as the "mother" (rather than "sister") of all Orthodox Churches and made no special mention of the witness born by his own Russian Church – Nikolai, now Metropolitan of Korsun, was clearly dismayed by the thought that this might indicate an intended change of allegiance,[8] a suspicion that tells us more about the mindset of the highly vulnerable and over-burdened old Exarch than about Anthony's loyalty to the Moscow Church, which never wavered. It does, however, highlight the fact that the new Bishop of Sergievo did not wish either native British churches or his fellow Orthodox to perceive the precipitate rise in prestige of the Russian Orthodox Church in England (an inevitable consequence of his promotion to episcopal status) as in any way nationalistic or triumphalist, but rather as a step towards pan-Orthodox reconciliation.[9]

As Metropolitan Nikolai had specifically requested, Anthony was simultaneously appointed Bishop Suffragan to himself as Exarch. The relationship between the two émigré priests continued to be one of mutual friendship and admiration, with Anthony, of course, very much the junior in age and ecclesiastic experience. From this time onwards, however, it was not altogether free from moments of distrust on the part of the older man and those closest to him in the Paris community, particularly after the Patriarchate decided to grant the old Exarch's request for retirement and appoint Anthony Acting Exarch and two years later Exarch in his stead. Meanwhile, subordinates who had grown impatient with Metropolitan

Nikolai's lack of practical acumen did all they could to enlist Anthony's support in administrative matters, while he in his turn did what he could to act as a buffer between factions, and all that was consistent with helping the Exarchate towards a viable financial policy in relation to the upkeep of a community of ageing ecclesiastics and of hard-pressed publishing and academic initiatives, and to the restoration or acquisition of church buildings for the more scattered communities of the Western European diaspora. "He has very good contact with all of us and we are full of hope for the future of the ecclesiastical life of our Exarchate, because Bishop Anthony has brought new life with him, he has great endurance, firmness of purpose, equilibrium, true love and intelligence," wrote Archimandrite Dionisii (Denis Chambault) to the Foreign Department of the Patriarchate,[10] shortly after the first council meeting to be chaired by their new Suffragan Bishop.

It was scarcely to be hoped one man could live up to such high expectations. Anthony could not spare the time from his London parish and other commitments as speaker and preacher to come to Paris as frequently as the diminutive Father Denis (a Frenchman who had converted in the 1930s under the influence of Vladimir Lossky) and his other supporters would have wished, and some problems, such as the state of the Russian Patriarchal Church in Holland, where conflict between parishes had gone beyond the control of an ailing bishop, and in Rabat, had become endemic and could not be solved "on the hoof". Clearly, the Bishop needed to free himself up at home, but this he had neither the means nor the will to accomplish in haste. To stand in for him while he grappled with new obligations laid on him by the Exarchate, he now stood in great need of a priest, but hesitated to impose his choice on the parish, feeling rejection would be too bruising an experience for an unprepared candidate. There was, of course, no money, and Anthony was not, at this stage, prepared to request a salaried pastor from the Patriarchate. He needed somebody from his own diocese prepared to serve as a non-stipendiary priest while earning his living in some other capacity, and he needed time not only to prepare the candidate and the congregation, who must be willing to accept him as pastor and confessor, but also the future *Matushka*, for he considered that to be wife to a priest was not just something that might happen to any believing Christian woman but "a special vocation, just as specific as that of a deaconess in ancient times".[11] He had in mind a suitable candidate, but proceeded slowly, allowing his laity to assume the initiative. On 21 September 1958 he consecrated Deacon Sergei Hackel, a young librarian from Cambridge whose father had authored a book on icons and whose mother, eventually, as a widow, took the veil. Father Sergei was priested, with the full backing of the parish, almost six years later, in June 1964, by which time he had published his PhD thesis on "Aleksandr Blok and The Twelve" and become a lecturer in Russian literature at the University of Sussex.

Chapter Six

In spite of all the conflicting demands on his time in the years immediately following his consecration as Bishop and appointment to assist the Exarch, Anthony's main interest remained the cure of individual souls and missionary outreach towards people of all denominations or none, for which he had such a special gift. This kind of non-proselytising outreach is featured most tellingly in an unpublished memoir by Dr Frank Johnson, who first heard him speak when he was a medical student at Newcastle University on "The Meaning of the Resurrection" and "Christ the Man", and was, some time later, taken by a friend to the Cathedral in London where he was impressed by the "tone and depth of worship", and after the service, introduced himself as a medical student who felt he had a monastic vocation. Clearly this resonated with Anthony who sought him out (on duty on the hospital ward!) next time he came to Newcastle. Johnson's friend, who had introduced him to the Cathedral but not known Anthony personally, had since succumbed to cancer of the pancreas and told him that the Bishop had come the very next day after receiving her letter telling him of the diagnosis and had spent four hours at her side, after which she had felt "at peace, happy to let go and die". These two acts of personal attention greatly impressed the future doctor, who had been raised between the Presbyterian and Anglican Communions and "taught that the reason why communism had taken hold in Russia was that the Church was so unchristian". In his own words, they "blew me off my feet". In Newcastle, Anthony spent three hours talking to Johnson and his friends, who had conceived the idea of founding a community of Christian doctors living together but comprising both single and married people serving and teaching medicine in the Third World. The foundation of such a community, he said, should be happy families, not supressed and constantly sacrificed wives; "I'd never before heard a celibate cleric speak in such a tone concerning marriage." A recommendation that the young doctor should further consult Sophronii at the Orthodox monastery in Essex was also enthusiastically followed up.

Two surgeons, one with further training in leprosy and hand surgery, another a paediatrician, together with Johnson, himself trained in obstetrics and gynaecology, did indeed form a community and were later joined by another physician, the Reverend Dr David Gill, whom Johnson introduced to Anthony before their departure. They worked together for many years in Africa, before which the Metropolitan spent a long evening with them, again in Newcastle, talking "about spirituality for busy people and it is by far the finest spiritual talk I have ever experienced". However, when Johnson asked at a later meeting whether he should become Orthodox, Anthony told him: "If it was God's will I went to Africa (and he did believe it to be God's will for us) then it was not right at this time for me to become Orthodox. What I should do, he went on, is to take into Anglicanism the things I liked in Orthodoxy. He said this with real affection and impressed me greatly. It inferred that he wasn't willing simply to grab skulls!"

After their return from Africa David Gill became an Orthodox priest and took a section of his parish with him, and Johnson joined the Orthodox Church at the same time. Both he and Anthony were extremely busy and met seldom, but he considers it still "one of the greatest gifts I've had to have been allowed by God to know him".

In 1958, Anthony attended the Lambeth Conference to further the cause of Christian unity. Exasperated by the cautious jockeying for position, the earnest efforts to work out a "minimal" agreement, he urged his fellow hierarchs to stop thinking negatively, in terms of negotiating a "marriage of convenience" which would entail regrettable compromise or closing ranks in the face of ebbing faith and dwindling congregations, and to recognise that "the unity destroyed by human frailty and sin can only be restored by God's almighty power and His Holiness". "Our hearts must change," he said, "for they are narrow. . . . [I]t is with suffering that our quest for unity must begin, to be divided from our neighbour must become intolerable suffering. And only then shall our prayer fly like an arrow and hit the mark."[12] People felt as though a window had been thrown open in a stuffy committee room. It got them no further in the tortuous debate, but they gratefully gulped the fresh air and found courage, together with the speaker himself, to go on to the next thing and to hope.

The next thing in the ecumenical field for the Bishop of Sergievo was the first attendance of delegates from the Moscow Church at a meeting of the World Council of Churches (WCC) at The Hague. This was a painful occasion as the choice of representatives was unfortunate and the Moscow contingent appeared to Western delegates more like well-nourished and rigidly cautious Soviet officials than hierarchs of a holy, suffering Church. Russian émigrés, including Bishop Anthony, were dismayed. There was, however, one moment when he felt an intense sympathy, indeed admiration, for one of the most unpopular Moscow delegates. Metropolitan Nikolai of Krutitsy and Kolomna, Head of the Patriarchate's Department of Foreign Affairs, had a reputation as a collaborator with Soviet State organs and, when he undertook to celebrate the Liturgy, there was an almost palpable atmosphere of hostility in the church. Anthony, who was concelebrating, saw the elderly priest, who clearly sensed the mood of those present, pull himself together and concentrate his whole being on the consecration of the bread and the wine. Whether or not thanks to the insight granted him at that moment, Anthony found a way to talk to his fellow bishops from the Patriarchate, schooled as they were and he was not in the arts of survival and compromise, and to make them understand without offence how counterproductive, even for the government-inspired peace offensive, to implement which they were now permitted to cultivate international contacts, was their over-emphasis on peace and disarmament and the stonewalling evasiveness of their replies to questions about freedom of worship in the

USSR.¹³ They did not change their tone overnight, but they did realise that the multilingual Bishop of Sergievo, with his effortless dignity, empathy and charm, was a God-sent intermediary between them and the vociferous, unpredictable gathering of prelates of every conceivable colour and creed, who clearly regarded them with profound reserve, exacerbated by reciprocal mistrust. Anthony was asked to join the Russian Patriarchal delegation in the capacity of interpreter at a conference in Delhi scheduled for 1961 at which they were to be officially received into the WCC. He also received a second, pressing invitation to visit the Patriarchal Church in Moscow which, in October 1960, he felt able to accept as part of a wide-ranging programme of foreign travel in his capacity as Suffragan Bishop to the Exarch.

Meanwhile, in the course of 1959, the Bishop of Sergievo was invited in his own right to speak about the Church in Russia at a conference for Christian unity in Switzerland, where he was subsequently remembered by one English delegate as the "pied piper of the conference . . . who charmed us all, this dignified black-clad figure with his piercing eyes and impressive beard, speaking usually in clear, measured French and occasionally in English all the more attractive for his foreign accent".¹⁴

This pied-piper-like ability to charm was even more in evidence at Grandchamps where, asked to address a youthful, educated audience before whom he could relax, linguistically and culturally, Anthony drew freely on his own reading and experience as schoolboy, undergraduate, soldier and doctor in pre-war and wartime France.

As the English delegate to Geneva wrote, it was not so much what the Russian Bishop had to say as the way he said it that had people eating out of his hand. He never spoke to the whole room but either seemed to be addressing each individual separately or looking over their heads, appealing for inspiration to some larger, more powerful yet shy, almost elusive intelligence. When, in Switzerland, he took questions from the floor, he answered directly, clearly seeking not to "field" the query to stump the questioner as politicians tend to do, but to establish God's truth between his own experience and his interlocutor's need to know. Speaking of the Church in Russia, he told his audience clearly what it could do (celebrate the Liturgy, administer the sacraments and maintain Church property) and what it could not (teach the children, visit hospitals and prisons, preach and publish without preliminary censorship). Concealing nothing, he infused all he said with respect and love for his brother clergy who were not at liberty to speak out abroad but who had upheld the faith through almost forty years of harassment and persecution.

In Grandchamps, his subject was "Mutual love between the children of God" ("*L'amour mutuel entre les enfants de Dieu*"). For the nascent "flower power" generation, the monastics had chosen their subject well – and their speaker. As always, Anthony made no attempt to adjust his vocabulary to "trendy" ideas and catchphrases, but spoke, simply, austerely and challengingly, from the heart, of his own experience of Christ's love which involves each and all, body and soul, in the sacrificial Trinitarian process of total engagement, of bearing one another's burdens, not from a sense of duty but from a true, in-depth perception of the divine potential of every human creature. His words were redolent of a profound sense, welling from within the Church but in no way confined to the Church, of our human responsibility for God's creation. As in Geneva, his audience was instantly attracted to this ardent person who told them the word "passion" was rooted in "passivity", yet radiated a "jealous", "zealous" love for each and every individual being, infinitely precious in the sight of the Lord, as well as a detached perception of his or her shortcomings. It was at once a fierce and an eirenic vision. When asked whether it was possible to love and disagree at the same time, Anthony emphasised the imperative to acknowledge that we can never know the ultimate depths of another's soul, which is perceived by God alone, and therefore it is possible to hold fast to one's own opinions, as far as they go, without in any way setting ourselves up in judgement on those who dispute them. True love, in his view, was never tyrannous nor possessive.

Things were happening at home, too, in the new diocese. The year 1959 saw the first diocesan children's camp, another occasion to play "pied-piper", if only to join in vigorous games of volleyball, in spite of a still troublesome back, and to share the joy of the outdoors with the children whom he visited. The initiative for the camp came from his old friend Tatisha Behr, who organised a beautiful site for it in Wales. A whole generation of diocesan activists, including future deacon Peter Scorer, drew inspiration from the atmosphere of joyous improvisation.

The young diocese was also graced by a contemplative offshoot of enduring beauty: the ex-Athonite, Father Sophronii, brought his community of monks and scholars, including some women and the nun Mother Elizaveta (Medvedeva), from their precarious self-financing existence in Paris to found an Orthodox monastery at Tolleshunt Knights in Essex, a house gifted to them by a wealthy convert. The initiative clashed at one point a few years later with the camp, when the Bishop, happily ensconced with his youngsters in the Welsh mountains, failed to respond to two telegrams from Father Sophronii demanding his presence at the patronal Feast of the Monastery. Only in response to a third telegram, in which Father Sophronii, who understandably considered his monastic initiative important and was sensitive to slights,[15] threatened to transfer them to the jurisdiction of the Ecumenical Patriarch, did Anthony realise he had given serious offence and set off helter-skelter on a crazy all-night drive to join his brethren in time to celebrate the solemn Liturgy on the day of the birth of John the Baptist, patron saint of the monastery.[16] It was a great sorrow to Abbot and Bishop that this incident in fact proved symptomatic of a relationship that was to prove unsustainable. After a

Chapter Six

Summer camp, July 1979

few years, the contemplatives found the tempestuous, financially hand-to-mouth existence of the Moscow Orthodox Church in Great Britain led by a Bishop burdened with the affairs of the Exarchate as well as the diocese to be incompatible with the concentration and stability to which they felt themselves called. Sophronii eventually sought shelter under the omophorion of the Ecumenical Patriarch. For the first five years, however, the monastery, which was to become a beacon of Orthodoxy in Britain, took root and prospered in the diocese of Sergievo, then Sourozh. Against his usual practice, Anthony obtained what monies he could for the monks from the Moscow Patriarchate (for instance, 1100 francs, by far the largest single item in his "personal expenses" claim for 1961[17]), but there was never sufficient foreign currency available to balance the books and, as it turned out, Anthony was no more successful in ensuring continuity and stability for the contemplative life in England than his predecessor Exarch Nikolai had been in France.

The first major event of 1960 was also connected to St John the Baptist, albeit to one of the Saviour's Feast Days, one for which Anthony particularly loved and honoured the Forerunner, the Baptism of Christ, before whom John, as the self-effacing friend of the Bridegroom, then and there consented "to decrease". This particular occasion, however, marked no falling off, but rather a new high point in Anthony's own service to Christ in Britain. He was honoured by an ecumenical invitation to celebrate, for the first time, the Russian Orthodox rite of the Blessing of the Waters, in this case of the Thames, an event that served to mark the degree to which his church had become acceptable to the community of London churches and, more particularly, to the territorial Anglicans.

The Blessing of the Waters of the Thames, 1960

The year 1960 passed as busily and successfully as had 1959 and, by the autumn, the Bishop felt sufficiently secure in the trust of his flock and the respect of his peers in the English, international Orthodox and wider ecumenical community to accept the invitation to Russia that it had formerly given him such pain to refuse.

On 6 October 1960, Bishop Anthony boarded the plane for Moscow and was wonderstruck by his first glimpse of his native land from the air: a small white church on rising ground amid field and forest, glowing in a shaft of sun. He was forty-six, a long time to wait for your first conscious sight of your own country.

Patriarchal protocol demanded that visitors from abroad were met and accompanied by a priest, who would be obliged to put in a detailed report to the Foreign Department: where they had been, what had been said, who had spoken with them by chance or arrangement. This was not exactly KGB supervision but a kind of insurance policy for the Church, who needed to know as much or more than their government-sponsored minders, who had the advantage of electronic equipment. Nevertheless, the unfortunate clerics involved were widely referred to, even in Orthodox circles, as *"stukachi"* (informers) and, when with Bishop Anthony, were not infrequently discomforted by people who came to see him on personal matters who would patiently wait until left alone – not infrequently in complete silence.

On his first visit, Anthony was met and accompanied by Father Evgenii Ambartsumov, with whom he promptly made friends and whom he insisted on visiting in hospital four years later in 1965 when he was a guest of the Theological Academy in Leningrad – not the easiest thing to arrange in a country where hospital visits by clergymen in their professional capacity were strictly taboo. His itinerary on this first visit comprised the Moscow Theological Academy at the Trinity St Sergius Monastery in Zagorsk, where it had been disbanded after the Monastery itself was "nationalised" as a museum in 1921 but reinstated in connection with the patriotic stance adopted by the Church from the onset of the German invasion of Russia in the Second World War; the Leningrad (St Petersburg) Theological Academy in the city where his mother had received her schooling; the ancient Hanseatic league cities of fabled Novgorod and Pskov with its remarkable Monastery of the Caves (Pskovo-Pechersky Monastery); and Vladimir, together with the neighbouring town of Suzdal, an outpost of Orthodoxy at the edge of the Tartar Steppes, where the grassland sweeps like the sea to beat against the forested escarpments of the Moscow region. This, not exotic Persia, nor *la douce France*, nor Austria with its glorious Alps where he loved to holiday, with a knap-sack and sleeping rough, nor sea-bound Albion with its mists and gales, was the country of his heart, and his heart opened to meet it – wound to wound, as he described the process by which the Christian is grafted to the true vine of Christ.[18] An outcast himself, he returned to his orphaned homeland, where the people were cut off and estranged from their own history no less than the diaspora were cut off from their native soil – and he loved them and they came in their hundreds for his blessing. Of course, there was no media coverage, but he was permitted to celebrate in the great churches and after services he would stand for hours, blessing all who came up to him, looking at each one with a love as demanding as judgement day and as non-judgmental as sun and rain.[19] "Haven't I blessed you before, Granny?" he afterwards recalled asking an old woman on her third time round. "Ah, Vladyka," she replied, beaming, "but it is so *wonderful* to be blessed."[20]

Another joy was meeting up with his relatives: his Scriabin cousins Elena and Maria and Elena's daughter Roxana Sophronitskaia. He introduced to them Tatiana L'vovna Maidanovich, the daughter of a returned émigré now living with her parents in bleak conditions in the little town of Zagorsk, formerly Sergievo, which had grown up around the Great Trinity St Sergius Monastery. He remembered her as an adolescent from her Paris church, for which she was desperately homesick. From the outset, Tatiana became an unofficial contact for members of the intelligentsia to find out where he would be celebrating or preaching, and they came in droves to hear this man of the Church who spoke neither in Soviet slogans nor in rotund ecclesiastic Slavonicisms, but in clear, cultivated twentieth-century Russian: "He has given us back our Russian language."[21] From 1966 onwards, Tatiana, the proud owner of a grotty little tape-recorder, trudged and bussed from venue to venue, recording Anthony's sermons and the informal question-and-answer sessions that soon began to arrange themselves in the crowded flat of the priest Nikolai Vedernikov – and, later on, of other admirers, such as the Utenkov family. Later, with the help of and, indeed, at the instigation of Tatiana's younger sister Elena, these modest recordings, scrupulously typed out, edited and passed from hand to hand in "*samizdat*",[i] were to become the basis for the greater part of Anthony Bloom's publications in Russian,[22] apart from those which are in fact translations from French or English by one or other of the sisters or their close friends.

Relations with Anthony's brother hierarchs were not always so easy to establish. From the outset, he had set himself a simple rule: "never to say there what I would not repeat here, and vice-versa".[23] He was quite open about the need to revise the behaviour of delegates to the international community; to "talk less about peace in order to make peace";[24] to answer politically awkward questions more openly and not to bat them back to their head of delegation, which gave the clear impression that junior members were afraid to speak out; to avoid, where possible, travelling in embassy cars which made them look like Soviet officials; and not to seek to make a good impression by emphasising the prosperity of the priesthood, which merely convinced their critics that the Church had "sold out" to the State. Father Evgenii reported back to the Department of Foreign Affairs that this extraordinarily outspoken émigré bishop said openly that he was a "monarchist", albeit not a politically active one, a declaration that Anthony was later to claim saved him from approaches from the KGB, who never

---

i. *Samizdat* (from Russian *sam*, "self", and *izdatelstvo*, "publishing"): literature secretly written, copied and circulated in the former Soviet Union.

attempted to recruit him.

Why was such an attitude taken in good part? Presumably because Anthony's criticisms were clearly aimed to improve, not to undermine, relationships with Christians outside Russia. Also because, though frank, he was not censorious.

Everywhere he went, "our Bishop of London", as Patriarch Aleksii still called him, won hearts and minds and, in spite of an initial wariness, felt himself accepted and surprisingly at home. It was his language and, for all their faults and foibles, these were his people. In his turn, he did his utmost to convey the love and loyalty of those abroad who had remained faithful to the Moscow Patriarchate. This in spite of the fact that he was not personally drawn to many of his brother bishops. However, Patriarch Aleksii, a transparent old gentleman of great culture, inspired him with a very real veneration and filial affection. Also, it was part of his personal self-discipline to wrestle with his own blindness to the divine in any particular person he met, and to overcome it. These were his people and he could, should and would love them and Christ in them.

It was an intensely experienced fortnight in which Anthony, though he had neither time nor opportunity to explore far beyond the tight-scheduled arranged programme, felt confirmed in the task he had set himself of representing the Russian Orthodox Church in the ecumenical community, in spite of the fact that a top-secret plan for the Department of Foreign Affairs was in direct contradiction to his advice. The official "plan" was that the Church should continue "to struggle for peace and disarmament"; to counter the "aggressive policies" of other denominations, particularly the Vatican; to cultivate all those individuals and societies known to be for "Peace and Friendship"; to explain Soviet law on cults and to counter anti-Soviet propaganda; to prepare actively for the Second World Congress for Peace as also for the International Patristic Conference to which academic theologians were encouraged to contribute; to activate the work of foreign representatives of the Patriarchate (presumably the exarchates) by encouraging them to expose the exaggerations of anti-Soviet propaganda and to reintegrate other branches of Russian émigré Orthodoxy; to summon the Exarch himself to Moscow to discuss ways in which this should be undertaken; to convene a congress of clergy and peace activists in early 1963; to invite groups of activists from émigré parishes to visit Russia and see for themselves the position of their Church; to activate the role of the Western European Exarchate, preferably by replacing the exarch in office with a bishop from the USSR; and to work towards greater outreach to the children and young people in Russian Orthodox parishes abroad.[25]

There was one point in this rather sinister-sounding programme that could have been prompted by consensus with such representatives of the Patriarchal Exarchate as Metropolitan Nikolai, Bishop Anthony and Bishop Vasilii Krivoshein (now Bishop of Brussels): this was to do with the current position of the Evlogian Church, which had remained under Greek jurisdiction in spite of their leader's dying wish for reconciliation with Moscow in the spring of 1960. Canonical questions arose owing to the death, in 1959, of Metropolitan Vladimir (Tikhonitsky), head of the "Western European Exarchate of Russian parishes under the Ecumenical Patriarch", which had been instituted by Constantinople to represent the Russian Orthodox within its jurisdiction and which still continued to function, as it now seemed to both Moscow and Constantinople, somewhat redundantly. By 1966, the two churches agreed on the disbanding of the rival "Russian" (Ecumenical) Exarchate. All efforts towards full reconciliation[26] with the "Evlogian" bishops, however, were to prove in vain. They regrouped to found their own, independent *Arkhiepiskopeia* and the Exarchate of Russian Parishes of the Ecumenical Patriarchate was re-established by the wish of this body in 1971.

As to the rest of the "secret plan" of the Department of Foreign Affairs, it ran contrary to Bishop Anthony's advice in almost every respect. He, however, regarded the Department, distinct from the Patriarchate itself, as a useful filter for communications, to whom he invariably referred peace-niks and other do-gooders who, from this time on, would ask him to put them in touch with Russian Christians or arrange trips for well-wishers to the Soviet Union. The Department could be relied on to sanitise direct contacts with the West from the point of view of the Soviet authorities and Dr Bloom's time in the Resistance had left him with a natural instinct for how to keep his friends out of trouble.

Nevertheless, Anthony was, from now on, involved in a two-way mission: to convey the love of the diaspora and the culture they had preserved to the Church in Russia and, in England and Western Europe, to hold high the standard of the Moscow Patriarchate as a true Church, proven in suffering and deserving the veneration of his own multi-cultural diocese which owed so much to Russian Orthodoxy. He was helped to tread this tightrope by his training as a monk in the world, a habit of mind rooted in self-discipline and self-abrogation, but perhaps still more by zealous love (quite the opposite, as he had made clear at Grandchamps, of cloying sentiment or passive passion) for his spiritual children in Britain, for the Russian Church that had nurtured him, and for the Russian people, to whom he belonged, "whose joys are our joys and whose sorrows are our sorrows".[27]

No such tightrope would have been there to tread, of course, had the moment in history been less prone to seismic change. The super-powers were engaged in a ruinous arms race; the ideological battle was blazing up like wildfire in ever-changing locations but burning low in Russia itself; and the Soviet Union was committed to a balancing act of preserving its great power status while making every effort at home and abroad to live down the horrors of Stalinism. In the West, many men and women of good will were hypnotised by the atomic threat, prepared to put their whole way of life at risk to preserve life itself: "Better red than dead." Many were socialists, though few "communists" of the Soviet variety. To some extent, it was precisely these people whom the Soviet state wished to cultivate and encourage and officials were intelligent enough to realise that they could not have a more desirable front than a comparatively young and personable Orthodox bishop, free-thinking and outspoken, who commanded media time on radio and television in four languages and who was a welcome guest in his own right at churches of the most varied denominations, schools, universities and international conferences. To continue to impress, he would have to be given free reign, but he could, of course, be used in the service of the Church which he regarded with such fierce loyalty; and the Church, in its turn, could by its very nature be given a certain amount of leeway to promote the entirely Christian ideal of peace in the international community in its own way. Also, some clergy and many lay Orthodox in Russia truly valued Anthony's input into the mind of their Church.

Indeed, Bishop Anthony's assignment to a delegation from the Patriarchal Church to the conference of the World Council of Churches in New Delhi in the winter of 1961, their debut appearance as full members of this institution, was soon to prove his worth. He acted as an adroit interpreter of the highly intelligent but unprepossessing Metropolitan Nikodim's answers to aggressive questioning from the world press and, in spite of residual stonewalling by the Patriarchal clergy, earned them the goodwill of the conference.

To Anthony himself, New Delhi came as something of an eye-opener – not the conference, which he was later to designate as a "talking-shop". Rather, he was devastated by the poverty of India – and surprised to find himself, logical as it might seem from his early appreciation of the Upanishads, more impressed by the Hindus than by the Malabar Christians who, it seemed to him, appeared to think of themselves as a social elite, a notion deeply foreign to his own understanding of religion as a cosmic and all-embracing truth. For Nikodim, he developed a respect that was to deepen into a genuine friendship, and he was profoundly amused by one of the senior Russian delegates Archbishop Sergii (Larin), who insisted on his pressing need to bring back quantities of coconuts as gifts to favoured parishioners and murmured, lost in admiration for a festively bedecked processional elephant, "What a model of dignity for an Archbishop!"[28]

Bishop Nikolai of Mukachevo and Uzhgorod, one of those at the New Delhi conference charged with reporting back to the Department of Foreign Affairs,[29] relayed Anthony's opinions with unreserved enthusiasm. Archbishop Sergii (at that time of Perm and Solikamsk), on the other hand, felt it necessary to enter in his report a caveat that Anthony was not so much motivated by the interests of the Russian Church as by personal, possibly purely subjective, émigré considerations. However, the shrewd old ex-*obnovlenets*[i] went on, though everyone knew that the Bishop of Sergievo

---

i. *Obnovlenets* (lit. Renewer): adherent of a modernising branch of the Russian

was not always "politically, only canonically, loyal", his opinions nevertheless deserved careful consideration . . . and the Archbishop proceeded to give a pungent exposition of Anthony's advice on how to avoid the impression that "our" delegates are "under police pressure" (his words) to give blatantly duplicitous answers to questions such as that of the closing down of seminaries in the Soviet Union – for instance, in Stavropol, "because believers had complained that the seminary was a breeding-ground for atheists"; or, in Kiev, "because they were short of accommodation so it made sense for them to amalgamate with Odessa". He also cited a whole list of inept replies to questions on the ongoing anti-religious propaganda campaign: "There hasn't been any for three weeks and anyway you can't really call it anti-religious – it's just the same old thing – every now and again they have a go at the clergy" – or on the closing down of churches: "Some have been shut down, true, but not all that many, just a few specific ones at the request of the believers themselves." These were replies, says the Archbishop, that Anthony categorised as "deceitful and sinful". One delegate, who had tried to deny any closing down of churches and monasteries in the USSR, had been put to shame by one of "the foreigners" producing an article from a Soviet journal that actually gave the statistics. "In the opinion of Vladyka [Anthony]," Archbishop Sergii concludes, "such inadequacies should be eliminated for the sake of the Russian Church and its authority in the international arena."[30]

So Anthony's views were sent echoing down the corridors of power without putting others at risk and without unseemly confrontation with his own church in front of the rest of the world, precisely because his advice was not only frank, but genuinely friendly. On 10 October 1962, the Patriarchate duly elevated him to the rank of Archbishop of Sourozh, Vicar of the newly constituted Diocese of the British Isles and thus senior Orthodox prelate in London. "What will the Greeks say?" wondered Satterthwaite of Lambeth Palace,[31] nervously contemplating problems of precedence. But more was to come. On 16 January 1963, the new Archbishop was appointed Acting Exarch of the Moscow Patriarch for Western Europe, in place of Metropolitan Nikolai, who was persuaded to request his own retirement, a request the old priest let it be known was made unwillingly and "with great sorrow", and, he suggested, because of government rather than Patriarchal pressure. At the very least, Nikolai's request for retirement had not been intended to include his work as Vicar of the Church of the Three Holy Hierarchs. As to the Exarchate, he admitted he would be relieved to lose responsibility, and endorsed Anthony as his successor in the role of Acting Exarch as "most worthy of the worthy",[32] at the same time making it clear he wished to continue as priest. In this he was supported by the overwhelming majority of

---

Orthodox Church, advocating co-operation with the Soviets and eventually declared schismatic by the Patriarchate. Archbishop Sergii rejoined the Patriarchal Church in December 1943.

his parishioners, including Father Sergii (Shevich), the compromise candidate to succeed him, who first offered to share the parish, celebrating on alternate Sundays, then backed down in the face of almost universal indignation and disapproval. Anthony himself, for the first time in his life, had to face the hostility of old friends and supporters when he visited his beloved *podvor'e* to receive confirmation as Acting Exarch from Metropolitan Nikolai and to concelebrate at the Church of the Three Holy Hierarchs with his old friend Father Aleksandr Turintsev, his and the Patriarchate's first choice as successor to Nikolai as vicar. But Father Aleksandr was initially rejected outright by the congregation, some of whom even threatened they would not take communion from his hands – the worst possible kind of schism.

Feeling that, as Acting Exarch, it would be his duty from now on to celebrate once a month in Paris, Anthony had decided to begin from the first Sunday in Lent, the Triumph of Orthodoxy. The inoffensive Father Aleksandr, as we have seen, had been rejected and Father Sergii refused; so the newly appointed Archbishop had to go it alone and was met at the door of the church by members of the congregation in which he had first served, come not to congratulate or welcome him but to express the general feeling that Anthony Bloom, whom they had all known and loved as an unassuming young monk of no ecclesiastical experience and the wrong sort of education, had, surprisingly, proved himself to be an ambitious ingrate, ready to sell his soul in return for rank and power.

Distressed, Anthony wrote to Nikodim that, at a subsequent parish meeting which he had called and chaired, he had been asked almost unanimously (a secret ballot had in fact shown thirty-four for, thirteen against and three abstentions) to request that the Patriarchate reinstall Nikolai as Vicar, which he was inclined to recommend they do, while making it clear the parish was not the Exarchate. The alternative was to impose the reappointment of Father Aleksandr Turintsev, but, in his opinion, neither Father Sergii nor Father Aleksandr had the firmness of purpose to hold the office, because of the great affection in which the Metropolitan, "a good and popular priest", was held by his parishioners. There was a real danger that the parish, the largest Patriarchal congregation in France, might disintegrate. For this reason, Anthony asked that the Patriarchate should reconsider.

He did, however, write a personal letter to Metropolitan Nikolai himself, reminding the old priest how genuinely overburdened he had felt and how he had in fact requested the Patriarchate more than once to allow him to retire. The last time they talked, Anthony continued, the Metropolitan had been actively looking forward to a monastic retirement in Villemoisson and to devoting his energies to writing. Anthony implored his old mentor not to split the parish by insisting he had been ousted against his will and his place usurped by Father Aleksandr, but rather to co-operate with him, Anthony, to defuse the situation. For his part, he had reported to the Patriarchate that the majority of Nikolai's parishioners wished him to stay on as Vicar of the

Church of the Three Holy Hierarchs; only Nikolai himself could persuade them to accept the Patriarchate's final decision as the will of God. He was not, Anthony concluded, asking this for himself, though he had been very unhappy to be counted as Nikolai's enemy and accused of duplicity; he was asking for Nikolai's co-operation to work together for peace among their flock. "I implore you," he added by hand, "pray for them and for me."[33]

With the support of Denis Chambault and Vasilii (Krivoshein), Archbishop Anthony succeeded in riding out this storm and was soon attracting back to the fold French-speaking priests and free-thinking Russians who had been thinking of defecting from the Patriarchal Church. Father Aleksandr did eventually become Vicar of the Three Holy Hierarchs and Metropolitan Nikolai retired gracefully to Villemoisson. The two old priests died within a few months of one another in the early 1980s.

The job of Acting Exarch, however, was to prove to be no bed of roses. The Patriarchal parishes and institutions were widely scattered and tended to be managed by ageing, often querulous personnel. All were materially insecure, many suspicious of Moscow and also of the rising generation of younger clergy and some of the old established francophone priests, whether or not of Russian origin, who threatened to outnumber the Russian native speakers and take the Russian Orthodox Church in Western Europe still further down the road to multiculturalism and multilingualism, on which Anthony had long been leading his own British diocese with such tact and loving care, gradually and by consent.

Moscow, however, appeared pleased with the efforts of their temporary appointee, granted him the symbolic distinction of the right to wear a cross on his high black hat and invited him to advise the Synod on their committee for relations with other Christian denominations. The closer relationship with the offices of the Patriarchate was not always comfortable. On 31 December 1963, Anthony was summoned in his capacity as Acting Exarch to precisely the kind of meeting he had always managed to avoid in England, with the First Secretary of the Russian Consulate in France. On the agenda was a discussion of how to nurture Russian patriotism amongst Orthodox youth and the still vexed question of the fragmentation of the Russian Church abroad, the Synodal Church and the nascent *Arkhiepiskopeia*. To judge by the Secretary's diary, "Antonio" (as he called him) defended his own moderate and gradualist position on both heads, without giving offence. Indeed, the entry states that, towards the end of the meeting, they touched on general questions of religious belief, such as the creation of the world, and talked for three hours in the presence of G.N. Vlasov, Secretary of the Consular section. One has the impression that the diplomat, although he took care to be suitably chaperoned, really rather enjoyed himself.[34] As usual, however, the meeting was, as the Russians say, "a stick with two ends". The rumour at once took wing that Anthony had been spotted "coming out of the Consular section of the Soviet Embassy in Paris where he draws his pay".[35]

In fact, as before, he drew no pay either from the Consulate or from the Patriarchate, and only claimed expenses from the latter. He was, nevertheless, obliged to present complex financial reports to Nikodim, now Metropolitan of Krutitsy and Kolomna and Head of the Department of Foreign Affairs, to justify expenditure on the property and on the dependants of the Russian Orthodox Church in France and elsewhere in Western Europe. There was never enough currency available to cover all needs and remittances were usually tardy. The Acting Exarch had to nag and beg – "like the importunate widow", as Anthony wrote wryly to Nikodim.

Fortunately for the Archbishop, his base in his home diocese and the community of churches in London remained secure. The Anglican Church had welcomed his appointment as Acting Exarch and also, explicitly, the fact that it would not mean his removing full-time to Paris, and he had received a letter of congratulation from his bluff, outspoken friend Michael Ramsey, now Archbishop of Canterbury, hoping "that your presence among us will continue to strengthen the bonds between the Holy Orthodox Church and our own".[36] His fellow Slavs also, in the person of M. Nikolich, appointed representative of the Serbian Orthodox Church in Great Britain, offered heartfelt congratulations and support for an Orthodox sister church "in these exceptionally difficult times" when, with the exception of Greece, the Orthodox throughout Europe were "oppressed by the terrible tyranny of Communism", and the Provost of the Greek Cathedral in London also expressed himself delighted at the appointment. Closer to his heart, Anthony's own beloved parish presented him with a thank-you letter for his continuing care for them with over 200 signatures.[37]

This happy state of affairs at home made it possible to prioritise the immensely complex task of cementing relationships with Russian Orthodox abroad, which entailed a rapprochement with the recently consecrated Bishop Aleksii (van der Mensbruegge[i]), originally a Roman Catholic from an old Flanders family, with whom Anthony concelebrated according to ancient Western (Roman) Orthodox rite, a goodwill gesture that appeared deeply suspect to not a few Russians of the Patriarchal Church in Paris. A pastoral visit to Italy, where the community was still reft by old scores dating back to the Second World War and the bloodthirsty fascist-communist feud still simmering throughout society, also sowed seeds of future strife. Anthony was at one stage even heard to complain that he simply could not cope with the Italian temperament, which turned the simplest negotiation to a scene from grand opera. There was also the longstanding conflict within the Russian Patriarchal Church in Holland to be attended to. This, eventually,

---

i. Aleksii was consecrated Bishop in Paris by the Exarch Metropolitan Nikolai, Anthony (still Bishop of Sergievo), Vasilii (already Archbishop of Brussels and the Hague) and Nikodim, Bishop of Podol'sk, in 1960.

involved installing Vasilii (Krivoshein), who was consecrated Bishop in London in 1959, as Bishop, then Archbishop, of Brussels and The Hague and allowing the Dutch Orthodox to be included in his diocese. Having by this time ironed out his difficulties with the French authorities, Vasilii, more scholar, perhaps, than pastor by inclination, in fact spent much of his time thereafter in Paris editing the Russian language journal *Le Messager de l'exarchat du Patriarcat russe en Europe occidentale*. He was assisted by a Father Kornilii (Fristedt), with whom he had, after the parting of the ways between the Russian Patriarchal Church and Father Nikolai Gibbes' jealously guarded home church in Oxford, been staying with Anthony in the none too spacious accommodation of 34 Upper Addison Gardens. Meanwhile, the Church in the Netherlands managed very well without the constant presence of a resident bishop and was at peace.

In the Parish House in London, Anthony was seldom alone, his door always open to the spiritually, mentally or physically needy of his parish. In this, he followed in the footsteps of Father Afasanii's predecessor at the Church of the Three Holy Hierarchs, Veniamin (Fedchenkov), who, living in a Spartan cell above his church on the premises of the old garage, had been known to sleep for nights at a time on the floor, having given up his bed to some homeless parishioner. Anthony enjoyed occasionally practising his medical skills. Thus he happily gave shelter and regular injections for diabetes to a youthful, stick-thin but beautiful and temporarily homeless young Georgian, a member of the choir at the Cathedral – until such time as the old guard of Orthodox matrons let it be known that this was cause for scandal amongst his flock, after which he meekly excluded single young woman as house-guests, but continued to see to it that anyone in need of a roof over their heads would be accommodated, if not by him, then by some more suitable member of the congregation. In spite of the ever-changing population of Anthony's house, he kept the place scrupulously clean unaided, but was still helped with some secretarial work and the housekeeping by the ever lamer but indomitably faithful (and, naturally, unsalaried) Barbara Morshead, who had shown such concern for his dying mother, knew his ways, and, when needed, drove a car.

More and more, the London parish, which celebrated the 250th anniversary of its foundation as chapel to the Russian Embassy in London on 26 October 1963, was finding its own new Anglo-Russian identity and, in June the following year, was sufficiently mature to celebrate the consecration of a priest from its own ranks: Father Sergei Hackel, already mentioned earlier in this chapter, the first of a series of appointments which were to give it an established, indigenous character, very much in contradistinction to the precarious outposts of the Russian Orthodox Church newly entrusted to Anthony's care in the rest of Western Europe. Circumstances, however, were never to allow him to sit back and enjoy the harmony so painstakingly established in his own backyard.

CHAPTER SEVEN
The International Arena, 1963-1974

The contemporary world sets us a challenge and the world is contemporary to every generation at every moment of their life.[1]

... an ideal is not a dream, an ideal is a challenge, something to be achieved.[2]

Michael Ramsey, Archbishop of Canterbury 1961-1974, first made friends with Anthony during his time as head of the Fellowship of St Alban and St Sergius. Worried that his highly valued brother in Christ might be perceived as condoning the evasions of representatives of the Moscow Patriarchal Church on the sore subject of the suppression of Christianity in Khrushchev's Russia, Ramsey did his utmost to persuade Anthony to make some kind of public gesture, albeit of a low-key and non-confrontational nature, to live up to his own conviction that there was no reason why the Russian Church abroad could not be the free voice of the Mother Church while yet preserving canonical loyalty. As a responsible Prince of the Church of England, Ramsey could understand and make allowances for the reticence of hierarchs from the Soviet Union, but world opinion could not ignore the glaring discrepancy between their bland cover-up statements and reports in the press, including the Soviet press. Ramsey's very love of the Holy Orthodox Church inspired him to urge his friend to make public intercession for Her at an ecumenical service[i] of prayer for persecuted Christians throughout the world to be held at the Church of St Dunstan's in the city of London after the now annual event of the Blessing of the Waters of the Thames.

Curiously, the World Council of Churches got wind of this initiative and, fearful it would be perceived as a provocation, sent a special envoy to warn Ramsey off,[3] so that he did not attend either service in person. Anthony, however, and Father Vladimir Rodzianko of the Serbian Church, went ahead,

---

i. In precisely this way, Metropolitan Evlogii had brought about his dismissal as Exarch for the Moscow Patriarchate in Western Europe in 1931.

and caused a sensation in the ecclesiastical press. Anthony confined himself to including a prayer for Eastern Orthodox Christians and their persecutors at the appropriate juncture of the Vespers service. Rodzianko's sermon, not agreed in advance with the Russian Archbishop, was impassioned and explicit. Naturally enough, this was perceived as a concerted action, a public statement by two Eastern Orthodox clerics resident in Great Britain against the oppression of their Church behind the Iron Curtain – "A call to the world to protest against currently increasing measures against Christians in Russia", as the *Catholic Herald* put it under an imposing photograph of "Patriarch Anthony" in full regalia.[4]

This and other only slightly less sensational headlines upset the picture that even the Soviet authorities were beginning to form of Anthony as a maverick but essentially non-political, even patriotic and certainly diplomatically talented representative of Russian Orthodoxy abroad. It exasperated Nikodim, who was now Head of the Department of Foreign Affairs and – it seems – genuinely fond of his London colleague. He rang up Anthony to express his displeasure, and the question of demanding the Archbishop's resignation as Acting Exarch was prioritised in the corridors of power around the gentle Patriarch.

On 21 January 1964 Anthony sat down to compose a full account of the context in which he had acted for Nikodim, in whose voice he had detected "some anxiety" about the content of the service at St Dunstan's. He also enclosed a letter from Rodzianko which, Anthony said, should be considered at the same time, as he had consciously avoided overlap. Rodzianko, who chose but was not obliged to explain himself to the Moscow Patriarchate, took sole responsibility for the sermon which, he wrote, had not been agreed in advance, was impromptu, "from the heart", and based on information obtained from Soviet publications. Anthony, in his turn, gave a detailed description of the impressive rally in Trafalgar Square, addressed by Eric Abbott, Dean of Westminster, in the presence of Cardinal Heenan for the Roman Catholic Church in England and Philip Potter, the Methodist, African Chairman of the World Student Christian Association. They had called for a two-minute silence in memory of all who had died for the faith and sang a hymn before moving on to the river bank where icons and ceremonial paraphernalia awaited the Orthodox celebrants of the Blessing of the Water, together with a Serbian choir of eight male voices who sang in Slavonic, Greek and English. The Serbian Archpriest Milosh Nikolich concelebrated and Greek Orthodox clergy also attended as observers, as did many representatives of other denominations. The service was broadcast by the BBC and widely reported (and Anthony here included press cuttings), after which those present moved off in solemn procession, led by the Second Secretary of the Anglican Department of International Relations and by Canon Satterthswaite, First Secretary and

Vicar of St Dunstan's, the church designated by Lambeth Palace especially for ecumenical prayer and put at the disposal of the Orthodox on this occasion by the Archbishop of Canterbury.

The procession was beautiful and impressive and the Serbian choir sang well. Rodzianko preached, after which Anthony included in the Liturgy a prayer of intercession inherited from a former representative of the Moscow Patriarch in Western Europe, Metropolitan Elevferii of Lithuania and Vilno (now Vil'nus):

> Again and again let us pray, remembering our Church, that it be confirmed and strengthened and that those who believe in Thee may receive steadfastness, courage and patience and be protected from all foes visible and invisible, all-powerful Lord, hear us and have mercy!
>
> Thou Who didst create this world to Thy Glory and eternal joy, grant that all those who oppose Thy word turn to Thee together with all the faithful to glorify Thee in truth and holiness; hear us and make haste to have mercy!
>
> As once the persecutor of Thy servants, Saul, wonderfully became Paul Thine Apostle, so now in the days of our sorrow look with mercy at those who hate and wrong us, on those who do and wish us evil, and may they not perish because of us sinners. Thou, Lord, even as Thou hast laid down Thy life for them, enlighten them with the Light of Thy Reason and speak peace to their hearts towards Thy Church and Thy people, we pray to Thee, Almighty Creator, Saviour of the World, hear us and make haste to have mercy!

"These words exactly express my position at these services." So Anthony affirmed his stance which, he continued, was shared by Orthodox Russians and others of the diaspora, who had been profoundly concerned to read the most distressing news not only of dissident churches in Spain and South America but also about new discriminatory legislation against the Orthodox Church openly propounded in the Soviet press. This was the reason for the decision to pray for believers in all countries and, in particular, for their Slavonic brethren. This was done in the context of a week of prayer for reunification, because it was felt it would be hypocritical not to pray for them and, indeed, for those who, like Saul, not knowing Christ, persecute Him.

He had not, Anthony added, known exactly what Rodzianko was going to say in advance, but what he did say had sounded entirely appropriate to the occasion. His subject matter was common knowledge and had received immense publicity. At the same time, he had been careful to distinguish between the legal, constitutional position of the Church in communist countries and failure to control the abuse of the Constitution by rogue elements at a local level. Silence and evasion was earning the Orthodox a bad reputation with all literate people, who had only to look at the journal

Nauka i religiia ("Science and Religion") to convince themselves that "there can be no achieving peace with the Soviet Union because of the declaration of war against Christians in Russia itself". At the same time, he reminded Nikodim, what was said had been said in an ecclesiastical, not political, context and he, Anthony, "deeply, with all my soul" loved "not only the Russian Church but Russia itself".[5]

The impact of these letters was complicated by Father Vasilii Borovoi's report on the role of the Archbishop of Canterbury and the intervention of Visser 't Hooft, General Secretary of the World Council of Churches, and his emissary, implying as it did the timely frustration of an Anglican plot to discomfort the Russian Patriarchal Church. Lambeth Palace, it was hinted, was offended that Patriarch Aleksii had twice declined their invitation to visit.[6]

While it was accepted that Anthony, by and large, had meant well and was doing his best in a very difficult situation, and that Rodzianko should, anyway, answer to his own Serbian Church, Ramsey's role seemed to require further explanation. Certainly, Anthony did mention pressure from the Anglican Archbishop when explaining his actions on his next visit to Russia in December 1965, but only as friendly criticism from a fellow churchman which it was impossible for him to ignore, not as a deliberate provocation. It is another matter entirely that Pyotr Vlasych Makartsev, the official from the Department of Religious Affairs to whom he elected to explain himself, chose to represent Canterbury's role as deliberate pressure and Anthony's rather as that of an innocent, confused and temporarily led astray by scheming foreigners. Possibly Makartsev was simply one of the unlikely people with whom the Archbishop succeeded in establishing a friendly human relationship (he is reported as having been scarlet in the face throughout their talk, overwhelmed by the unaccustomed frankness of his interlocutor) and that he was doing his bureaucratic best to put a good face on Anthony's actions for the authorities to whom it was his duty to render account.[7]

In spite of these rumbling repercussions, the letter to Nikodim immediately after the service at St Dunstan's was enough to put the life of the Russian Church in Western Europe temporarily back on course. Bishop Kiprian from Moscow paid an official visit to the Acting Exarch and preached a sermon which, Anthony informed Nikodim, was a "joy and an enrichment". In the same letter of March 1964, he thanks Nikodim, somewhat wryly, for the "brotherly scold" contained in his most recent letter, and promises "to think about it".[8]

Their "brotherly" relationship was, perhaps, first established by having taken part together the previous summer, from 19 June to 2 July 1963, in a delegation to Mount Athos, the Holy Mountain, the fabled monastic republic then celebrating the millennium of its foundation. The vicissitudes of the burning sun, the surprise of being introduced to the delights of iced Coca-

CHAPTER SEVEN

The Holy Mountain, Athos, 1963 ("the perils of riding small donkeys")

Cola in the capital Karyes, the fascination of the beautiful monasteries and legends of ascetic prowess attached to them, the perils of riding small donkeys along steep mountain paths (the burly Nikodim, Anthony recalled with delight, had persuaded his sagging mount to keep further from the edge of the precipice by dangling grass on a stick before the cliff-ward side of its nose) had combined to forge a bond capable of surviving even this present shock.

Nevertheless, pressures on the Patriarch "to resolve the question of Bloom" continued to mount. The Archbishop's defenders in Moscow were not helped by a hail of complaints from members of the Russian Patriarchal Church in France and Italy, disgruntled for one reason or the other and frequently for mutually exclusive reasons. The Archbishop of Sourozh was proving a disappointment as Acting Exarch. He did not come to Paris often enough and, when he was there, spent too much time meeting people and too little on the affairs of the Exarchate. He did not answer letters. He preferred his British diocese and indulging his genius for talking to non-Orthodox and even non-believers on radio and television to the administrative grind of exarchal duties. Archbishop Bloom, wrote his recent houseguest Kornilii Fristedt,[9] whom Anthony had helped get a visa to England to assist with the Oxford and London Orthodox parishes and then appointed to assist Vasilii Krivoshein, Archbishop of Brussels and

The Hague, should never have taken on the job: "the demon of ambition had got the better of common sense." He does not have the physical stamina, declared Kornilii, and suffers from heart and back trouble. When he can tear himself away from his own beloved diocese, he wastes time indulging the "lady psychopaths" who are always lying in wait for him in Paris or slopes off to take refuge with personal friends, an accusation borne out to some extent by those same friends, who mention the Archbishop's attempts to hide out from his female admirers and the waiting list of people who wished to complain to him of one another.[10] Kornilii's criticisms, however, were far from friendly. Things, he writes, were going badly wrong; he complains that Bishop Aleksii van der Mensbruegge's liturgical Old Catholic experiments, countenanced by the Acting Exarch, are a bad influence, and that Anthony's affection for Father Georgii Shumkin leads him to ignore the fact that the old priest is in his dotage and completely under the thumb of his wife, who is making a profit from the administration of the youth camps and Thursday Russian school attached to the church at Clichy, from which they should both be retired. Princess Antonina L'vovna Meshcherskaia, patron of the old people's home, Kornilii continues, is at loggerheads with her priests, Archimandrite Silouan and the more recently appointed Father Sergii. As a result, the old people are without a pastor and Anthony is doing nothing about it.

In fact, Father Silouan's own letters to Nikodim state that Anthony listened at length to his complaints of the Princess and gave him spiritual council and moral support, but could suggest no way to resolve the precarious material position of himself and his friends, who were resident at the home and had nowhere else to go. The Princess, on the other hand, was refusing the Patriarch's candidate for the position, Father Pavel Statov, who needed to prove employment for a *permis de séjour* in France, in favour of her own, Father Vladimir. As for Mme Shumkina, she repaid Anthony's loyalty to her husband by storming off to complain of him to the Soviet Consulate:[11] the Archbishop, she told them, lays too much stress on belief in God and not enough on the attitude of young people towards the Motherland. He is soft on the Constantinople faction (those who did not return to the Moscow Patriarchate after Evlogii), and may well eventually cross over to them himself. For instance, he insists that the Exarchate Thursday school and camps should be open to *all* Orthodox and objects to their making use of Soviet textbooks to teach literature and geography. Those faithful to Moscow, she continued, are worried by the circulation of Rodzianko's sermon and of pamphlets with clippings from the Soviet press about anti-Orthodox activity; she feared Anthony was countenancing a campaign to alienate his own flock from the Patriarchate. In conclusion, the redoubtable lady actually told the First Secretary that she would be happy were he to pass on her observations to the Soviet Council for Religious Affairs, to which he had the grace to reply that she should write to them herself. He did, however, send in a copy of his protocol to Nikodim (i.e. the Patriarchate's Department of Foreign Affairs) on 18 June 1964.

Still more poisonous was a letter to Nikodim from Italy, penned by one Dom Eusebio in the form of a "brief" commentary to a genuinely brief letter from the Acting Exarch ordering him back from his ex-monastery at Montal'to Dora, whither he had returned to "make trouble" pending the resolution of a disciplinary hearing, and to await the decision of the Exarchate in the diocese of Aleksii (van der Mensbruegge) in Villemoisson. It is common knowledge, Eusebio writes, that "Antonio" is a fascist, a monarchist and a great enemy of the Soviet Union, who is too busy taking tea with rich old Englishwomen to attend to his correspondence or the affairs of the Exarchate. He and Bishop Aleksii should be excluded from all part in these affairs. At Villemoisson, they regularly pray for the Tsar. "Antonio", moreover, is a crook who receives 660,000 francs a month and 2 million for travel expenses (always by air and first class), while many poor priests live in poverty. He himself, for instance, gets 15,000 a month, of which 10,000 goes to the monastery for his keep. It would no doubt be better for him if he were an ex-fascist and pervert like Gregorio Baccolini, the only Italian priest in whom "Antonio" appears to place any confidence and with whom Bishop Aleksii is trying to replace him in Montal'to Dora.[12]

To make doubly sure, the hyperactive Dom Eusebio also wrote to the Soviet ambassador in France, asking him to recommend the Patriarchate send no more money to the Paris Exarchate and relieve "Antonio" of his duties there.

To confuse the issue further, Anthony was involved in a genuine setback on the home front, where he had failed to raise the necessary funds or attract patronage to secure the future of Father Sophronii's monastery in case of the old Athonite's death; he had recently suffered a serious illness. The monastery itself had been dismissed as "immoral" by some Orthodox die-hards of the Paris Exarchate because it comprised both monks and nuns, and, in spite of a growing reputation as an intellectual and spiritual centre and place of pilgrimage, had never received adequate funding from them. Anthony had always, on principle, run his own diocese as financially independent of Moscow, though he had made the occasional exception for Sophronii and claimed subsidies towards the upkeep of the monastery as "expenses". However, this was not enough to provide the security required and Sophronii and his brethren now undertook to obtain their Bishop's reluctant agreement to change their statutes. Anthony had suggested three possibilities: (1) to wait a while in the hopes that God would provide; (2) to move to the jurisdiction of the Metropolitan of Thyateira Athenagoros II, Exarch of the Patriarch of Constantinople in Great Britain; or (3) to move to the "Pan-Orthodox Bishop's Council", which was still a dream project and had no canonical jurisdiction. Possibly, Sophronii also thought that to ask for more financial support from Moscow would entail shouldering unwanted political obligations, though he refrains from suggesting this in his letter to Patriarch Aleksii but rather, stressing the sadness of the decision for those who had spent decades in prayer for the Russian Orthodox Church, he encloses copies of his appeal to the Ecumenical Patriarch and to St Paul's Monastery on Athos, of this monastery's reply to him and of their submission to the Ecumenical Patriarch agreeing to take under their wing the Stavropigial monastery at Tolleshunt Knights. Pressures of daily life, Sophronii wrote, were such that the monastery could not wait, so he had entered into bilateral negotiations with the Greek Archbishop Athenagoros, who had himself suggested they become a daughter-house of St Paul's, a solution most pleasing to the brethren. On 27 May, he and Anthony went together to Athenagoros (he does not actually explain that he had confronted his own Russian Bishop with a *fait accompli)* and Anthony had "orally" agreed to their change of allegiance but afterwards, unexpectedly, made a last appeal to them to stay with the Russian Church, which was why Sophronii now felt it necessary to involve the Patriarch.[13]

On 14 July 1964 Anthony addressed a letter to three of the monastics who had written to him, stating how hard the decision had been for them: "Where do you stand?", he had asked them. Priest-monk Irinei replied for them and for himself with a life history: he had been born in Athens and christened in the Greek Orthodox Church, where he had remained until, in 1947, he had become a student at the Theological Institute of St Sergius in Paris on the advice of Sophronii, who had become his spiritual father in 1946. Here, he had come under pressure to choose a new spiritual father when Sophronii was excluded from the Institute for belonging to the Russian Patriarchal Church, but had chosen to remain under obedience to Sophronii and so come under the Moscow Patriarchate himself, a move that was never officially documented and which did not affect his Orthodox faith. Father Sophronii taught his spiritual children to love the Russian Church and partake of its sufferings, but Russians in England had shown no interest in the monastery, and the community in fact comprised eight or more different nationalities. They had no wish to break with a Church they loved and honoured. On the other hand, when Russians take vows on Mount Athos, they have to accept the jurisdiction of Constantinople and even take Greek citizenship, and no one accuses them of disloyalty. Archbishop Anthony had appealed to them on the grounds of the Russian Church's need for priests, abroad as much as in Russia, but, Irinei wrote, "I want to be a monk and my service with you (in spite of your fatherly love and care for me) taught me that it was virtually impossible to keep the monastic way life as a parish priest. I beg you not to face me with the difficult choice of obedience to you and fidelity to my spiritual father as happened in the Seminary and to let me go in peace. . . ."

Anthony yielded (how could he not? – they had chosen that "good part" which was denied to him), but it was a bitter blow to lose the prayers of his brethren at this difficult juncture, and, in the long term, to lose the monastery that might have provided him with a successor after his own heart.[i] Neither, of course, was the loss of Tolleshunt Knights "to the Greeks" calculated to enhance his prestige in Moscow. He had once said that his monastery down in Essex gave him so little trouble, and was so "remote and quiet", that he sometimes tended to forget about it.[14] Given the backbiting and quarrelsomeness of the Exarchate at large, Anthony must now have wished most devoutly he could have done more for his tranquil monastics, direct spiritual descendants of his beloved, oft-quoted St Silouan of the Holy Mountain. To care for the laity and priests prepared to minister to them was, however, the service to which he had been called, willingly accepted and faithfully performed. An exchange of letters between Archbishop and Abbot, initiated by the former at the beginning of Lent (Forgiveness Sunday) 1982, indicates the establishment of a new, more remote, but still cordial relationship. Anthony writes that although, by his fault, they have not met for some time, he prays to God, "seriously and sincerely", that the community's trials are now at an end and that "a new spring has begun". "With sincere love," the letter ends, "and in the hope of your prayers and love." Sophronii replies in a minor key that he, in his turn, hopes for Anthony's continued support in what he feels is a climate of general hostility. He is still vulnerable, because of his anxiety for his community. "But we, that is I and all who are mine, entrust ourselves lovingly to your prayers and blessing."[15] Sophronii, who retired as Abbot in 1974 to become confessor and spiritual guide, eventually died in 1993 two months before his ninety-seventh birthday. In spite of his misgivings, the Holy Monastery of St John the Forerunner continues to thrive as a centre of scholarship and beacon of Orthodoxy to this day.

* * *

One way and another, then, the Committee for Religious Affairs had plenty of ammunition to fuel a campaign within the Patriarchate to rid them of their ambivalent Acting Exarch. In September, Patriarch Aleksii came at last to visit the Anglican Church and his new diocese of Great Britain and Ireland, under considerable pressure to discipline the Archbishop. Anthony, who nurtured a genuine, filial devotion to the old man, maintained steadfastly that, in private, Aleksii in fact gave him his blessing to make what use he saw fit of the independence conferred on him by his well-established London diocese and French citizenship for the good of the Church in Russia. In

---

i. An Orthodox bishop must be a monk. At that time there was no bishop-in-waiting in the Diocese of Sourozh and, as things turned out, this was to prove a gap impossible to fill without a sharp break in continuity.

exchange, as it were, for this tacit approval, Anthony wrote a brief letter offering to resign as Exarch on the grounds that he could not satisfactorily perform all his duties because of increasingly frail health (his health was indeed deteriorating as a result of constant travel and stress), but requesting he be permitted to continue to serve on as Archbishop and Head of the Russian Church in Great Britain and Ireland. The Patriarch, it was agreed, would only accept his resignation if pressure from the lay authorities were to prove irresistible. Vasilii Krivoshein, now Archbishop of Brussels, Holland and The Hague, who appears to have believed that the Patriarchate was considering him as an alternative candidate for the Exarchate (a posting he would not have accepted because of Anthony's great popularity) gives an alternative, amusing but somewhat mischievous account of events.

According to Archbishop Vasilii, Anthony was indeed, in spite of his outstanding personal qualities as pastor and preacher, not really well-fitted for administrative work: the tendency not to answer letters, not to spend more time than was absolutely necessary in Paris and to delegate the day-to-day running of the Exarchate had entailed a flood of complaints. The Archbishop of Sourozh's position in England, however, remained unassailable, so it was assumed the Patriarch would demand only his resignation as Acting Exarch. This, nonetheless, had been enough to alarm Vitalii Borovoi, permanent representative of the Russian Church at the World Council of Churches in Geneva, who boarded the plane taking the Patriarchal delegation on from Geneva to Paris on their way to London and spent the whole journey dissuading Nikodim, who accompanied the Patriarch in his capacity as Head of the Department of Foreign Affairs, from demanding the resignation on the grounds that any such move would have catastrophic consequences for the reputation of the Russian Church in the international community. He succeeded, as he subsequently told Vasilii, in convincing the powerful cleric, and even extracted a promise.

In Paris, Borovoi's arguments were reinforced by representations from Vasilii himself, who also handed Nikodim a letter from Denis Chambault who, in spite or because of being saddled with much of the day-to-day work of the Exarchate, enjoyed the fact that Anthony was prepared to delegate responsibility without mistrust and now hastened to assure the Patriarch that, whatever he might have heard to the contrary, they had all "breathed a sigh of relief" when the Archbishop of Sourozh was appointed to replace the tetchy Metropolitan Nikolai. In London, Vitalii Borovoi and Vasilii found Aleksii (van der Mensbruegge) staying with Anthony and the three met up the next morning to hear how their host had fared at his evening audience with the Patriarch. According to Vasilii, Anthony had been tricked into offering the letter of resignation by Daniil Andreevich Ostapov (officially the Patriarch's personal secretary but in fact "a hereditary lackey of the Simansky family, a legendary personage nicknamed 'Daniil of all

With Patriarch Aleksii I, 1960 ("a genuine filial devotion")

the Russias' or even 'by Him all things were made that were made'"). This "legendary personage" met Anthony with sympathetic enquiries after his health and how he was managing as Exarch, which Anthony answered at face value, and, before he rightly knew what was happening, had extracted the promise of a letter tendering his resignation "for reasons of health" on the strength of his honest response.

Anthony, Vasilii records somewhat waspishly, appeared to feel compelled to submit the required document to Patriarch Aleksii that very morning, after which he was presented with the highest Patriarchal award, the Order of St Vladimir First Class, supposedly for organising the visit to London but in fact to sweeten the pill of resignation. Borovoi, he says, had commented wryly that Ostapov was doing the work of the KGB and of Kuroedov, Head of the Council of Religious Affairs, combined.

Indignation waxed high among the Orthodox clergy abroad. Vasilii himself, without mentioning that the letter of resignation was subsequently shelved for the next ten years or recording any tacit agreement between Anthony and Aleksii, of which he may indeed have been unaware, rounded off his reminiscences of the London visit with a vivid account of the clash between Nikodim and Archbishop Ramsey, who enraged the Russian dignitary by informing him to his face that, although, as a statesman, he could sympathise with diplomatic caution, a bishop should – by virtue of his calling – avoid outright lies. The memoir, moving from England to Vasilii's own later visit to the Soviet Union, goes on to imply that the acceptance of Anthony's resignation and appointment of a successor was only finally removed from the Patriarchate's agenda after Vasilii himself had made quite clear his own disinclination to step into the shoes of "the well-beloved Archbishop Anthony".[16]

Be that as it may, the existence of the letter of resignation soon became public knowledge. In Paris, where rumour was, of course, already rife, Anthony broke the news of it in person at the next meeting of the Exarchate "to a resounding silence". According to Father Kornilii, only Vasilii Krivoshein protested *pro forma* that he should not go. However, within a matter of days the Archbishop's shocked colleagues had rallied and dispatched a letter, bearing all their signatures, begging him not to insist on resigning as there was no one to replace him. Denis Chambault was particularly supportive, so much so that Kornilii, who although half-Swedish-Finn described himself as a "Scythian" and a "Slavophile", renewed his campaign to discredit Anthony with the Patriarchate, this time for favouring Father Denis, a man – according to him – bent on introducing a note of "French chauvinism" into the Russian Church.[17]

On 2 March 1965, Olivier Clément, a convert to Orthodoxy under the influence of Anthony's old mentor Vladimir Lossky and a distinguished theologian and thinker, voiced the support of the French Orthodox so eloquently it seems only right to quote his letter in the original, all the more so as Lossky's son Nikolai held that Clément's style was so quintessentially French as to defy translation![18]

> Durant mon récent séjour à Marseilles, pour le congrès de jeunes Orthodoxes du midi de la France, j'ai pu mesurer le rayonnement bienfaisant de votre passage, de vos conférences. Des Grecs, des Russes, des Français m'ont parlé de vous avec enthousiasme vrai – d'hommes qui ont été touchés au coeur. Vous avez bien servi l'Orthodoxie et l'Eglise russe, je veux en être témoin, je suis prêt à l'écrire à Mgs Nicodème pour exorciser tant de lettres ignobles ou mesquines envoyées de Paris – si cela vous semble utile et mon nom n'est pas une hypothèque!
>
> Nous sommes plusieurs, je tiens à vous l'assurer, d'avoir une grande vénération pous vous, à être fiers de vous avoir pour évêque. J'ai dis cela au père Denis. Je vous supplie de [rester?] à votre poste de combat, aussi longtemps que ce sera possible, malgré les hommes infectés [?] (pour parler comme Dostoevsky) qui s'acharnent sur vous – simplement parce que vous êtes un homme vrai, un veritable évêque, notre Pasteur que nous aimons.[i19]

---

i. "During my recent stay in Marseilles for the congress of young Orthodox in the South of France, I could evaluate the salutary light of your passing through, of your lectures. Greeks, Russians, French spoke of you with the unfeigned enthusiasm of men who have been touched to the heart. You have done good service to Orthodoxy and the Russian Church, I want to bear witness to it; I am ready to write to Monseigneur Nikodim in order to exorcise all these knavish or

This letter and the antagonism between Kornilii and Chambault are indicative of a certain distrust between the new francophone ecclesiastics and their ageing White Russian colleagues. This was, if anything, exacerbated by the 1968 appointment of Pierre L'Huilier, a French convert, as Bishop of Korsun and thus as first among the Russian Orthodox clergy in France. The French were culturally less Russophile yet often more sympathetic to the Soviet Union which, they understandably felt, was no longer the dictatorship it had been under Stalin and, indeed, had achieved much since the end of a war from which it had emerged victorious but financially devastated. The intercession for "our much-suffering land of Russia" used in the litanies was no longer, perhaps, thought of solely in terms of political oppression but also in terms of simple hardship. Anthony himself, as he came to know Soviet officials and to meet more ordinary and not necessarily Orthodox people in Russia, had begun to perceive them as individuals and therefore as children of God: "I am really rather fond of Pyotr Vlasych," he is reported as saying after the gruelling interview with P.V. Makartsev about the Blessing of the Waters incident; "he is a nice man. We have our differences but at least we have talked openly."[20]

The early 1960s was a time when – the Cuban missile crisis notwithstanding – people in Western Europe and in Russia itself had begun to talk and write of possible ideological "convergence". Archbishop Anthony, who had long since trained himself to love his enemies and whose special gift was to talk convincingly of religion to the unbeliever, was at once open to convergence – at a depth few could attain without an attack of psychological "bends" – and doctrinally uncompromising. In his political opinions he remained distinctly right-wing, but never sought to impose these on his flock. There was, however, one aspect of the Soviet agenda for the Orthodox Church in the international field that he was temperamentally quite incapable of supporting. This was "the struggle for peace" and the encouragement of movements for unilateral disarmament. Though a hereditary diplomat, he was by nature a combatant and saw nothing wrong in opposing force with force, though he admitted this might be a fault in his nature. Yet Christ, after all, did not tell the soldier to lay down his arms, only not to use them unjustly and to be prepared to suffer violent death: "Those who live by the sword die by the sword"

---

petty letters from Paris – if that strikes you as serving a good purpose and my name is not an obstacle.

There are several of us, I wish to assure you, who have a great reverence for you and are proud to have you as our Bishop. I said that to Father Denis [Chambault]. I beg you to [remain] [original illegible] at your post as long as possible in spite of the possessed people (to speak like Dostoevsky) who are trying to bring you down just because you are an honest man, a true bishop, our pastor whom we love." [Translation my own.]

– a fate Anthony could contemplate without dismay as, indeed, he could contemplate the end of the world, whether or not brought about by nuclear fission. Eternity would be there at the end of time as at the beginning. Disarmament, on the other hand, might be wise but, to be meaningful, it had to be bilateral or it was merely another word for surrender. Evil was not in the atomic bomb any more than it had been in the invention of dynamite or, indeed, in any other scientific discovery such as contraception or artificial insemination; evil was in human sinfulness which misused such inventions for power, greed and lust, thereby desecrating the material world, which is of God and has been entrusted to the stewardship of man.[i]

Yet, in spite of the fact that Anthony had never been and was clearly never going to be an agent pliant to the hand of the Soviet government or those in the Russian Orthodox Church whose business it was to maximise co-operation with the State, the overwhelming support of Orthodox abroad for the Archbishop as Exarch of the Russian Church, albeit for want of anyone better and in spite of the flow of complaints, was not altogether unwelcome either to the Patriarchate or to a Soviet establishment upset by instability on the Chinese border, unenthusiastic about the war in Vietnam and genuinely anxious to find points of contact with the non-communist world that might eventually lead to some let-up in the arms race. This man, with his faithful love of Russia and his own Mother Church and extraordinary "missionary" outreach, was one such point. Already, the English were calling him "the face of Russian Orthodoxy".[21]

So, perhaps unsurprisingly, a later visit to Russia from 7 to 23 December 1965 went even better than the first. Anthony was invited to meet students at the Theological Academies of Leningrad and Moscow, to talk to them and discuss their work. On a visit to Elokhov Cathedral, he stood for a long time at the tomb of Patriarch Sergii, the man who had guided his Church through the most virulent years of persecution and the desperate days of the Second World War. Afterwards, he made the acquaintance of Archbishop Pimen and established contact with this simple man, who had experienced arrest and internal exile at first hand, by a mutual agreement to pray for one another's parents. "It's extraordinary," he said, "how that brings people together."[22] He also confirmed a promising friendship with Father Vsevolod

---

i. Out of context here but pertinent in essence was Anthony's reply to G. Percy Junior of the BBC of 18 December 1985, referring back to an earlier letter to Elizabeth Satess, who had asked him for a statement on the Russian Church's view on nuclear weapons. Anthony explained to Percy in detail his own views on the subject, which, he believed, corresponded to those of the great majority of his congregation, though he neither would nor could claim them as the views of his Church, since "as a body of believers we have no binding policy concerning political problems: every member of the Orthodox Church is free to hold any view compatible with the Christian faith".

Spieler, at whose church he attended a Liturgy on his name day, and with Nikodim, with whom he concelebrated at the consecration of Bishop Ioann (Snychev) and at the tonsuring of a monk, occasions that he found genuinely moving. He felt he had taken part in the everyday life of the Church more than on his first visit, when he had been conveyed from place to place "like an egg in a shell". At the same time, he made strenuous efforts to enable those who loved him, the Patriarch in particular, to leave the letter of resignation in abeyance. For instance, an elderly woman approached him with a packet of written material at the church in Mariny Roshchi and, because his hands were occupied, it was taken by the priest acting as his official escort who, he knew, would have to report it to the Department of Foreign Affairs. Back at the hotel, Anthony, suspecting the envelope contained information on the persecutions which might well get the writer into serious trouble, relieved the priest of his burden, tore it across and across, strode into the en suite and crammed it down the plug, saying sweetly: "There you are, you can bear witness I didn't even read it."[23] Another priest reported with great sympathy how when, in Leningrad, the ebullient Archbishop Sergii (Larin), in the middle of a banquet in Anthony's honour, launched into a diatribe against Russian drunkenness, saying the only cure would be to introduce prohibition and to shoot bootleggers and their customers out of hand, the Archbishop from England had lowered his eyes in shame for his colleague and blushed, adding from himself "and indeed it was unpleasant to hear an Orthodox hierarch say such things". Afterwards, he goes on, Anthony expressed the devout hope that neither Sergii nor anyone like him would be included in the Patriarchal delegation invited to attend the consecration of the new cathedral at Coventry, a monument to Christian reconciliation.[24]

The Archbishop of Sourozh's relations with the unfortunates who had to report on him were astonishing. Far from evading or despising them, he maintained a courteous, indeed compassionate respect for their invidious position, while leaving them in no doubt that he perfectly understood their obligations. The resulting reports are genuine curiosities, redolent of an almost enamoured goodwill. They relayed his sermons and public utterances with relish, but more often than not left him alone with friends and relatives, noting merely "and what they said then I don't know".[i] The priest who reported to Nikodim on the autumn 1971 visit, Father Mikhail Turchin, in his report of 5 October 1971, even ventures an opinion as to why

---

i. When I was living in Russia in the late 1960s, Vladyka Anthony came (by car in *mufti*, presumably a borrowed suit, smart but old-fashioned) to visit myself and my husband and our small daughter in the village of Kupreianikha, not far from Moscow in the direction of Domodedovo Airport on the River Pakhra. He looked like an aristocrat at home on his estate and sparkled with pleasure at the illicit adventure. I do not know how he managed this, but the visit went unrecorded in any report that I have seen.

the sermons work so well: "Metropolitan Anthony is a psychologist and for this reason it is easy for him to break through the invisible barrier which exists for believers between the history of Holy Writ, the lives of the saints and their own lives. M.A. [Metropolitan Anthony] easily and harmoniously 'ties in' these two lines in his sermons: bringing the exalted down to the simple for the sake of understanding and raising the simple into the sphere of the exalted, so showing us a practicable path to salvation."

Finally, on this visit, Anthony, as was his wont, took the bull by the horns and himself requested the interview with P.S. Makartsev of the Council for Religious Affairs, which has already been mentioned. He made it quite clear that, though the Soviet government had no hold over him as a French citizen, he truly loved his country and, were it not for his responsibilities to his British diocese, would be only too glad to spend the rest of his days and leave his bones there. They could, therefore, rely on his genuine desire to serve the Patriarchal Church as a worthy representative abroad – to the best of his ability but by his own lights.

It is scarcely surprising then, that, after celebrating Christmas in London, Archbishop Anthony was recalled to the Soviet Union where, on 27 January 1966, he was confirmed as Exarch of the Russian Orthodox Church in Western Europe and raised to the dignity of Metropolitan Bishop.[25]

That the State authorities were still anxious as to how he would behave was confirmed by three meetings with Makartsev's superior, Kuroedov, Head of the Soviet Council for Religious Affairs, which did not so much as dent the independence of Anthony's position. Why, Kuroedov asked him, did he have such a "mania" for publicising the closure of churches? Why, the Exarch retorted serenely, did he keep closing them? When asked what he thought of the *Journal of the Moscow Patriarchate*, he replied that it was really too boring to read – all ecclesiastical protocol. It would gain immensely in human interest and be a better advertisement for the liberalisation supposed to be taking place in the Soviet Union were they to publish material on the two "dissident" priests, Gleb Yakunin and Nikolai Eschliman, or even a lively account without pompous jargon of the elderly Pimen's recent tour of his diocese on skis over unpassable roads![26] On this visit, Anthony stayed until 9 February and was invited to lecture at the Moscow Theological Academy on "Inner experience of the knowledge of God" to an audience enchanted by the outgoing contemporaneity of his thought and translucent spirituality, as also by the obvious joy he felt to be among young Orthodox educated in the Soviet period, of whom he and his fellow émigrés had virtually no experience.[27]

After the strain and stress of the preceding year, 1966 was all achievement. It saw the publication – to instant international acclaim – of Metropolitan Anthony's first book, *Living Prayer*, like its successors a collection of recorded and transcribed talks.[28] The Metropolitan became a member of the Central Committee of the World Council of Churches and of the WCC

*Unofficial talks on the Anglican priesthood, London, 10-11 November, 1966.
From left to right: Archbishop Vasilii Krivoshein,
Archbishop Michael Ramsey, Metropolitan Anthony, Bishop
Vladimir Sabodan, Archpriest Vitalii Borovoi*

Christian Medical Commission, as well as of the Patriarchate's Ecumenical Commission. In July, he attended a conference on "Church and Society" and, in August, a summer youth camp in Normandy, always more pleasure than duty. It was in this year that the Patriarchate of Constantinople temporarily, as it turned out, disbanded its rival "Russian" Exarchate in Paris, which once again raised hopes of a lasting rapprochement with Evlogii's bishops and their Orthodox flock, which included many fine priests and scholars, much-needed potential allies. Meetings, however, were already under way to form an independent *Arkhiepiskopeia* and hopes for any kind of reunion between the advocates of this development and the Moscow Patriarchal Church had to be put on hold.[29]

By 26 November Anthony, exhausted but in high spirits, was back in Russia, where he lectured at the Leningrad and Moscow Theological Academies and attended English examinations at the latter. The Patriarchate actually arranged for medical treatment and a brief rest in the south, where he visited Odessa, Sympheropol, Yalta and his own "virtual" diocese of Sourozh, now Sudak in Crimea. It seemed that he was now indeed a trusted member of his own Church and he even succeeded, through Father Vsevolod Spieler, in arranging a meeting formerly denied him by Kuroedov, with the two "dissident" priests, at that time already banned from their ministry, Gleb Yakunin and Nikolai Eschliman.[i] Although sympathetic to many of their concerns, he had seen all too much of the harm that had come to the Church in the emigration through the vehemence of the centrifugal Russian temperament and regretted the confrontational tone that had arisen between them and the ecclesiastical authorities. Before leaving, he concelebrated the Liturgy with Patriarch Aleksii and Metropolitan Pimen in the Bogoiavlensky Patriarchal Cathedral, and was fêted by Nikodim at a farewell dinner in the Department of Foreign Affairs.[30]

* * *

The ensuing years of service to diocese and Exarchate were extremely busy at home and abroad. The Metropolitan's public life was divided as ever between his own diocese and calls to preach at other churches, schools, universities, medical and even military academies; to appear on television and to speak on radio; to work towards the reconciliation of all Orthodox churches; to bring the Orthodox faith to Westerners who knew neither Moscow nor Constantinople, neither Synodal Church nor the Patriarchate, nor the new but firmly independent *Arkhiepiskopeia*; and to participate in conferences at European and North American venues in English, German, French and Russian. It will, however, put all this in proportion if we take advantage of a last glimpse, afforded us by a visiting hierarch of the Moscow Patriarchate from Belarus, of Anthony at home in 34 Upper Addison Gardens, where he had lived so long with mother and grandmother.

---

i. Fathers Gleb Yakunin (1934-2014) and Nikolai Eschliman (1929-1985) caused a furore in the press in 1965 by addressing an open letter to Patriarch Aleksii I, challenging the Patriarchate to show more leadership in shaking off State control of the Church. Both were forbidden to continue serving in their parishes the following year, but Yakunin, the more politically active of the two, was allowed to serve again as a priest after a term of exile and imprisonment for anti-Soviet activities (1980-1987) until 1992, when he again clashed with the Church leadership for publishing compromising material about the Patriarchs of Kiev and Moscow (Aleksii II) discovered in KGB archives in the course of his service on a commission to investigate the failed 1991 coup. For this he was excommunicated in 1993. In 1996 he was elected delegate to the Duma, representing the Democratic Russia Party. Eschliman, an artist and a fine singer, suffered no state repressions but was never reinstated as a priest for private reasons (he divorced and re-married) and died before the onset of *glasnost'* and the fall of the Soviet Union. The letter of 1965 was widely circulated in *samizdat*. See also Glossary of Proper Names.

Chapter Seven

Addressing the Moscow Theological Academy, December 1966

Archbishop Anthony Mel'nikov spent a month and a half "in our Church house" in London in the summer of 1968 and, within two weeks of his return, jotted down his impressions of the simplicity and accessibility which were the keynote of this establishment.[31] A house, he begins, tells us much about the character of its master, and here the master was "a luminary, a man of great spiritual energy [*podvizhnik*], and an ascetic".

He goes on to describe it room by room: you enter through a narrow hall with books, candles and a money-box. All the rest of the ground floor, the best space in the house, is taken up by the Church of St Sergius.

On the landing of the first floor there is a portrait of Alexander II, the Tsar-liberator, a leather sofa and a huge mahogany wardrobe. Opening off the landing are a modest sitting room and Anthony's study with lots of books and icons, a large table piled high with books, a smaller writing table, and a sagging armchair. There are photographs of Patriarchs Sergii and Aleksii, and of Father Afanasii (Nechaev). A table lamp was "a present from Shaliapin's grand-daughter". On the same floor is a kitchen-cum-dining room. The Metropolitan, Mel'nikov comments, eats simply and very sparingly.

The top floor has three rooms, the largest with two beds for guests. The empty fireplace, he suspects, is a front door for ghosts, and owls hoot at night from the garden behind the house. In the smaller room, which was allotted to him, he could hear canaries greeting the morning from the house next door and see the garden from the window. The third room was occupied by "a very kind old priest" who lived in a state of perpetual "philosophical chaos".[i] The staircase up to these rooms was damp with flaking plaster and had ancient velvet curtains at the window. In the basement, used for meetings and socials, things were cosier. There were portraits on the walls, photographs, one or two reproductions of famous pictures.

The atmosphere throughout was welcoming, peaceful.

The Metropolitan works day and night and has nothing for himself, no personal pleasure, no divertissements. Neither radio nor television.

People flock to him from all sides for spiritual consultation, and each leaves comforted and renewed. . . . He greets them all gladly, goes to meet each and every one with an open face and sparkling dark eyes. He has found Christ and Christ's love overflows generously. Best of all is just to look at his beautiful face and you see that it is the face of his spirit in the widest and deepest sense.

He has no *keleinik*.[ii] The only person he has to help him is his secretary-cook-chauffeur who is about 60 and walks with a stick, an Orthodox English-woman called Barbara. . . .

The visiting dignitary goes on to recount a train journey to Taunton which, he claims, resembled nothing so much as the epic voyage of *Three Men in a Boat*. Wearing their cassocks,[iii] the visitor tripping over his unaccustomed skirts, laden "like camels" with hat-boxes and odd-shaped parcels containing ceremonial regalia and staves, the two clerics bundled themselves, their baggage and "the invalid Barbara" into an old-fashioned second-class carriage on a train which, to Anthony's delight, actually departed some minutes before schedule. Enquiries of their fellow passengers, however, established it was not the right train and they had to change at Reading, sitting for what seemed an age in the station buffet of the city where, the well-read visitor was awed to discover, Oscar Wilde had once languished in gaol. Punctuality was important as the founding father of the Orthodox monastery of St Elias, the Welsh monk Varnava (Barnabas), was waiting for them to consecrate a new Orthodox church in one of his recently established south-western Orthodox parishes. His welcome, when they arrived, was enthusiastic but, for a hierarch of the Moscow Patriarchate who was distinctly peckish after the long journey, ascetic to the point of dismay. Indeed, for one quite unaccustomed to carrying his

---

i.   Probably Father Aleksandr Belikoff; see Gillian Crow, *op. cit.*, p.119.
ii. Monk who keeps the cell of a bishop or of an elder in a monastery – a kind of ecclesiastical batman.
iii. Forbidden at the time on public transport in the USSR.

own gear, travelling second-class or sitting, chummily befriended by an appealingly hungry dog, at a station buffet with a fellow bishop and an arthritic Englishwoman, the whole outing was clearly a cathartically comic experience. It was counterbalanced by the traditional beauty of Oxford and Cambridge colleges, the intellectual sparkle of Orthodox Oxford, the solemnities of the Lambeth Conference and, on 29 July, by the Queen's garden party for the delegates, at which Bishop Anthony (Mel'nikov) was presented to Her Majesty, who enquired, graciously if predictably, how he was enjoying England. On 15 August he concelebrated at the Greek Cathedral with Athenagoros and was entertained to a splendid dinner in a "fine, rich house".

By that time, however, the visitor had grown accustomed to the higgledy-piggledy poverty of the Russian diocese, whose members, he wrote, "were very well-disposed to the Moscow Patriarchate. Very important is that the whole large parish lives as it were as one family, taking to heart their common joys and sorrows."

This was Anthony's great achievement and it is against this familial background, this unpretentious, dedicated everyday life, that we must evaluate his worldwide success as missionary and preacher and his more debatable efforts as Exarch, organiser and disciplinarian, in which last capacity, as Nikolai Lossky said, though he never put a foot wrong orally, he had no special talent for expressing himself on paper and could sound unexpectedly categorical, if not downright harsh.[32]

An unfortunate example of this was the appeal he had addressed to the *Arkhiepiskopeia* in 1966, which had sounded to them like a threat of excommunication calculated to drive them into schism and did not, as it well might have done, bear fruit during his exarchate, or indeed thereafter. Anthony, after all, was from the same stable: the Russian emigration, the flowering of religious thought that Nicholas Zernov called "The Russian Religious Renaissance",[33] and Evlogii's Russian Church. His attitude to the Greeks was conciliatory and based on mutual respect and the mutual hope of ever greater pan-Orthodox convergence – this in spite of the fact that so many Russians after Evlogii, including Sophronii and the remarkable Orthodox convent consisting of three nuns under the Swiss Mother Maria,[i] eventually took refuge from the political strains and financial discomforts of allegiance to Moscow with the enviably emancipated and well-provided-for Patriarch of Constantinople. In the case of the nuns, Anthony's efforts to include them in the care of his extended family of the diocese by organising retreats for unhappy individuals "before we had even taught ourselves to say the services properly and to keep the hours"[34] were to prove an additional reason for the break-away, although they continued to look on him with the greatest affection and to listen – tearfully – to his voice on radio

---

i. See Chapter Five, p.50 and footnote i.

broadcasting the midnight Easter service from the Cathedral in London. Metropolitan Anthony was, in himself, potentially a perfectly acceptable rallying point for the sadly fragmented Russian Orthodox Church abroad, but, although he was on cordial terms with almost everyone he actually met, his success in uniting his fiercely independent Orthodox contemporaries under the Moscow Patriarch was confined to individuals, and in rare cases to priests who came over to him with their whole parishes. Here, though, it was a case of win some, lose some. Father Yves Dubois, for instance, who had relieved the London diocese of the care of Orthodox in Guildford, in 1975 betook himself and his flock under the jurisdiction of the Greeks "after a disagreement with the Metropolitan"[35] and the brilliant, supportive Olivier Clément joined the *Arkhiepiskopeia* in the late 1960s because he felt Anthony and the Patriarchal Church were not as vocal as they should be in denouncing the suppression of religion and free thought in Soviet Russia.[36] On the other hand, in 1972, in Holland, an entire diocese of the Synodal Church, together with its bishop, Iakov, rejoined the Patriarchal Church. Indeed, Metropolitan Anthony's defence of that church at the Moscow Council of 1971 at which, after Aleksii's death in April 1970, Pimen was elected Patriarch, undoubtedly laid the foundations for its potential reconciliation with the Patriarchate.

The fact that the Russian Orthodox seminary of St Sergius in Paris remained firmly in the domain of the *Arkhiepiskopeia* naturally limited the Metropolitan's choice of priests for his ever-growing diocese, but here he made a virtue of necessity. Small Orthodox communities were springing up all over the British Isles and Metropolitan Anthony appointed non-stipendiary priests, proposed by the congregations to which they were to minister. Sergei Hackel, with a job as a teacher at Sussex University and active in the BBC Russian Service, was soon looking after a community of his own which served Brighton and Eastbourne. From 1969, Michael Fortounatto, the Cathedral choir-master who had taught at the University of East Anglia, was ordained priest to help Anthony in London and, shortly thereafter, gave up the university to devote himself full-time to his new duties, which came to include running the summer camps for smaller children. In 1971, Professor Michael Beaumont established a parish in Dublin, where he died, much mourned, after only two years. In 1973, at the request of the Oxford parish, Basil Osborne was ordained priest having served for four years as deacon; also in 1973, Father Benedict Ramsden, founder of the unique community of St Anthony and St Elias which cares for the unwell in mind, was ordained and graduated from acting as deacon at the monthly English-language liturgies at the Cathedral to a parish of his own in Devon, where he was later joined by Father John Marks. Father Benedict, a protégé of the first ex-Anglican priest Father Kirill (Taylor), was rare among converts in that the Metropolitan accepted him into the

Orthodox faith at once at first request and astonished Father Kirill by acceding, again at once, to his ensuant desire to be ordained: "[O]f course. That's why I told you to receive him!"[37] Nicholas Behr, a son of Anthony's old friend Tatisha, was ordained and assumed responsibility for a parish in Bristol. Father Alexander Fostiropoulos, a Greek married to an Irishwoman, Patsy – who, like Michael Fortounatto's wife Marianna, was an accomplished icon painter and also a genius with children at the summer camps – served in London as deacon and remained attached to the Cathedral as priest. He was later appointed Orthodox Chaplain to the University of London. In 1979, Father Alexander was joined at the Cathedral and the camps for older children by the steadfast and good-humoured Father John (Lee), an American of Ukrainian Eastern Rite Catholic origin, the first qualified male midwife to work in England, who was married to an Indian woman, also a professional nurse. In Wales, whither Archimandrite Barnabas eventually retired from Exeter to his monastery hermitage of St Elias, Father Deiniol energetically promoted the Celtic tradition and the undivided Church. The ever-growing number of Orthodox enclaves with no permanent priest included the lovely retreat centre at Jennywell in the Lake District and a community at St Andrews in Scotland. British converts, in a word, were appearing at all points of the compass. The policy of encouraging local parishes to elect a priest they knew and trusted from among their own number rather than imposing a seminary-trained stranger ensured a continuing familial yet cosmopolitan atmosphere in the diocese as a whole, which worked well so long as Anthony had the stamina to serve as full-time representative hierarch at the highest level.

For the moment, whatever his difficulties in his capacity as Exarch, the Metropolitan was riding high indeed. At the Congress of Youth at Taizé in 1967 he spoke on what it means "To pray today" and was clearly the preferred preacher for the young, who gave him an overwhelming ovation. They believed him because it was impossible to doubt his faith and he gave the unambiguous impression that "this inner fire which devours him" was something well worth sharing.[38] Appearing on television on a serial Monday evening programme on the same subject of "faith", he earned a glowing tribute from the Roman Catholic *Tablet*. Earlier in the series, their reviewer remarked, belief in God had been presented as an extremely thorny problem, whereas, with Anthony's appearance on the small screen, it became something solid and completely natural: "I kept asking myself the reason for such a change. And I told myself it was because Archbishop Anthony, from beginning to end of the broadcast, was in the presence of God."[39] On 25 May 1967, *The Radio Times* praised his "guest of the week" appearance on *Woman's Hour* for "his power, his compassion and above all his humanity".[40]

Although the deliberations of the ecumenical movement seemed to him to hold little promise, Anthony embraced every opportunity to foster real, open-hearted relationships with other churches. In 1968, he spoke at the Fourth Assembly of the World Council of Churches at Uppsala on "Divine Worship and a Christian Lifestyle", addressing problems raised by "radical" theology's depersonalisation of God and the resultant crisis in public worship and personal prayer – especially at a time when many words no longer mean what they meant at the time traditional prayers were formulated. As to the Christian life: detachment from the things of this world, which gives freedom and impartiality, is not to be confused with estrangement or coldness. "At the centre of the conscious life of a contemporary Christian stand the words 'solidarity' and 'responsibility'!"[41] That same year, the Fellowship of St Symeon invited him to preach at the Consecration of an Orthodox Chapel at the Roman Catholic boarding school of Ampleforth. The occasion sparked a moving sermon, acceptable across the denominations, on the Church as any actual enclosed consecrated material space, where a God, Who had nowhere to lay His head in an estranged world, could dwell and be at home, welcome amongst men; a space, however small, deep and high enough to accommodate all creation. To make his own Orthodox church accessible, as building, ceremony and gateway to the Eternal, to bustling city-dwellers of the modern world, he sought to simplify and streamline the lengthy episcopal services. He entered into discussions with Bishop Jonathan of the Orthodox Church in America on hypothetical liturgical reform and collaborated with him to obtain a relaxation of the fasting rules from the Patriarchate so that the working laity might take part on occasion in a vesperal "liturgy of the presanctified" without having to go without nourishment from midnight the preceding day. The Synod gave permission to fast on such occasions for no less than six hours, but could not resist adding that a fast from the previous midnight was still "most praiseworthy". Long ago the Byzantine Greeks had complained that their Russian converts must have "iron legs" to remain standing throughout services of monastic duration, and Archbishop Athenagoras, faced with the same problems of multi-culturalism among the Greek diaspora as had arisen among the Russians, proved a sympathetic ally in the cause of a flexibility which, while not touching on basic questions of dogma established by the Ecumenical Councils, would open up new possibilities in the liturgical and administrative practice of the Orthodox Church. He informed the Russian Archbishop about a questionnaire he was circulating to establish a broad consensus of opinion on such initiatives[42] and Anthony, too, consulted his priests and congregation about their thoughts and requirements. The balancing act between maintaining this innovatory impulse and not offending the sensibilities of the Church in Russia, which, deprived of outreach, had become inordinately jealous of tradition, was an arduous task – "with men", most probably, an impossible one, though with God's help Metropolitan Anthony did achieve a monumental step in the desired direction – at least within his own diocese – over the course of the

Chapter Seven

Blessing the congregation in the Church of St Nicholas in Khamovniki, Moscow, 1969

last thirty-five years of his life. This could only have been done from inner conviction, that rare combination of solidarity with his contemporaries and profound awareness of "Jesus Christ, the same yesterday, today and forever; Jesus Christ in a changing world", which was the subject of his address to the Seventh General Assembly of Syndesmos in Beirut in 1968.

Although Metropolitan Anthony never sat down to write a book, the success of his publications over the next decade contributed greatly to his international renommée. *School for Prayer* came out in 1970, to be followed almost immediately by *God and Man* (1971), *Meditations on a Theme – a Spiritual Journey* (1972) and *Courage to Pray* in 1973.[43] All these little books were made up of recorded, transcribed and edited talks, using primitive, labour-intensive equipment, masterminded by Anna Garett the church warden, and, in some cases, translated from the French (*God and Man*, for instance, contains a chapter based on lectures given at the University of Louvain in Belgium). More and more, Anthony worked on editing the transcripts himself, but his first tactful and unobtrusive editor and collaborator from his own flock was Esther Williams. All subsequent editors and translators shared respect for what Gillian Crow calls his "Antonian English"[44] and the books read as a homogeneous sequence, the prose conveying the warmth of his voice and the moments of hesitation, of almost apologetic lyricism and quick humour. It was a matter of fond amusement and much hard work for his editors that Vladyka, preparing, would jot down ideas pell-mell in four different languages with energetic lines linking one to another or separating sequences, encircling metaphors, rather in the manner of Dostoevsky's rough plans for his novels, and would seldom check his sources or, indeed, keep to his "plan".

One devoted publisher's editor, who became a personal friend and introduced the Metropolitan to his wife and children, whom Anthony presented with Russian toffees, was Richard Mulhern of Mowbrays. Early on in their relationship, Mulhern wrote coaxingly to his publicity-shy author: "I know you said when we last met that you were not particularly keen to let us use a photograph on the jacket of *Meditations on a Theme*: can I persuade you to change your mind? Your face is, if you will forgive me for being personal, a rather salable commodity."[45] He need not have worried about saleability. By the beginning of 1972, Mowbray's had sold out a first edition of *Meditations* (10,000 copies in advance orders) and were running off an additional printing of 5000 before the book reached the shops.[46] They and Darton, Longman and Todd, the Metropolitan's other main publishers, were beset by requests for translation rights from France, Spain, Germany, the Netherlands, the Scandinavian countries and beyond – as far as Japan. Each book, moreover, was republished separately in North America. They were widely reviewed and in great demand as "devotional aids", though it was noted that the very fact that they originated from recorded talks not only ensured their spontaneity but inevitably entailed a certain amount of repetition.

The range of these talks, on the other hand, was extraordinarily wide. On Radio Three Anthony spoke with George Harrison of The Beatles, their Sufi yoga master and a medical doctor in a programme called "Fact and Fantasy, Prayer and Meditation" and, in the same year of 1970, gave a recorded interview with Julia Gonzalez on Spanish radio entitled "Jesus maestro". A newspaper commented on one of his appearances on French television that, in the person of a French cardinal who featured in the same programme, they beheld "a man of the church", in Metropolitan Anthony "a man of God". The BBC interviews with the agnostic Marghanita Laski, also broadcast in 1970 and printed as an introduction to *God and Man*, were a great popular success, in spite of the BBC's reservations that Anthony's certainty was too simplistic for the modern mindset. His reply to the Broadcasting Corporation was the same as it had been to Miss Laski herself: "To me, God is a fact." Curiously, given this categorical conviction, he was at his best addressing the uncertain and unconverted (i.e. the majority of the modern world). In Oxford, he actually organised a series of lectures specifically for unbelievers and supplemented appearances in the auditorium with impromptu preaching on the steps of the Bodleian Library, where he attracted a small crowd of hippies and entertained them to an improvised demonstration of "who is my neighbour" by inducing them to counter the cold by standing closer and closer together like penguins in a blizzard!

In 1972, David Sparrow invited him to talk at St Catharine's College, Cambridge, on "God and Man" and "Life in Christ". Sparrow's flyer announcing this event stated: "He is one of the most impressive human beings I have ever met." He stayed at the college for a week from 6 to 12 February, making himself available from 10:00 to 12:30 every morning to talk to anyone wanting a private discussion in the senior common room and lecturing in the evenings.

University audiences suited his direct, challenging, *ad hominem* style of speaking and he remains the only preacher to have been invited three times to give the Hulsean lectures at the University Church of St Mary's, Cambridge – the first time in 1973, in which year he was awarded an honorary doctorate by the University of Aberdeen for "the preaching of the word of God and the renewal of spiritual life in this county". Indeed, he was in constant demand to "preach the word of God" in Methodist, Anglican, Baptist and Evangelical churches, at Quaker Meetings, and also at women's and men's societies ("Cruise" and the Men's Association of the Church of England), where he taught the essential equality while lyrically celebrating the particular qualities of the male and the female in the complete human being.

The ethics of medicine were, of course, an obvious field of expertise, and the Metropolitan was asked again and again to address hospital staff, nurses, doctors and psychiatrists,[47] and to speak to wider audiences on bereavement and death.[48]

In England and within the confines of the Exarchate in Europe he was in demand to speak in schools, monasteries and convents of various denominations, even, in 1972 in Numia, to young offenders and their families at a penal institute. Only on its own home ground in Italy did the Roman Catholic Church object to this kind of activity as "proselytising" … and Anthony was duly thankful when the Patriarchate relieved him of his obligations as Exarch in his grandmother's difficult country by instituting a new, central European exarchate in 1970.

In other parts of the world, however, the Russian Orthodox Metropolitan was welcomed by Protestants and Roman Catholics alike. He is said to have particularly enjoyed talking to soldiers and addressed officer cadets at both Sandhurst and St Cyr. Because invitations often involved residential sessions away from his diocese he had to turn down many requests, particularly to run residential retreats which, in the Cathedral, he would organise on an external basis in the form of a series of Lenten or Advent talks, interspersed with periods of silence, opportunities for questions and, in Lent, a general confession in which he would take the lead, confessing aloud his own sins and, in so doing, reaching to the depths of others' consciences. The terrifying compulsion he had felt to lay out his own soul like a stall in the marketplace when he first became a priest was put into practice, not only in these quiet and reverend confessional sessions, but every time he rose to speak, in whatever language, whichever country. Sometimes he felt he was wearing thin, always repeating himself,[49] but he retained the ability to spark light and inspiration from each encounter with his fellow creatures and to draw power from unfathomable depths, finding refreshment in that place where "the cross is at the heart of the Trinity".

This quotation from *God and Man* was used as an epigraph to an Anglican priest's poem on "The Trinity". On 15 January 1973 the Reverend N.W. Havoc of Sevenoaks, Kent, who had read Anthony's books, seen him on television, listened to him on the radio and seen him in person addressing a local school, but who, with typical English reticence, hesitated "to add to your fan-mail", asked permission to dedicate another poem to him. This poem not only expresses something of its subject's unique quality but also of his appeal to those for whom religion had become an affair of the mind rather than the heart.[50]

> The Risen Christ we know, – but wonder how
> On earth Jesus as man had ever been
> Tempted, as we are, yet exempt from sin,
> Knowing love's tensions in the here and now.
> If neither lovely Mary nor beloved John,
> Nor any other lover stirred His passion
> To be committed in our human fashion,
> To have one special love to dote upon,
> Was it not in encounters far and wide,
> Offering salvation to each and every soul
> Or group, He wrought Love's perfect whole,
> The Bridegroom's full involvement with the Bride?
> Love's four dimensions, redeeming the world's strife,
> We still may witness in some dedicated life.[51]

Good deeds, Anthony taught, must have their origin in the love of Christ, which is the only thing that makes them "forgivable" to those on the receiving end. He said it to the youth of his diocese[52] and to the Quakers, with whom he had a particularly warm mutual relationship. His own strength was a combination of straightforward, down-to-earth honesty, human vulnerability and this puzzling "perfect whole" of love, an ardour that welled from deep places essentially beyond understanding.

This did not mean that even now, at the height of his powers, his judgement was always perfect. A cool head and a restraining hand were as welcome as in the days of church warden Korenchevsky. Here, Anthony was fortunate in his friends: gentle Michael Fortounatto; practical, humorous John Lee; of the laity, most notably the Garret family (the

Chapter Seven

Metropolitan Anthony answering questions at an informal private meeting in Moscow, 1971 or 1972 ("never spoke to the whole room but seemed to be addressing each individual separately or else appealing for inspiration to some larger, more powerful yet shy, almost elusive intelligence")

longest-serving church warden Anna Garret was a tower of strength to the whole congregation); and Irina Kirillova, whose remarkable gift for spontaneous interpretation relieved him of the necessity of always giving two sermons, one in Russian and one in English, and who succeeded Barbara Morshead as his driver and got him from place to place swiftly, efficiently and, when he needed it, in silence – there were always plenty of volunteers to drive him and enjoy a nice chat on the way. These were, by and large, old friends from the original tiny parish he had inherited from Father Vladimir Theokritoff. There were English converts too, who could, as Vladyka Anthony said when asked to describe the typically English virtues, "usually be relied on to keep their word" and were good at organisation and finance, as well as providing a solid body of regular attenders. The Behr family were still a part of his life. Then there were the von Schlippes, of Baltic baron stock as their name indicates. Irina von Schlippe at that time worked with the BBC Foreign Service and her political judgement restrained the Metropolitan from offending his Russian Church, once again the object of media criticism for the silence with which Patriarch Pimen had greeted Solzhenitsyn's "Lenten letter", an open "dare" to the Patriarchate to champion freedom of speech, at least on religious matters, which had been circulated abroad and, clandestinely, in the USSR early in 1972. The Russians have a saying: "Silence is a sign for agreement", and, under the circumstances, silence was the only possible reply. Irina von Schlippe shared Metropolitan Anthony's indignation at the attitude of the Western press, which chose to jeer from the sidelines at the helplessness of the Russian Orthodox Church in their own country. Anthony, grateful that the old Patriarch Aleksii, before his death, had reached out beyond ethnic boundaries to grant autocephaly to the Russian Orthodox Church in America and to canonise two "missionary" saints, and conscious as always of the long agony of a Church in bondage, undertook, at his parishioners' instigation, to address these issues on the BBC Russian Service. However, he delivered himself, unscripted as usual, of such a wholeheartedly supportive view of Solzhenitsyn's critique that Irina von Schlippe asked him to re-record a more moderate version – unless he intended to renounce his allegiance to the Patriarchate. Having listened to the play-back of his talk, Anthony could only agree![53] The resultant, more considered broadcast was a resounding affirmation of the duty of the Church first and foremost to guarantee continuity of worship, to serve as a window onto Eternity and to refrain from meddling in politics *ex cathedra*. Individual members should be free to take whatever part their consciences called upon them to play in secular, sociological and political affairs.

In this Metropolitan Anthony was, in fact, being absolutely consistent, reiterating the stance he had adopted together with those émigrés who remained true to the Mother Church in Russia back in the 1930s and, once again, refraining from saying "here" what he would not have said "there" and vice versa. Adverse criticism in the English press died away, until such time as it was reignited by the gratuitous contribution of Metropolitan Seraphim of Krutitsy and Kolomna to the Soviet campaign of vilification against Solzhenitsyn leading up to the writer's expulsion from Russia in 1974. Seraphim took it upon himself to add his voice, as if from the Church as a whole, to the clamour instigated against the intrepid collator of the *Gulag Archipelago*, which was already circulating on the illegal book market in Russia under the promising title *Treasure Island* and was in the process of being published abroad, in the so-called *tamizdat*,[i] a cardinal sin in Soviet eyes. This was a worldwide scandal of quite other proportions to the Lenten letter, and Metropolitan Anthony, seizing on the fact that the Patriarch himself had kept silence throughout, took the unprecedented step of disassociating himself, his clergy and his parishioners from Metropolitan Seraphim's view of Solzhenitsyn whom he had accused of being a neo-fascist, disloyal to Russia and the Russian Church. On the contrary, Metropolitan Anthony insisted in an open letter to *The Times*, Solzhenitsyn's love of Russia was evident precisely in his "fearless struggle for human dignity, truth and freedom". He did not stand alone "in this love and endeavour" among his countrymen at home and abroad.[54]

Keston College, with which Anthony had had an uneasy relationship since he wrote of its founder, Michael Bourdeaux, that his original purpose of "giving a voice to the voiceless" had, in Anthony's opinion, led to its publications becoming the mouthpiece of extremely vocal dissidents, organised a service of intercession on 7 February 1974 which, for all his reservations, he felt obliged to attend, praying, as always, for the persecutors as well as the persecuted.[55] Anthony, somewhat reluctantly, felt obliged to take part, praying as always for the persecutors as well as the persecuted. On Easter Day, 14 April 1974, finding himself increasingly torn between loyalty to the Orthodox Church in Russia and the imperative to disassociate it from what appeared to many at the time to be a recrudescence of Stalinist oppression in the USSR, Metropolitan Anthony announced his resignation from the official position of Exarch. He spoke at the Cathedral, having dispatched the following letter to Patriarch Pimen, which he proceeded to read out to the congregation:

> Your Holiness, deeply revered and dear Lord Bishop. Ten years ago, before his departure from England, I submitted a request to be released from the duties of Exarch to the most Holy Patriarch Aleksii. The reason for this request was the bad state of my health.

---

i. In Soviet times, the term *tamizdat* was used for Russian material published abroad and clandestinely circulated in the Soviet Union.

Since then a whole ten years have passed and my health has significantly deteriorated, my strength is ebbing and I am no longer fit enough to endure travel, nor even the labours of a full working day. The doctor no longer advises, but insists upon a radical curtailment of my activities.

For this reason I am addressing to Your Holiness a most urgent plea to relieve me of my position as your Holiness's Exarch in western Europe by Easter or immediately thereafter, leaving me as Ruling Archbishop of the Sourozh Metropolia where I hope to be useful still to Orthodoxy and my mother Church. The temporary management of the Exarchate for western Europe I suggest you entrust to the most Reverend Archbishop Filaret, Exarch for Central Europe, whose periodical visits to Paris will be met with lively appreciation and be of undoubted spiritual benefit.

Asking for the holy prayers of Your Holiness and your Patriarchal blessing on your flock abroad, I remain with sincere love your loyal and devoted brother and concelebrant, Metropolitan Anthony of Sourozh, Exarch for Western Europe, London 21 February 1974.[56]

Anthony was, in fact, not quite sixty years old at the time, but his doctor had told him that he had driven himself so hard over the years that his physique was that of a much older man.

Chapter Eight

The Consolidation of the Second Diocese of Sourozh, 1974-1989

> *In this parish we have gone through a succession of periods and each period was seemingly complete, and then God sent us a challenge to make our security explode; and every time we had to learn something about venerating and loving our brother and sister.*[1]

> *Every circumstance that we meet with in this life is willed by God. We should enter into the situation and make God present in it through our own presence and our prayer.*[2]

Free at last from his complex duties as Exarch, Metropolitan Anthony concentrated his energies on his role as Head of the Russian Orthodox Church in Great Britain and intercessor for the future of Orthodox Christianity in the world at large. He was in even greater demand, at home and abroad, in his own right, than he had been as Exarch and representative of the Moscow Patriarchal Church in Western Europe, his serenity and conviction at a premium in a world of shattered convictions and tottering values.

Temporarily, however, the Metropolitan was *persona non grata* in his native land. On his next visit, in December 1974, he was not allowed to address the students of the Moscow Theological Academy, who were all, he was informed, on vacation, though he was invited to dine with their teachers, to say Vespers in the Academy chapel and to concelebrate the Liturgy in the Refectory Church at Zagorsk and at the Church of St Peter and St Paul in Lefortovo, Moscow. Once again, he was conveyed from place to place "like an egg in its shell", yet even this, together with the fact that official invitations to revisit Russia appeared to have dried up, even to the extent of rescinding a visa already granted, failed to dismay him. As he said: "I live within a situation, and become totally engrossed in it. I stake my life on what I believe, on what I am saying – the results are God's concern."[3]

The London congregation were, of course, delighted that their beloved Vladyka could now spend more time with them, and invitations poured in from other quarters. As "one of the most stimulating and charismatic

In Finland, 1974

personalities on the British scene today" who "has exercised a remarkable ministry among students in the past few years",[4] he had been invited in 1973 to give the following year's Hulsean lectures at the University Church of St Mary in Cambridge, where he became a popular and frequent visitor.

Chapter Eight

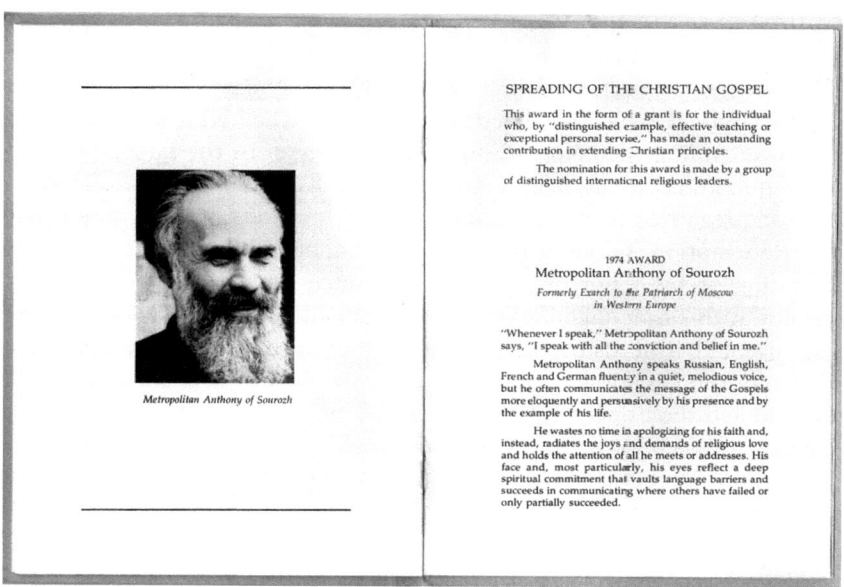

Report of Browning Award for Lifetime Achievement, 1974

He was asked to address the Association of Headmistresses before their annual conference at St Margaret's, Westminster, from 7 to 8 June 1974 and, in that same month, to visit Finland which, to judge by the happy, windswept photographs, he appears to have keenly enjoyed. In October he was invited to give a lecture tour in the United States, where he was honoured by the Browning Award for Lifetime Achievement. The citation reads:

> Metropolitan Anthony speaks Russian, English, French and German in a quiet, melodious voice, but he often communicates the message of the Gospel more eloquently and persuasively by his presence and the example of his life.
>
> He wastes no time in apologising for his faith and, instead, radiates the joys and demands of religious love and holds the attention of all he meets and addresses. His face and, more particularly, his eyes, reflect a deep spiritual commitment that vaults language barriers and succeeds in communicating where others have failed or only partially succeeded.[5]

The respect in which the Metropolitan was held by his peers, however, suggests an intellectual edge to his preaching not quite conveyed by this rather cosy evocation of a charismatic teacher. In July 1973 he had received a doctorate *honoris causa* from the University of Aberdeen – the first of four. The Moscow Theological Academy followed suit in 1983, the University of Cambridge in 1996 and the Kiev Theological Academy in 1999.

In August 1974, Anthony was asked to preach, in German, at the opening service of the Berlin meeting of the World Council of Churches. His sermon, in marked contrast to the politically correct preoccupations of the Council, which appeared primarily concerned with racism, sexism, and overcoming the "North/South divide", began in the far past, with a long quotation about participation in the Eucharist of the undivided Church, regarded as participation in every step of Christ's passion and the Redemption. Without this participation, he asserted, there can be no reuniting of the Churches. Yet there is much that we *can* do. Since we cannot at this time take Communion together, he said, let us do what we can: live and, if needs be, die for one another in the greater community of Christ's disciples. Only when "at the centre of the world stands the Throne of God and the Supper Table of our Lord" will the apparently infrangible barriers between us dissolve as if of themselves.[6]

Also in August that year, the Metropolitan attended the theological conference at the opening ceremony for the Berlin Congress of the Central Committee of the World Council of Churches and from 30 August to 3 September a conference in Sweden on the activities of the Church in the year 1974. In November, he spoke at an Orthodox youth conference in Dijon, the official language of which was French. Here, he exercised his customary direct and simple appeal to the intellectually wide-awake young people in search of challenge and adventure who constituted his audience.[7] The fact that he himself was not boring, however, did not render him immune from boredom after what must have been something of a surfeit of such solemn confabulations. At Dijon, when a small bird fluttered into the conference chamber and bumped into a window-pane in an attempt to regain the open air, he passed a note to an appreciative Russian neighbour: "The Holy Spirit hovered over the Ecumenical Councils in the form of a dove and all we get is a sparrow!" Levity, yes, but no dereliction of duty. Bone weary, he gave up every spare moment on this occasion to hearing confessions from young people he had, more often than not, never seen before and would, most probably, never see again.

Back in the United Kingdom, the Metropolitan buckled down to meeting the demands made upon his time by the host country. He arranged a series of monthly lectures to run from October 1974 to August 1975, timed to follow on from Orthodox Vespers at St Basil's House for the Fellowship of St Alban and St Sergius, in the course of which he himself was to speak on the "Theology of the Resurrection", and he agreed to give the twenty-first jubilee lecture of 15 January 1975 at the Pushkin Club, an émigré cultural centre not specifically affiliated to any ecclesiastical jurisdiction. A request to conduct a Christmas retreat for the St Simeon's Fellowship he passed to Father Basil Osborne who, according to the Fellowship's annual journal, led a "successful and relaxed retreat". Indeed, he encouraged the clergy

Chapter Eight

of the Patriarchal diocese to function more and more as a team, ready to stand in for one another or for their Bishop. This had become necessary during his enforced absences as Exarch and continued to be so because his increasingly frail health did not permit him to satisfy the overwhelming external demands on his time and to look after his own people.

This last, for him, remained *the* priority: he avoided outside appointments on Sundays and feast days and invitations to take retreats that meant staying away. Thus he continued as a dependable presence, ever more firmly anchored in the Cathedral church that was at the heart of his growing and changing diocese, a shepherd who could still boast he knew all his sheep by name. Towards the end of 1975 he moved into a modest bed-sit situated at the back of the church to the right of the altar, to balance the vestry on the left-hand side, where tea was served after the services and where, from now on, he was to receive visitors. The busy, hospitable parish house at 34 Upper Addison Gardens went to the choir-master and priest, Father Michael Fortounatto, and his wife Marianna.

To Anthony, it was an intense relief to have the nights and early mornings free to put himself in the presence of God and to serve and care for the beautiful, spacious building consecrated to that presence. He would say happily that he now fulfilled the functions of caretaker and night watchman – and did so with a cheerful lack of ceremony that sometimes nonplussed visitors, particularly those from Russia, who did not expect the bell at the door of the church to be answered by a senior hierarch in a rusty black cassock. What, to him, was of inestimable value was that now, in every twenty-four hours, there was a central core of silence and solitude. From this he drew strength for the unrelentingly busy days.

In January 1975 he was, as usual, invited to play an active part in the Week of Prayer for Christian Unity, this time by the Camberwell Council of Churches, under whose aegis he addressed an evening meeting at the Salvation Army Centre on the 17 January and gave the blessing and a sermon at a United Service for Christian Unity on the 22nd of the same month, then preached on the 25th at Westminster Abbey before the Lord Mayor of Westminster and various dignitaries of the churches of England, Scotland and Rome and of the Free Churches, stating the need for Christians of various denominations to be simply, humanly aware of one another's existence, not "to pass by on the other side", as we all tend to do every day, only too eagerly accepting the defensive "I'll be alright, thanks," from people obviously in dire need of help. In a sense, he was repeating to these grandees of the Church and the civic order the message of elementary human solidarity he had once tried to convey to the gaggle of Oxford hippies who he had persuaded into a penguin huddle for mutual warmth on a cold winter's day on the steps of the Radcliffe – and he used this story to illustrate his point!

Ce chant est à toi, toi l'Auvergnat
Qui m'a donné un bout de bois
Quand dans ma vie il faisait froid.[8]

He was never far from the cold and hungry days of his early life, and he recalled vividly how, during the war, he would hoist fifty kilos of firewood on his back to store in the attic to keep his grandmother warm. It was, after all, *la condition humaine*.

On 27 January 1975, Metropolitan Anthony preached at a Service of Dedication of the Sacred Heart Convent of St Margaret. The second series of Hulsean lectures to Cambridge undergraduates that followed on 21 and 26 January and 4 and 10 February took as their subjects "Believing", "A God of Love", "A Responsible God", and "God and the Cosmos". There was a record attendance. During Lent, closer to home, a series of lectures was arranged by King's College, London, on the distinctly "with-it" subject of "Meaninglessness".

Invited to appear within the framework of "Les grandes conférences de Notre Dame de Paris", Metropolitan Anthony was the second Orthodox to be thus honoured after Olivier Clément, who had preceded him the previous year in addressing the conference after a question and answer session in the crypt of the Great Cathedral Church. Anthony's subject was "The Holy Liturgy, the Place of the Spirit". The order of service, for many but vain repetition, remained for him a well-spring of inspiration and here, as on so many other occasions, he proved adequate to the task of infecting his audience with his own awed enthusiasm. Yet back home, on a pastoral Eastertide visit to the house of a sick parishioner unable to attend church, he spent the preceding reception fooling with a rowdy six-year-old. Only when the service was due to get underway, did he order the child to hush: "It is now my turn to make a noise. . . ."

In June 1975 Metropolitan Anthony addressed the Royal Air Force Chaplains' Annual Conference at Airport House and in October he was awarded the Lambeth Cross in recognition of his contribution to the promotion of understanding between the Russian Orthodox Church and the Church of England, an honour by which he set much store and which commemorated not only his service with the Fellowship of St Alban and St Sergius but also the excellent personal relationship he had struck up with two Archbishops of Canterbury: Michael Ramsey and his successor Donald Coggan, who presented the award and agreed to be present at the diocesan Eucharist on Friday 26 September 1975 as part of the ongoing celebration of the twenty-fifth anniversary of Anthony's service as Vicar of the London parish.

These celebrations had been fittingly inaugurated by the first Sourozh Diocesan Congress in May that year, an innovation the necessity for which had arisen from the number of new priests ordained to serve the far-flung Russian Orthodox communities and parishes which had now sprung up all over the British Isles. Describing the process, Anthony was to say at a later conference:

> They were born not through systematic, concerted missionary action, but "from the ground", they were born by an act of God which called out believers in a particular place and called out of the midst of those believers men whom they chose as their spiritual guides, their pastors, their liturgical leaders. So we grew into a body, but a body without shape: things happened in one place or another but they only related to one another because they related to me and because the priests and the people related to one another in personal friendship and the joy of meeting in a community of life, sharing their problems and their joys. A moment came when all these bodies reached a maturity assessable by the fact that each body was alive with its own life . . . with a sense of belonging together and being made alive by the power of the Spirit. Then we undertook a first venture. The clergy began to meet regularly, several times a year, and in the course of four years we had to learn to know each other in order to understand each other. We had clashes and tensions, they were resolved at times with great difficulty and at times miraculously by the opening of our hearts and minds. We conceived the thought of a diocesan conference as a means of bringing together not only the priests and deacons, but also the people who had given them birth, a body of people mature, intellectually adult, knowledgeable in Orthodoxy, filled with love and respect for their Church, understanding the ways of God on their home ground in their country. . . .[9]

To those who took part the conference provided an opportunity to live and worship together for a few festal days in a relaxed, informal atmosphere, in close contact with their priests and their bishop. The venue was provided by a hospitable and benevolent community of Roman Catholic teaching nuns during the half-term break of the summer term at their convent school in Effingham. Anthony, at ease and bareheaded in his plain black cassock, made himself generally available, carrying his own plastic trays of food from the buffet, sitting on the grass with groups of youngsters or standing in a familiar pose, very upright with arms akimbo and hands supporting his bad back, wholly absorbed in whoever he was talking to. The point of the conference, however, was not just to provide a much appreciated opportunity to talk informally to the Metropolitan, but to stimulate discussion among his parishioners. Each conference was themed[10] and sensibly organised as a series of panel discussions in English or Russian, with round table free-for-alls to conclude.

The twenty-fifth anniversary of Metropolitan Anthony's service as Vicar of the London parish was celebrated on Sunday 12 October 1975 by a full episcopal Liturgy. The Metropolitan was received at the west door and ceremonially vested by his assembled clergy. After the service a reception was held at Holy Trinity Church, Brompton House, always hospitably open to diocesan events including the annual bazaar at a time before the Cathedral built the extension at the back of the church which now serves as a church hall. There was an exhibition of nostalgic photographs arranged by the parishioners and their gifts of some cash, an album of photographs of Old Moscow, a new typewriter and a tape recorder were presented by the church warden Anna Garret. Father Sergei Hackel and Alexander Pickersgill spoke warmly of the Metropolitan's years of service and all he had meant to them personally and to the parish that had grown up around him, as it increased and prospered and became a diocese. They would have liked, they said, to have him all to themselves but, realising the importance of his vision for Orthodoxy in the rest of the world, undertook to do their best not to monopolise him.

Anthony responded with a moving address to his spiritual children, first in the Russian which had been the language of his original little flock, then, with an injection of quiet humour, in English. He felt, he said, like Abraham surveying his herds, his family,[i] and he thanked them "for our mutual love, your patience with me". Fittingly, he remembered their dead:

> But the Church is an army which cannot be overcome. The Church does not die with the death of Her members on this earth, God is the God of the living, not of the dead, all are alive before Him and, standing here, we stand not only amongst ourselves, not only we here visibly, sensibly present, but all those who, whenever it was, were of one mind with us, one flesh and blood. This Church is full of those we bear in our hearts and those who loved us more than we love them, who, perhaps, we have forgotten, but who do not forget a single one of us before the throne of God. . . .[11]

Aware of disaffection with the Mother Church amongst his flock and, at the same time, full of sober gratitude to Patriarch Aleksii for his tacit permission to his Church to remain true to itself and speak its mind when, in the Soviet Union, the Church could not do so,[12] Anthony continued with passion:

---

i. This was no mere figure of speech. Anthony, who would joke that a wise woman in France had once predicted that he would never marry but have many children, often stood godfather to his converts. He bluffed his way in to visit Tatiana Maidanovich, newly hospitalised with tuberculosis and all alone in England, out of visiting hours and hot-foot from a conference in central London by placating the indignant ward sister with a totally convincing: "But I am the next of kin!"

*Break in talks with a Methodist group in Kemble,
2 June 1984 ("familar pose")*

I thank God for the love of our people and our Church and hope; how I wish you to understand it and to give thanks together with me, to trust and to have faith in this church of the martyrs and the confessors, not to be afraid, not to be ashamed, to glory indeed in the fact that we belong to it. . . .[13]

Loving fealty to the Mother Church, quite unaffected by the temporary coldness of the Patriarchate towards him, was part of the very fabric of Anthony's nature. In a letter written that same year to a trusted friend, he wrote: "I believe that disloyalty is one of the major sins – all betrayals are founded on it: the betrayal of one's friends, of one's convictions, and ultimately of Christ."[14]

Not, as we have seen, that he needed the rank of Exarch of the Moscow Patriarch to boost his international renown. It was not until early 1976 that health problems forced him to cut back drastically on travel abroad, which he had lately found increasingly exhausting, even without the administrative responsibility, financial worries and political infighting that went with the job of Exarch. Thus he decided not to attend the Congress of the World Council of Churches in Nairobi, but instead gave an interview suggesting the Council would do better to confine its activities to speaking out against religious persecution and to preaching the Gospel "without theological vagueness" rather than to supporting and even financing political liberation movements: "There is a confusion between Christ making us free from sin and Christ allegedly calling us to political and social freedom – which I do not think He did."[15] He was, however, active as before in the January Week of Prayer for Christian Unity in London, though both here and at other venues he began to speak more often of the erosion of Christian doctrine throughout the world and within the Churches themselves. Taking as his theme the "Crisis in Christendom", he spoke out against the mindset that makes it "fashionable to be perplexed, and out of date to be certain", a mindset that feared above all to appear bigoted and so to stand up and affirm: "Yes, I believe that God does exist and that this must make a radical difference to my life." Christians, he maintained, should be like the Apostles, ready to "turn the world upside down". They should not strive to keep a low profile and blend in with the status quo. "One felt almost thankful that there was a crisis which could evoke such a deeply spiritual and reassuring talk," commented one of his listeners.[16]

As one of the speakers at a study course for church leaders from 2 to 4 February, Metropolitan Anthony was asked back to deliver one of the Lenten sermons given at the Wednesday lunchtime services at St James, Piccadilly. Cambridge also invited him to preach again at St Mary's and to give the Jane Harrison Memorial Lecture at Newnham College, where he spoke on "The Fools for Christ's sake in the Russian Church". In March, he conducted a two-day School of Prayer at the PLH Portland Building and was one of the main speakers at the Second National Symposium of the Society of Friends, where he tackled, from his own experience as priest and doctor, the difficult subject of "the bereaved parent" – emphasising, as ever with English listeners, that to "keep a stiff upper lip" is often merely to interiorise negative feelings of guilt and rage; better to seek help, to understand and share grief, not to blame and punish, but to keep in mind the great positive significance of death as baptism into New Life. During their April-May meetings he spoke at Chelsea Methodist Church's Open House on "Liturgical Prayer", as also at the RC Brentwood Diocesan Liturgical Commission.

This busy schedule shows the sheer diversity of Christian communities anxious to involve the Russian Orthodox Bishop and should be considered as offshoots of his fundamental service of celebration at the Cathedral, where he not only conducted services but, in Advent and Lent, continued to run retreats for his own congregation, separately in English and Russian, which took the form of three-hour sessions comprising a talk, a question-and-answer session and communal prayer, sometimes silent. Though no longer fit enough to attend the remarkably successful children's camps, which he now entrusted more and more to enthusiasts from among his own clergy and parishioners, he responded to an initiative from adolescent attenders to have their own question-and-answer sessions under his personal guidance and sought to point them in directions in which they could make their own contribution to the life of the parish in their own way. He also continued to receive many people for private talks although, increasingly, these had to be arranged well in advance, something that a happy propensity to put off answering letters until God provided the answer made increasingly difficult. Sometimes it was felt that the Metropolitan relied too much on God to sort out what was really important, but he was, after all, only human – and the demands on his time, in spite of his parishioners' best resolutions not to trouble him with trifles, were unrelenting.

Books, too, were now claiming more and more of his attention and he was asked for contributions and advice on a number of publishing projects. The new typewriter and tape-recorder were in constant use and he found himself attending unlikely venues, such as Foyles' Luncheon at the Dorchester organised by Enoch Powell to mark the launch of a compendium on "Medicine and Politics: 1975 and afterwards". Richard Payne of the Paulist Press wrote to ask advice on their current series "On Spirituality" and to suggest an autobiography, a proposal that prompted a vehement recrudescence of Anthony Bloom's private self, the very retiring self he had submissively set out like a stall at market when he first became a priest:

No! I CANNOT write an autobiography: all my life and work are entangled with the life and problems of people; to write about myself apart from them is impossible, yet, to speak of others, who have entrusted their most intimate thought and emotions, the light and darkness of their lives, is not permissible; if I was to write about my own self apart from them there would be nothing left; a shell, or a cymbal without a sound! Beside, my dream is to be forgotten, and, if something of me survives after my death, that it be a vision of God through a "window" noted for a minute, but forgotten for what it discloses.

The request for advice on the compendiums "On Spirituality" he suggested passing on to Archbishop Vasilii of Brussels, "a deeply spiritual Patristic scholar".[17]

Richard Mulhern of Mowbrays wrote frequently about such issues as plans to re-issue *Meditations on a Theme*; the German translations he had seen in Landeck and Innsbruck; a request from Editions Akninos for the Greek rights to a translation (particularly important in his view because of the way the regime imposed by "the Colonels" had made the Orthodox Church odious to all but the most hidebound traditionalists); and a new manuscript, long "in preparation". Anthony's first Russian-language book of sermons and talks, *Propovedy i besedy*, was published in Paris in 1976, to be followed by *In the Name of the Father, the Son and of the Holy Ghost* ("*Vo imia Otsa i Syna i Sviatogo Dukha*") in 1982.[18] Caroline Scott wrote asking the Metropolitan's co-operation on an authorised biography in a series including Richard Shepherd and Trevor Huddleston but was, like Richard Payne, politely refused. Robin Baird-Smith from Anthony's other regular English publishers, Darton, Longman and Todd, sent him the Italian versions of *School for Prayer* and *Living Prayer* together with a proposal for a new collection of unpublished talks to be edited by Irina Kirillova. Willum Holmström of the journal *Ortodox Tidning* asked permission to reprint their own translations from sermons and talks published from tape-recordings in the London parish newsletter. Modest honorariums trickled in from various publishers. These were to be put to good use when the next financial crisis overtook the Cathedral.

In the meantime, notwithstanding all these opportunities to build up an enduring literary legacy, Anthony continued to respond generously to more ephemeral demands on his time: he contributed to a well-received series of talks on Scottish television entitled "Patterns of Faith" and spoke, to some acclaim, to the Church of England's Men's Society in Loughborough.[19] Here he provided an antidote to mounting mutual antipathy between men and women by urging a renewal of confidence in masculine identity in counterpoint to his own consistent, albeit cautious, strategy of increasing female contributions not only to the organisation of the diocese but to the liturgical life of the Orthodox Church.

Indeed, Metropolitan Anthony considered that the ordination of women was a subject due for serious reconsideration by Orthodox theologians who had been too quick to reject the idea as unprecedented and therefore undesirable. To the dismay of those Anglican opponents to its introduction in their own Church who had thought to find a safe haven in Orthodoxy, Anthony declared himself potentially in favour of the project, though he refrained from hurrying his own congregation to accept innovations for which they were not ready, such as allowing qualified girls to serve with boys in the Sanctuary – a proposal that they actually voted down. He did, however, encourage a study group to discuss women's role in the Church and to submit their findings in writing for his consideration.

No one could accuse the Russian Metropolitan of being an exclusive aesthete with his head in the clouds. In the course of 1976, he spoke in Newcastle at the Imperial College of Science and Technology, and at the Polytechnic in Enfield. In Cambridge, he spoke in the quiet room at Newnham College on a subject to which he often returned: "Can modern man pray?" – a theme particularly apt for a college whose enlightened founders had constitutionally forbidden the introduction of a chapel unless a majority voted in favour.

The Metropolitan, one would have thought, had as much to cope with in his day-in, day-out routine as could reasonably be expected of any man in his mid-sixties who had regularly overtaxed his own strength since adolescence. Neither was he, by temperament, one to provoke a crisis. In teaching and preaching, as in his administrative initiatives in the life of the diocese, he took a thoughtful, gradualist approach and tended to respond to rather than to impose new ideas. When crisis burst in on him, it was from without. However, he was not slow to shoulder responsibility and take command . . . and the next emergency to arise in the life of the diocese was a direct threat to its physical core, its very heart: the Church of All Saints and the Dormition in Ennismore Gardens, hard won and lovingly maintained, consecrated to the worship of God and, now, the Metropolitan's own home, office and centre of pastoral care.

As far as his landlords, the Church of England, were concerned, it appears to have been a case of the right hand not being fully aware of what the left hand was getting up to. The lease was running out and somewhere in the hard-pressed financial administrative centre of the Anglican Church Commission it had been decided that such a prime piece of Knightsbridge real estate should no longer be leased "to the Russians" at a peppercorn rent but should either bring in a proper annual income or be sold outright. Valuers were accordingly sent in and, before long, the Metropolitan was confronted with a copy of their report detailing the various uses to which the building might be put: storage, a dance-hall, a Chinese restaurant. Anthony had never lacked imagination and before his scandalised inner eye there promptly arose a vivid picture of tables served by Chinese waiters around the gallery and a busy dance-floor in the body of the church with nice space for a cabaret in the altar, the floor of which had been specially raised to accommodate Orthodox ceremony.[i] He fired off indignant protests to the men he knew in the Department of Foreign Affairs and to the Archbishop of Canterbury, who had the grace to exhort Foreign Affairs to persuade their business people to show more consideration for "Anthony's sensitive soul"[20] and came to tea to see how he could help – the matter, however, was already out of his hands. Negotiations had to be conducted through the far more hard-nosed Church Commissioners and London diocesan funds.

Representatives of these institutions did explain, with painstaking condescension, that the potential uses to which the building might be put were not what was actually envisaged but rather constituted hypothetical suggestions offered by the independent valuers in support of the London diocese's claim. It was, they said, nevertheless clearly in the interests of the Church to sell off the property or to renegotiate the rent at a realistic rate. Anthony sensibly decided that a realistic rental might well prove beyond the future means of the diocese but, in defiance of all common sense, decided to buy. "On our bones we will establish this Holy place for those who come after us," he told a doubtful parishioner and again, as twenty years earlier when he had accepted binding financial responsibility for the upkeep of the building, rallied his congregation to contribute every penny they could to meet the bill and to support his launching an appeal, of which his old friend Michael Ramsey, now Lord Ramsey of Canterbury, consented to be patron. The Church Commissioners were persuaded to agree an offer of £80,000, a not unrealistic but very moderate sum even in the 1970s for so central yet secluded a property. The offer was made, of course, on condition that the building would continue to be used as a place of worship, in which capacity it had, most embarrassingly, become redundant for the Church of England before it was offered to the Russian Orthodox.

Again the diocese came in firmly behind their Bishop. Bazaars, concerts, contributions, and greatly increased sales of "Ikon" recordings of Orthodox church music sung by the Cathedral choir and of books from a shop at the back of the church ensued – people gave all and more than they could afford, because Anthony told them once again that they had to justify their independence rather than accept the offer of the Mother Church in Moscow to fund the purchase of the building via the Soviet Embassy. Nor, he said, should they go hat in hand for assistance from a wider public in England

---

i. This, at least, is how he envisaged the possible fate of the Cathedral on several occasions after the event!

Interior of the Cathedral in Ennismore Gardens. "London has many beautiful places and a few holy ones. This is both." (Patrick O'Donnor, The Observer, May 1878*)*

and elsewhere until they had truly exhausted their own means. He set an example by contributing all his royalties and lecture and television fees – even what he could skim off his travel expenses. By the time they had raised more than half the required sum, £46,000, the resources of the London parish and the diocese as a whole were exhausted. It was then, on 18 May 1976, that the Metropolitan launched the appeal in *The Times* and *Christian World* in an open letter entitled "Cry for help".[21] The target he set for the appeal, to cover not only the shortfall for the Cathedral but the costs of urgent repair, the construction of a parish hall and the purchase of a small house for a married priest, was calculated to leave the diocese firmly on its feet and able to face the future: not £35,000 but £75,000 – an ambitious target, indeed, but one carefully calculated to meet future needs. The letter, to the mortification of the Church of England, caused a resounding scandal. Anthony's appeal was vigorously upheld from within the Anglican community by one Henry Franklin of Wells Cathedral in *The Times* and by Janet Brown and other sympathisers in *The Observer*.[22] Martha Gellhorn contributed a spirited letter, emphasising the contribution already made by the diocese, and Franklin went so far as to say: "I think every paid priest would forego the few pounds that would come to him if the Russian Orthodox congregation could continue to use Ennismore Gardens; just to say 'thank you' for the tremendous contribution Metropolitan Anthony has given the Church of England." A generous gesture, he suggested, would contribute more to the ecumenical cause "than lots of ecumenical conferences".[23]

Anglicans, in other words, felt deeply embarrassed, and the Archbishop of Canterbury was inundated with distressed letters, telling him that, as the Christian head of a wealthy established Church, he should instruct his financial advisors to waive the difference, and with less friendly ones from people of other confessions or none, writing scathingly of a dog-in-the-manger attitude towards a church the Anglicans could not even fill. Dr Richard Lamerton fired off an irate letter to Archbishop Coggan, promptly forwarded to the Bishop of London as "rather absurd". "Have you not," Dr Lamerton demanded, "an embarrassment of buildings, rotting and empty, on every side? Then why take this one which is at least used and loved! How could this émigré community find so large a pound of flesh as £100,000? You should give it to them."[24] In an icily polite reply, the Bishop of London told Lamerton he had been misinformed and that surveyors from both sides had yet to meet to discuss a fair solution. "I told the Bishop of London of the Archbishop's concern for the Russian Orthodox Cathedral," Michael Moore reported on 19 May 1978. "We came to the conclusion that once commercial negotiation had started it had become too late for generous and imaginative gestures. The Bishop drew my attention to Metropolitan Anthony's letter of appeal in today's *Church Times*. He made the point that if the Diocese yields to one foreign Church it would have to yield to others. We agreed, however, that the Russian Orthodox Cathedral was a special case because emotions were aroused by the plight of Russian Christians in the Soviet Union and because of the special regard in which Metropolitan Anthony was held."[25] The General Secretary of the Church Commissioners,

A.S. Oswald; the General Secretary of the Diocese of London, Derek Hayward; and the Treasurer and Chairman of the Fund all wrote in to *The Times* in what reads like a concerted attempt to justify their position.[26]

Their tone, however, was condescending to the point of brush-off and provoked a spirited response in a joint letter from the Reverend J.M.W. Wilmington and the surveyor acting for the Diocese of Sourozh, Arthur Turnbull, deploring their "cautious and almost gnomic contribution" to the debate, and pointing out that the £80,000 agreed by both sides was a fair commercial price and not, as they had claimed, 20 per cent below that first mooted. Alexander Schouvaloff, intervening on behalf of the Orthodox congregation, reminded readers that the church was a listed building and, as such, subject to restrictions in the uses to which it could be put which was bound to affect its "commercial" value. He also objected to the General Secretary's attempt to play on xenophobic sentiment by continually referring to them as "the Russians". "The congregation," he wrote, "is Russian Orthodox but, by now, we are all English."[27]

Indeed, the British Christian public did not feel Metropolitan Anthony and his flock to be aliens, and the idea of their being turned out of a building from which, for many years now, the Russian Easter and Christmas services had been broadcast to their deprived co-religionists in the Soviet Union and to anyone else who wished to tune in to the BBC's late night broadcasts exacerbated a strong feeling of shame, not least in Anglican circles, that such a situation should ever have arisen. The spectacle of their own securely established national Church threatening an impecunious and insecure minority simply did not accord with British notions of fair play.

The scandal in the newspapers, however, was not allowed to affect cordial relations between the Metropolitan and the spiritual leaders of the Church of England. In 1978, the Cathedral at Ennismore Gardens demonstrated how at home it had become in the host country by celebrating, for the first time, a special service in honour of British saints. Here, Anthony spoke inspiringly of his great vision for the future of the churches and the One Church, and how that future might germinate from a shared past. He also described how, in France, Sainte Geneviève herself had appeared to a Russian Orthodox woman before the founding of the francophone parish of Ste Geneviève and the Mother of God Joy of all who Sorrow, and how the Orthodox community had felt:

> We are no strangers; in this land thousands and thousands of men and women have shared our faith. We are strangers in no land because the oneness of the Church hundreds of years ago unbroken made us the kin of those who are heirs to their resplendence and their glory. . . . And now for the first time we have celebrated here after the Sunday of All Saints appointed of old to be kept after Pentecost, after the Sunday

of All the Saints of Russia that is celebrated as a consequence of the decision of the Council of 1917-18 at the moment when the revolution was breaking all that had been standing, we have kept now the Sunday of all Saints of the British Isles. Unbeknownst to the world we have begun a tradition which will not die, we have resurrected the memory of those who are our brothers in the Faith, examples for us to follow in our lives, those people on whose prayers we can count, who are at one with us. . . . Let us never forget this oneness of the Church of God, let us not forget how the saints of the west have addressed themselves to us through St Geneviève of Paris. Let us never forget the loving wisdom of Patriarch Sergius who called on us to be like a seed sown in the west . . . because our generations are growing thin and those who were children who came out of Russia are now among the old. Let us remember faithfully, lovingly, and build on the foundation of the Saints . . . a Church whose mark will be love, offering of self; readiness to die that others may live, full of joy, open, tender and true. Amen.[28]

Never, surely, was there a man who could fight so hard for his own side without either alienating, or being alienated from, his opponents.

Far from losing touch with his friends in the Anglican hierarchy, he did his best to damp down "the row" in the press, stating in an open letter of 18 August that the Anglican Church was not, as had been rumoured, trying to "price us out of our Church" and the idea of selling the building for secular purposes had been quickly dropped. "There is therefore no row over the future and no possible scandal, although there is without doubt a great need for sacrifice on the part of our people and of generous help on the part of our friends."[29]

"Help on the part of our friends" was forthcoming, as had been the required "sacrifice on the part of our people". The response to the appeal was overwhelming. The situation in the diocese was under constant review, with a Scottish accountant, Alistair Macpherson, appointed to monitor donations. These came pouring in, especially from conscience-stricken individual Anglicans, but also from all over the British Isles, France, the Low Countries, Greece, North America and Japan. One pensioner in an old people's home sent his wedding ring,[i] another his gold teeth, a third two crumpled pound notes, all with the warmest good wishes, words of thanks and appreciation, with many generous souls disclaiming the need for receipts or thank-you letters. Ministers of various denominations took special collections for the Russian Church and sent in meticulously counted donations in pounds, shillings and pence. Anglican bishops, including Archbishop Coggan himself, offered private contributions of widely

---

i. Anthony felt unable to sell this very personal gift and eventually gave it to an engaged couple who could not afford a ring themselves.

varying amounts, all of which were gratefully received.[30] Yehudi Menuhin, "as a Jew",[31] gave the entire proceeds of a concert; John Tavener contributed the takings from the first performance of a new setting for the Orthodox Liturgy given in Westminster Cathedral on 30 November.

The accompanying letters that came with these donations are worthy of publication in a separate album. An agnostic, "ashamed of the Church I grew up in", sent £17 with the caveat "please don't tell Tamara I sent it" and "best love". One mildly eccentric letter in spidery handwriting came from a Welsh donor who claimed to have inherited "not a feud but a faith" and so considered himself basically Orthodox. The letter enclosed £5 and informed the Metropolitan that his Cathedral appeal had been added to the "list of good causes" for local fundraisers and so might hope to receive modest annual donations in the future. A correspondent from St Albans wrote: "When I was in much distress, and . . . concerned about my son Martin, you said you would pray for us and in doing so you conveyed something of the love of God for us in a way I have never forgotten. I still remember with gratitude that insight into Eternity." Others recalled attending services in the Cathedral: the "wonderful sense of peace" that should be preserved at all costs. A lady who had seen the appeal in *Christian World* contributed £5 in cash as "a small offering for your many books which I have found most helpful". A valiant Quaker, Albert Bell of Manchester, wrote: "I am sorry to read in today's *Times* about the threat to your Cathedral. The grounds on which this is based are shameful in the extreme. I have written to the Archbishop of Canterbury to tell him so . . .", and enclosed £5, adding: "My wife and I have great comfort and strength from your books and your broadcasts, and we remember you in our prayers." A "retired nonagenarian Anglican priest" sent two guineas. Mrs A.F. Mackenzie remembered the Metropolitan's wonderful address in Salisbury Cathedral on "Dying a Holy Death" and enclosed £2, expressing her sadness "that our Anglican communion can allow such a state of things to come about", a sentiment echoed by many. The Rev. E.W.T. Dickson of the Warden's House, Nottingham University, contributed £5: "Your work for the glory of God and the benefit of the Holy Church cannot be allowed to be put in jeopardy." R. Fox, "a Catholic myself", also contributed £5, because "if enough Christians respond you will reach your target I'm sure" and "it would be a tragedy if you could not keep your church". This idea that small contributions would add up was widely shared and emboldened individuals to send what they could. Corporate institutions, too, stepped in with considerable sums, as did several anonymous donors. Eventually, the future of the Cathedral and its future financial viability was assured from a source no one had known existed: a fortune left by a nonconformist businessman in the form of a trust for the charitable purpose of promoting the spreading of the Gospel and the worship of God. The executors of the Trust came to interview the

Metropolitan and reached the conclusion that to bestow the entire bequest upon so outgoing and, at the same time, so genuinely and desperately needy an institution as the Russian Diocese of Sourozh was the best possible use to which they could put the money.[32]

By 8 June 1978 Metropolitan Anthony was writing to *Christian World* that the astonishingly generous response to the appeal had reached £55,000, which left him "deeply moved" – "I never thought we mattered so much." By 7 July, the total was £62,000 and again a letter of thanks was published, mentioning especially the accompanying letters to which it was impossible to reply individually.

In order to operate and service funding on this scale, it became necessary to register the diocese as a charity; this, in turn, involved the elaboration of a constitution. A committee was appointed from among the parishioners, consisting of people nominated by the Metropolitan himself and comprising professionals of considerable legal and financial experience as well as men and women of good will and proven loyalty, and scholars with a sound knowledge of the history and doctrine of the Orthodox Church in Russia. Their task was not only to advise on the wisest use of material resources but, prayerfully and thoughtfully, to work out a series of statutes to govern the appointment by election of priests and bishops, the role of the laity in the administration of the Church, and the direction of policy towards other national Orthodox confessions. There was no question of breaking away from the Moscow Patriarchate, who were to retain the final veto, after the Metropolitan Bishop, on major decisions such as the appointment of bishops. These last, however, were initially to be decided in a manner unprecedented for the Russian Church, on a one person, one vote basis according to a franchise that included all adult members of the diocese, the laity as well as ecclesiastics of all ranks.

Democracy, as ever, entailed a deal of bureaucracy but, encouraged by a Bishop who defined himself as their centre rather than their leader, they worked away manfully to elaborate a forward-looking, open-ended, yet legally watertight constitution along lines mooted by the 1917-1919 Council of the Russian Church and the Autocephalous Orthodox Church of America, which openly aimed to accommodate all Orthodox, whatever their national origin.

The Metropolitan set out his concept of the need for this new and, at first sight, rather un-Russian[i] and cumbersome legislation in an open letter

---

i. It had been a favourite tenet of nineteenth-century Slavophile thought that "constitutions" and legislation of all kinds were essentially foreign to the Russian mentality, which worked much better within the framework of a loving, familial relationship between an anointed Tsar and a free people. The Slavophiles, who, as Florensky pointed out in a review of a book on Khomiakov, were all related among themselves and so thought everything

to the Diocesan Conference of May 1979, and he began with the story of how the London parish he had inherited gradually changed from a group of elderly émigrés faithful to the Moscow Patriarchate to comprise not only an anglicised second generation of émigré Russians and their children but also their spouses, often of neither Russian nor Orthodox origin, and friends from the Society of St Alban and St Sergius and, eventually, further afield, who wished to be received into the Orthodox Church. The story of how they came to require a written constitution and the considerations entailed is best told in the Metropolitan's own words:

> It became a parish of many facets, with a variety of currents that related it more and more profoundly to the actual reality in which people lived and not to the Russia of before the Revolution. What we preserved faithfully, and with great love and reverence, was the spiritual tradition of the Russian Church, not in distinction to the tradition of any other Orthodox Church, but because Russian Orthodoxy has its particular and precious characteristics which must, together with the particular and precious characteristics of other churches, form an even greater and more perfect harmony of beauty, truth and living.
> In the course of this process, other parishes were born. . . .
> Then another need became apparent, the need to have a body of people who would meet regularly and think carefully, attentively, deeply, as deeply as the Spirit of God would lead us, about the nature of the Church, our place in the world, how we could serve our own members and make our life so to shine that God be given glory. But to do this it was essential to educate people in their ability to think dispassionately, to listen respectfully, to share daringly, to become unanimous in the

---

could be settled in the friendly atmosphere of their drawing and dining rooms, tended to make fun of their equally Russian rivals, the Westernisers, who were ardent advocates of a political constitution as a first step to liberalisation and democratisation. Rebel soldiers, they insisted, led by the reforming Decembrists against the accession of Alexander I's reactionary heir Nicholas I, when told to shout for a constitution, raised their voices in support of Nicholas's brother Constantine "and his wife Constitutsia". Metropolitan Anthony undoubtedly regarded the Kingdom of Heaven as a family: a God who had "loved us into being" and from whose fatherly love we cannot contract out by any transgression of the law, which, in the last analysis, is merely a set of rules given us as a guide "because of the hardness of our hearts", just as we can never contract out of the obligation to go on building the Kingdom or, however worthily we may have laboured "from the first hour", deny right of entry to apparent layabouts who only joined us at the eleventh. From this point of view, no "constitution" is an absolute and every rule is a compromise, a concession, which, even if it purports to guarantee our liberties, limits our ultimate freedom.

love of God,[i] and this is what we conceived to be the just aim of our Diocesan Assembly: to learn to listen to one another, and to grow into a body of aware and responsible laity, a body that would be capable of thinking, with all the responsibility this implies, both of the present *and* the future of this community of Orthodox that we are.

At this juncture there occurred something apparently trivial, but which I believe was an act of God. It became imperative for us to be registered as a charity. One may say, what has that to do with God creating a Church? It has a great deal to do with it, and you must help others understand. *To be registered as a charity we needed Articles of Association, or Statutes, which we could present to the Charity Commissioners*, and we set out to prepare them. We appointed a group of people who could think of a way in which our Church could be given expression in legally correct terms, but without betraying its mystery and substance, or the Divine Presence in it or the human response to it. This led to something which to me is a wonder and a miracle, for this group of people who set out to work on Articles of Association rather than on the theology of the Church, discovered they could not do it without betraying God, the Gospel and Orthodoxy, if these formulations were not an expression, as profound and true as possible, of our faith, in particular of our dogmatic faith in Orthodoxy, in the Church and in spiritual experience. In the course of several years, this group came repeatedly to the priests' meetings and presented us with drafts for the Statutes and commentary on them which was a disclosure of what the Church is. It was an act of worship, an act of prayer, an act of adoration of God to look at these elements and to see how we could express, not only in human terms but in terms of Law, (not Old Testament Law, but the Law of Christ of which the Apostles speak) the mysterious and ineffable reality of the Church. . . . This work has gone on for several years. It has involved more and more people; as soon as we had a section ready, we turned to the Council, which was a smaller body elected by the Assembly, and asked it to reflect and comment on it. Then we brought the complete draft Statutes to the Assembly to discuss, line by line, and it became for the members of the Assembly a revelation of what theology, incarnation can be, that is the work of the Spirit seizing upon the flesh and making it into a body which is the Body of Christ, enlivened by the Power of the Spirit. . . . We have taken great care to prepare Statutes which in no way contradict the universal canon of the Orthodox Church, or which even give it a more faithful expression than in various other countries, where conditions have been too easy or too tragic. We have tried to take this into account because we belong to the Russian Church and our life,

---

i. These words might well serve to define the elusive Russian word *"Sobornost"*.

our spirituality and this document must be rooted in the experience of a Church whose history has been more tragic than glorious in spite of centuries of seeming resplendence. We examined attentively the rules established by the Council of 1918/19,[i] we studied the statutes of the Orthodox Church in America, which is the first church in the non-Orthodox world to be born as an independent Church.

Lastly, we considered our own local circumstances. These come under two headings: on the one hand, this country in which we live, its law and the concrete body of people we are; on the other hand, – the fact that in the Orthodox Church behind the Iron Curtain, where they have been stripped of everything which is not the substance of Church life and where they have been forced to look only at essentials, it is now considered that all the churches of Eastern Christendom, those we call the Mother Churches, should relinquish their jurisdiction on the bodies born of them and that these bodies should become culturally, nationally and politically distinct and set up as independent bodies, while remaining faithful in love, in faith and in the awareness that they were born of the Mother Churches. *This is not a question that can be resolved by any church singly or immediately, it may take years.* . . . It cannot be done by decision or enforcement, these things must grow and happen of their own accord. . . . The Statutes we have been working on are an attempt at providing a first draft of a possible vision of a Church of Great Britain, or at least in Great Britain, or a first challenge to other bodies to think in the same terms, creatively, inventively, in humility, with total faithfulness to the Mother Churches and yet with a vision of what Orthodoxy is to be in the future.

So when you read these Statutes keep in mind all I have said, because they are not formal articles of association, they are not addressed to the Charity Commissioners, although they will read them in a form understandable to them. These statutes must be a vision of how we can incarnate what I have tried to convey when I spoke of the Church in forms, but in forms which are not immobile and petrified, but vital and dynamic, and that lose none of their vitality and strength by being united, intertwined and brought into harmony with each other. These Statutes must be a framework in which we can create life, a life which may not as yet be perfect, for it must follow the course of its own natural, free development, but it must be in the Spirit of Christ and nothing but Christ and His Spirit.[33]

It took the Committee close on twenty years to elaborate, but eventually the statutes were formulated in print and accepted as the Constitution of the diocese. The Moscow Patriarchate gave tacit approval for the

---

i. Usually dated as 1917-1918.

implementation of the document within the diocese but never accepted its possible implications for Russian Orthodoxy as a whole, nor, indeed, ratified it officially for the Diocese of Sourozh.[i] Although the statutes still arouse intense interest within the Orthodox Church in Russia, there was too much democracy, too much participation in the government of the Church by the laity, too inclusive an attitude to all Orthodox irrespective of nationality or cultural tradition, and too much emphasis on a wholeness comprising not uniformity but unity in diversity for the tradition-bound Muscovites to take on board even in the post-Soviet 1990s. Grassroots attempts to include Sourozh practices such as the election of priests in Russian parishes were actively discouraged. Metropolitan Anthony was in no position to hurry his colleagues in the USSR or later in the Russian Federation and was careful, as always, to avoid direct confrontation, insisting, for instance, on obtaining the blessing of the local Metropolitan and Archbishop before countenancing the foundation of a congregation representing the Diocese of Sourozh in the present Sudak, which wished to organise itself according to the Sourozh statutes. Receiving no answer to several letters raising the subject with the hierarchs concerned, he felt bound to write – albeit sadly – to the representatives of this initiative that his courtesy title did not give him the right to intervene between them and their local authorities.[34]

Indeed, from the moment of his resignation as Exarch, Anthony had made every effort to mend fences with the Moscow Patriachate. The death of his successor Metropolitan Nikodim in 1978 provided a catalyst. Metropolitan Anthony, in his capacity as Nikodim's predecessor as Exarch, firmly asked himself to the funeral for which it was evidently felt impossible to deny him a visa, and, in his genuine grief for his rather unlikely friend, re-established personal contacts and the regular invitations to visit Russia which were of such importance to him personally and to his ever increasing circle of friends and followers there. As usual, he made no compromises. In the thank-you letter he dispatched to the Patriarch for receiving him on this occasion, the Metropolitan deplored the fact that lingering disapproval in certain quarters had ensured his presence at his successor's obsequies was not mentioned in the official bulletin. However, Nikodim's successor as Exarch, Metropolitan Philaret of Minsk and Belarus, accepted an invitation to London, where he was warmly received, and Metropolitan Anthony again became a frequent and welcome visitor to Moscow.

The combination of imperturbable firmness of purpose with a non-confrontational approach seemed to be working: all doors were still open. Even the intransigent Solzhenitsyn, who had clashed with the Metropolitan at their first meeting in Zürich just after his exile, admitted that, at the time, he had been on the rebound from many years' gagged resistance, which was

---

i. At the time of writing the Constitution for the Diocese of Sourozh has, alas, been officially abrogated.

the reason he had harangued Anthony for not taking every opportunity to speak out against the suppression of Christianity in the USSR at the top of his voice. Only now, in exile, was he beginning to understand Anthony's "guarded, profound look with a spark in its depths" and his careful reply: "But surely you don't mean a break with the Patriarchate that would make it impossible for me to have any influence from the tribune entrusted to me?"[35] Now, from the tribune entrusted to him, he continued to pursue a policy of influencing his Mother Church from within and supporting Her from without. The ascetic way, to him, was never to close doors but to remain open and vulnerable in everyday life no less than in the life of prayer.[36]

This is not to say that he never said a sharp word to anyone nor that he was never rebarbative in setting out his own concept of what was right, or what was right for a certain person in a given situation. Just how he understood the Constitution's advocacy of the election of priests he made very clear in a rather forbidding letter to a francophone convert who wrote to him in the summer of 1980 asking to be ordained as a hieromonk to serve in the London parish. The request is refused outright on the grounds that proficiency in Russian and English are essential prerequisites for the job and that all clergy in the diocese are self-financing and their candidature has been put forward by the congregation.

> I advise you first and foremost to acquire a qualification which will make you self-supporting and independent (you strike me as a man who lacks stability). Then settle down as a faithful Orthodox in a parish that suits you; if the worshippers discover in you a man to whom they would naturally turn for advice, for support in their prayers; if, in time, they feel they would willingly make their confessions to you – they will ask the Bishop to enrol you and appoint you to that parish. The priesthood presumes the Call from God. "Are you ready to drink the Cup from which I must drink?" and a Response to this question (and not to the one many young men believe they hear: "Do you wish to go and preach to the nations?"), together with recognition by the people of God, the presbytery and the Bishop, of both Call and Response. . . . A priest is a man who gives himself to God without reserve, his Eucharistic sacrifice begins with the offer of self. "Lord, do with me what you will, my life (and all its circumstances) and I myself am yours without reserve." A monk is "a soul that stands face to face with God" (Theophanos the Recluse). . . .
>
> Don't run from one Bishop to the other in search of someone who will take you on; God will find you when He needs you.
>
> Forgive me this harsh letter; I am answering yours in all honesty.
>
> May God keep you and guide you – attach yourself to ONE church and one priest and study assiduously to live the spiritual life. . . .[37]

The fact that Metropolitan Anthony was temperamentally quite capable of administering a bruising fatherly scold, a sharp one-line reprimand or even a punch in the teeth[38] does not mean, however, that his gradualism did not spring from profound conviction or that his non-confrontationalism was not rooted in the will to love his fellows, *all* his fellows, as he loved God. Even on his own home front he implemented the ideas advocated in the new statutes with tact and caution, over many years. Not all shared his vision and laity and clergy alike had to be gently guided into co-operation.

The study group considering the veneration of British saints of the undivided Church, for instance, had not worked with one mind. Some were inclined to a selective approach, particularly to those local saints and martyrs modern scholarship had declared mythical or semi-mythical and whose claims to sanctity were based on legends not their own, whose very historical existence remained doubtful. They were also cagey at the thought of venerating other well-documented figures, such as St Augustine of Canterbury, too closely associated for their comfort with the authority of Rome. Other members of the group, on the contrary, felt that they, as twentieth-century amateurs, had no mandate to pick and choose from among saints hallowed by local tradition. Among these, not surprisingly, was the linguistically gifted Welsh priest Father Deiniol who, in his turn, had to be reminded that he could not dwell for ever in the Celtic twilight but was also called to co-operate with the rest of the Orthodox Church he had chosen. The Metropolitan chivvied Deiniol into attending the Diocesan Liturgical Assemblies as well as the thrice-yearly meetings of clergy:

> [W]e are trying to build Orthodoxy in this country, a body multinational, multicultural, yet one in God and in the one Church; and you have a distinctive contribution to make as an heir to Celtic Orthodoxy. We need you; and you need us all.[39]

He had, Anthony continues, intended to confer the epigonation on Deiniol at the Liturgy, the failure to attend which had elicited this letter. He gives dates of further meetings and assemblies in the coming year, but adds ironically that, if Mohammed will not come to the mountain, then the mountain, "readily and gladly", will come to Mohammed; he proposes to visit the reclusive priest's parish on 12/13 May 1984 on the third Sunday after Easter. Would Deiniol, in his turn, represent the Moscow Patriarchate and the diocese at a forthcoming conference for monastics, to which an invitation was enclosed?

So he coerced and persuaded disparate individuals into a greater loyalty, not just to him as a beloved pastor, but to the Russian Church he loved and to a concept of Orthodoxy open to all nationalities.

Icon of the saints of Great Britain and Ireland

Some other problems Anthony set before his diocese failed to generate a corporate response. The group nominated to discuss the role of women in the Church, for instance, turned out to be far from ready for the task and eventually asked permission to disband itself. Anthony was left very much alone to cope with incidents such as the curious little spat in *The Church Times* over the ordination of women, occasioned by Eric Yates, for the "Anglo-Catholics", quoting an Orthodox statement agreed at the Pendeli Conference to the effect that the idea of women priests was unprecedented, ergo unacceptable and, indeed, unthinkable within the framework of the Holy Orthodox Church. Writing "as an Orthodox Christian", Elizabeth Moberly disputed this opinion in the same newspaper on 31 August 1984, saying the pronouncement was not authoritative doctrine defined by a Church Council, but simply the over-hasty reaction of a few conservative clerics to an idea to which they had given no serious consideration. She was publicly supported by Bishop Kallistos of Diokleia (Timothy Ware) but execrated in a private letter by Father Columba Flegg, who told her she should "crucify her intellect", repent, and publicly confess that she had no mandate "as an Orthodox Christian" to defy the Pendeli pronouncement. Both sides involved Anthony,[40] who did his best to broker a peace, regretting Father Columba's intemperate style and the rumours that he had threatened Elizabeth with ex-communication. Father Columba moderated his tone, though he insisted that he truly believed the Pendeli pronouncement to be representative of Orthodox doctrine. However, both Kallistos and Anthony put their point of view – that the question was not settled but open to debate and deserving of serious, imaginative and creative consideration – so diplomatically that what might have become an ugly inter-Orthodox stand-off was defused without undue scandal.

The vexed question of the ordination of women did not, of course, go away. Metropolitan Anthony had come close to pre-empting consensus in his own diocese with a public declaration of his position on the subject in a 1967 preface to Elizabeth Behr-Sigel's book in French on the position of women in the Church: she opens the subject, he says, "with humility and boldness", and the book requires from its readers an "inner emancipation and deep communion with the vision and will of God in prayerful silence". Even here, he was reluctant to enter the lists to champion a cause for which the majority of his fellow Orthodox were not ready and to which many were positively hostile. It was, he felt, not the most pressing task on his agenda, but he insisted consistently in public and private that women's role in the Church should be reviewed in accordance with late-twentieth-century attitudes and that he himself saw no reason against their ordination as priests. Of this he expressly warned Anglicans seeking refuge from the introduction of women priests and maintained firmly that the question should be decided on its merits and not on the basis of whether or not it might hinder the ecumenical process. He set out his views clearly when addressing the young people of his diocese and in a letter to a research student who sought his advice about her thesis on Galatians 3:28, which, he said, spoke to us directly of the essential equality of man and woman: "this equality is totally absent from the practice of the Church, which is completely man-centred and man-dominated, and you might make a play, nay, lodge a claim Urbi et Orbi for a new appraisal of Christ's work of salvation and the place of women in the economy [in the sense of God's plan for our salvation]."[41] The question of the ordination of women, he told his correspondent, had yet to be raised from within the Orthodox Church. It had been presented "from without" and the Church had issued a number of statements without giving due thought to a problem that deserved to be studied on merit, not on precedent.

In fact, the Metropolitan seems to have seen it as his duty to prepare hearts and minds in his own diocese to do just this. When a women's group was formed to produce and discuss papers on the subject, he found their initial contributions very unfocussed and suggested they take as set texts Evdokimov's *Le Mariage, Sacrament de L'Amour* and *La Femme et le Salut du Monde* (for which he himself had declined to write an introduction, pleading insufficient knowledge of Jung), and Troitsky's *A Christian Philosophy of Marriage*. They should, he said, consider man's role in parallel to woman's (as indeed he was to do himself in a series of open lectures in the Summer Forum Centre of Pushkin House: "Man and woman in creation", "Man and woman after the Fall", "Man and woman in Christ") and decide "on a subject that is directly relevant to your own lives within not only the Church but in the wide and complex world, full of greatness and tragedy, in which we live and of which we are an integral part".[42]

In the Orthodox press, he continued quietly to lobby behind the scenes without provoking a polemic – as in his letter to the editor of a French revue *Nouvelles de la Fraternité* objecting to an article by a certain Père Cyrille, from whom he had expected a more enlightened attitude: "To refer to Tradition is only justifiable if one can show that the origin and the *raison d'être* of that tradition has an eternal validity or, at least, one destined to last as long as history. . . . It is essential to provoke fresh reflection, free and in depths, on a number of Orthodox themes – and on the question of the ordination of women in first place."[43]

When, in 1988, Elizabeth Behr-Sigel was invited to attend an inter-Orthodox consultation on the subject, called by the Ecumenical Patriarch in Rhodes for 30 October-7 November with the remit "to confirm the theological basis of the impossibility for the Orthodox Church to ordain women",[44] she wrote to Metropolitan Anthony asking whether she should accept so forbiddingly worded an invitation. Most unusually for him, he answered by return of post, advising his "dear Lizelotte" to accept but to register an immediate protest against the way in which the organisers of the "conference" appeared to have pre-empted their own decision by the formula "to confirm . . . the impossibility" and, secondly, to bear in mind that Christ, like the first created human being before the Fall, contains the fullness of both man and woman "without confusion, without separation", that the priesthood is the prerogative of God alone, but that the Mother of God participates in the priestly function through obedience, dedication and the sacrifice of Her Son, and that this is remembered in the Liturgy. "Bon courage," the letter concludes, "et que Dieu lui-même te vienne en aide, car nous pouvons attendre bien peu des évêques et des théologiens."[i]

So, with the patience of a good gardener, Metropolitan Anthony sowed the seeds for the eventual realisation of his vision for the future of the Orthodox Church in Great Britain. Later, presented with the opportunity to explain this reality and this hope to his fellow Russians on the BBC Russian Service, he began by telling them why he had been particularly pleased to receive the title "of Sourozh" when he became Archbishop, because Sourozh, in Crimea, had once been a missionary outpost of Byzantium:

> I saw our role in the West as a missionary one. Not in the sense that I thought of converting all the English to the Orthodox faith: that is, first, unimaginable and, second, I would even say undesirable, because

---

i. "Be of good courage and may God Himself come to your aid since we can expect very little from the bishops and the theologians." (Metropolitan Anthony of Sourozh, letter of 30 March 1988 to Elizabeth (Lizelotte) Behr-Sigel. Copy in the MASF Archive.)

> a quick move from one confession to another is seldom stable. Our mission, as I and now my fellows understand it, is like this: we here are the voice of the Orthodox Church in the Russian tradition, we are not bound to convert people to Orthodoxy, but we should impart our understanding of Orthodoxy to them, the love of Orthodoxy, and give religious people of various confessions those particles, those shards of the truth of Orthodoxy which they are already now in a state to absorb, understand and experience.
>
> What will come of this does not concern us in the least in so far as it is the business of God. Our business is *to sow*. How the earth receives our seed, how God will nurture it – is not our responsibility. There is even a saying which is very dear to me – a Latin proverb: Fructuat, das [*sic*] pereat, – let it be fruitful so that, in its own good time, it may disappear. . . . I don't know what will happen to our diocese. I think that, at some time or other, it may serve as the seed of future Orthodoxy here and that all Orthodox will merge and that it is possible there will be no diocese of Sourozh or of Thyateira, the Greek diocese, or of the Serbian diocese, but there will be something new, perhaps the Orthodox Church of Great Britain and Ireland.

He went on to tell his Russian listeners, as always humorously and in vivid detail, how the present Diocese of Sourozh had grown from two small parishes comprising 300 people to over 1000 and how the ethnic and cultural mix had gradually changed. Now, he concluded:

> A congregation has gathered about our Church that is, I would say, 80% English-speaking and we have children of 12 to 15 born of parents who made their own decision to become Orthodox. As a result the congregation is profoundly educated in Orthodoxy, because there is no-one there who was simply born Orthodox, christened in an Orthodox Church and just stayed that way from inertia; almost all of them have become Orthodox from <u>personal</u> conviction and thanks to <u>personal</u> inner change.[45]

As he approached his seventieth birthday, Anthony continued to cultivate his garden, an unremitting and exhausting labour for one who conceived his place at the apex of the pyramid of the diocesan hierarchy quite literally to be at its base – as servant of all, homeless caretaker of the great Cathedral that lodged him, employing neither domestic help nor secretarial staff. He even personally blessed and oversaw the work of volunteers who came to clean the church, dust the icons, polish the candle stands, scrape candle wax from the floor, and clear out the occasionally blocked sink in the vestry. The last two functions, indeed, he had been known to perform himself. He liked to leave the candles burning right down after the services, both to fulfil their symbolic function of prayer and to warm the premises – a lofty, draughty English Italianate building, not a well-insulated, cosily domed and vaulted Russian winter church. He had no personal or official car and, on the rare occasions when neither his priests nor Irina Kirillova, chauffeur of choice from among his parishioners, could transport him, he would use public transport – always wearing his cassock, because "people talk to you and you get into the most extraordinary conversations".[46] Gillian Crow describes him as "just the sort of man you could imagine running for a bus",[47] and another parishioner recalls him, the skirts of his cassock gathered up in one hand, jumping the puddles in a sudden downpour and gleefully "whistling through two fingers" at the (inevitably engaged) London taxis.[48]

For all he was accustomed to strenuous activity, the strain of the appeal and the ongoing work both of repairing and redecorating the body of the Cathedral and of building up the diocese took its toll, and the Metropolitan became subject to recurrent illness. His back gave constant trouble. Chest infections repeatedly escalated to pneumonia. He suffered three separate attacks of extremely painful shingles – an illness often associated with nervous strain. When he was laid up, a notice would appear on the door of his room that he would not celebrate, would not hear confessions, and was not seeing people: "do not leave notes unless it is of unavoidable necessity." The backlash to such retreats was that, when he re-emerged, there was invariably a long queue for confession and he would be kept standing in the body of the church until the last possible moment at the Liturgy. Outside engagements, on which he was increasingly cutting back, were subject to cancellation, sometimes at the last moment. He was seriously trying to avoid foreign travel, with the exception of his visits to Russia, cancelling an appointment with French television and a second lecture tour in the United States. Reluctant to refuse the constant calls upon his time, he would, nevertheless, often overbook his schedule, then cancel, desperately seeking a last-minute replacement from among his increasingly unwilling clergy, who not only had obligations of their own but also did not relish the role of disappointing substitute. The up-shot of all this was that Metropolitan Anthony, formerly so exceptionally available to his flock, became notoriously hard to get hold of. People began sending in a third or fourth request for an interview or query about a book with the ominous ending: "we will assume your agreement in case of no reply. . . ."

Prolonged bouts of illness entailed some relaxation of his regime. He would allow himself more rest and occasionally watch television. As in his youth, he read widely. True to his upbringing in pre- and post-war France, Anthony's taste in literature was existential. Creativity, he felt, should be based on experience; he responded to integrity and challenge, rejecting what he felt to be unconvincing spiritual comfort, whether in the form of Dostoevsky's *starets Zosima* or the Yeshua chapters of Mikhail Bulgakov's *Master and Margarita*, but embracing the former's agonising moral dilemmas and the latter's soaring, romantic fantasy. Poetry he read for pleasure, especially the German poets. His favourite among the Russians was the hard-thinking and morally exigent Baratynsky, but he also loved the romanticism of Lermontov and Blok, their tragic sense of history, their insatiable longing for a purity and perfection beyond "the lack-lustre songs of the Earth" ("skuchnye pesni zemli"). Of the French prose-writers, he read the classics and, among the moderns, Camus, Simone Weil and Bernanos, but had little stomach for Sartre. He often quoted from Jean-Marie Vianney (Le Curé d'Ars), as he did from the English works of C.S. Lewis and Charles Williams, fiction and non-fiction.

He had loved Dickens as a boy and some Dickens characters still cropped up in his own discourse, though now he found the great novelist's style excessively sentimental. Mind and ear responded to the sonorities of Shakespeare and the King James Bible and he found it completely natural to give an epigraph to his introduction to Sergei Hackel's book on Mother Maria (Skobtsova) from Shakespeare's *The Tempest*: "Ah, I have suffered with those that I saw suffer." Anthony's preference for the Authorised and Revised Versions over modern translations of the Bible worried his English publishers, who feared quotations from these venerable sources would put off the modern reader, but, wherever possible, he insisted on retaining them, protesting that he found more recent versions "flat".[49]

This disinterested browsing through books bore fruit not only in the examples he drew from them to illustrate his talks but in his remarkably sophisticated contributions on beauty to the T.S. Eliot Memorial Lectures at the University of Kent, a series of four concluding with "The Significance of Ugliness".[50] The weakness of body that kept the Metropolitan confined to his room and obliged him to rest up in solitude thus allowed him to absorb fresh nourishment for the mind. Even the television could be nourishing and he derived from the antics of dogs in training not only amusement but an apt metaphor for spiritual obedience, which should be given – he said – not in a penitential spirit of resignation but joyfully with wagging tail, eager attention and a great desire to please![i]

Gradually, then, even as he "girded up his loins" (an expression his publishers felt was particularly obscure) for the task of building up an Orthodox diocese in Great Britain that would withstand the buffeting of time and, he hoped, outlast him, Metropolitan Anthony became more withdrawn and reclusive, which is not to say either slack or lethargic. An elderly parishioner once confided in him comfortably that her doctor had told her she must give due consideration to her ageing body and take things easy. "Of course," he replied. "The body is like a donkey. One has to take care of it, feed it and rest it. But its primary function is not to be ministered to but to perform, so long as it is able, the tasks you require of it."[51]

---

i. In fact, he owes this image to Evelyn Underhill – see *Trudy* 1, 880.

Anthony's seventieth birthday celebration, June 1984 ("... all of us went up to kiss the cross, and he stood with it to the very end – and looked, and looked tirelessly. In that concentrated look he simultaneously welcomed each of us into a very intimate, close, real communication, – and at the same time was strikingly stern, demanding, exacting. It was not easy to meet his eyes.")

That was certainly how he treated his own much mortified flesh and his frail health was public property not because he complained or fussed but simply because he lived in the church, in the public eye, at the mercy of all those who loved and needed him – many disinterestedly and with reverence but some, inevitably, out of their own neediness: well-meaning busy bodies, failed suicides, depressives, addicts, the mentally unstable and, of course, the dying. When he could not meet all these needs, there was nowhere he could quietly withdraw, no buffer between him and the world; there were just the notices pinned to the door of his "guard-room" in the Cathedral or pleas relayed through his clergy to allow him some minimal time for rest and recreation.

So he soldiered on through the 1980s, shouldering as much as he could carry of the everyday burdens of the diocese and fulfilling his outgoing mission to the rest of the world, teaching and preaching with all the remarkable stamina he had trained himself up in since boyhood. Neither did he skip the required austerities, though he never made a parade of them. Indeed, he confided to one parishioner, he never "thought about food and sleep so much" as during Passion Week, when it was his habit to deprive himself of both to the extent he feared some people might actually notice him swaying on his feet from sheer exhaustion. Few did – he took care to present a smiling face and welcoming presence whenever he appeared in public.

The year 1988, however, the year of the millennium of Christianity in Russia, taxed him beyond his strength. He attended both the preparatory Council for the celebration in March and the official commemoration of the event in June that year. The solemnities, involving long hours of standing and processing in full regalia, embarked upon on an empty stomach and followed by unaccustomedly heavy and lengthy feasting, were exhausting. So much so that, come autumn, he felt the need to take an unusually long holiday retreat. On his return in time for Russian Christmas 1989, Metropolitan Anthony addressed a direct appeal to his own parishioners to spare him as much as possible the constant individual demands they were still accustomed to making on him personally. They should, he said, get used to making their confessions to the priests they had chosen and he had consecrated – and try not to overwhelm them, either, with problems they ought to be able to solve for and among themselves. It was time, he said, to grow up and to bear one another's burdens as mature Christians.[52]

Meanwhile, he had not forgotten and was never to forget the surge of love and solidarity his diocese had received from the British public during the crisis over the purchase of the Cathedral. In January 1983, nearly five years after the launch of the appeal, Metropolitan Anthony had dispatched a new letter to *The Church Times* to render account of the use to which the money raised had been put and to thank all those "individuals and parishes of all denominations" who had shown such profoundly moving support: "I would invite them to join us at our service of thanksgiving on Saturday January 29 at 2.30pm that they may see for themselves what they have achieved – the fabric of the Cathedral structurally sound, the interior freshly cleaned and decorated – that we may express our gratitude both to God and to them and rejoice together."[53]

So, in joyous fulfilment and mutual courtesy, albeit in exhaustion for Anthony himself, culminated the saga of the physical and territorial establishment of the Diocese of Sourozh of the Russian Patriarchal Church in Great Britain. The Constitution, according to which it was to live for the next twenty years, was fully elaborated and ratified by the diocese, if not formally accepted by the Mother Church. Yet this seeming stability was undermined from the beginning by the explosive build-up of ongoing geo-political cataclysm within and without the ecclesiastical world.

Chapter Nine

Mission to Russia and New Problems in England, 1983-2003

I believe, Lord, and confess, that you send the fire of trial that we may emerge purified and transfigured, ready to build life anew.
I believe, Lord, and confess, that every effort we make to live in truth and in the light of faith in Thy Wisdom brings close the hour of universal resurrection and prepares the Way for Thy coming.
Consciously and at every hour I wish to take part in the redemption of the world, remaining a light amongst the storms, to be one of Thy lighthouses.
I go, Lord, into the world to do Thy will, all my desire is to stand firm as a faithful servant at the post to which Thou didst appoint me, in order to meet Thee worthily.[1]

The Constitution of the Diocese of Sourozh was first mooted in a world that appeared permanently divided between militantly atheistic communist states and tolerant but increasingly secular democracies. In the course of the 1980s, however, the situation began to change and nowhere were the immediate repercussions of this change to be felt more acutely than within the Diocese of Sourozh and, indeed, in the heart of its chief pastor. Increasingly, it was not only his own beloved flock who required his attention, but a whole generation of his own countrymen, an ever increasing number of whom were arriving in London throughout the last twenty years of the century, some to seek guidance, but many, no less in need of pastoral care, for reasons of their own: political, economic, or just because it had become possible to see the world.

Not unnaturally, the influx activated the strong sense of self-preservation which, in British public opinion, has always militated against immigrants.

Danger signals, like bubbles rising to the surface of a lake, popped and fizzled, scarcely disturbing the surface calm. As the Soviet Union began to relax its grip on the populations of Russia and Eastern Europe, first trickles, then waves of enterprising individuals, hungry for freedom of information but also for the consumer goods of all kinds that had been so hard or impossible to obtain throughout their lives in their own country, and, in many cases, on the lookout for a foothold that would ensure them a long stay, if not permanent residence, beyond the confines of communism, gave the people of Western Europe a new reason to beware of "the Russians". As G.K. Chesterton once wrote, before the onset of communism, Russia had never been popular in England, neither with the Liberals, because it was an empire, nor with the Conservatives, because it was *another* empire. Big countries, as Peter Ustinov, who loved the land of his fathers, remarked in his urbane and sparkling *My Russia*, are not cuddly. Anthony was to compare the reaction of people once full of compassion for the "victims of communism" to that of visitors at the zoo, who coo over the tiger cubs in a cage only to discover that, in their natural state, these sweet, kittenish creatures bite and scratch.[2] Having long execrated the oppressive isolationism of the one-party state, people now shied away at the prospect of being engulfed by tough and wily immigrants whose cherished aim was to escape it and, one way or another, to ensure their own material survival in the free enterprise economy. These people were not, it seemed, even to co-religionists at first disposed to welcome them with all sympathy, of the stuff of martyrs. Quite apart from this, success breeds resentment and, as early as 1981, the success of the Cathedral appeal together with Anthony's great personal popularity was causing the occasional backlash in the press. Nicholas Coleridge, for instance, writing in *The Tatler*, chose to treat the extraordinary response to the Metropolitan's appeal for the Diocese of Sourozh, with its "nominal allegiance to Patriarch Pimen and the compromised Soviet Church", as a fashionable fad, on a par with the sudden rash of Russian restaurants, "good hunting ground for KGB agents", and the illicit trade in icons (forged or smuggled) that had sprung up as a result of relaxed Soviet controls over the movement of goods and people. Metropolitan Anthony, who looked, said Coleridge, not unlike Ayatollah Shariatmadari, was, he implied, a clearly bogus hot-gospeller "instrumental in the charismatic resurgence of Russian Orthodoxy". "Cosseted by a plethora of first, second and third generation Russians . . . Bloom has proven that Orthodoxy can still reap where it Soviets. . . ."[3]

Wisely, Anthony left it to his indignant parishioners to deal with this charivari of old anti-Soviet and new anti-Russian prejudice, but it was symptomatic of things to come, above all of an increasingly widespread distrust of the "new emigration" which was made possible by the gradual liberalisation of Russia that preceded *perestroika* and *glasnost'*, was greatly accelerated by the official adaptation of these policies, and attained the velocity of a riptide after the fall of communism.

For Anthony, watching the gradual lightening of the atmosphere, refraining from comment, determined to do nothing that might provoke a backlash or undermine the seemingly miraculous process of emancipation, this easing open of the sluice-gates of the communist-held human reservoir was something to be treated with the utmost care and reverence – the perilous breaking of the waters that heralds the advent of new life.

Such was the background to the disagreement between him and his old ally Vladimir Rodzianko, whose broadcasts to Russia over the years had shown an increasing tendency towards dramatisation and sensationalist foregrounding of dissident causes which people of the Church found embarrassing. When Anthony, in his capacity as chosen confessor and spiritual guide, pointed out that it was not good practice to make a spectacle of services of intercession featuring a beautiful girl holding a candle, Father Vladimir had replied hotly that he must be speaking under the influence of the KGB. It was with total approval, therefore, that, after the death of Rodzyanko's wife, Anthony welcomed the fiery cleric's decision to withdraw from public life and political broadcasting and to seek spiritual renewal in the Orthodox Seminary of St Vladimir in the United States. Rodzianko was professed monk with the name of Vasilii in the Cathedral of the Dormition and All Saints and, in 1980, the parish saw him off to his new retreat with all solemnity and not a little relief.

By nature a man of action rather than a contemplative, Vasilii soon moved on to be consecrated Bishop and to serve in a diocese of his own in the States. But he did not settle and Anthony was dismayed to hear that he felt he was being "eased out" of his new diocese and that his real vocation, after all, was recalling him to the service of the BBC. Surely, the Metropolitan replied with the asperity he appears to have exercised only towards his brothers in holy orders, Rodzyanko should devote himself to the episcopal care of his flock and to prayer rather than to political activity. In no uncertain terms, Anthony insisted on the "strongly negative reaction" of many people both in the Soviet Union and in the Orthodox diaspora to his broadcasts. At the BBC, he was neither "indispensable nor essential". Also, it was not easy to accommodate him in the ecclesiastical context. If he were to return to London he should expect to concelebrate at Ennismore Gardens "only by invitation" as there were people who found him "a very disturbing celebrant", whose flamboyant style was "quite opposed to that which had gradually and consciously been created". "My advice to you, therefore," the letter concludes, "is to have a sincere and repentant talk with the Primate, to become a Father to your flock, patient and humble, and to give up those of your activities for which both the OCA[i] and the Orthodox [in general?] are forced to carry a responsibility which they do not wish to carry, as they have not put you in charge either of their ecumenical or their political work: *Amiture Plato, sed major amica Veritas.*"[4]

This very sharp letter was not his final verdict on his old ally, who he remembered with fondness on hearing of his death in the autumn of 1999 on the morning of the day he had been due to be sworn in as a citizen of

---

i. Orthodox Church of America.

the United States. All who loved Bishop Vasilii, he wrote to the parishioner who gave him the news, were much saddened: "he will be remembered for his devotion to Orthodoxy and to Russia; for his directness and open-heartedness."[5] Their disagreement should be seen in the context of new hope for civic change from above in Russia. There had been many false dawns and blighted "thaws" followed by sharp relapses into winter in the history of the Soviet State, as in that of its relationship with the Russian Orthodox Church. Anthony did not want to see another relapse precipitated by Orthodoxy's well-meaning advocates from without.[6]

Indeed, the Metropolitan ushered in the millennial year of the Baptism of Rus', 1988, with a penitential sermon: there was, he felt, naught for our comfort in looking back over what Orthodox Russians had made of their 1000 years, or, for that matter, what all so-called Christians had accomplished in their nigh on 2000.[7]

The very fact that the millennium of the conversion of Russia was permitted to become something of a media event within the country, as well as an opportunity to show hospitality to other Christian churches worldwide, was made possible by the increasing openness of Soviet society and a marked relaxation in the regulations affecting both visiting foreigners and travelling Soviet citizens. There was already a noticeable increase in the number of individuals who had, metaphorically speaking, touched the hem of Metropolitan Anthony's cassock as he passed through Russia and who were now showing up in the Cathedral in Ennismore Gardens, having arranged to come to London as tourists, on business or on various cultural schemes. They longed to see more of this man who spoke of the half-forgotten faith of their ancestors as of a living religion capable of relinking and reconciling past and future, and who offered a bewildered generation a way to make sense of their present, to recover a sense of purpose.

Anthony was acutely aware of these expectations and of how inadequate to the demand, with a few lustrous exceptions, were the hierarchy, clergy and, indeed, the laity of the Orthodox Church in Russia, for so long now a closed community, always on the defensive, refraining on principle from contact with the non-Orthodox, forbidden to engage in open debate and condemned to the role of (often curmudgeonly) guardians of ancient truths, that it would seem dangerous and almost blasphemous to take out and re-examine in the light of contemporaneity. The Church as a whole was neither ready to educate those who sought baptism nor to communicate with the hesitant, nor, even, to set a moral example. Astute managers of the small, enclosed world left to them within the bounds of Soviet legality, the priesthood and the hierarchy had come to share something of the rest of their society's preoccupation with material things and to look upon the welfare of the Church as their responsibility while shouldering none whatsoever for that of the community. In theory, at least, it was the State that provided family allowances, pensions, free medical care, education and, in general, cradle-to-grave security – even the social reintegration of criminals, all in the name of the building of communism, an ideology that suffered no competition. Now, to replace this ideal with the building of the Kingdom (an interior as well as exterior exercise in which the end never justifies the means) required total readjustment, among the shepherds no less than among the milling multitudes of their scattered and alienated flock.[8] As Metropolitan Anthony wrote to an English correspondent:

> Changes had been creeping in for some time before the *Perestroika*. The attitude of society had been changing: many, disillusioned in communism, had begun to ask themselves first, then one another, two sorts of questions. "Is there any world view other than Communism that has failed us which could make sense of life, make it worth living?" and "Why are these people, law-abiding, earnest, possessed of an ideal whereas we have lost ours, why are they ostracised and persecuted?" . . . With the New Thinking and *Perestroika*, the fear that has kept people out of churches and silenced their questioning has vanished, speech becomes free and daring, questioning a normal process of thinking; and the State, in the face of a horrifying moral disintegration of society, has turned to the Church as the only organised body possessed of an ideology and unbending, solid moral principles. This has created a new climate and opened new avenues. Unfortunately, the Church is not ready for the challenge and for the task. Its structure has been broken or damaged by more than 70 years of Communist dictatorship; we lack people trained for a dialogue with unbelievers, people who can teach and train children, youngsters and adults; charitable work was forbidden before Gorbachev came to power as it was said that to help the poor would be a way of bribing them to become believers. An immense upsurge of energy is visible, mainly among the intellectuals, who are trying in many unrelated ways to meet the immense needs of the day. Doctors are forming associations of Christian doctors and investigating the possibility of evolving a Christian psychiatry. Hospices are being founded, volunteers are offering their services in hospitals, prisons can now be visited by members of the clergy and re-education work is beginning there; schools and universities are inviting believers – lay or not – to give lectures and new courses. Hope is growing, but problems grow as fast. Brought up under a dictatorship that allowed no independent thinking, most people have to learn to make choices, take decisions and be answerable for them, and this is not easy to learn. (It took 40 years for the Jews to cross the peninsula of Sinai under Moses so a whole generation could die and the remnant forget "the way of slaves" and become free men and women.)[9]

Naturally, the great need of Russian society as a whole, as well as the coming and going of individuals in his home diocese, added to the burden of obligation under which Metropolitan Anthony, with his plummeting blood pressure and uncertain heart, was already staggering. It was a new challenge, an opportunity beyond his wildest dreams when, as a youth, he had studied so hard in order – someday, perhaps – to be of service to Russia, an opportunity to be embraced with sober gratitude and quiet enthusiasm. He was needed, as never before, by his Mother Church and the Russian people. The unprecedented exposure to Russian and Eastern European initiatives, however, also entailed fending off tiresome "business propositions" such as Metropolitan Pitirim's suggestion that he should approach Maxwell to publish an English version of the sumptuous album *The Trinity and Saint Sergius Monastery*, which could be sold at the Cathedral bookshop, the proceeds going to the Russian Orthodox Church in Great Britain. This Anthony declined to do on the grounds that Maxwell was involved in the organisation of conferences that were notoriously anti-Christian and specifically anti-Orthodox.[10] On the other hand, as his own books began to come out legally in Russia in the early 1990s, so pirated translations cropped up all across Eastern Europe, and he had to exhort his English publishers to stand firm for his own author's rights. Inevitably, the Metropolitan and members of his congregation were beset by requests for assistance in getting jobs, work or residence permits, for hospitality or pecuniary help, and for permission to use their telephones (a service that had cost next to nothing in the Soviet Union and was thoughtlessly abused by visitors from it).[11] Apart from those who looked to the church for enlightenment, guidance, spiritual comfort and truth, there were not a few who saw it as a location to contact fellow Russians well-established in Great Britain or even, simply, as a soft touch. Core members of the diocese were at first at a loss, then began to grumble and resent the new demands made upon the time and strength of their Bishop as an imposition on his goodness and other-worldliness: here, though, they undoubtedly underrated his shrewdness, psychological penetration and his far from rosy, essentially tragic worldview.

All of these were amply demonstrated by the Metropolitan's firm, albeit usually patient and benevolent, handling of individual cases. He would never, he wrote in 1990 to Father Simeon of the monastery at Tolleshunt Knights, send anyone to them "as a means to stay in this country". Far too many people recently had been trying "to use the Church as a source of income, or as a provider of accommodation or as a guarantor". Equally, when, as did occasionally happen, the odd enterprising individual turned up purporting to collect money for Christians in Russia, he was quick to check their *bona fides* with the Russian Church at home.

It was, of course, only natural that the wider English public and, indeed, the international community, soon began to turn to Metropolitan Anthony to elucidate shifts in Soviet policy and, above all, what they meant for the Orthodox Church in his own country. At first, he was cautious, declining invitations to speak on *glasnost'* on the grounds that "as far as the Church in Russia is concerned the situation is not clear enough for me to make a responsible contribution to your discussion – both believers and hierarchy are full of hope, the atmosphere is much lighter, but the future is still wrapped in uncertainty".[12] In July 1988 he was unable to attend a lunchtime meeting of Anglican chaplains to discuss the impact of *glasnost'* on religion in the USSR, but suggested they invite a lay scholar, Irina Kirillova, in his place. He likewise regretfully declined to speak about the changes in Russia at a conference on the millennium of Russian Christianity at UNESCO headquarters on 28-30 June 1988 or even to send a representative of his diocese, but passed on their invitation to the Exarch of the Russian Orthodox Church in Western Europe, Metropolitan Vladimir. Towards the end of the year, however, he agreed to speak in the context of the millennium to the LSE at King's College on 19 October and at the Church of Christ the King on 9 November.[13]

As always, the Metropolitan felt more confident speaking and acting in an ecclesiastical context and readily consented to celebrate the millennium with an Orthodox Liturgy on 11 July 1988, and to host the annual Festival of Anglican and Eastern Churches at a Liturgy at the Cathedral and afterward at Holy Trinity, Brompton, at a reception in their hospitable church hall.[14] In Russia, he attended both the pre-millennial Conference of Bishops in May 1988 and the Solemn Commemoration of the Baptism of Rus' later that summer.

As far as relations between the Diocese of Sourozh and the Moscow Patriarchate were concerned, it was unfortunate that the latter declined Anthony's suggestion that Militza Zernova accompany him to the millennium celebrations as a representative of the laity – not so much for her sake as because he wanted his Russian colleagues and their people to see the concentrated beauty of her face as she stood in church! The refusal was seen as something of a snub to the women and intellectuals of the diocese. Still, the celebrations – however exhausting – were magnificent and deeply touching, and from now on Anthony embraced every opportunity to share his pastoral experience with colleagues in Russia. Priests, he regretted, were taught theology in the seminaries, but not pastoral practice. At the same time, he defended his Russian colleagues fiercely against uninformed criticism: "You never had to live their lives and wouldn't want to," he would cut short criticisms from members of his own congregation. This did not mean, however, that he lost the opportunity to go in for constructive advice – on the contrary.

For the first time, his printed works began to be legally available in the USSR. The millennial year saw the publication of a modest enough article in the newspaper *Semia* ("The Family"). Anthony's message was primarily

Chapter Nine

Celebration of 400 years of the Moscow Patriarchate, October 1989 ("long hours of standing and processing in full archiepiscopal regalia")

that freedom – so talked about at this time in Russia – was something to be established from within, the "perfect freedom" of learning to live simply, within one's means, in the service of Christ and in constant readiness to lay down one's life. This freedom was not something that could be taken away by other people.

At his last visit before the millennial year in May 1987, he had been asked to lecture on spiritual direction, an opportunity to speak out against a worrying trend among inexperienced pastors to assume premature responsibility for and authority over penitents, putting unready souls "under obedience" to youthful "elders" (*mladostarchestvo*). As always, he taught that the relationship between penitent and spiritual director should be voluntary and involve helping the one who had sought direction to go on, on his own, to meet his God. It seemed, in his teaching, that priests were not a race apart, but human beings like everyone else with the same high calling to restore the image of God in themselves and their flock. The message, directly and simply conveyed, as always with love and humour, was avidly received.[15]

In October 1989, there was another great ecclesiastical anniversary in Russia, the fourth centenary of the foundation of the Moscow Patriarchate, entailing more dressing up in all the splendour of his Metropolitan episcopal gear, the high white hat and heavy robes, worn for hours through the long, standing services and shuffling processions, as well as attendance at a seemingly endless "solemn act" (according to Anthony's lively and irreverent Deacon, Peter Scorer, "boring beyond belief"),[16] at which delegates delivered themselves of lengthy speeches in the foyer of the Rossiia Hotel. As usual, however, Anthony made good use of the ceremonial visit to make himself available to his fellow countrymen and, this time, the watchdogs of communist ideology appeared to have given up fencing him off from the wider public. He was actually allowed to speak at a lay gathering at the House of the Artist in Stoleshnikov Pereulok in central Moscow – his one and only non-ecclesiastical live public appearance in Russia. There was not enough room for all those who came and one of those present recalled "we only dispersed because it was time to shut down the venue".[17]

As was evident from Anthony's address to the clergy and people of the Diocese of Sourozh in the winter of 1989,[18] he was exhausted. In theory, he could have retired as ruling Bishop in June that same year at the age of seventy-five, but the Patriarch asked him to stay on and it was not until the following year that he acceded to the Metropolitan's persistent requests to allot him an assistant bishop to help look after the increasing numbers of Russians in the London diocese and, in the fullness of time, God willing, to provide a successor who had had "time to experience and accustom himself to the Church in Great Britain". His choice had fallen on a quiet, kindly and learned monk at whose enthronement as Bishop he himself had assisted. Vladyka Anatolii had served the Russian Church in Damascus and Lithuania, acting with tact and circumspection in strained situations between Christians and Muslims, Orthodox and Roman Catholics, and had been well-respected by all parties; as Bishop of Ufa, a largely Muslim area, he had actually been proposed to stand for the new Russian multi-party elected Parliament, an honour he had refused in the interests of his ecclesiastical duties. "I first addressed myself to him himself to find out if he would be willing to become my Vicar Bishop while I am still in charge of the Diocese," the Metropolitan informed his flock, "and then, if he and the diocese come to love one another and unite in a creative alliance of mutual trust, respect and unanimity in the understanding of God's ways in the west, become heir to my diocesan throne."[19]

On obtaining Anatolii's consent, he approached members of the Synod of the Russian Church, individually and officially, expressing his readiness to continue in office – on condition he was allotted a suffragan bishop – and, after due discussion, the Patriarch himself.[20] At last:

> I received a telegram informing me of the appointment of Bishop Anatolii as Vicar of the Diocese of Sourozh with the right to succeed me if that be the will of God and the Orthodox people, the faithful of our diocese. By this decision the future and independence of our diocese are assured. Rejoice with me![21]

The faithful, however, did not rejoice. They had never had so much as a priest appointed from without the diocese, never mind from Moscow, and it was widely considered Anthony had acted like a real old-fashioned *despota* without prior consultation and against the spirit of their statutes. Even his old friend Militza Zernova wrote in from Oxford to protest. Their Metropolitan's plea that he had sought in vain for a suitable bishop in the Patriarchal Church in Europe and the Orthodox Church of America, that the influx of Russians made it essential that his suffragan should be at home in the language, that the diocese lacked monks and that Anatolii was a good man, chosen with care, did not altogether mollify them. They disliked being presented with a *fait accompli* – even by their beloved Vladyka.

Thus Metropolitan Anthony's first attempt to insure the future of a truly Anglo-Russian Orthodox diocese got off to a rocky start at home in London. Though naturally his vicar, when he arrived, was met with due courtesy and caused no offence, he was never totally assimilated into the multi-cultural yet essentially homogeneous Sourozh community in London.

Meanwhile, Metropolitan Anthony's popularity in Russia – both among the disorientated Soviet intelligentsia and within the Church – was on the up and up. When Patriarch Pimen died on 5 May 1990, he attended the *Sobor* convened to elect a new Patriarch in the company of Anna Garret, the church warden, for the laity, and Father John Lee. "We thought we were going to lose our Bishop," Anna Garret reported back to the flabbergasted diocesan council. Protopriest Boris Pivovarov, Chairman of the Department of Religious Education in the Diocese of Novosibirsk, supported by the young Hieromonk Ilarion (Alfeyev) who had been studying for a PhD in Oxford and so knew the Diocese of Sourozh and its Metropolitan at first hand, got up to propose from the floor the candidature of Anthony, Metropolitan of Sourozh, as Patriarch of all the Russias. For the proposal to go forward, however, it would be necessary to abrogate article 17 of the fifth chapter of the 1930 Statutes of Governance of the Russian Orthodox Church, which stated that any candidate for the Patriarchate must be a citizen of the USSR. If this point could be annulled, it would clear the way for the Metropolitan of Sourozh who had "all the spiritual distinction" necessary for the role of Archpastor. The Russian Church, his proposers insisted, was losing whole parishes if not dioceses because of the decline of the hierarchy's spiritual authority, a decline that the election of Anthony would reverse. Financial cupidity and a supine attitude to authority verging on collaboration in the "period of stagnation"[i] had led to this loss of moral authority. Anthony, respected throughout the world, politically non-confrontational, a man of moral and ascetic integrity and living spiritual experience, would re-establish respect and could and would do much to heal the rift between the Patriarchal

---

i. Roughly coinciding with Brezhnev's time as Premier.

Church and the Russian Church abroad. It might be argued that he lacked experience in Russia, but, with the co-operation of the Synod, this could be overcome. He might, at seventy-six, be considered old for the job, but think of John XXIII, elected at eighty! Also, he was not retired, but known to be coping capably with a huge pastoral workload. "So," Pivovarov concluded, "I ask for the inclusion of Metropolitan Anthony amongst the candidates for the Patriarchate."[22]

Point 17 of the Statutes was, however, upheld, and Anthony's candidature did not, therefore, go forward. He was instead appointed with acclaim to oversee the counting of votes, in itself a homage to his international reputation and perceived integrity – as well as to his seniority; he was now the longest-serving hierarch in the Moscow Patriarchal Church.[23]

Several names were put forward and the vote went to a recount but, eventually, went in favour of the 62-year-old Aleksii, born in Estonia during that country's inter-war period as a free republic and, like Anthony, of émigré parentage. Preaching on the election of the Patriarch in London after his return from Russia, Metropolitan Anthony, as he had so often before, quoted St Paul on strength through weakness and that same Apostle's "I can do all things through Christ that strengtheneth me":[24]

> This is what we should pray for, when we think of our Patriarch! We should surround him with love, veneration, but also with heartfelt prayers that, if needed, we will give him all the support of which we are capable.
>
> We will remember him every day, because his task is so complex. The Lord grant him wisdom so that he may distinguish the signs of the times, but not with the eyes of the world, deciding the questions which arise before him with unedified common sense, but rather that he should make out the signs of the times and the ways of God in our time! God grant him the suppleness to perceive, year in, year out, in ever changing circumstances, the footsteps of God along the paths of history. The Lord grant him to become a true intercessor for the Church, for every human soul, believing and unbelieving, for the land which is now so tragically torn apart, which is falling apart before our eyes; for the country in which he was born and the other countries which lost their freedom: Lithuania, Estonia, Latvia, Georgia, Moldavia, – and for all the people who long for a freedom which, it may be, they themselves do not truly understand when they look for freedom on a worldly scale, in a worldly dimension. And we must pray, and he will pray for that freedom, which is the freedom of the children of God. <u>Know the Truth, and the Truth will make you free</u>, says Holy Writ.
>
> Let us pray for him: let us sing him "Many years", that the Lord

should grant him long and fruitful life, should give him strength and steadfastness of heart to carry his cross, that is our cross. And let us, like Simon of Cyrene, keep close beside him to offer a shoulder when and where needed, so the cross should not crush him, should not prove too heavy, so that we all together should be saved and, when the day comes, he should be able to stand before God and say: these are the children you gave me, – saved, all saved. Amen.[25]

These were not empty words. In October 1991, Patriarch Aleksii II attended the Conference of European Churches in Durham and visited his Diocese of Sourozh and Lambeth Palace from 28 to 30 October. Accompanied by Metropolitan Anthony, he was received by her Majesty Elizabeth II – an unthinkable event but a few years earlier. True to the exhortation in his sermon on the enthronement of the Patriarch, Anthony from then on, with all his failing strength, was to endeavour to keep close to his side and to offer a shoulder when and where he judged this to be needed: to advise and criticise as a good colleague, as concerned with the fate of the Orthodox Church in Russia as in Western Europe. When he was not well enough to attend the annual Episcopal Conference, he wrote to the Patriarch – personally, frankly and incisively – on matters of Church policy. Indeed, so absorbed was he by the stirring events in Russia that he even wrote to Boris Eltsin on the Feast of the Transfiguration 1991 after he so memorably faced down the August coup that turned out to be a last-ditch attempt to restore communism, distressed not to be present "in these days of heroism and the resurrection of Russia. Boris Nikolaevich, God give you the strength, the courage, the firmness and the wisdom, which you so unforgettably demonstrated in those August days and which you need now on the long, hard and thorny road to love, to Transfiguration, that Russia must tread."[26]

The letters to the Patriarch deal with problems arising along this "long, hard and thorny road". The first, which raises questions he would have broached at the Bishop's Conference in 1991 had he not been unable to attend for reasons of health, is primarily devoted to the highly volatile state of the Orthodox Church in Ukraine. Roman Eastern Rite Catholics (or Uniates) were reclaiming church buildings confiscated from them under the Soviets and the Ukrainian Orthodox Church was itself divided between nationalists who stood for autocephaly and loyalists who adhered to the Moscow Patriarchate. Anthony advised that autocephaly, or at least maximal autonomy, should be granted as soon as possible. Independence freely given makes for reconciliation, but independence that has to be achieved by struggle, for bitterness and estrangement. A new leader should be elected by a local council comprising not only senior hierarchs but reflecting the whole complexity of the situation on the ground. To heal division within the Orthodox Church "the widest economy" should be practised, for excommunications and taboos lead only to lasting disaffection. Readiness to take the initiative and to apologise for mistakes "we ourselves" may have made in the past will gain the moral high ground for the Moscow Church, whose reputation is now on the mend worldwide. As for the Uniates, he adds in a characteristically mistrustful *post scriptum*, dialogue with both them and Rome itself is not to be avoided but should be approached with caution. Rome's final aim, he has been told, is the elimination of Orthodoxy and, as Vladimir Solov'ev says, "When I meet my brother I always ask myself whether his name is Cain or Abel."[27]

The theme of Orthodoxy in Ukraine recurs in a letter of 5 June 1992, in which Anthony endorses the removal of Philaret, Metropolitan of Kiev, in favour of the appointment of Vladimir, at present of Rostov and Novocherkask, to the throne of an independent Church of Ukraine. On a more sensitive issue, he advises that the small commission set up to investigate the co-operation of bishops with the KGB should be "transparent but merciful", aiming for reconciliation and mindful of the terrible pressures to which individuals are subjected. "Such justice should not dare to become a witch-hunt" – but neither, if the Church wishes to keep the respect of the people and stop the drift towards various heresies, should it be a cover-up.[28]

Defections from the Russian Orthodox Church had indeed become a problem in the unprecedented situation of freedom of religious propaganda in the newly formed Confederation of Independent States. Missionaries of the most varied Christian and non-Christian creeds, some genuinely anxious to reclaim a spiritually hungry populace for their own understanding of the religious life, others, less reputable, scenting potentially rich and virtually unguarded fields to harvest, inundated the country, and their success was proportionate to lingering distrust for the officially tolerated Orthodox Church and to its lack of outreach, especially to the young, who were attracted by the exoticism and friendliness of the various missionary movements. Anthony, with a lifetime's experience of interfaith society and of readiness to talk to anybody from hippies to charismatics to militant atheists, was in a position to advise.

The third letter to the Patriarch preserved in the MASF Archive, however, was confined to preoccupations proper to his own diocese and to his own representative role for the Russian Church in the United Kingdom. Prince Philip, whom Anthony had met on the occasion of his receiving an honorary doctorate at Cambridge University and with whom he got on very well indeed, was to come to Russia the following year to attend an ecological conference and to facilitate the Russian Federation in cleaning up pressing ecological problems resulting from industrial pollution. It would be fitting were he to receive a personal invitation to visit the Patriarch. In mid-July, Anthony continues, he will be sending Basil Osborne, recently widowed, to familiarise himself with the workings of the Patriarchal Church and to improve his Russian. He asks permission to accept Osborne's vows as a monk prior to consecrating him Bishop in the presence of his children, so that they could wholeheartedly go along with his new dedication without the bitter feeling that their father was being taken from them so soon after the loss of their mother. Bishop Anatolii, he adds, is providing invaluable support to the many new arrivals from Russia.

In the Cathedral bookshop, August 1995

This letter signals a changing situation in London, where Anatolii was to devote himself increasingly to caring for the ever-growing russophone congregation, whereas long-term members of the diocese felt more at home with the newly consecrated Bishop Basil, who had emerged, via the Oxford parish, from their own ranks. Anthony's attempt to acclimatise him to the Russian Church through a period of further study in Moscow was, perhaps predictably, not altogether successful. The new Bishop, sensitive and intellectually fastidious, did not find it easy to fraternise with the down-to-earth, in part stubbornly conservative Russian hierarchy. He did not "speak their language" and tended to keep to his own sort.[29]

Anthony, however, did not give up. His next letter is a concentrated attempt to share his own cosmopolitan, twentieth-century vision with the Russian Patriarch. There had been an ecclesiastical meeting in the Danilov Monastery where, as Anthony had been told, a strong current of opinion had been expressed in favour of locking the Church firmly in the traditions of times past. There was a difference, he argued, between the veneration of tradition and false "traditionalism":

> Tradition (*predanie*) is the living memory of the Church creatively active from generation to generation. Traditionalism is the moribund observance of what was done in the past. . . . As you know, I am not a supporter of "modernisation of the Church", but the Church is obliged to look into the needs and problems of the contemporary world and to respond to them in a language comprehensible to those who put the

questions. That is what the Fathers of the Church did – seeking "the mind of Christ" and recognising both the reality and the justice of the demand for new ways of thought. This applies to all spheres of life, in particular to the language in which we proclaim the truth: too often sermons are pronounced in the dry language of scholastic theology and make no impression on the listeners. The services themselves it seems should only be allowed to be celebrated in Church Slavonic, not particularly comprehensible if not totally incomprehensible to the modern person. Thank God Byzantium understood this at the dawn of Christianity in our own country! Otherwise we would all still be praying in the Byzantine Greek dialect, which is no longer fully comprehensible even to modern Greeks. . . .

The harassing of Father Georgii Kochetkov, who advocated services in modern Russian, and now of Father Aleksandr Borisov, had, the Metropolitan wrote, a distinct whiff of the fabled Roman Catholic inquisition.

Among other questions he felt bound to raise were the Russian Orthodox Church's attitudes to the ecumenical movement and to the need for an "inner Renaissance in our own Church".

Ecumenical work is not a betrayal of the Church and does not have to involve any compromise. . . . We need to be there, amongst those of other Confessions, so that they should encounter Orthodoxy and their own root faith, but also to listen thoughtfully to the reproaches levelled at us, the accusations. . . .[30]

The second question, he writes, the need for "inner Renaissance" and moral renewal among the clergy, should not be glossed over. It is precisely the perceived subservience and cupidity of the Moscow Church that is causing many Orthodox in Russia to turn to the Russian Orthodox Church outside Russia – and this at a time when Anthony himself and the ROCOR Archbishop Mark of Berlin and Germany are doing all they can "to acknowledge our ideological closeness and to co-operate wherever possible in care for the Old and New Russian Emigration".[31]

True, he goes on, there will be no re-unification of the Russian Church outside Russia with the Moscow Patriarchate as long as the former is led by Metropolitan Vitalii, who looks upon all who acknowledge the legitimacy of Patriarch Sergii as children of Satan. Nevertheless, the groundswell of opinion is now such in both Churches that re-unification is bound to come. Could we not therefore, even now, establish mutual tolerance and intercommunion with them as we do with other national Orthodox jurisdictions? This would pave the way to eventual reconciliation.

The question of the infiltration of Russian Orthodox by other confessions is a related one and should not be countered by "legal action" unless what is being preached is, indeed, illegal or harmful; on the contrary, the Orthodox should learn to meet proponents of other confessions on their own ground, not "holed up defensively in their churches but on street corners, in football stadiums" – as he himself had once preached in the docks of Aberdeen and London, in the streets of Oxford. It is necessary to learn to think quickly, to speak the language of doubters and hostile people, "to penetrate their psychology, to translate the Truth into their language, which will make them able to receive it, and so save them". To counter infiltration of minds and hearts by the Roman Catholics, whose appeal is often to the educated,

> ... it is necessary to create in all haste yet not hastily but thoroughly trained activists of wide culture from laity and clergy, who are capable of responding "well" to the intellectual and spiritual quests of our fellow-countrymen.

And one last thing that requires to be said:

> The Church, that is Her members, need to think deeply about the question of anti-Semitism. We need to separate politics from theology, the state of Israel from what St Paul calls God's Israel – and make it clear to priests and laity that we do not tolerate those who sow enmity: doctrinal, national, even political.[32]

Some letters were written merely to keep the Patriarch in touch with the problems of the Sourozh diocese and the clergy at their disposal. Others were to request favours for Orthodox clerics who had been working in Europe and who wanted to serve in Russia.

In 1997, the Metropolitan again missed a meeting of bishops "for health reasons" and sent "some thoughts" to be conveyed by his suffragan bishops Anatolii and Basil. This year, he informed the Patriarch, the diocese will celebrate, "or bewail", the fortieth anniversary of his own consecration as Bishop. Acutely aware of the possible loss of direction after his death, Metropolitan Anthony officially requested that the Patriarch designate his successor, Bishop Basil having by then emerged as the most wished for and, to his mind, most suitable candidate, and he asked the Patriarch to take a good look at him and, if he would, to give his blessing to his taking over the day-to-day running of the diocese while he, Anthony, was still around to ease the transition. "I really am failing!" ("Deistvitel'no sdaiu!")[33]

However, as we have seen, Bishop Basil appears to have had no more natural empathy for his Russian colleagues than had Bishop Anatolii for those core members of the English diocese who had initially resented his appointment. The attempt at grafting these divergent sprigs of the community, so successful in Anthony's own vulnerable person, was still at the cut-and-bandage stage. Both men were essentially shy, retiring, scholarly and non-confrontational, and their natural tendency was to continue as long as possible under the benevolent wing of their Metropolitan Bishop, each complementing the other's input but retaining their separate identities. However, from now on Bishop Basil did increasingly shoulder the burden of the day-to-day administration of the London diocese, though the Metropolitan continued to lead retreats and be a central presence in the life of the Cathedral.

In 1998, however, aware of the impending council summoned to revise the Statutes of the Russian Patriarchal Church imposed upon them by the communist government in 1930, the Metropolitan took the opportunity to send Patriarch Aleksii II a copy of the statutes of the Diocese of Sourozh, vigorously recommending them for the consideration of those who were to take council for the Church in Russia:

> We are aware that the Council (Sobor) of 1999 is to review and, perhaps, to reconsider the present Statutes of our Church and that, in the light of the conclusions to which they come, changes will be introduced both in the Statutes of the Russian Church as a whole and in our Statutes; but we sincerely believe that the particular vision expressed in our Statutes may deepen and broaden the vision of the local Council. . . .

In the accompanying letter, Anthony made an eloquent case for the Sourozh Constitution: it is, he says, his testament, inspired by the work of the Local Council convened under Patriarch Tikhon, who is now canonised as a Saint of the Orthodox Church:

> But the task before us was not just to adapt the immutable rules of the past to circumstances which could not have been foreseen and which could not have been pre-decided. We immersed ourselves in the study of the past of our Church in a thoughtful and creative attempt to perceive what in our ecclesiastical regulations expressed eternal, unchanging Truth and what was justifiably conditioned by historical, that is national and cultural, but also political circumstances.
>
> We clearly realised that the diaspora, in which we lived, was not merely a transient moment in the life of various local churches to which we belonged, was not a fortuitous development that could be straightened out through the reorganisation of Ecclesiastical administration under the leadership and authority of those historic Churches from the depths of which a New Reality had been born. We came to the firm conclusion that the Orthodox Dispersion, Diaspora, had brought us back to that time when the Christian world, the Church of Christ, was a living, all-embracing Flame of Life; a society of people who were at one despite all human boundaries, being at one with Christ and in Christ, a single Body living by one and the

same Spirit, a Body in which "all are children of God by faith in Jesus Christ" . . . where "there is neither Jew nor Greek, there is neither bond nor free, there is neither male nor female: for ye are all one in Christ Jesus." (Gal. 3:26-28).

The statutes, in other words, amounted to a new declaration of unity throughout the Orthodox diaspora:

> [A]ccording to this vision, this was no longer merely the presence of representatives of various native Churches in non-Orthodox countries but rather a Church in itself, alive, simultaneously "in a state of becoming" and already complete in unity in Christ.
> Strictly observing the rules of the Church but aware that tradition is "the living memory of the Church", calling all to greater maturity, enlightened by the wisdom of the past, the common past of all Orthodox Christians, yet capable of expressing in unprecedented circumstances the Eternal Newness of the Divine Life, poured out upon us and accepted, giving us a New Vision, new only because it is an Eternal vision and so present in the time we live in and permeating it. "Behold! I make all things new."[34]

A letter written in the same year to the Orthodox church in Oxford, which the Russians actually shared and do still share with the Greeks, on the occasion of the twentieth anniversary of its consecration, showed how dearly the ageing Metropolitan valued this vision of Orthodox unity and the reconciliation not only of the splintered Russian Orthodox Church but of all national Orthodox churches. The Oxford community, he said, was "an expression of Unity beyond all barriers, but we have not yet achieved this purpose, to create a Church where all Orthodox are at home and at one because they are Christ's own people, yet bringing a multiplicity of gifts and a variety of experience born of our various historical pasts. May God grant you, and, indeed, all of us, to become more perfectly one, yet unique, as the voices of a choir – all different, blending in a single, glorious harmony."[35]

This holistic vision was, at the turn of the century, more than an old man's dream. It was in process of embodiment through unremitting labour, triumph and failure, trial and error . . . but it was not, as Anthony rightly foresaw, a hope to be realised in his lifetime. Neither, to his sorrow, did the impetus that he had done so much to create appear destined to survive him in a changing world. As one of his most ardent admirers, the Russian scholar and poet Sergei Averintsev once remarked of his own work: "While we are building bridges over huge rivers of ignorance these rivers are changing their courses."[36]

Indeed, the local Council in Russia did not so much as consider the Sourozh statutes. For quite different reasons, Anthony's next letter to the

Patriarch was written "for the first time . . . not with joy, but with pain". Its subjects were the cautious failure of the leaders of the Patriarchal Church in Russia either openly to honour the past or wholeheartedly to defend the new: the internment of the remains of the royal family in St Petersburg and the burning of allegedly heretical books in a ceremony reminiscent of the notorious Black Hundred which – to the scandal of the whole Christian world – had been enacted in the very city in which the Tsar and his family were executed: Ekaterinburg. Why, asked Anthony sorrowfully, did the supreme hierarchy of the Russian Church boycott the internment of the royal family? Why did they have to be more cautious than Boris Eltsin? The absence of the Church hierarchy on this occasion had been most painful to the Russian Church abroad. As to the book-burning: the Patriarch's letters to himself and other representatives of the Russian Orthodox Church in the West were "unconvincing". The Church should disassociate Herself clearly and completely from so barbarous a ceremony, Anthony asserted. Please, he implored Aleksii, send at least a private letter which I could show to individuals to comfort the worried and confused.[i] Forgive me, he adds, this "bitter" but "just" letter.[37]

Metropolitan Anthony's health was failing. For many years now he had been "doing everything in spite of pain".[38] He walked with a stick and, during service, with a ceremonial staff. Yet his letters to the Patriarch continue in a vein of active day-to-day co-operation. On 1 July 1999 he wrote asking Aleksii to receive Stephen Platt, Secretary of the Anglo-Orthodox Fellowship of St Alban and St Sergius, who would be presented by Father Ilarion (who had, of course, got to know him in Oxford), and to thank the Patriarch for the "truly missionary" award of the Order of St Inokentii recently bestowed upon himself.[39]

Another distinction conferred on Anthony in this same penultimate year of the twentieth century was an honorary doctorate from the Kiev Theological Academy which, he wrote to their President Metropolitan Vladimir, he was happy to accept "*amoris causa*", but was in no state to travel to Kiev to receive: "My health has got shaky and I've not much strength."[40] "Look after yourself," they replied. "You are dear to us and we need you."

Indeed he was, and they did, and it was not only the hierarchy of the Church in Russia which looked to the beloved, now venerable figure who, it seemed to very many, was in every sense their contemporary, yet had "the words of Eternal Life".

"It is as if he stood at the very brink of the first source" is the title of a 2000 article by the psychologist Fedor Vasiliuk. The article, located "London-

---

i. Among the books destroyed were works by Alexander Schmemann, the Orthodox theologian now living in the United States, who Anthony had known as a younger candidate for the priesthood in Paris, and other émigré theologians from the Orthodox Church of America.

Moscow" and published in a Parisian émigré newspaper, is by a Russian author who had read Anthony's books, listened to tapes, seen videos, but, nevertheless, found their first meeting face to face (at one of the Effingham conferences) "exceeded all expectations". How? Superficially speaking: his simplicity and the immediate feeling of entering into "some kind of very close contact".

> Also, among the immediate impressions: temperament, the passion of his speech, the passion of his presence in a conversation is such that here, in Russia, even had they experienced any such thing, most people would have thought it only proper to suppress it.... More than anything, come to think of it, I was impressed by something which seemed to go against all the laws of psychology. The man never ceased to wonder, every time afresh and anew, at spiritual events ... it's as if this was something outside normal time, not a repeat of something already told and retold. It was an immersion of self in that sphere of feelings, thoughts and happenings, particularly from the Gospel, where he was once again actually present. But this presence is, every time, for the first time. What happens to me, then, as I listen to him? I begin, thanks to the way he tells the story, to be present there with him.... There are absolutely no laws of psychology which can explain this absence of accustomisation ... it is a break with those laws.

The oft-repeated story of his conversion, told always as though *sub specie aeternitatis*, suggests an immediate, apostolic calling which explains that "shattering freedom which imbues his texts.... It is as though he always stands at the very brink of the first source and, because of this, is speaking for the first time.... And hence the impression of freshness, of ever self-renewing youth, because only the unjaded view of a 17-year-old youth could be so full of wonder."[41] This stumbling yet exceptionally cogent effort to explain the appeal of Anthony's speech far exceeds national, temporal, or cultural boundaries. What the Metropolitan of Sourozh meant precisely to educated Russian Christians brought up in the Soviet Union is, however, well-documented.

By chance, Aleksandr Ogorodnikov, a God-seeking but still godless Soviet-educated youth brought up to think the Church was the exclusive province of the ignorant, the superstitious and, above all, the superannuated, but with aspirations to change the world, stumbled upon a service in Moscow, where there was a press of people ("*educated* people, you could tell by their faces") about the Church. Consumed with curiosity, he managed to work his way into the building, where Anthony was celebrating – "not even preaching, just celebrating". For the first time he felt at one with all that was going on here, and went up with the others to take communion. Afterwards, he began organising his with-it, dynamic young friends to attend religious seminars, underwent brutal persecution as a dissident Christian that sparked off worldwide protests, and made friends with the Bishop whose living faith had given direction to his life.[42]

There are so many stories of the difference Anthony made to the lives of those who became his spiritual children and even of those who simply caught a glimpse of him in passing, of people helped by his prayers or encouraged by a timely phone call or letter expressing unexpected, absolute solidarity at moments of crisis. Some of them, such as the account written by the Russian film-director Valentina Matveevna, are extremely personal:

> About 20 years ago misfortune struck – I fell ill. The doctors gave me one year. My friends decided I should get christened. "What's the point?" I asked. "I'll soon be dead." "All the more reason to get christened", they replied. There was no Bible and – in those days – no getting hold of one, but I needed some preparation. And so somebody brought me – on fragile copy-paper from a wonky old typewriter: "Metropolitan Anthony of Sourozh. Sermons and talks". . . . I began to read. And a kind of warmth entered my cramped, twisted soul, sickened as it was by unshed tears, and it was as though someone had lit a fire, temperate, not burning but warming, and I felt physically that the pain and darkness were receding. "That man has met God", I thought. "If he believes in Him, so will I." Ten years later I met Bishop Anthony in England, 15 years later made a film about it and called it "Vstrecha" (Meeting or Encounter).[43]

More objective is the witness of the much-loved scholar Sergei Averintsev, one of the first members of the new Russian Parliament to be elected from the Academy of Sciences and author of later partially rescinded legislation on religious tolerance, who made a point of attending church whenever the Metropolitan was known to be serving in the Soviet Union and of seeking him out privately when it became possible to travel:

> But by common consent for all of us, for several generations of Russians alive today, the embodiment of Christ's authentic, pure Gospel, incompatible either with Phariseeism or with dumbing down in the spirit of the times, has become, or so it seems to me, this man: Vladyka Anthony. His spiritual presence in the mirky atmosphere of the post-Soviet decades – I mean, of course, his visits to Russia, his sermons, talks, but also the reading of his sermons in self-published copies (v samizdatskikh spiskakh) and simply the awareness that there is such a man in the world, – was not something anybody else could have given us. Let others tell what his labours meant for Orthodoxy in England . . . but I was only there as a traveller accustomed from the cradle to all kinds of hardships but, also, to the conveniences, the mental comfort of non-freedom. Vladyka reminded us not only by

what he said but also by what he was that we are all, in the words of the Apostle Paul, "called unto liberty" (Gal.5:13). Liberty is demanding; according to the same New Testament text, we must "stand fast" in it (Gal.5:1) – and yes, indeed, there can be no sitting back, no lounging about here, you just have to stand and to stand fast, with all your might. For Vladyka, this was some kind of central theme. (I remember how I hurried to consult him on some of my post-Soviet problems and received the austerely-spoken reply: "Learn to be free!" And the way he looked at me: no more need for words.)[44]

Casting his mind back to Soviet times, Averintsev recalled, as did many others,[45] the difficulties put in Anthony's way by the authorities, the demonstrative surveillance and attempts to intimidate both the man himself and those who wished to talk to him privately – and how triumphantly these were evaded and ignored by this priest of God, who, though careful of the harm he might do to others, gave absolutely no thought to his own safety or convenience:

> In the days he came to Moscow the flood of visitors to his hotel room would begin to dry up well after midnight; and then the hotel staff would come knocking at his door, simply to have a word. If there is anything harder to give up than property, possessions, then it is surely the minutes one can live for oneself, at peace. He gave them up.[46]

More detailed and analytical again is the witness of Aleksandr Kyrlezhev, a member of the Synodal Biblical-Theological Commission in Moscow:

> In our opinion, Vladyka Anthony's particular, specific influence in Russia is bound up, amongst other things, with his complex "identity". We cannot say exactly how many people he converted to believe in the Church back in Soviet times, – through personal encounters face to face, but still more through the *samizdat* texts and radio broadcasts, together with stories of those who had met him, seen him and listened to him at church or at meetings in people's flats (meetings like that were arranged as often as possible whenever he came to Russia; in certain circles when people said "Vladyka" they meant Metropolitan Anthony and no other, – because there was simply no contact with other Vladykas). There is no doubt that, in Soviet conditions, when no religious preaching at all was possible, his message was absolutely unique – in style, in intonation and even, in a certain sense, in content (at least as regards semantic emphasis).
>
> Totally Russian and one of us in the ecclesiastical sense, he was still, of course, perceived as an alien, a visitor from some other planet. He was free of all our Soviet and anti-Soviet complexes. He was a bearer of high Russian culture, but did not deploy the Aesopean language, which many here were obliged to speak. He was a Prince of

the Church, but not a "leader from the religious ghetto". His devotion to the Church was not channelled into a parallel course from the rest of life, so that before our very eyes the "Berlin Wall" between the "Christian cosmos" and the "Soviet cosmos" came tumbling down – a wall which, at that time, divided not only the Church from the rest of society but constricted the inner life of all Orthodox people (the laity, particularly but not exclusively: it would be hard to overestimate the impact of his lectures in the Moscow Theological Academy addressed to future priests). . . . This is religion proportionate to the personality of man and in the context of encounter and engagement with other persons; in freedom from any outward ideological pressure, not to be reduced to politics, or to sociological achievement or failure.[47]

Anthony could speak directly to the heart of his Soviet and post-Soviet contemporaries from the depths of his Russianness but also from the detachment of his upbringing in the non-communist world, from the contemporaneity of a life of hardship, poverty and engagement with all the problems of the modern world and from the centrality of his timeless Christianity. There could be no question, with him, of allowing the Church to be used to rally a disaffected population, totally disillusioned as to the Marxist beliefs in which they had been indoctrinated.

There is no room for a utilitarian approach to Christianity, so widespread, alas, amongst us now at a time when people are beginning to look on faith as a means to an end, as a mechanically effective instrument for the rallying of public morale, Russian identity, and so forth. . . . Is Metropolitan Anthony our contemporary? Yes, in the best way, he is more contemporary than many of us: in his distrust for all that is decorative, formalised, artificial, superfluous; in that concentration on the essential that springs from suffering. Not a shadow of pious pose, not one sugary intonation . . . he understands modern men from within, without need for words. . . . But if contemporary means to keep up with the times, to adapt to them, then Vladyka Anthony, like any other Christian worthy of the name, cannot in any way be called contemporary. . . . The flame of faith burns bright in him as it burnt in quite, quite other times. Everything changes, but fire is still fire. . . .

Maybe he will, after all, succeed in explaining to our believers and unbelievers that faith is neither a folksy enamel box, nor parapsychology, nor a brand of what might be called parapolitics, nor the pretentiousness of that "true Orthodox believer" who, as Brodsky once remarked, says: "Now I'm the boss." In general, it is not a new kind of master-key to all our worldly problems, nor a pretty make-believe. Faith is completely real, nothing more so. It is fire and, at the same time, most importantly, fire that can kill. . . .[48]

So wrote Averintsev. Kyrlezhev writes in much the same vein, affirming that, in a Russia over-run by missionaries of various American and Korean cults, not to mention followers of Eastern religions, Metropolitan Anthony is the only effective Orthodox missionary. His voice and whole personality demonstrate that "it is possible to be a contemporary person, a member of contemporary western society, and, at the same time, a member and bearer of the ancient tradition of the Orthodox Church".[49]

Two years later, Kyrlezhev wrote: "Belief in man as a result of an experienced meeting with God – that is Metropolitan Anthony's logic. . . . Russianness, for him, is openness to everything that is not our own without undervaluing what is ours. . . . The most important, the most significant thing about this priest is how he matches up to the condition of the world as it is and of man in it."[50]

It was this feeling of belonging to their world, yet speaking from a totally different perspective, that enchanted educated Russia. They also appreciated the fact that Anthony spoke their language as they felt it ought to be spoken, without the acronyms, barbarisms and bureaucratic-cum-media clichés that now corrupt it, but also without pompous ecclesiastic jargon, and that he did not talk down to them – but spoke as man to man:

> We all felt straight away that one of the totally new things in the way he addressed us was that, in contradistinction to the usual sermonising, he talks to us as grown-up people.[51]

The fact that Metropolitan Anthony had received a scientific education also worked in his favour. Iurii Vilensky, in an article written for the journal *Doktor*, lists other men of God who had also been men of science: Pasteur, Pavlov, Archbishop Luka (in the world Valentin Voino-Iasenetsky). Retelling the youth of Andrei Bloom and the story of the essay about his ambition to grow up to be a monkey, which earned him the reputation of a Russian barbarian, Vilensky continues hotly: "That 'barbarian' became one of the most educated and attractive personalities of our difficult twentieth century" and quotes Anthony's own words:

> I understood my scientific education and scholarly work as a part of theology, that is the study of God's works, the study of God's ways. . . .[52]

This was a change indeed from the conviction inculcated by Soviet anti-religious propaganda that it was impossible for a scientist to be a believer.

Not only the Metropolitan's personality, but also the fruits of his labours impressed those Russians who had the opportunity to see the diocese in England for themselves: how it functioned as "a collective", to use the Soviet term. Nikolai Balashev, who visited the children's camp run by Father John Lee and Deacon Peter Scorer at the invitation of Father Michael Fortounatto, wrote:

... to speak of the daily "lessons" I was lucky enough to attend, I was particularly delighted by their dialogical character, the teachers' freedom from didactic stuffiness. ... The frankness, spontaneity and freedom, tempered by discipline and community spirit – these went to make up the chief lesson I took with me from the camp.[53]

Naturally, there were – particularly among conservative ecclesiastics – people who profoundly distrusted this "frankness, spontaneity and freedom". Some, objecting to the Metropolitan's conviction that it is not only those who say "Lord! Lord!" who can be saved but, ultimately, all those who sincerely seek God and strive to do His will, and also to his assertion that we are saved not by our own faith but rather by the Saviour's redeeming love, even cried heresy. Metropolitan Anthony believed, and clearly formulated on many occasions, that Christ's last cry on the cross, "Why hast Thou forsaken me?", expressed a genuine experience of death, not as a "falling asleep" but as the absence of God Who is life, a proof of His total solidarity with mortal man that made possible the Redemption. To some, this was blasphemy, Nestorianism. First mooted by an anonymous Greek monk in the journal *The Shepherd*,[54] the controversy also raged in Russia during Anthony's lifetime,[55] although here voices within the Church, notably Archimandrite Ilarion's, were raised in whole-hearted support of his understanding of this most tragic moment.[56]

Among other vituperate attacks was one launched on the internet under the headline "Metropolitan Anthony (Bloom) advocates the permissibility of abortion". The writer stated that, with the support of the "heretically-inclined theologian Ilarion" and others in the Russian Church who considered themselves his followers, the Metropolitan had escaped proper criticism for his "modernism" and support of the ecumenical movement but, in a BBC interview with Sergei Hackel, had now gone too far by actually allowing that, given the state of medical science today, in some cases, where a child in the womb could be diagnosed as diseased to such an extent as to be quite incapable of normal life, there might be a case for abortion – thus, thunders the writer, Anthony allies himself with the Nazi doctors who experimented on unborn children: a child killed in the womb is deprived of eternal life.[57]

Anthony seems to have made it a rule not to enter into polemics and, indeed, to have been rather amused by his fire-and-brimstone opponents, though humanly irritated by their insistence on foregrounding his un-Russian surname. He had, he said, received a letter from a monk in Russia actually seeking his advice. The writer had been expressly warned – or so he confided to Metropolitan Anthony who was, after all, a dignitary of the Moscow Patriarchal Orthodox Church and not of some émigré "Church abroad" – to beware the heresies propounded by Alexander Schmemann,

Chapter Nine

John Meyendorf and Anthony Bloom. The first two he knew, but who, please, was Anthony Bloom? It sometimes seemed, Vladyka joked ruefully, that he, who had once dreamed of martyrdom for the love of Christ, was more likely to be burned at the stake as a heretic.

However, he was irreplaceable.

The Patriarch showed no sign of wishing to grant his request for retirement, nor even to disassociate the Russian Church from their Metropolitan's more unconventional opinions. On the occasion of the celebration of Anthony's forty years' ministry as Bishop in 1997 he had written:

> For many Orthodox people in Russia, your sermons have become important spiritual guidelines; they help them to preserve their faith in the complex contemporary world. Your talks, coming as they do from an active spiritual experience and from a living, loving heart, are also perceived by people in their hearts, tangibly conveying the sense of your solidarity and fatherly care. Your acute sense of Christian responsibility before God for each human soul has taught you to discern in every human being the ineffable image of God which is the foundation for spiritual growth and divine sonship.

Metropolitan Kirill, the head of the Patriarchal Department of Foreign Affairs, destined to become Aleksii's successor, followed suit:

> ... the ability to see the spiritual meaning in different circumstances of life, a sensitive attitude to God's world, and a vibrant, loving heart, help you to perceive the inner truth of man and to find the precise words which are able to penetrate the most hidden depths of a man's soul and which can awaken it and search it out.

Speaking at the same fortieth anniversary, Archbishop Anatolii contributed in his capacity as a member of the Diocese of Sourozh and as a hierarch of the Moscow Patriarchate to the chorus of appreciation:

> ... Joy attracts people's hearts and souls. They recognise in you a spiritual shepherd and a person of complete integrity.

Anthony's own long-serving priest and choir-master Father Michael Fortounatto spoke warmly of his Metropolitan's acceptance of Sophronii's concept of the Church as a reversed pyramid and of his influence on clergy and laity in Russia; Bishop Basil borrowed his image of the Eastern shepherd who walks before his flock and joked:

> Now I don't want to suggest that we are all sheep, it is not the case, but I think it is simply true that in a strange way at every point Metropolitan Anthony has been ahead of us and I have a strange feeling it will always be the case.

The Russian ambassador to Great Britain sent polite congratulations and the Georgian ambassador, in a warm statement read out by his wife, envied him, "as a politician", his rare ability to bring people together "in friendship and in love".

Fondly, Anthony's friend the Bishop of London, Richard Chartres, added his voice from an Anglican viewpoint:

> ... while you have been loyal, an ambassador of your own Russian Orthodox tradition, and there has never been any doubt about that, you have been received and respected by all manner of other Christians as simply a strong, deep voice of the Christian Gospel here, and a great influence well beyond the Russian community.[58]

In this way, Metropolitan Anthony's well-grounded popularity in the West served as a firm foundation to the respect accorded him in Russia – and the other way about.

At a meeting of the Russian Orthodox University, also in honour of the fortieth anniversary of his episcopal ministry, this point was made by the Rector, Igumen Ioann (Ekonomtsev), whose opening speech stressed precisely the universal popularity, in Russia and abroad, among Orthodox and Christians of other confessions, of this

> most charming personality, who is all that we all aim to be: a combination of spirituality, intellect, knowledge, profound faith and devotion to Orthodoxy, together with broadmindedness. . . .[59]

At the same meeting a priest, Father Sergii Shirokov, recounted his impressions of the London celebrations, stressing Anthony's modesty and approachability and telling how he himself would lend his books to the doubting intelligentsia among his congregation. He compared Anthony's personality to "the gentle light" of the evening hymn. Elena Maidanovich gave a highly intelligent summary of the proceedings, signalling out the Patriarch's key-word "*Tsel'nost'*" (integrity), and adding that Metropolitan Anthony was not just a "gentle light" but a burning fire. Father Christopher Hill told how, having first heard of the Metropolitan of Sourozh from a Russian priest in the 1980s and then seen him on television, he had sought him out and found "the ideal priest". Liudmila Viktorovna Borodina voiced the feeling of many representatives of the post-Soviet intelligentsia that his witness had restored their faith – in God, in their own immortal souls, and in their country, culture and language. Summing up, Igumen Ioann confirmed that Anthony had indeed given them back their language, and said:

> It would have been the simplest thing to say with indignation that all this was the Evil Empire and to break off relations with the Russian

Orthodox Church and with Russia. But, happily, this was not what he did, he acted with great wisdom, and for that reason the part he played in the history of our Church over the last decades can scarcely be over-estimated.[60]

In all appearances, everything was coming together and Anthony's long life of service was proving equally fruitful in the country to which his Church had appointed him in 1949 and in his Russian motherland. His belief that all sincere Christians would, eventually, "not *construct*" but "*grow into* unity through increasingly full and perfect fidelity to the Gospel" and that "it is not through *uniformity* that we wish to become one, but through *unity* which is possible only through *uniqueness*" (italics my own),[61] provided a guideline that the world not only required but was ready to welcome. He, too, was more than ready to pass on the baton in the great race that had still to be run.

Chapter Ten

Agony

The aim of the Christian life is to become disciples, people who learn from Him, not only obedient in the sense of being well-drilled but obedient in the sense of being able to listen deeply, to understand His thought, His heart, and to grow into the full measure of our humanity, which is His humanity.[1]

The Gospel is not a success story. Failure, the unravelling of a lifework, death – I suppose it is all a part of growing into the full measure of our humanity, which is His humanity – but it is hard to write about, as it must have been hard to endure. As Anthony himself once said to the students of the Moscow Theological Academy: "But such a God Who becomes man, such a God Who takes on Himself the total defencelessness, the total weakness, the total vulnerability, the total apparent defeat of a man, could only be 'invented' (if one can express oneself in that way) by God Himself, could be presented only by God."[2]

Before such an unfathomable mystery, he goes on, "we can only stand in silence . . . that condition of the human soul which stands before a mystery totally convinced that in this divine darkness shines an unattainable light – and remain silent".[3]

It is not the part of the chronicler, however, to stand in silence, but to tell the story, to set out the facts as far as they can be established, seeking neither to blame nor to exculpate, nor to speculate on possible misunderstandings or might-have-beens, and it is, perhaps, some comfort that Anthony's grand vision of a united, autocephalous Western Orthodox Church sprung from a Russian Church purified by experienced suffering, in which all post-Revolutionary factions would at last be reconciled, should actually have come to be shared, at least as far as the reconciliation of the Russian émigré churches under their own elected Metropolitan was concerned, by the Moscow Patriarchate during his lifetime. The Mother Church was aware that only Metropolitan Anthony had the stature to implement their attempt to found an autonomous Metropolia of Western Europe in place of the Exarchate of the Moscow Patriarchal Church. The Metropolitan, however, was a dying man, and the authorities, dreaming of transforming his grand vision into an administrative reality, did not have his insight into the time-span needed for old wounds to heal and new shoots to take root and grow. The project was still born – but to this we will return in context.

Meanwhile, we have the witness of close friends, Irina Yanovna von Schlippe and her husband Vladimir Borisovich, as to how old age and physical weakness affected his ministry which, in turn, offers an impartial and neutral explanation as to why his own parishioners were beginning to feel he was neglecting them in order to accommodate the influx from Russia.

Irina Yanovna: "I have been telling you the same thing over the last 40 to 50 years", he would complain, recounting stories from his own experience. "I have no more words" . . . and, however often we told him that we do understand, in as far as we are able, and are doing what we can, it grieved him profoundly that he had to keep on repeating himself. And the second thing was the evolution from a state of burning to a state when he just seemed like a light. And again there was this uncertainty as to whether he were doing all he could, in spite of the fact that great crowds of people gathered round him as if he were their only priest. It's now there's 40 of them in the Diocese. I think that state of mind was the result of dissatisfaction with himself – a natural enough state in a Christian.

But there is another detail. The closer we worked with him, the more seldom we got to speak to him. I was talking the other day to one of his closest collaborators, she said: "But he never spoke to me at all over the last years." And Alena,[i] I may say, translated all his sermons from English into Russian.

He permitted that to no-one else, although he never answered her queries.[ii] I think he was just sure that if he'd entrusted her with the task, she would manage. That, too, was very typical of him. . . . "You know, my view is that, if there is an affinity, one doesn't need physical contact". . . . I believe that many people were not admitted to personal contact with him anymore because they were all more or less able to steer their own boats.

---

i. Elena L'vovna Maidanovitch.
ii. Metropolitan Anthony had actually refused a highly reputable St Petersburg translator permission to publish a book of translated sermons, saying: "I don't speak like that in Russian." In fact, the majority of Metropolitan Anthony's sermons in English were translated into Russian by Tatiana Maidanovich for the ongoing Russian version of the parish magazine and the two Paris-published Russian books. Elena helped out and eventually took over this task in response to demand in Russia after it became possible to publish there.

> **Vladimir Borisovich:** But I do think the main reason was the growth of the Diocese and the London parish itself. There were more and more clergy who had to be looked after, so there was less and less time for the laity.
>
> **Irina Yanovna:** But, you know, he always found time for misfortune. To help anyone who was in trouble he could even skip attending church for an important service. I know individual cases. . . .

And Vladimir Borisovich goes on to tell of the shock it had been to Anthony's parishioners when he installed the answering machine, and how one of the best ways of securing his company for a few uninterrupted minutes was to drive him somewhere he had been invited to preach or talk:[i]

> [H]e would always tell some story or other on the way. Pity that at the wheel it's hard to remember anything. Only the gist and the tone stay in one's head.
>
> It was usually things from life seen as only a man of wisdom with a sense of humour could see them. Vladyka Anthony imbued these stories with some kind of spiritual content but, at the same time, they made you want to laugh for joy. . . .

And Irina Yanovna added that you could see the influence he had on his priests "not just by example but by loving, yet highly exacting trust". There came a time, they said, when he could no longer spend many hours confessing his spiritual children and his priests had to take over. But, added Irina Yanovna, in a way every meeting with Anthony was confession. "You and I," he would say, "will immerse ourselves in Eternity and see what's going on."

> He lived in Eternity and, in contact with him, it was sometimes possible, if you really tried, to touch on Eternity yourself and to see yourself in it, which was amazing. . . . He celebrated far quicker than the average priest. But the impression remained that he was in Eternity, time had simply dropped away.[4]

Gillian Crow, who, as secretary to the diocese, was closely concerned with day-to-day life in the Cathedral, records that Metropolitan Anthony suffered from chest infections throughout February and March 2000 and had a bad fall in the street, followed by slight concussion or possibly a minor

---

i. Father John Lee claims Anthony was, in fact, intensely grateful for silence on such occasions, though he would sometimes begin chatting of his own accord. He was, in fact, quite capable of driving himself and John had seen him at the wheel of a tractor – but, of course, his £3000 a year stipend would not extend to a car.

stroke, for which he was under observation at the neurological department of Brompton Hospital. At the end of July he "came close to collapse during the Liturgy" and, a few weeks later, underwent an operation for a pacemaker, from which his recovery appeared, both to himself and to his parishioners, painfully and unexpectedly slow.[5]

No doubt the very real problems of this exhaustion of a physical organism long weakened by exigent demand were compounded by worry for the future of the diocese. The many new Russian parishioners were pushing hard for more Russian-speaking priests, and the Metropolitan upheld the general feeling that the second generation of this new "economic" immigration should be encouraged to maintain their culture and their language,[i] rather than allowing themselves to be assimilated without trace by the country in which they or their parents chose to live. This, after all, had always been the émigré ethos – however different the circumstances.

The London parish, however, had no russophone candidates they wished to put forward for the priesthood and, towards the end of Lent 2000, Metropolitan Anthony ordained Father Mikhail Gogoleff from the recently established Orthodox community in Bristol – on his own initiative. As with the appointment of Anatolii as Suffragan Bishop, this "highhandedness" was resented by those who had long unstintingly given their time and energy to working out the statutes of the diocese and to the struggle to implement the democratisation of twenty-first-century Orthodoxy, though pressures were such that the ever-changing situation called for quick decisions not always compatible with slow-growing democratic procedures.

The demands of the incomers exceeded the potential of the grassroots, and linguistically qualified clergy prepared to work for nothing, or for a minimal stipend, did not spring up from the London earth. The Metropolitan, moreover, in frail health and coming up ninety, was, quite simply, overwhelmed with the responsibility of reconciling the vision of a

---

i. It is symptomatic of the scale of the "second generation" problem today that the British Educational Authority has introduced a GCSE in "Russian for native speakers". There was also the problem of teaching sons and daughters of Soviet Russians the language of the Church. As a university teacher in the 1990s, I came across native-speaker Russians who translated the Day of the Saviour from Russian into English as "Spasov's Day" and the Communion Service from English into Russian as "poslednii uzhin" (a very workaday rendering of "the last supper"). This linguistic confusion naturally fuelled the conviction of many non-Russian Orthodox in the Diocese of Sourozh that their services, to be accessible to all comers and more especially to the younger generation, should be conducted mainly in English – something that Metropolitan Anthony had always understood but resisted, seeking a balance between the beautiful language with which he had grown up and to which his original parishioners were deeply attached and the requirements of those to whom it was no longer comprehensible.

Western Orthodoxy growing from Russian roots, towards which he had so gently and gradually, yet with such burning inspiration, been leading his beloved diocese, with the pressing needs of the influx from his native land, many of them recent converts, with whom his and their own Mother Church hardly knew how to cope. They were, like the crowds that came to hear Jesus on the shores of the Sea of Galilee, like sheep without a shepherd, and the old pastor was driven by the need to tend them.

Meanwhile, in a series of talks given in the Cathedral from October 2001 to June 2002, he made one last, sustained effort to share the fruits of his life and thought with the English-speaking parishioners whom he had already nursed to a certain maturity and who, he felt, could – paradoxically – contribute knowledge of Orthodoxy to the passionate hunger for faith brought to the Church by his Russian flock. "The thoughts I have been presenting you in previous talks," he says at one stage, "are not a teaching but my own reflections and questionings about matters of faith, not in the sense that I doubt things in the negative sense but I want to be true, I want to understand and when I don't understand I want to be frank and open with God, with myself and with you."[6]

There is a video of one of these talks: Anthony, his face somewhat disfigured by old age, the eyes strained and dull, the once springy hair wispy and limp, struggles hard to enunciate and formulate the experience of a lifetime. "I want to say things which have accumulated in my mind and heart over the years but I don't know whether I will be able to do it properly. So I will do my best to express these things and I will ask you to do your best to hear beyond the words in your heart and your experience of life what I ought to have said. . . ."[7] At the end of the talk, he rises with difficulty from behind the table where he has been sitting and turns to the icons behind him in prayer. The voice is once again the voice we had all known so well over the years: sonorous, deep and resonant, every word clearly spoken. Turning back to his listeners, once more a very old man but no longer struggling, lovingly and spontaneously, with a smile about the eyes, he blesses them, dismissing them like beloved children after a dreary lesson, to take a rest "from all this talking".[i]

What he had to say in these last talks was truly amazing. He always taught that, when reading the scriptures, you should pay special attention to passages that resonate with you as true and inspiring and to passages that you

---

i. This film was shown to maximum effect at the end of the one-day conference to mark the tenth anniversary of Metropolitan Anthony's death at the Serbian Church in London, October 2013. The impression from that last blessing was that of a window being opened wide on a stuffy classroom to let in the spring air – exactly, incidentally, the impression my late husband Kirill Sokolov took away from his very first meeting with Vladyka in a Moscow hotel (see *O mitropolite surozhskom Antonii* (2013), p.104).

find difficult or unacceptable. In these last talks, it is to these problematic[i] passages that he devotes consideration: to how a loving God could have created a creature capable of sin, a world destined to fall; to doubt; to the twilit condition of the fallen world; to faith as the memory of fleeting but real experience ("the certainty of things unseen"); to the Church, as on the one hand "the place where God dwells" and, on the other, as a body of "people, who are frail and in the making";[8] to sin as "unfaithfulness to the One Who created us in an act of love and Who, in an act of love, has become one of us";[9] to the story of the creation from chaos, understood as a state of infinite potentiality, and of the Fall, here perceived as a "parable", a term stemming from the geometrical term "parabola", the second centre of a broken circle projected into infinity. Anthony speaks of the Book of Genesis, citing Bulgakov, as not history but "meta-history" that tells, "in the language of the fallen world which is ours, the mysteries of the world before the fall".[10] In that world there could have been no inclination to sin, to be unfaithful – only love, trust and aspiration. He argues that neither Eve nor Adam intended evil when they ate the fruits of the forbidden tree of knowledge, "not the tree of death but the tree of search". Rather, they accepted the challenge of an alternative, tragic route to salvation through human effort, study and creativity, a way on which their Creator, knowing their weakness, was ready to join them:

> The one tree, the tree of life, let us call it so, is the way that consists in renouncing, turning away from everything except God Himself, communing with Him, acquiring what St Paul calls the Mind of Christ, discovering God, discovering God's creation including oneself and mankind in and through communion with God, through the mind of God, through being at one with Him. And the other is the possibility of making the same discoveries but by looking deeply, trying to understand the world that surrounds us, to find the Creator through His creation.

Yet the tragic guilt of humanity's choice of this latter way has brought about a situation in which "the creation itself has become a problem".[11] We are no longer in the simple, unbroken light of revelation but in a twilight through which we have to puzzle our way step by step, generation after generation:

---

i. According to Metropolitan Anthony in *God and Man* (London, Hodder and Stoughton, 1974): "When one uses the words 'problem' and 'problematic', one means things that had seemed to be absolutely clear to the generation before but which have now unfolded themselves in a new way and have acquired a depth of vision which requires new thinking." (Translator's note to "On the Light that Shineth in Darkness", this same series of talks in Russian *Uverennost' v veshchakh nevidimykh*, p.55.)

A scientist may be a believer, a scientist may not be a believer but in desperate search for meaning and this gives us such hope that the world is not open only to the ascetics and to the saints, that *all* the roads may lead to the discovery of God.[12]

He qualifies this statement as from and for himself:

> I believe passionately in the communion with God which is offered to us in prayer, in a life worthy of His holiness and His love for us, of all He gives us; but also we are merged with and we are part and parcel of a fallen world and it is through this turmoil we must find our way.[13]

Through the twilight that enveloped the world when we chose this way of tragic enquiry "the light of God still shines".[14] We are, indeed, descendants of Cain, he says, but it is "Cain and his family who began to build cities, who discovered industry, who created art and music. All that could not have been done out of nought and out of evil."[15] Indeed, "there is nothing human that is alien to God in essence".[16] Even Judas, when he slinks off to betray his Master, goes at His bidding. Surely even this act cannot be ascribed to intentional evil. Anthony's defence of Judas (that he may have wished to provoke a "crisis" through which Christ would be put in a position to "prove" His Messiahship and, tragically, did not give himself time to repent and recover his trust, his love towards the Son of God, as did Thomas and Peter) failed to satisfy at least one listener, Gillian Crow, who addressed to him a cogent critique closely based on the Gospel texts. True to the concept of "questioning" that underlies the whole series, he praised her well-reasoned thesis that Judas, a thief from the beginning, typifies mankind's darkest desire to be rid of a God Who sees through them, acknowledged it might serve as a corrective to his own thought, and read out her letter to his audience.[17] Perhaps, he concedes, she is right, at least in part – his hearers must judge from themselves – but he still holds to his basic insight that, although "the situation of mankind is a mist, a twilight, a blurred situation",[18] "God and mankind have never been ultimately separated from one another by human sin . . . because our oneness with God, our closeness to Him is based on the divine love and not on ours."[19]

The task of humanity is to restore the situation, to bring back the light. "We are people sent by Christ into the world to transfigure it, not to reorganise but to transfigure it. . . ." This is something dimly felt in all the great religions, a hazy memory of how things were and should be. The world, the Creation has been entrusted to us. He quotes Khomiakov:

> We speak of the body of Christ, we do not say, and he uses the word itself, the "meat of Christ". It [the Host] becomes Christ – how? Because the whole world is called to become the place of Incarnation, Incarnation itself visible, perceived, accomplished.[20]

This vision he seeks with his last strength to impart to his flock:

> Do you see how wonderful these things are? I can not express them, I am sorry, I am so sorry, but it is so beautiful to think and to know that in this world of twilight, in which we live, there is the plenitude of fulfilment, of light. . . . We do not see it because we are blind, we do not see enough but there are saints to whom it was given to see.[21]

The restoration of our vision, however, to which we are called, demands all we have to give. He passes on to the "problem" of the hard saying that he who does not hate his parents cannot follow Christ, suggesting the word "hate" (Slavonic etymology) means "not to see". The eye must be single. At the same time, believing in Truth, loving Truth, dedicating oneself to the discovery of Truth, one cannot hope to express it fully in words in our fallen situation.

> I do believe that the Orthodox Faith to the extent it can express things is true, but I cannot believe any more after many years of life that someone who does not embrace it cannot find salvation. . . . So often, people cannot believe in what we believe to be true because we are to them a proof that our words are untrue. . . . We can be within the truth only if we live it.[22]

As to those who hold to other faiths, or none: "We can leave it to God to know, but be sure that if He became man and died for all those who need salvation we can hope."[23]

The penultimate talk is devoted to the intractable "problem" of Christian disunity in a twilit world where it is impossible to discern the absolute; as ever, Anthony calls for transfiguration rather than reorganisation. Then, in the final address of the series in which he has been speaking "almost exclusively of questioning, of doubt" he tries to say "something about certainty",[24] the certainty "of contemplative silence", "a direct perception of the depths of inwardness, of silence, of prayer", telling story after story from his own life, from the lives of the saints, of the momentary vision of light that makes a twilight of darkness and which, "having seen once, we have seen forever, having perceived once, we have perceived for ever, it has become our experience, it is us".[25] "Do not try to perceive anything," he says. "It is enough for you to know that God is there"[26] and "the surrounding dark becomes like a mist through which one can walk because one knows that beyond the mist there is the perfect light of the sun".[27]

In that surrounding mist, however, even Anthony's attempts at reorganisation quite failed to bring about transfiguration. People do not become saints just because they convert to Orthodox Christianity, and a mutual irritation sprung up within the community which deeply distressed their pastor. Many of the old-timers felt their parish was getting too big and unwieldy, ceasing to be a family freely interacting with a loving, albeit exigent father. Their Metropolitan was, it seemed, at least as much concerned with the newcomers and their spiritual welfare as he was with his own "children" – and it was clearly all too much for him. As to the newcomers, they did not always understand Christianity as Anthony had taught it but tended to see their Church as an island of "Russianness" in the alien seas of Western Europe and to emphasise the importance of outward things such as traditional dress and custom (which can be absorbed so much more quickly than the essence of the Christian life). The vexed question of language, always an emotive one in the life of the diocese, was thus compounded by cultural differences and different attitudes to the function of the Church. An attempt was made to found a separate church in Clapham with Father Alexander Fostiropoulos, which would provide more space but was hardly calculated to resolve problems of integration. Why should the Russians join a parish whose vicar was a Greek, however successfully he had fulfilled the function of Orthodox university chaplain? Why should the core parishioners leave their bishops and their hard-won, much-loved Cathedral in Ennismore Gardens for a church elsewhere? At best, the unassimilated mixture as before would be perpetuated in both centres. The Metropolitan's attempts to inspire the ex-Soviet Russians, among whom there was no lack of spectacular wealth, to endow a new church specifically for Russian speakers within the community got nowhere. It was, anyway, not what he really wanted, which was *unity* at a depth where English and Russian would commune with their God together and not even know what language was being used. As to the oligarchs, they tended to turn up only for the great festivals and for private occasions such as weddings and christenings, or so it was felt by those for whom the Church had long been the centre of their lives and had long taken for granted their co-operation – financial, organisational, charitable, artistic and intellectual. Anthony, seeing his suffragan bishops beset by problems not of their own making, with which they were temperamentally ill-equipped to deal, turned to Moscow for help.

While Anthony was still recovering from heart surgery, still struggling to deliver those extraordinary last talks, in November 2001, the Chairman of the Patriarchal Department for Foreign Affairs Metropolitan Kirill came to London with Igumen Ilarion, the Oxford-educated priest-monk who was one of the Diocese of Sourozh's most ardent admirers among the younger Russian clergy. At a meeting with Bishops Anatolii and Basil and some other clergy of the diocese they discussed the organisation of pastoral work for the English-speaking and Russian-speaking communities. The initiative appears to have been a response to problems shared and perceived by all, not the sinister first move in a Moscow take-over which subsequently suggested itself to the minds of some,[28] but it was, nevertheless, an initiative perceived as having been taken from without the parish and electoral college envisaged by the diocesan statutes. So, when, towards the end of December, Metropolitan Anthony, after celebrating only the second or third Liturgy since his bypass operation, announced the forthcoming changes mooted at the November meeting, they came as a thunderclap. To begin with, he spoke first and at greater length in Russian – always a sensitive issue. Secondly, Archbishop Anatolii, by now generally accepted and well-liked, had "asked" to be retired from his position as Assistant Bishop, though he was to stay on indefinitely in England to continue his pastoral work in Manchester, where he later organised the building of an Orthodox church, and among the Russians in London.[29] It was felt that he had been *asked* to request retirement and there was some shock that his place as Suffragan Bishop was to be taken by a younger man: Ilarion (in English, Hilarion), a scholarly theologian of proven intellectual ability with a higher degree in music, a lively interest in film and an excellent knowledge of English from his years in Oxford, who was to arrive as the newly consecrated Bishop of Kerch (Anatolii's old title) and take over the latter's duties as Vicar-Bishop. Ilarion would also, in the tradition of the diocese, supplement his stipend by lecturing at the Orthodox Institute in Cambridge University. Metropolitan Anthony, as his spiritual advisor, personally recommended him to the congregation.

Problem solved, one might think – however much the diocese, which Metropolitan Anthony himself had nursed and coaxed and scolded into maturity and independence, might initially resent the *fait accompli*.

Bishop Ilarion was duly consecrated on 14 January 2002 in Moscow, with Bishop Basil representing Metropolitan Anthony, and arrived in England at the beginning of March. "Everyone was struck by the extreme youth of the new bishop. He was not yet 36 and no-one knew how he would mature."[30]

From the start there was misunderstanding. Ilarion told Anthony that he felt his consecration had endowed him with "power" and, whatever he may have meant by this, the Metropolitan was deeply shocked and took it to mean the power to rule, the very opposite of his own understanding of the Bishop's function as "servant of all". Out of step with the émigré tradition of poverty, Ilarion had a mother to support and was not slow to claim he needed more money than had been envisaged and to advocate a more structured policy of financing and rewarding clergy throughout the diocese. More serious for his relationship with other clergy was his insistence on celebrating the full episcopal Liturgy, except when Anthony was actually present to modify it in the now customary manner. Ilarion later said he felt he had fallen among "sectarians", who adhered rigidly to their own idiosyncratic practice and regarded his more traditional approach ("I celebrate as I have been taught") with positive hostility.

The zealous young Bishop's academic duties in Cambridge which, it had been hoped, would absorb a part of his energies and render his introduction to Cathedral affairs more gradual and less confrontational, appeared to interest him but little. Indeed, he was to claim they had little use for him and, when he arrived, had not fixed either duties or salary. On the contrary, he saw his primary task as the reorganisation of the diocese. With Anthony's blessing, he undertook a tour of the provinces, during which he became the focus of dissatisfaction in some small Orthodox communities which had, over recent years, felt either neglected or misunderstood by the Metropolitan, creating, as Gillian Crow records, "a faction". In the provinces myself at the time, all I remember of this was some talk of appointing new full-time priests salaried from Moscow, which may well have been anathema to those who still feared any dependence on Russian money, but seemed quite a good idea to scattered Russian Orthodox dependent on Greek-speaking parishes for their services – and, of course, on the occasional visit from or trip to London. There were, however, it seems, pockets of actual personal resentment; Irina von Schlippe says this was because Anthony, far from being the sugary, universally beloved figure sometimes depicted, could be "stern and exacting".[31]

Be that as it may, the atmosphere in the diocese as a whole very soon became adversarial and the clergy, accustomed to familial, brotherly relationships, were deeply shocked and upset, as was their Metropolitan. They called a meeting to discuss the situation when it was thought Ilarion would be out of London.

He, however, got wind of their intention and, mindful of the old Soviet adage that it is easiest to "eat" a man when he isn't there, appeared unexpectedly to "confront" them at the meeting.[32] This resulted in a most distressing show-down, followed by a decision from Moscow on 17 July 2002 to confer honourable relocation on Ilarion to another post in Western Europe as representative of the Russian Orthodox Church to the European Union in Brussels, and to reinstate the peaceable Anatolii as Bishop of Kerch. Ilarion, hurt and acrimonious, published an apologia for his position in *Nezavisimaia gazeta*, and Anthony replied, but, as was natural to him, directly, *ad hominem*, in the form of an open letter to an errant spiritual son who had himself chosen to publicise their differences.[33]

Exhausted and distressed by all this unprecedented ill feeling, on 12 December 2002 the Metropolitan convened an extraordinary meeting of the Diocesan Assembly to discuss his own wish to retire. "I cannot carry on" were his words at the meeting and, with one exception, the Assembly voted to accept his resignation. It was also voted to petition the Synod right away to appoint Bishop Basil as permanent diocesan bishop,[34] though Anthony had made it clear that, while they could "offer" Basil, the final decision must rest with the Patriarch.

Towards the beginning of 2003, however, it became evident that all these failed attempts had simply served to exacerbate the differences in the diocese and steps were taken to try to reconcile the separate groups that had come into being. A committee of eight people was formed – which sat for three solid hours with no result. "When I accompanied Metropolitan Anthony back to his own room," recalls Father John Lee, "he banged the service book he was carrying down on the table and said: 'If we can't manage love, surely we should at least be capable of making peace.' He was at the end of his tether and very upset, as indeed were the majority of us."[35]

On the following day, after the Liturgy, which he somehow found strength to celebrate, Metropolitan Anthony announced the decisions reached the previous December and added that he was due to go into hospital to undergo an operation. The congregation was not told until after his admission a week and a half later that he had been diagnosed with cancer of the bladder, possibly long dormant and originally caused by service in a radiology department in wartime Paris without proper protective clothing. He was accompanied on all visits to the doctor and to the operation itself by Father John Lee – sensible, humorous, a close friend and a trained nurse – whom he had designated "next of kin".

The Metropolitan was back in his room in the Cathedral within ten days and was soon to be glimpsed hobbling indomitably about the building with the aid of two sticks, chatting with the cleaners. On 27 April he celebrated Easter for the last time, leading the traditional procession to announce the Resurrection before the doors of the darkened Church and afterwards, in a blaze of light, censing the congregation: "Christ is risen." "You should have seen his sheer joy at Easter," Peter Scorer told those attending the Fourth International Conference in Moscow. "His face shone and he would shake and swing that censer as though he were going to let the incense fly across the Church."[36] He managed to read the wonderful address of St John Chrysostom welcoming all those who have laboured from the first hour and those who came only at the eleventh, those who have kept the fast and those who have not, to rejoice at the festival of the Resurrection – then retired, apologising to the congregation that he had no more strength and must leave his bishops to celebrate the Liturgy and to greet everyone individually at the ambo.

This was the last service he was to celebrate with them.

Meanwhile the Synod, their next meeting abrogated because of the serious illness of the Patriarch himself, had failed to respond to the petition about his retirement and the appointment of Bishop Basil as his successor. It seemed they were simply not prepared to face up to Anthony's mortality. In a letter dated 1 April 2003, the Patriarch had floated a proposal for the establishment of a semi-autonomous Metropolia of Western Europe which, it was hoped, would replace the Exarchate and absorb the European branches of the Russian Orthodox Church outside Russia (the Synodal Church) and the mainly France-based *Arkhiepiskopeia*. This Metropolia would eventually elect its own bishop, but, in the meantime, the only candidate who conceivably commanded sufficient respect to unite all these disparate elements was Metropolitan Anthony of Sourozh.

This initiative, though it came at a time death was already staring him in the face, signalled a huge step towards the conversion of the Moscow Patriarchate to a project for Orthodoxy in the West which was all he had hoped and worked for and, even though, once again, it was an attempt at organisation rather than transfiguration, the honour could not be refused. Metropolitan Anthony wrote to all those involved, explaining that he was at present too weak to travel, but inviting them to come to London for consultation. The invitation was taken up at once by his old associate from ROCOR, Bishop Mark of Berlin, but the initiative began to flounder when the American wing of that Institution – who had, understandably, been omitted from the original blueprint for a West European Metropolia – began to take an active interest. The *Arkhiepiskopeia*, too, were clearly going to prove hard to wean from their comparative autonomy under the Patriarch of Constantinople. Then the Metropolitan of Sourozh himself fell out of the equation.

A new tumour. The discovery of a new tumour was followed by six weeks of radiotherapy, which seemed at first to offer hope of at least one or two years in remission, but Anthony did not think so. That winter, his grandmother had appeared to him in a dream, looking more solemn than when she came to read him the stories that had delighted his childhood, and had begun to show him a calendar: at first flicking through the dates, slowing down in July and, eventually, holding it open at the 4th of August. He believed her and they were right. Father John records:

> Then began a lengthy course of treatment. I drove Vladyka to the daily sessions for almost eight weeks. He was prescribed heavy doses of painkillers. However, the treatment brought no relief.[37]

Nevertheless, not yet relieved of his duties, he managed two last public occasions. On 5 June he was guest of honour at the Nikaean Club at Lambeth Palace, where he was awarded the Nikaean Cross for the second time by Rowan Williams, who, at the end of the evening, knelt to receive his blessing. Too weak to attend the Queen's banquet at Buckingham Palace in honour of Vladimir Putin, he was represented there by Bishop Basil, but managed to be present at Putin's thank-you reception at the no longer off-grounds Russian Embassy. By the end of June, though, Anthony was back in hospital in a four-man ward undergoing a further course of radiology.

"He's charmed them all in there," Father John informed a meeting of anxious parishioners. Nevertheless, he would have preferred to die in his own "cell" in the Cathedral. Arrangements were made for Macmillan nurses to attend him there but, on their first visit, he denied them admittance, and when, over-persuaded, he agreed to let them in the following day, they found his condition cause for grave anxiety, recommended he be admitted to residential care and, on 23 July, secured him a place at Trinity Hospice, Clapham, where he was kept heavily sedated. On 30 July, the Synod at last granted him official retirement and officially appointed Bishop Basil to take temporary charge at the Cathedral. Anthony, looking towards eternity, declined to take any further part in the still vexed question of the succession and the future organisation of the diocese, though he did continue to care profoundly and to take thought for individual members of his flock. A few, who, one way or another, had trodden parts of the long road alongside him, were, at Father John's discretion, permitted to sit in quiet prayer by his bedside and take their leave. He confided to his chosen priest a list of those whom he had always remembered with a request to keep it a secret but to continue praying for them. John spent whole days beside him, "heard his last confession and gave him Holy Communion and the Last Rites. Soon enough thereafter he lost consciousness. . . ."[38]

On 2 August, a statement was issued to this effect to the parish. A special service of intercession (*moleben'*) was sung twice daily at the Cathedral. It was a stiflingly hot summer and, on 4 August, it was Father Michael Fortounatto's turn to keep vigil:

> Metropolitan Anthony died very peacefully. When I arrived at the hospital where they were looking after him, he was lying relaxed in bed. When the nurse saw me, she invited me to sit down and left. And so I stayed for several hours praying, thinking and looking at him. He did not move and no-one came to see him. Eventually, I realised that he had passed away, and that eternity had begun for someone who had been a father to a multitude of believers. And so I went to make a telephone call to say that, instead of a *moleben'*, we should sing a *panikhida* in church that evening.
>
> Father Anthony, as he was easily called in the old days, was a whole and complex man, both fragile and strong, sometimes tormented and sometimes fired up, and totally trusting and calm. I lived in his shadow for more than 40 years; I suffered with him, I rejoiced with him, and above all I learned a lot. He was pastor to a multitude of people, a theologian and a teacher of the faith. He was also a voracious reader, not only of theology, but also of literature, poetry and science. He knew six European languages. I would say, to sum up his teaching in a sentence, which I hope others will develop one day, that his faith was in a God, Who sustained complete trust in humankind, His creature. I say this straight away in order to set him from the start in the context of what was deepest and most endearing about him. On the face of it, this idea [of God's faith in humankind] is crazy, given the paradoxical and contradictory course of the story of humankind on earth from our

Anthony's committal, 13 August 2003, with Deacon Peter Scorer in the foreground

creation and right through our history. But the absolute centre of this tumultuous history is the coming in the flesh of the Son of God, to live willingly among men. The Lord Jesus was the vital heart of all Father Anthony's concerns. And the focus of his consciousness.[39]

It was still stiflingly hot on the day of the funeral. Anthony, looking small and vulnerable in his massive regalia, lay, as Orthodox tradition demands, in an open coffin in the centre of the church for his people to come up one by one to take leave of him. He was surrounded by clergy: his own diocesan priests and bishops, representative hierarchs from the Moscow Patriarchate, from other churches, and Rowan Williams in person from Canterbury. Solemn tributes were read but, according to his own wishes, the rite was simple and austere, as for a monk rather than for a prince of the Church. The singing, "Give Rest with the Saints" and other funeral chants, as always endowed the whole ceremony with a quiet but essentially joyous sense of liberation. This continued as his priests bore him from the hearse on the last lap of his journey to the re-opened grave where his mother and grandmother had long lain under a simple Russian cross in the very un-Russian Old Brompton Cemetery. "Christ is risen from the dead, and to those in the grave He has given life." The Easter hymn, struck up spontaneously around the grave, was taken up by the long, long procession of people, informally dressed in light summer clothes, some pushing babies in prams, who came to sprinkle earth on the lid of the coffin, closed at last on the servant of God,

Anthony, now at rest.

Endnotes

Acknowledgements
(pp.xi-xii)

1. Published as *Uverennost' v veshchakh nevidimykh. Poslednie besedy 2001-2002*, "Dukhovnoe nasledie Mitropolita Antoniia", "Nikeia", Moscow, 2012.
2. The references for English-speaking readers are as follows:
   "Metropolitan Anthony of Sourozh: Publications", *Mitras*, http://www.mitras.ru/eng/eng_publ.htm;
   "Anthony Bloom", *Amazon*, https://www.amazon.com/Anthony-Bloom/e/B001HCS4V2;
   "Metropolitan Anthony (Bloom) of Sourozh", *Goodreads*, http://www.goodreads.com/author/show/224474.Metropolitan_Anthony_Bloom_of_Sourozh.

Chapter One
(pp.1-7)

1. Archimandrite Anthony, letter of 8 April 1957 to Archbishop Nikolai (Eremin) of Clichy. Copy in the Archive of the Metropolitan Anthony of Sourozh Foundation (MASF); see further MASF Archive.
2. "Voskresenie i krest", *Trudy* II, p.326.
3. Metropolitan Anthony of Sourozh, "Without Notes" in *Encounter*, trans. from the Russian by Tatiana Wolff, Darton, Longman and Todd, 2005, p.171.
4. From an unpublished letter from Tatiana Maidanovich to her sister Elena.
5. Metropolitan Anthony of Sourozh, "Without Notes", pp.173, 181.
6. Gillian Crow, *This Holy Man: Impressions of Metropolitan Anthony*, Darton, Longman and Todd, London, 2005. (See further Gillian Crow, *op. cit.* See also "Without Notes", pp.171-3.)
7. Metropolitan Anthony of Sourozh, "Without Notes", p.195.
8. Metropolitan Anthony of Sourozh, *Coming Close to Christ*, SPCK, 2009, p.106.
9. "Iz zapisok pravoslavnogo Alekseia, raba bozhiia", *Russkii Dom*, No.11, 2000, pp.26-7.
10. Fr V. Vinnikov, "Ia poveril ot rozhdeniia v Bogoroditsyn pokrov", "Zarisovki", *Rusak*, 2000, p.194.

11. Fr V. Pereventsev, "Mitropolit Antonii", *Prikhodskoi listok pravoslavnogo prikhoda Sviato-Nikolaevskogo Khrama*, No.7, November 2000.
12. Metropolitan Anthony of Sourozh, "Without Notes", pp.174-5.
13. *Ibid.*, pp.176-7.

Chapter Two
(pp.8-15)

1. Metropolitan Anthony of Sourozh in an interview with Anthony Wilson, *The Church Times*, 10 July 1970, Archive ref. 1970-06-12-1 – *The Church Times*. Also the introduction to *School for Prayer*, Darton, Longman and Todd, first pub. 1970, p.xvii.
2. Oral communication. Metropolitan Anthony frequently retold the story of the reception of his monkey essay and it is recounted in detail in "Without Notes", p.179.
3. Metropolitan Anthony of Sourozh, "Besedy 2002 goda", *Trudy* II, V., Praktika, 2007, p.34.
4. Told at the Third Metropolitan Anthony Conference in Moscow, 2011, by Aleksandr Semenovich Filonenko.
5. See Metropolitan Anthony, "Without Notes", pp.184-5.
6. For Andrei's correspondence with one of these leaders, see Hieromonk Silvestr's very supportive letters to him of 1938-1941, four of which are preserved in the MASF Archive. The first letter regrets Andrei's change of allegiance and remembers him as "always and everywhere the model Vitiaz" (Letter of 1938-08-27, 1-2). The second reassures him that taking French citizenship should not exclude him from the organisation as he seems to think, though the writer understands that being a leader might be hard to reconcile with his aspirations to become a monk, something Silvestr knows from his own experience. The third sympathises with Andrei's difficulty in reconciling the great love he bears his mother with the demands of his monastic vocation and the last, written in 1941 under the occupation, tells how many of his parishioners have been arrested and again offers comfort for the young man's feeling that he is neglecting his religious calling for medicine, which, he says, is also a God-given talent.
7. Copy dated 30 October 1958 in MASF Archive. This is in fact the date of a warm letter of condolence to Shumkin's widow, who was to prove a thorn in Anthony's side, vigorously opposing his advocacy of multicultural and so multilingual summer camps and even complaining to members of the Soviet Embassy in France that the Exarch of the Moscow Patriarchal Church was against the use of Soviet textbooks for teaching history and geography in those camps. Anthony, however, remained steadfast in his loyalty to her husband's memory, the first letter to whom here preserved is dated 1954.
8. Interview with Timothy Wilson, *Living Prayer*, first published 1970, p.XL. Also Metropolitan Anthony, "Without Notes", pp.192-3.
9. Perhaps most vividly in French during an interview with Léon Nadeau for Paris-Canada on 23 September 1977: "La découverte d'un sens à ma vie intérieure qui s'exprime en prière." (*Nouveau Dialogue – Revue du Service Incroyance et Foi* (SIF), 01:01: 1978, pp.4-7.)

10. This account is from a 1960s interview with Timothy Wilson used as an introduction to the book *School for Prayer*, first published 1970, here quoted from the 10th impression, Libre Books, 1976, p.xii – see note 1.
11. S. Averintsev, "Vstuplenie k publikatsii avtobiografisheskogo rasskaza Vladyki Antoniia", "Bez zapisok", *Novyi mir*, No.1, 1991, pp.212-3.

Chapter Three
(pp.16-31)

1. Metropolitan Anthony of Sourozh, letter of 8 March 1936 to "Margot", who had written to thank him for an inspiring address to Durham University students, MASF Archive.
2. In 1921 Russian bishops in exile met at the invitation of the Serbian Church in Sremskie Karlovtsy and decided that the final authority for ROCOR (The Russian Orthodox Church Outside Russia) should be vested in a Holy Synod of "free" Bishops who would foregather yearly to monitor local situations and relations with the Mother Church in Moscow under the presidency of Metropolitan Antonii (Khrapovitsky), former Metropolitan of Kiev. At the same time they declared themselves for the restoration of the monarchy.

    Patriarch Tikhon, under arrest in 1922-1923, issued a statement of dissatisfaction with this overtly political group and named Evlogii of Paris to work out a new plan for the governance of the Russian Church abroad, then established him together with Bishop Platon (Rozhdestvensky) of North America as his own personal representatives or exarch. Tensions arising around the election of a new Patriarch after Tikhon's death led to a final split between the exarchs and the Sremskie Karlovtsy Synod (Karlovtsy or Karlovchane as they came to be called), who professed no confidence in Sergii as *locum tenens*. They claimed that the decrees of a Patriarchate under communist control lacked canonical validity and, in 1927, signed a condemnation of Evlogii and Platon. In 1928 they formally abjured obedience to Sergii following a demand that the Church in Exile should secede from all political activity. Sergii reconfirmed Evlogii as Exarch of the Moscow Patriarchate in Western Europe but, in 1930, he was relieved of his duties for subscribing to interfaith criticism of the anti-religious activities of the Soviet government and betook himself not to the Synodal Church whose meetings he had attended until 1924, but under the protection of the Ecumenical Patriarch of Constantinople, and was again followed by a majority of his flock. Relations between the Moscow Patriarchate and ROCOR (the Karlovchane or Synodal Church) became increasingly bitter throughout the Soviet period, but a reconciliation finally took place in 2007. Evlogii sought a personal reconciliation with Moscow after the war, at the end of his own life, but the majority of his flock stayed with Constantinople, who until 1966 maintained a separate Russian ecumenical exarchate. Improved relations with the Russian Patriarchal Church led to the closing down of the somewhat anomalous body and the creation of a third faction of the Russian Church – now calling itself not the Evlogians but the *Arkhiepiskopeia*, and still canonically attached to Constantinople, which re-

established the Exarchate in 1971. It should, however, be emphasised that the boundaries between these separate jurisdictions of the émigré Orthodox Church were, in practice, rather porous and there was considerable movement from one jurisdiction to the other among both parishioners and priesthood. See, for instance, Antoine Nivière, *Pravoslavnie svaschennosluzhiteli russkoi emigratsii v zapadnoi i tsentral'noi Evrope 1920-1995, Biograficheckii spravochnik*, YMCA Press, Moscow-Paris, 2007, pp.30-35. See also Chapter Six.
3. Interview for the BBC Russian Service of 30 July 1996. It was, in fact, Evlogii in 1928 who had worked out this formula with Moscow, insisting that his parishioners, who were not Soviet citizens, owed no "loyalty" to the Soviet government as such, but that the Church could promise to refrain from introducing politics into their services.
4. For more about Archimandrite Afanasii see *Arkhimandrit Afanasii (Nechaev) Ot Valaama do Parizha*, Fond Dukhovnoe nasledie mitropolita Antoniia Surozhskogo, Minsk, 2011.
5. See Metropolitan Anthony of Sourozh, "Ob Arkhimandrite Afanasii (Nechaeve)", first pub. in the collection *Propovedi i besedy*, Paris, 1976, here quoted from the book *Arkhimandrit Afanasii*, p.204.
6. A copy of this prayer, preserved together with a Gospel inscribed on the flyleaf from Father Georgii Shumkin to "our dear Andriusha Bloom" and the date he was consecrated altar-boy, 1931, is preserved in the MASF Archive.
7. Metropolitan Anthony, "Without Notes", p.203.
8. This story Anthony told several times. There is an accessible if slightly different version in the journal *Sobornost'*, Vol.1, No.3, 1979, pp.8-18.
9. Interview with Clementine Rehbinder, 2010.
10. *Ibid.*
11. Anna Garret, *Priskhodskoi listok*, No. 165, June 1984.
12. Oral communication, early 1960s.
13. Written deposition by Marina Fennel for Clementine Rehbinder, 2011.
14. Undated talk transcribed by Tatiana Maidonovich, MASF Archive.
15. One of his pupils was Tatisha Zakharova (later Behr), a memoir by whom is preserved in the MASF in Moscow. It tells how the well-brought-up, rather shy medical student Andrei Bloom would come to her home and struggle, largely in vain, to inculcate her with an understanding of mathematics, and how mortified he was when he spilt a mug of cocoa set before him by the mistress of the house. See "From St Petersburg to Sydenham", 1900-00-00-0 EEA – RCO4 – 028 Tatisha Behr.
16. Letter of 14 May 1981 to Diana Winsor, thanking her for her sympathetic profile "From Russia with love" for the *Telegraph Sunday Magazine*, No.238, 19 April 1981, of which she had sent him a pre-publication copy asking for comments or corrections and in which she called him "a small man". "I am 5 feet 8 inches, perhaps of medium height, rather than short."
17. See Metropolitan Anthony of Sourozh, *Tainstvo liubvi, beseda o khristianskom brake*, Satis', Sankt-Petersburg, 1994, prepared by E.L. Maidanovich from talks given on the Russian service of the BBC in 1971 and 1986.
18. This witness about Metropolitan Anthony as a young man by an émigré writer

named Karpushko is taken from the book *The Other Russia: The Experience of Exile*, edited by Michael Glenny and Norman Stone, Viking Press, 1998.
19. Metropolitan Anthony of Sourozh, interview for his eightieth birthday on the BBC Russian Service, 26 June 1994. Copy in MASF Archive.
20. According to his own account and the editor's preface to the book *Arkhimandrit Afanasii*, pp.5, 7. According to memoirs published by Metropolitan Anthony of Sourozh and by the nun Genofeva, both included in this work, he was born to a peasant family, pp.204, 213. Possibly this was the impression they gathered from Afanasii himself. Village priests were officially encouraged to resemble their flock, to be self-supporting and till the land, not to waste time on distractions like newspapers and monthly journals.
21. *Arkhimandrit Afanasii, op. cit.*, p.18.
22. *Ibid.*, p.11.
23. Metropolit Antonii of Sourozh in *Arkhimandrit Afanasii*, pp.203-212.
24. *Ibid.*
25. *Ibid.*, p.59.
26. *Ibid.*
27. Cf. Metropolit Antonii of Sourozh, "O dukhovnichestve" in *Pastyrstvo*, ed. E.A. Sukhova, Taganrog, 2005, pp.169-238.
28. Metropolitan Anthony of Sourozh, "Besedy 2002 goda", *Trudy* II, p.40.
29. Max Kovalevsky to Alexis van Bunnen in a dissertation published in Lausanne, *Une Eglise Orthodoxe de rite occidental L'Eglise Catholique Orthodoxe de France*, Folius 83-4.
30. Elizabeth Behr-Sigel, *Lev Gillet: A monk of the Eastern Church*, translated by Helen Wright, Fellowship of St Alban and St Sergius, Oxford, 1999; letter of 24 July 1928, p.143.
31. Quoted by Elizabeth Behr-Sigel in *op. cit.*, p.146.
32. Lev Gillet from a text anthologised in the book *Orthodoxie et tradition française*, Paris, 1957, quoted by Elizabeth Behr-Sigel, *op. cit.*, pp.150-51.
33. But see his preface to Sergei Hackel's *One of Great Price: The Life of Mother Maria Skobtsova, Martyr of Ravensbrück*, London, Darton, Longman and Todd, 1965, pp.vii-viii. "The Spirit of Truth that dwelt in her led her to criticise sharply all that is deficient, all that is dead in Christianity and, particularly, in what she mistakenly conceived to be classical monasticism; mistakenly, for what she was attacking was an empty shell, a petrified form. With the perception of a seer, she saw the hidden, glorious content of the monastic life in the fulfilment of the Gospel, in the realisation of divine love, a love which has room to be active and creative in and through people who have turned away from all things and – above all – from themselves in order to live God's life, to be his presence among men, his compassion, his love. . . . Mother Maria is a saint of our day and for our day."
34. Metropolitan Anthony of Sourozh, address at Father Lev Gillet's funeral in the Greek Orthodox Cathedral in London. Quoted by Elizabeth Behr-Sigel, *op. cit.*, p.9. See also Anthony (Bloom), "My monastic life", *Cistercian Studies Quarterly*, cf. 1973, pp.187-97, and Fr Michael Plekon and Fr Lev Gillet, "The Monk in the City: A pilgrim in many worlds", Spring-Summer 2000, Jacob Well's website *The Orthodox Church in America Diocese of New York and New Jersey*: http://www.jacwell.org/spring_summer2000/father_lev_gillet.htm.

Chapter Four
(pp.32-44)

1. Archimandrite Afanasii (Nechaev) in a Christmas letter of 19 December 1943, preserved in the MASF Archive.
2. Metropolitan Anthony of Sourozh, "On Death and Dying", talk in English, 1982, and oral communication. Metropolitan Anthony's archive contains a certificate of burial: Cimetière Parisien de Thiers, 05:06:1937, 6 Division, 4 ligne, 38 tombeau.
3. Anthony Bloom, "My monastic life", *Cistercian Studies*, VIII, 7, 1973, pp.191-2.
4. The source for these stories is Metropolitan Anthony himself, told to various people on various occasions.
5. Karpushko in Michael Glenny and Norman Stone (eds), *The Other Russia: The Experience of Exile*, Viking Press, 1990.
6. See Madame Claude Gaklan's letter of 15 January 1978, preserved in the MASF Archive.
7. Metropolitan Anthony, "Without Notes", pp.212-13.
8. *Ibid.*, pp.208-10.
9. Interview with Veronica Lossky recorded by Clementine Rehbinder, Paris, 2010.
10. Interview with Marina Fennel recorded by Clementine Rehbinder, 2011.
11. From the Introduction to André Bloom's "Considérations sur la voie d'abord vagino-périnale dans le traitement des fistules vesico-vaginales", no.215, thesis for the degree of Doctor of Medicine at the University of the Sorbonne presented 28 July 1943, a copy of which was kindly obtained for me by Clementine Rehbinder in 2011.
12. Metropolitan Anthony of Sourozh, *Russian Orthodox Spirituality*, 2 September 1987.
13. See Metropolitan Anthony of Sourozh, "Ob archimandrite Afanasii (Nechaev)", in *Ot Valaama do Parizha*, pp.209-10.
14. *Ibid.*, p.212.
15. Nikolai Lossky, interview with Clementine Rehbinder, 2010.
16. Veronica Lossky, interview with Clementine Rehbinder.
17. Dr André Bloom, "Contemplation et ascèse: contribution Orthodoxe", *Etudes carmélitaines Technique et Contemplation*, Desclée de Brouwer, Aschède Brouver, Paris, 17 June 1949, pp.49-68 (translation from French my own).
18. *Ibid.*
19. Antoine Arjakovsky, "La génération des penseurs réligieux russes", *La révue* La Voie (Put') *1925-1940*, Kiev-Paris, L'Esprit et la Lettre, 2002, p.30.
20. Metropolitan Anthony of Sourozh, from his talks with Iasenishevich materials, from MASF Archive.
21. Ksenia Nikolaevna Scriabina, letter of 10 July 1948 to Metropolitan Seraphim of Finland and Vyborg, MASF Archive.
22. Metropolitan Seraphim Lukianov, Patriarchal Exarch to Western Europe, letter of 31 December 1948 to His Holiness Aleksii, Patriarch of All Russia. From the State Archive of the Russian Federation (GARF); copy in the MASF Archive.

Chapter Five
(pp.45-67)

1. Metropolitan Anthony of Sourozh, letter of 22 July 1989 to Peter Mugleston, who wrote to him on 15 July 1979 asking for "any advice" he might be able to give him as to one who hopes to become a priest. From MASF Archive.
2. Metropolitan Anthony of Sourozh, "Speaking personally", *The Courier and Advertiser*, Friday 30 November 1973.
3. See *Sobornost'* (Organ of the Fellowship of St Alban and St Sergius), series 3, No.6, Winter 1949.
4. Copy of a newspaper report of 9 October 1949 in MASF Archive.
5. Cuttings from *Evening Telegraph and Post* of 11 October 1949; *Scottish Guardian*, *Aberdeen Evening Standard*, and *Times* Folio. All nos from MASF Archive.
6. Metropolitan Anthony of Sourozh, "Besedy 2002 goda", *Trudy* II, p.43.
7. This letter from Father Anthony Bloom to Metropolitan Seraphim is of 13 October 1949, MASF Archive.
8. Father Anthony Bloom, letter of 22 November 1949 to Father Nikolai (Eremin), MASF Archive.
9. Report by Boris Stark to Patriarch Aleksii of 19 June 1952, State Archive of Russian Federation (GARF), R699 1, op. 1, D997, list 53-65. Copy in MASF Archive.
10. MASF Archive. In some other European patriarchal parishes *panikhidas* were celebrated but many of the congregation demonstratively walked out. In France, the powerful Communist Party imposed three days of official mourning on the state.
11. *Evening News*, 7 February 1956, MASF Archive.
12. Christmas letter from Hegumen Anthony to his parishioners dated 1 January 1956 (Christmas was celebrated according to the Old Russian Calendar and fell on 7 January), MASF Archive.
13. Cf. Metropolitan Anthony of Sourozh, "Speaking personally", *The Courier and Advertiser*, 30 November 1973.
14. Report by Anthony Bloom to the Exarch of the Russian Patriarchal Church in Western Europe, Archbishop Nikolai (Eremin) of Clichy, on relations between the Russian Patriarchal Church and other local Orthodox churches in London, MASF Archive.
15. Archbishop Nikolai of the Russian Exarchate in Paris, letter of 18 July 1954 to the Very Reverend H.M. Waddams, MASF Archive.
16. Archdeacon M.A. Hodgins, letter of 4 October 1954 to Igumen Anthony Bloom. Copy in MASF Archive.
17. Draft of two letters (one unsent) from Hegumen Anthony Bloom to Archdeacon M.A. Hodgins, 5 October 1954, MASF Archive.
18. Cf. note 17.
19. Hegumen Anthony, letter of 24 September 1954 to Archbishop Nikolai, MASF Archive.
20. Cf. Hegumen Anthony Bloom, letter of 22 January 1956 to "Dear Father" (presumably Waddams), recapping the course of negotiations, MASF Archive.
21. A. Baikalov, "Novyi obman", *Novosti Rossiiskogo Ob'edineniia v Velikobritanii*, No. 9, 39, September 1955.

22. G. Benigsen in *Novosti Rossiiskogo Ob'edineniia v Velikobritanii*, No. 8, August 1955.
23. P. Mironov, letter of 19 August 1955 to the Russian National Association of Great Britain, MASF Archive.
24. Hegumen Anthony, letter of 27 June 1956 to Archbishop Nikolai (Eremin), MASF Archive.
25. Cf. OC file 2351-4 copy of memorandum to Patriarchal London Parish 19 October 1954 on Father Bloom's wish to ordain Cyril Taylor. Also report of A. Allen, Warden of the London Church, to his Grace Archbishop Nikolai, 21 October 1954, MASF Archive.
26. A. Allen, as in note 25 (above).
27. Hegumen Anthony, letter of 8 February 1955 to Archbishop Nikolai, MASF Archive.
28. Hegumen Anthony, letter of 12 June 1956 to Archbishop Nikolai.
29. Lambeth Palace, OC file 2 35/1-4, 6 October 1956. Copy in MASF Archive.
30. Hegumen Anthony, letter of 12 June 1956 to Archbishop Nikolai, MASF Archive.
31. Hegumen Anthony Bloom, letter of 21 December 1956 to Philip Hatfield, MASF Archive.
32. An account of the ceremony appeared in *The Church Times*, Friday 21 December 1956. See also the Exarch's report to the Moscow Patriachate of 25 March 1957, F.P. 1991-2 *donesenie* 19, ML 165-170.
33. Letters from Archimandrite Anthony Bloom, dated 23 August 1957, to the Bishop of Fulham and Canon Waddams, Lambeth Palace. Copy in MASF Archive.
34. Ksenia Nikolaevna Scriabina, letter of 14 June 1953 to her son Andrei (Anthony), preserved together with her French passport and other odd papers in the MASF Archive. I have translated the terms of endearment "nenagliadnyy", "moi rodnoi mal'chik" freely in an attempt to render the English as natural (if poetical) as is the original Russian.
35. Cf. Hegumen Anthony, letter of 27 February 1956 to Archbishop Nikolai asking for his prayers, letter of 11 March from Ksenia Nikolaevna thanking for them and letter from Anthony to the same of 19 April 1956.
36. Barbara Morshead, letter of 4 May 1957 to Archbishop Nikolai, MASF Archive.
37. Hegumen Anthony, letter of 27 May 1957 to Archbishop Nikolai, MASF Archive.
38. Archimandrite Anthony, letter of 5 July 1957 to Archbishop Nikolai, MASF Archive.
39. Oral communication. A version of this story was retold by Metropolitan Anthony in the very amusing, self-deprecating talk he gave on the occasion of the fortieth anniversary of his consecration.
40. Archimandrite Anthony, letter of 8 April 1957 to Archbishop Nikolai, MASF Archive.
41. Archimandrite Anthony, letter of 22 October 1957 to Archbishop Nikolai, MASF Archive.
42. Speech of the newly consecrated Bishop Anthony at the Pastoral Gathering of the Russian Patriarchal Church in Paris, 16-17 December 1957.

43. Bishop Anthony, letter of 3 February 1958 to Archbishop Nikolai, MASF Archive.
44. I have no source for this story, clearly written down and typed out verbatim from Bishop Anthony's own words. It was sent to me by E.L. Maidanovich.

Chapter Six
(pp.68-88)

1. Bishop Anthony of Sergievo on returning from his first visit to the Soviet Union, speaking at the 96th anniversary of the Foundation of Eastern Orthodox Churches and the Anglican Church, 19 November 1960.
2. This is a close paraphrase of Archbishop Nikolai's letter to Metropolitan Nikolai of Krutitsy and Kolomna, which is available together with Bloom's curriculum vitae and terse letters from the Soviet Foreign Office (MiD), dated 17 May 1955 and 27 November 1956, and with the minutes of a discussion held on 2 July 1957 culminating in the edict appointing Archimandrite Anthony Bishop and Suffragan to the Exarch. Copies in the MASF Archive.
3. See letters of 2 August and 23 September 1957 from Archimandrite Dionisii (Denis Chambault) to Metropolitan Nikolai of Krutitsy and Kolomna, expressing the hope that Anthony would breathe new life into this and other aspects of the work of the Exarchate.
4. Cf. Archbishop Nikolai, letter of 30 September 1957 to Metropolitan Nikolai of Krutitsy and Kolomna containing a translation into Russian of Anthony's letter to Iakovos of Apamea and of the latter's reply. Copies in the MASF Archive.
5. Letter from the Archbishop of Canterbury to Metropolitan Nikolai of Korsun, 23 September 1957. Copy in the MASF Archive.
6. Protopriest Mikhail Bel'sky's account of the consecration, *Messager de l'Exarchat du Patriarche Russe en Europe Occidentale*, 20 February 1957, No.28, pp.241-2.
7. Archimandrite Anthony (Bloom)'s letter of acceptance to Metropolitan Nikolai of Krutitsy and Kolomna published in *Prikhodskoi vestnik*, No.4, 1957. Cf. *Zhurnal Moskovskoi Patriarkhii* (Journal of the Moscow Patriarchate), No.2, 1958 for an account of Anthony's letter of acceptance and address at the ceremony of consecration.
8. Cf. Metropolitan Nikolai of Korsun, letter of 1 December 1957 to Irina Maidanovich. Copy preserved in MASF Archive. It was, of course, the Ecumenical Patriarch who had accepted the allegiance of a large part of the Russian Church under Evlogii in the early thirties. In 1957 there was still a rival Exarchate of the Russian Church maintained by the Ecumenical Patriarchate in Paris.
9. Bishop Kallistos (Timothy Ware) recalled Anthony's consecration as a "pan-Orthodox occasion" in a tribute for the fortieth anniversary of his service as Bishop.
10. Cf. Father Dionisii, letter of 23 January 1958 to Metropolitan Nikolai of Krutitsy and Kolomna, reporting on a "very good meeting of the council of the

Exarchate" chaired by Bishop Anthony of Sergievo on 14/27 December 1957. See GARF Dels 1/3. Copy in MASF Archive.
11. Bishop Anthony of Sergievo, letter to Metropolitan Nikolai of Korsun, 1958, MASF Archive.
12. For Bishop Anthony of Sergievo's speech at the Lambeth Conference see *Christian Illustrated*, May 1958.
13. See the account of the WCC in The Hague in the *Zhurnal moskovskoi patriarkhii* (Journal of the Moscow Patriarchate), No.9, 1958, p.27. For Metropolitan Nikolai of Krutitsy and Kolomna see Metropolitan Anthony's touching account of their relationship in "Obrashchenie k chlenam eparkhial'nogo sobraniia".
14. Mark Gibbard, *Twentieth-Century Men of Prayer*, SCM Press, 1974. See also V.I. Borovoi, letter to V.S. Alekseev, Head of the European Department of the Russian Foreign Office, marked "secret" but now available in the State Archive of the Russian Federation (GARF), informing the diplomat that, while in Geneva in August 1959, Anthony had asked him, as representative of the Moscow Patriarchate at WCC headquarters there, to find out how the Russian Orthodox Church would react to the idea of an autocephalous Russian Church in England if, as he had reason to believe possible, twenty-five high Anglican clergymen were to convert, some bringing their parishioners with them. It was agreed to ask the Soviet ambassador in Paris to contact the Exarchate on this tricky question, which does not, however, appear to have had any real consequences. Copy in MASF Archive.
15. See Archbishop Nikolai of Clichy's letter to the Patriarch deploring Sophronii's tendency to take personally the lack of funding available to his community. The letter, dated 29 August 1958, explains, distressfully, that, while all acknowledge that Sophronii, who came from Athos to France in the hopes of founding a monastery, is an industrious scholar and would like to help him, he and those of his monks who do not have private means subsist on state pensions, or work for the Sainte Geneviève old people's home, or have other work of their own outside the community. Sophronii, he laments, is inclined to take lack of financial backing as opposition to or at best indifference towards his project, which is why he wants to remove with some select followers to England where he hopes they will be more financially secure. Copy of letter in MASF Archive.
16. At the Third Conference in Memory of Metropolitan Anthony of Sourozh in Moscow 2011, Peter Scorer remembered this drive as the occasion when he came to know and love Anthony as a man, not just venerate him as a pastor.
17. See Anthony Bishop of Sergievo, letter to Metropolitan Nikodim, GARF, F6991, op-.2, d.430. Copy in MASF Archive.
18. Cf. Metropolitan Anthony of Sourozh, *The Living Body of Christ*, Darton, Longman and Todd, 2008, pp.15-19.
19. Cf. Sergei Averintsev, "Po tu storonu traditsionalizma i liberalizma. O novykh publikatsiiakh besed I propovedei Mitropolita Antoniia Surozhskogo", 1966: "When the liturgy finished he stood holding the cross and looked separately – absolutely separately! – at each of us who came up to kiss the cross: looked as if each and every one of us were the only one, the only one in the church, the only one in the whole world. (And, naturally, a good few hundred of us had crowded into the church and all of us went up to kiss the cross, and he stood

with it to the very end – and looked, and looked tirelessly.) In that concentrated look he simultaneously *welcomed* each of us into a very intimate, close, real communication, – and at the same time was strikingly stern, demanding, exacting. It was not easy to meet his eyes."

20. Oral communication. This was one of the stories Metropolitan Anthony retold several times to his London parishioners.
21. Cf. R.M. Iuzhakov, "Russkie pravoslavnye v Anglii: Nikolai Zernov i Antonii Surozhsky", *Russkii Mir*, Prosvetitel'skii al'manakh, No.2, 2000, pp.219-28, and Liudmila Borodina and Rector Ekonomtsev in Stereogramme of meeting of the Russian Orthodox University on the occasion of the fortieth anniversary of Metropolitan Anthony of Sourozh's episcopal service, 29 October 1997. See also S. Averintsev, "Vstuplenie k publikatsii avtobiograficheskogo rasskaza Vladyki Antoniia 'Bez zapisok'", *Novyi Mir*, 1991, No.1, pp.212-13.
22. Cf. Tatiana Maidanovich. In 1974, Tatiana finally left Russia for France, where she restored her French citizenship and continued to work for the Russian Orthodox Church at the Exarchate, in London, and at the WCC in Geneva where she earned enough money to finance (with help from friends) the first publication of Anthony's sermons in Russian: *Propovedy i besedy*, Paris, 1976. Elena Maidanovich has remained Russia-based and was President of the MASF in Russia until early 2015, and editor of the two-volume *Trudy*, Moscow, 2002 and 2007, and of many other publications. The fullest account of the sisters' co-operation with Metropolitan Anthony appeared 12 June 2014: Elena Maidanovich, "Neuzheli ETO nikto ne zapisyvaet?", interview with Alisa Strukova, *Pravoslavie i mir*: http://www.pravmir.ru/elena-maydanovich-neuzheli-eto-nikto-ne-zapisyivaet/.
23. Oral communication.
24. Bishop Anthony of Sergievo, letter of 4 March 1958 to Metropolitan Nikolai of Korsun, MASF Archive.
25. GARF, F. 6881, opis' 1, delo 228. The "secret" mark on the back of this document is stamped over: "rassekreshcheno".
26. See correspondence between Metropolitan Nikolai of Krutitsky and Kolomna and Metropolitan Nikolai of Korsun, letters of 2 February 1960 and 1 March 1960, GARF, F6991, op.2, 1.296 and F6881, op.2, delo 236, ll.74, copies in MASF Archive. The letter of 2 February 1960 contains a copy of "a brotherly exhortation" from Metropolitan Nikolai, Anthony and Vasilii (Krivoshein) to all adherents of the Russian Church who sought refuge with the Ecumenical Patriarchate to return to the Mother Church, which was now permitted a normal relationship with her adherents outside Russia. The fact that representatives of the Ecumenical Patriarchate took part in Bishop Anthony's consecration goes to show, it reads, that the way is open to them to follow Metropolitan Evlogii back to their native church without offence to the Greeks. The Exarchate desires nothing more than to have peace with both its fellow Russian Orthodox and the Church in Constantinople. Further to this, see the "Zaiavlenie" dated 31 March 1966, Paris, addressed by the Patriarchal Exarchate to the Arkhiepiskopeia (précis in *SEPI* No.12, 21 April 1966) and sharp reply with many signatures in *Messager Orthodox*, 1-II-1966. Also see Metropolitan Anthony of Sourozh in *Contacts*, 1967.

27. From a letter from Anthony dated 21 January 1964 to Metropolitan Nikodim, GARF, F6881, opis 2, delo 356, 1-20. Copy in MASF Archive.
28. That was the story to which I was treated. Another version was: "How splendid it would be to have one in the Easter procession!" Possibly the one followed from the other.
29. A batch of reports from various sources is filed in GARF, F6991, opis.2, delo 425, pp.144-51. Copies in MASF Archive.
30. Archbishop Sergii of Perm and Solikamsk, report on WCC conference in Delhi to Department of Foreign Affairs. See note 28.
31. Letter of 1 November 1967. See OC file 2391/4 Lambeth Palace. Copy in MASF Archive.
32. Metropolitan Nikolai's announcement of Sunday 10 March 1963 to his flock in the Church of the Three Hierarchs.
33. There are several versions of this letter, dated only 1963, in the MASF Archive.
34. V.S. Kazin, First Secretary to the Soviet Consulate in Paris, to *Dnevniki*, 31 December 1963. Copy in MASF Archive.
35. Anthony himself relayed this story on his next visit to the Patriarchate late in 1965. See Father A. Kaznovetsky's report to the Department of Foreign Affairs. Copy in MASF Archive.
36. Letters from Michael Archbishop of Canterbury to Anthony, Archbishop of Sourozh, of 7 February 1963 and 13 February 1963. Copies in MASF Archive.
37. Letters of congratulation to Archbishop Anthony of Sourozh on his appointment as acting Exarch dated 21 January 1963 are in MASF Archive.

Chapter Seven
(pp.89-120)

1. "The Challenge of Contemporaneity" is here quoted from *Trudy* II, p.712, first published in Russian in the journal *Tserkov' i vremia*, 2001, No.4 (17).
2. Metropolitan Anthony of Sourozh, sermon at Westminster Abbey, 25 January 1975.
3. See report by Vasilii Borovoi, permanent representative of the Russian Church in Geneva, dated 26 February and recorded by Filippov for the Foreign Department of the Patriarchate 20 March 1964. Copy in MASF Archive.
4. *The Catholic Herald*, 24 January 1964.
5. Archbishop Anthony of Sourozh, letter of 21 January 1964 to Metropolitan Nikodim. Rodzianko's letter, a copy of which is enclosed, is dated 6/19 January 1964. GARF 6881, opis 12, delo 56, ll.20. Copy in MASF Archive.
6. See note 4. A letter of 26 January 1956 in OC File 235/1-4 in Lambeth Palace (copy in MASF Archive) suggests the Anglicans were in fact somewhat flustered when the Moscow Patriarch accepted their invitation. "It looks as though we are to have competition in Patriarchal visits."
7. See Pyotr Vlasych Makartsev's report of the conversation, GARF, F2, delo 537, ll.115, dated 2 March 1965, and Archpriest Kaznovetsky's report to the Patriarchate's Department of Foreign Affairs, which states clearly that Anthony himself sought the meeting with the blushing Makartsev in order to "have things out" with the State as well as with the Church. Copies of both documents

in MASF Archive. See also Anthony's confidential report on the conversation to Lambeth Palace OC File 235/1-4, undated; copies of all three documents are in MASF Archive, which records a second meeting at which Makartsev said he had never been spoken to so frankly before and respected Anthony for it.
8. Archbishop Anthony of Sourozh, letter of March 1964 to Metropolitan Nikodim. Copy in the MASF Archive.
9. Father Kornilii (Fristedt), letter of 16 April 1964 to Archbishop Nikodim, MASF Archive.
10. Nikolai Lossky, interview with Clementine Rehbinder, 2010. An affectionate private letter from an employee of the Exarchate refers to him as "holed up at the Losskys' like a brigand and not answering the phone".
11. See V.S. Kazin's diary for 23 March 1964. Copy in MASF Archive.
12. Translation into Russian of letter from Dom Eusebio to the Patriarchate in Moscow, dated 3 June 1964 and readdressed to Comrade Filippov of the Council for Religious Affairs with a note stating that "in many things" Eusebio was correct and "the matter of Bloom" could not be indefinitely deferred. Copy in MASF Archive.
13. Abbot Sophronii, letter to Patriarch Aleksy, 1964. Copy in MASF Archive.
14. Statements about the Russian Patriarchal Church and the Synodal Church to the press, preserved as cuttings in newsprint but without date or attribution in the MASF Archive.
15. Copies of this exchange of letters between Anthony and Sophronii in the spring of 1982 are preserved in the MASF Archive.
16. Archbishop Vasilii Krivoshein, *Vospominaniia Pis'ma*, Izd-vo Bratstva vo imia sviatogo kniazia Aleksandra Nevskogo, Nizhnyi Novgorod, 1998.
17. Father Kornilii (Fristedt), letter to Metropolitan Nikodim, undated 1965. Copy in the MASF Archive.
18. Andrew Louth, oral communication.
19. Olivier Clément, letter of 2 March 1965 to Archbishop Anthony of Sourozh. Copy in the MASF Archive.
20. Compare note 7 for Makartsev. In a note of 9 February 1967 Canon Edward Avery mentions "two remarkable talks given by Metropolitan Anthony in Canterbury last week" which "for various reasons . . . cannot be published", in which he made a case for compromise, which was "not necessarily evil" and spoke of the benefits of Christians keeping in touch with atheist friends and relations. Note in OC File 235/1-4 Lambeth Palace. Copy in MASF Archive.
21. But see Bishop Antin's report to the Lambeth Council of Foreign Relations of 27 June 1966 that Anthony, because of his extreme conservatism, was not to be relied on "too much on any Anglican-Orthodox theological matter of importance". Copy in MASF Archive.
22. Oral communication.
23. Father Grishin, report on Archbishop Anthony's second visit to the USSR in 1965 to the Department of Foreign Affairs. Copy in MASF Archive.
24. See the reports of Father A. Kaznovetsky on Metropolitan Anthony's 1966 visits to the USSR. Copy in MASF Archive.
25. The ceremony and other details of Anthony's visit were reported in the *Zhurnal Moskovskoi Patriarkhii* (Journal of the Moscow Patriarchate), No.3, 1966, pp.15-18.

On 6 March he was greeted by Father Aleksandr Turintsev on his return laden with these new honours and by the church warden Alexander Pickersgill, to whom he replied warmly, recalling his youthful service to the Moscow Patriarchate in the Churches of the Three Holy Hierarchs and of the Mother of God Joy of all who Sorrow and Ste Geneviève and reaffirming the continuity of his attachment to his native church and his long and stable service to his flock in Great Britain, thanking God and his many helpers along the way for the joy of that service and the martyrs of the Russian Church for their steadfast example.

26. See Anthony's account of this meeting in OC File 235/1-4 in Lambeth Palace. Copy in MASF Archive.
27. For this visit see the report of Father A. Kaznovetsky to the Department of Foreign Affairs. Copy in MASF Archive.
28. Books published in English in his lifetime include:

   Archbishop Anthony Bloom, *Living Prayer*, ed. Esther Williams, Darton, Longman and Todd, 1966.
   Archbishop Anthony Bloom, *School for Prayer*, Darton, Longman and Todd, 1970.
   Archbishop Anthony Bloom, *God and Man*, Darton, Longman and Todd, 1971.
   Metropolitan Anthony of Sourozh, *Meditations on a Theme – A Spiritual Journey*, Mowbrays, 1972.
   Metropolitan Anthony of Sourozh with Georges Lefebvre and Father Benedictus, *Courage to Pray* (based on talks to a French audience), trans. Dinah Livingstone, Darton, Longman and Todd, 1974.
   Metropolitan Anthony of Sourozh, *The Feasts of the Christian Year: From Talks*, ed. Pegeen O'Sullivan, Ikon Books, 1979.
   Metropolitan Anthony of Sourozh, *Death and Bereavement: From Talks*, London, ROC, 1984.
   Metropolitan Anthony of Sourozh, *The Essence of Prayer: Living Prayer; School for Prayer; God and Man*, Darton, Longman and Todd, 1986.
   Creative Prayer: Daily readings with Metropolitan Anthony of Sourozh, introduced and selected by Hugh Wybrew, Darton, Longman and Todd, 1987 (Modern Spirituality series).
   Nicholas Chapman, *Practical Prayer: an interview with Metropolitan Anthony of Sourozh*, Conciliar Press, 1989.

29. Discussions were reported in the Russian language Paris newspaper *Russkaia mysl'* for 6 March 1966, 19 April 1966 and 10 June 1966. The last, no.2479, contained an indignant response from the *Arkhiepiskopeia* to Anthony's appeal to its members to reunite with the Moscow Patriarchal Church.
30. For official details of this visit see *Zhurnal Moskovskoi Patriarkhii*, No.3, 1967, pp.5-7. For Metropolitan Anthony's view of Yakunin and Eschliman, see his letter to Father Vsevolod Spieler of 25 August 1967, and Shpliller's reply of 16 December 1967, in MASF Archive.
31. *Vospominaniia Metropolita Antonia (Mel'nikova)*, 1968, archive of the diocese of St Petersburg (Leningrad), F3, opis' 6, 37pp. Copy in MASF Archive.
32. Nikolai Lossky, interview with Clementine Rehbinder, 2010. Cf. also Michael Bourdeaux, Obituary for Metropolitan Anthony of Sourozh, *The Guardian*, 7 August 2003.

33. See Nicholas Zernov, *The Russian Religious Renaissance of the 20th Century*, London, 1974. See also Canon Satterthwaite's note of 21 July 1966 of a conversation with Nicholas Zernov on the "unhappy position in Paris", in which Zernov made it clear that the Archbishop was upset by the continuing estrangement (copy in MASF Archive). Even the support of Oxford intellectuals such as Zernov and Prince Dmitrii Obolensky, who served as one of three church wardens at the Cathedral (with Anna Garret and Mrs Sevier, the wife of Geogy Sevier, a deacon currently helping out with the London parish), could not reconcile the Moscow and Constantinople contingents. See Dmitrii Obolensky's letter to Metropolitan Anthony of 6 March 1967 advocating an "advisory committee" to put an end to their divisions and, concurrently, the foundation of a group of laymen from all separate jurisdictions to identify and iron out old grudges. This, says the Prince, is essential, because their disagreements "distort the voice of Orthodoxy": "Of course, we Russians should neither become alienated from nor deny the Church in Russia, especially in this time of her present trials; but neither should we forget that, in the first place, we have been called in some measure or another to establish Orthodoxy in the west – ORTHODOXY and not just the Russian form of it! As they are doing now in America, so should we in England be arranging regular meetings between representatives of the National Churches (Greeks, Serbs and Russians: to start with) to discuss our common Orthodox Faith." This remarkable letter sets out Anthony's own policy over the ensuing years and is preserved in the MASF Archive.
34. Mother Thekla, successor to Mother Maria as Abbess of the Monastery of the Dormition of the Mother of God near Mulgrave, North Yorkshire. Oral communication.
35. See Gillian Crow, *op. cit.*, p.151.
36. That Anthony was well aware of and sympathised with this position, but preferred to try to influence his own church from within, is shown by his letter of 10 October 1968 to Patriarch Aleksii, deploring an overtly political missive from the Patriarch to the World Council of Churches: "Your flock abroad is becoming more and more convinced that their convictions, as far as the Mother Church is concerned, simply do not exist. Called to be apolitical within the Church, we are being drawn into a blatantly political one-sidedness far beyond every measure of tolerant neutrality." It is, he adds, virtually impossible for the Patriarch's "multi-ethnic flock" to keep faith with the Mother Church and, far from being in a position to heal the splits in the Church, she will be abandoned by individuals and whole parishes. He ends by imploring the Patriarch to leave him that "freedom of conscience" conferred on him at the anniversary of his consecration as Bishop in a personal interview – when the Patriarch visited England.
37. "Archpriest Benedict Ramsden", *Sourozh*, No.108-109, 2012, p.14.
38. "La rencontre de Taizé", *Informations Catholiques Internationales*, No.296, 15 September 1967.
39. Quoted from a French version in "Actualité réligieuse", *La Croix*, October 1967.
40. *The Radio Times*, 25 March 1967, p.2.
41. Metropolitan Anthony of Sourozh, "Of Divine Worship and a Christian lifestyle", *Encounter*, pp.239-40.

42. On 21 May 1969 Archbishop Athenagoros wrote to Metropolitan Anthony that he had been asked by the journal *Concilium*, edited by Henry King in Geneva, to write an article "Towards a reforming renewal of the Orthodox Church", had found the title absurd but had devised, together with a group of theologians and leaders of the Orthodox Church, a questionnaire on the desirability of liturgical and administrative reform.
43. See note 28 for a list of books published in English during Metropolitan Anthony's lifetime.
44. Gillian Crow, *op. cit.*, p.137.
45. Richard Mulhern, letter of 22 June 1971 to Metropolitan Anthony of Sourozh, MASF Archive.
46. Richard Mulhern, letter of 3 January 1972 to Metropolitan Anthony of Sourozh, MASF Archive.
47. Anthony became Vice President of the London Medical Group in 1966. In February 1963 he presided over a seminar on "Preparation for death", one of four at a conference arranged by the group for medical and theological students. This was to be a recurring theme, but by no means his only subject. Lectures under the auspices of the group include:

"Preparation for Death", 13 May 1965, London University Medical College.
"Christian Objections to Secular Medicine", 18 November 1965, Middlesex HMS.
"Preparation for Death", 13 January 1966, St Thomas' HMS.
"Preparation for Death", 28 February 1967, Charing Cross Hospital Medical School.
"Preparation for Death", 19 March 1968, Royal Free Hospital School of Medicine.
"On Being Human", 20 March 1969, Middlesex Medical School.
"Touch in Religion and Medicine", 25 November 1969, Charing Cross Hospital Medical School.
"The Significance of Physical Contact in Human Relationships", 23 February 1971, Guy's Hospital.
"Facing Death (IV: Preparation for Death)", 9 January 1973, London Hospital Medical College (Researcher's note: "this series not found in LMC programmes" [ES]).
"A Preparation for Death", 4 March 1975, St Mary's Hospital.
"Death: The conspiracy of silence", 6-7 February 1976, 13th Annual Conference of the London Medical Group.
"Preparation for Death", 3 November 1977, St Thomas' Hospital.
"Preparation for Death", 25 January 1979, Westminster Medical School.
"Preparation for Death", 18 March 1980, UCH Medical School.
"Preparation for Death", 19 January 1982, Charing Cross Hospital.
"Preparation for Death", 13 May 1986, University College Hospital.
"Preparation for Death", 2 April 1987, London Hospital.
"Preparation for Death", 3 March 1988, St George's Hospital.
"Preparation for Death: A Russian Perspective", 7 March 1989, Middlesex Hospital.

This list was compiled by Elena Sadovnikova from data provided by Amanda Engineer of the Welcome Library, London and Brenda Collaghan SJ of Heythrop College, University of London, which holds the records of the Institute of Medical Ethics.

Further talks and publications, the dates and venues of which are not always noted, comprise:

"On Death", 1954.
"On Stigmata", 1963.
"On suffering", 1964, Hospital Chaplains' Conference, Oxford.
"Body and Matter in Spiritual Life", 1965.
"On suffering", 1966, Guild of St Barnabas, The Oxford Conference.
"Body and Matter in Spiritual Life", 1967, FSASS.
"Medical Ethics", 1968.
"On Facing Suffering", 1969, University Church of St Mary the Virgin, Oxford.
"Care of Individuals", 26 March 1969, David Kissen Memorial Lecture (published in *The Care of Individual People and Cancer: The problem of relevance in cancer research: Two meetings*), ed. Dr G. Bennette, London, British Cancer Council, 1969, pp.54-60.
"On Death and Life", 24 May 1970.
"Theology of Suffering", 1971.
"Suffering and death of children", rtf, 6 September 1971.
"Prayer", Christian Medical Society, rtf, Christian Medical Commission Annual Meeting 1972.
"Remarks on Death", rtf, 3 February 1973.
"Man alive", rtf, 5 March 1973.
"Life and Death", rtf, 3 February 1973.
"Forgetting the dead", rtf, 1974.
"On pastoral work and death", rtf, May 1974 May 1974.

48. Some of his talks on these subjects are collected in a very helpful booklet of the same title: *Death and Bereavement: four talks*, London, ROC, 1984. A fuller list of talks for medical groups and/or on subjects related to medicine and care for the sick was compiled by Elena Sadovnikova from holdings in the MASF Archive. Her list notes a further twenty-seven Russian language titles. Not all the talks are precisely located as to date and location but each can be ascribed to a particular year; "rtf" means simply that they are available in the archive on tape.

Rough notes towards some of these talks have also been preserved in the archive and show the speaker's readiness to engage with the thorniest subjects: not only how to live with the human condition of suffering, ageing and mortality, but how to respond to hard questions such as abortion, euthanasia, genetic disease, AIDS, mental illness, "normality" and "abnormality".

"Death of Children", Hampstead, 14 January 1987.
"Death", Medical Group, 4 April 1987.
"On Healing", University Chaplaincy, 25 November 1987.
Untitled, Freudian Society, 25 November 1987.
"Holiness of Body", rtf, 7 February 1988.
"Preparation to [for] Death", London Medical Group, 3 March 1988.

"Death", rtf, 13 June 1988.
"Healing", rtf, 17 July 1988.
"Preparation for Death", London Medical Group, 26 May 1989.
"On Healing", rtf, 23 July 1989.
"Life and Death and On Prayer", Bagshot [Military Academy?], 21 November 1989.
"On Death and Life", rtf, February 1990.
"Quality of Life. Medicine - Palliative Medicine", rtf, 25 June 1990.
"Psychology and Religion", Sion College, London, 10 December 1990.
"Dying into Eternal Life", King's College, London, 5 March 1991.
'Workshop on Medical Ethics', rtf, 30 July 1994.
"Illness, Health, and Peace and War", rtf, 1995.
"The Whole Human Person", rtf, 25 May 1996.
"Humans Values in Medicine", British Medico-Chirurgical Society, 8 May 1974.
"Pastoral Care of Sick and Dying", rtf, August 1974.
"Spiritual and Psychological Realms", rtf, August 1974.
"How to Suffer", St Botolph's, Aldgate, 25 February 1976.
"On Death", Birmingham, Compassionate Friends, 26 March 1976.
"The Signs of Hope in Death", Newcastle, 16 November 1976.
"On Death", rtf, 1978.
"Bereavement", rtf, 1979.
"Afraid to be alive and afraid to die", Regional Cancer Organisation, Southampton, 10 April 1989.
"Memory of Death" ["Mindfulness of Death"], rtf, 30 November 1980.
"On Death and Dying", rtf, 1980.
"Pastoral Care", rtf, 7-11 February 1982.
"On Dying", rtf, 7 March 1982.
"On Death", Nurses Education Centre, Reading, 23 March 1982.
"Prayer and Suffering'", rtf, 17 April 1983.
"On Death", St Christopher's Hospice, 7 July 1983.
"Modern Man Facing Death", rtf, 6 September 1983.
"On Death", Anglican Society, 18 February 1984.
"Guide to Pastoral Psychology", rtf, 5 April 1984.
"Modern Man Facing Death", Cruise, 9 April 1984.
"Mind, Body, Soul and Spirit. Meaning and Value", Winchester Cathedral, 8 April 1984.
"Death", rtf, 12 April 1984.
"The Experience of Death", The Fellowship of St Andrew, August 1984.
"Answers to Questions", MacMillan Nurses Cancer Relief, 16 November 1984.
"Spirituality of Ageing", Christian Council on Ageing, Epworth Ho, Stuart St, Derby, 1985-6.
"Quality of life", rtf, May 1985.
"Bereavement", rtf, 6 February 1986.
"Violence", rtf, 16 April 1986.
"On Death", Allan Hall Seminary, 15 May 1986.
"Holiness of Body", rtf, 3 August 1986.

"Death", London School of Economics, 17 November 1986.
"Body as Temple of Holy Spirit", rtf, 24 May 1997.
Untitled paper for Gerontology Conference, Bournemouth, 17 September 1999.
Untitled paper for Moscow Hospice, ref, 8 June 2000.
"On accidental death", London Cathedral [of All Saints and the Dormition of the Mother of God], 19 October 2000.
"Unity in Death", ref, 5 November 2000.

49. Oral communication.
50. See Anthony's own answer to a question frequently asked by Russians: what is it Westerners find in Orthodoxy? Metropolitan Anthony of Sourozh, radio talk in Russian on Orthodoxy and the West, 1981, in *Besedy o vere i Tserkvi*, selected and edited by E.L. Maidanovich, Interbook, M., 1991, p.276.
51. I have not been able to ascertain if this poem was published. The text is from the Rev. N.W. Havoc's letter to Metropolitan Anthony of Sourozh of 15 January 1973, MASF Archive.
52. Irina Sokolova-Snegir, oral communication.
53. For Irina von Schlippe's role in this incident see Gillian Crow, *op. cit.*, pp.146-7. She herself retold the story at the 2013 International Conference "Metropolitan Anthony of Sourozh – Learn to see" in Moscow.
54. For the English publication of Seraphim's "Open letter to Solzhenitsyn" see *The Times*, March 1974, and for Metropolitan Anthony's letter *The Times*, 7 March 1974. Subsequently, Metropolitan Anthony lost no opportunity to combat the impression that he had "quit over Solzhenitsyn" or was in any way at odds with the Patriarch or his Mother Church as such. Most extensively, he wrote to correct a French newspaper (*ICL*, No.467, 1974) which had so interpreted his resignation and the appointment of Nikodim as Exarch in his stead: "A la page 30, dans le paragraphe encadré que vous avez consacré au Métropolite Nikodim, vous laissez entendre, après bien d'autres, que j'ai démissioné en liaison avec l'affaire Solzhenitsyne. Il n'en ai rien: j'ai pri son parti très dèliberément mais s'il s'était agi de le défendre; je n'aurais pas quitté mon poste: j'aurais combattu; j'ai exprimé librement l'opinion d'un homme libre et n'ai pas reçu aucune remonstrance de la part de l'Eglise russe. Si j'ai donné ma démission c'est réellement pour raisons de santé: j'ai été l'exarque d'Europe occidentale pendant treize ans; constraint à voyager au moins huit mois par an, et ni mon âge ni ma santé ne le me permettent plus; j'ai un diocèse qui éxige de plus en plus d'attention (il s'acroit numériquement, s'étend dans l'espace, englotte un nombre croissant de jeunes et d'intellectuels, attaint des couches nouvelles de la population . . .). Et je me dois à ce travail pastoral avant tout autre. La simultanéité de ma démission avec mes déclarations publiques sur Solizhenitsyne n'a pas eu lieu de cause en effet. . . ."

Unlike *The Times*, who failed to publish a sharp protest against the sensationalist way they had reported the Exarch's resignation, the French newspaper gracefully apologised and printed this correction (undated cutting from the *ICL*, No.467, 1974, in the MASF Archive.) To *The Times* he had written on 13 May 1974: "Once more a Church under trial is charged with betraying its duty to mankind by insinuation, if not explicitly. In justice to the Russian Church I must state that I have been under no pressure and have received no expressions of disapproval or displeasure. Statements like yours can ruin my relationship with the Russian

Patriarchate which could legitimately, on the strength of your report, accuse me of duplicity, falsity, disloyalty and underhand behaviour. I should be grateful, therefore, if you would publish, with the same prominence, with the right name [he was waging an ongoing battle to be styled Metropolitan Anthony of Sourozh in the correct fashion and not Anthony Bloom as he was so widely known] and the true facts, a correction of the original report. . . ." Copy in the MASF Archive.

55. Further, for Michael Bourdeaux's attitude to Metropolitan Anthony, see also Bourdeaux's Obituary in the *Guardian*, 7 August 2003.
56. The letter was published in full in the *Journal of the Moscow Patriarchate*, No.6, pp.11-12.

Chapter Eight
(pp. 121-155)

1. Metropolitan Anthony of Sourozh, in answer to a question recorded in the parish newsletter, No.286/287, July-August 1995.
2. Metropolitan Anthony of Sourozh, "Uber die Vergebung", *Orthodoxe Stimmen*, Ubernationale Orthodoxe Zeitschrift, April 1974, pp.2-8.
3. Metropolitan Anthony of Sourozh, speech on the occasion of the Browning Award for Lifetime Achievement, received October 1974 for "spreading the Christian Gospel". Text in MASF Archive.
4. From the pre-publicity put out by the University church. Copy in MASF Archive. For Metropolitan Anthony in Cambridge 1969-1979 see Canon John Binns, "Zhivoe svidetel'stvo very. Mitropolit Antonii i ego sluzhenie studentam", *Chelovek v bogoslovii mitropolita Antoniia. Doklady Vtoroi mezhdunarodnoi Konferentsii 11-13 sentiabria*, 2009, M., Fond "Dukhovnoe nasledie mitropolita Antoniia surozhskogo", Dom russkogo zarubezhia imeni, A.I. Solzhenitsyna, pp.22-33.
5. The citation, together with the Metropolitan's answering speech, is preserved in MASF Archive.
6. *Orthodoxe Stimmen*, 21 Jahrgang, 3 Vierteljahr, 1976, No.883, pp.13-17.
7. For accounts of this conference see *Contacts*, No.89, 1974, and *Sophia*, No.1, 1975.
8. Juliette Gréco, *L'Auvergnat*, a song of the late 1940s.
9. Metropolitan Anthony of Sourozh, "On the need for Statutes for the Diocese of Sourozh in Great Britain", report to the Diocesan Conference at Effingham, 27 May 1979.
10. Some idea of themes discussed over the years can be obtained from the following (incomplete) list:

    1975, 23-25 May. What it Means to be Orthodox in Great Britain today.
    1976, — (dates unknown). Baptism, Chrismation and the Eucharist.
    1977, 3-6 June. Sacraments of Repentance and Anointing.
    1978, 26-29 May. The Church.
    1979, 25-28 May. Orthodox Spirituality and Sanctity.
    1981, —. In an Alien World.
    1982, 28-31 May. The Royal Priesthood of the Laity.
    1983, 27-30 May. Jesus Christ, True Man.

1984, 26-29 May. Christian Living.
1985. 24-27 May. Orthodoxy in a Non-Orthodox Land.
1986, —. The Church of the Holy Apostles.
1987, 22-25 May. The Church of the Councils.
1989, 26-29 May. Living with Oneself.
1990, 25-28 May. Orthodoxy and Ecology.
1992, 22-25 May. The Secularisation of Religion.
1993 (at Hawkhursts). The Royal Priesthood: The Role of Lay People in the Church.
1995 (at Headington). Our Orthodox Presence in Great Britain.
1996, 24-27 May. An Orthodox Understanding of Personality.
1997, 23-26 May. The Experience of Incarnation: The Church as the Body of Christ.
1998, 22-25 May. Where Have We Orthodox Failed in Our Calling?
1999, 28-31 May. The Gifts of the Holy Spirit. The Church as a Aequel to Pentecost.
2000, 26-29 May. Confession. Repentance.
2001, 25-28 May. Christianity at the Dawn of a New Millennium.
2002, 31 May-3 June. Men and Women in the Church.
2003, 23-26 May. Life with the Living God: the Orthodox Community of the Future.

11. Metropolitan Anthony, address on the occasion of the celebration of twenty-five years of service as Vicar of the Russian Patriarchal Church in Great Britain, London, October 1975.
12. See Chapter Seven, note 36.
13. *Op. cit.* See note 11.
14. Metropolitan Anthony, letter of 3 June 1975 to "Chris". Copy in MASF Archive.
15. Photograph and interview with Valerie Carroll, "Orthodox view of WCC's role", unidentified news cutting for 2 January 1976, MASF Archive.
16. *The Fairview Chronicle*, school magazine for the Ursaline School in Brentwood, 7 February 1976, pp.15-16.
17. Metropolitan Anthony of Sourozh, letter of 17 June 1976 to Richard Payne of the Paulist Press. Copy in MASF Archive.
18. *Propovedy I besedy* (1976), preceding, as it did, all other Russian-language publications of the Metropolitan's works, had a profound if slow-working impact on the Russian-speaking world. Together with its successor *Vo imia Otsa i Syna i Sviatogo Dukha* (1982), it was enthusiastically reviewed, in the émigré press and in *Vestnik russkogo zapadno-evropeiskogo ekzarkhata*, No.109-112 for 1982, pp.289-91, and mentioned in Archimandrite Evlogii (Smirnov)'s encomium for Anthony's preaching for the Moscow Theological Academy meeting at which it was decided to grant him a doctorate *honoris causa*: see MDA *Zhurnal*, No.4, "Zasedaniia Soveta MDA i seminarii, 31 ianvaria 1983". For the way in which these books were reproduced and distributed in *samizdat* see "Neskol'ko svidetel'stv", *Chelovek v bogoslovii Mitropolita Antoniia Surozhskogo. Doklady vtoroi mezhdunarodnoi konferentsii. 11-13 sentiabria 2009 Moskva*, Fond "Dukhovnoe nasledie mitropolita Antoniia Surozhoskogo", Dom Russkogo Zarubezhia imeni A Solzhenitsyna, M. 2013, p.324.

19. See Metropolitan Anthony of Sourozh, "Men should become men again", *The Church Times*, 17 September 1976.
20. See copies of letters from Lambeth Palace Archive in MASF Archive, particularly the Archbishop's letter of 11 January 1977 to Fr Michael Moore and Moore's to him of 8 November 1977.
21. Metropolitan Anthony, "Cry for help", *The Times*, 18 May 1978, and *Christian World*, 18 May 1978. On 19 May *The Catholic Herald* quoted Anthony's eminently reasonable: "If this place were needed by the Anglican Church for worship I would not hesitate to walk out at once because we have no claim against an Anglican congregation. But that a place of worship, which is well-attended, should be considered only as a building which could be put to commercial use is something that shocked me very much." *The Church Times* chimed in on the same day, 19 May, with detailed instructions on how to respond to the appeal, where to send cheques, how to make covenants and, on 22 May, featured a photograph of Anthony flanked by a male and female representative of his flock. A week later M. Gellhorn published details of how much had been collected and of the shortfall; hitherto uninformed people began writing in, most of them crying "shame!" on the Anglican Church and the controversy ran and ran under the title "A Church under Notice" in the correspondence columns of the British press.
22. Also Janet Brown, "Threat of Church Closing", *The Observer*, 21 May 1978 and Patrick O'Donnor's piece in the same paper, featuring a photograph of Anthony in the Cathedral: "London has many beautiful places and a few holy ones. This is both. . . ."
23. Henry Franklin of Wells Cathedral, "A Church under Notice", letter of 19 May 1978 to *The Times*.
24. Letter from Dr R.L. Lamerton to the Archbishop of Canterbury of 15 December 1977, and from Archbishop Coggan to the Right Reverend Gerald, Bishop of London of 22 December 1977, Lambeth Palace archive. Copy in MASF Archive.
25. Report from the Reverend Michael Moore, Lambeth Palace Archive, of 19 May 1978. Copy in MASF Archive.
26. Cf. S.P. Oswald, letter to *The Times* of 17 May 1978 and Derek Hayward, "A Church under Notice", also in *The Times* correspondence columns, protesting that the Russian Orthodox Cathedral was the subject of discussion between surveyors representing the interests of both Churches and was not "under notice to quit", and the virtually identical letter from J.N. Edwards, also to *The Times* for 26 May 1978.
27. J.M.W. Wilmington and Anthony Turnbull, letter of 30 May 1978 to *The Times*, and Aleksandr Schouvaloff, letter of 31 May to *The Times*.
28. Metropolitan Anthony of Sourozh, sermon for the first celebration of All Saints of the British Isles republished online by the MASF on 13-14 July 2013, originally 7 September 1978.
29. Metropolitan Anthony of Sourozh, letter to *The Times* of 18 August 1978. See also Michael Moore's thank-you letter to Anthony: "Perhaps we realize a little what it must have cost to write it: but only you could have done so and we are very grateful. I have drawn all the correspondence to the attention of the Archbishop."

30. Letters and records of donations are preserved in the MASF Archive. Most date to 1978, though a few stragglers were still writing in in 1979 after the appeal was closed.
31. Cf. 1976, Yehudi Menuhin's letter to Archbishop Coggan (Lambeth Palace pp.222-242), and Coggan's letter to Anthony of 25 May telling him of this offer.
32. Oral communication. The donors wished to remain anonymous. Their contribution, as listed by Alistair Macpherson, the fund manager, on 28 December 1978 was a round £20,000.
33. Metropolitan Anthony of Sourozh, "On the necessity of Statutes for the Diocese of Sourozh", report to the Diocesan Conference at Effingham, 27 May 1979. See also *Diocesan Statutes*, St Stephen's Press, with an introduction by Metropolitan Anthony of Sourozh dated 26 June 1998. Invaluable for the understanding of the statutes is E.V. Belyakova, "Kanonicheskie osnovy ustava surozhskoi eparkhii", *Dukhovnoe nasledie mitropolita Antoniia Surozhskogo. Materialy pervoi mezhdunarodnoi Konferentsii 28-30 sentiabria 2007*, Biblioteka-fond "Russkoe Zarubezhie", M. 2008, pp.82-98.
34. Correspondence in the MASF Archive relates to Anthony's 1997 attempts to involve Patriarch Aleksii II as mediator between him, Archbishop Lazar of Sympheropol and Crimea and Metropolitan Vladimir of Ukraine, whose blessing he required, and the parish in Sudak that wished for closer ties with Sourozh under an elected priest without breaking with their immediate hierarchical superior Archbishop Lazar. Metropolitan Anthony wrote repeatedly to all three but I could find no trace of an answer. The initiative foundered on the Archbishop's refusal to deal with their elected priest and the congregation's refusal to accept, in his stead, an appointed pastor.
35. A. Solzhenitsyn, "A grain between two grindstones: Sketches of exile, Part I (1974-1978)", first published in Russian in *Novyi mir*, No.9, 1998, p.60.
36. See Anthony's remark to Jacob Needleman recorded in the latter's chapter on their meetings in the book *Lost Christianity*: "In prayer one is *vulnerable*. You must not be enthusiastic, nor rejecting – but only *open*. This is the whole of asceticism –'to become open'," a dictum quoted by A. Filonenko in "The Russian Church in Great Britain" translated by Jonathan Sutton in the journal *Religion, State and Society*, Vol. 27, No.1, 1993.
37. Metropolitan Anthony, letter of 16 July 1980 to Father Marc Lotegen. Copy in MASF Archive (original in French, translation my own).
38. See Chapter Two, note 4.
39. Metropolitan Anthony of Sourozh, letter to Father Deiniol, 1983. Copy in MASF Archive.
40. The correspondence is preserved in the MASF Archive in the form of letters addressed by the participants to Metropolitan Anthony in September 1984 and copies of his answers.
41. Metropolitan Anthony of Sourozh, letter of 6 September 1988 to Marina X. Copy in the MASF Archive.
42. Metropolitan Anthony of Sourozh, letter of 12 September 1985 to "Effie". Copy in MASF Archive.
43. Metropolitan Anthony of Sourozh, letter of 22 June 1989 to "Père Jean", editor of *Nouvelle de la Fraternité* (original in French, translation my own). Copy in MASF Archive.

44. Achimandrite Melita, letter to Elizabeth Behr-Sigel inviting her to attend the consultation in Rhodes, which she forwarded to Metropolitan Anthony on 30 March 1988, MASF Archive.
45. "Surozhskaia eparkhiia". Talk by Metropolitan Anthony of Sourozh on the BBC Russian Service, June/September 1991. He was to return to the subject on 17 June 1995 and to emphasise their desire to keep the Russian language and Slavonic services in spite of the preponderance of English speakers.
46. Oral communication.
47. Crow, *This Holy Man*, p.9. The Metropolitan himself elicited the comment by remarking meditatively, as he surveyed the bewhiskered and rigidly upright portrait of his own grandfather, that "He seems so dignified: not the sort of man who would ever run for a bus".
48. Tatiana Maidanovich, private letter to her sister Elena.
49. "I find the New English Bible so flat," he wrote apologetically to a publisher who had asked him if they might substitute quotations from it for the Authorised Version in one of his books (Metropolitan Anthony of Sourozh, letter of 16 September 1971 to J. Purcel, editor of *Meditations on a Theme* for Mowbrays of 16 September 1971. Original of rough copy in MASF Archive).
50. T.S. Eliot Memorial Lectures, 1-14 November 1982 at the Cornwallis Lecture Theatre, University of Kent.
51. Oral communication.
52. Metropolitan Anthony of Sourozh, "Obrashchenie k prikhodu", 8 January 1989, published in Russian and English in the newsletter for that year. The exhortation to grow out of dependence was not a reversal of policy, but rather a generalisation of the principle of leading people out of themselves and himself into a direct and independent relationship with God. "I asked him if he would be my spiritual director," recalls Dr Frank Johnson, the co-founder of a remarkable medical and religious, teaching community "for service in the Third World", and he replied that he might get me into a situation where he could no longer help me and would prefer to do something less formal. . . . Some people claim that Metropolitan Anthony created a dependency in some people, but I certainly never sensed anything of that sort. In psychoanalysis sometimes, however hard the analyst struggles not to allow a dependency to take place, it nevertheless occurs. It all depends on the attitude of the person being analysed. I think the same thing can take place in the relationship between priest and people." Frank Johnson, unpublished memoir of Metropolitan Anthony, 2014.
53. Metropolitan Anthony of Sourozh, letter to the editor of *The Church Times* published in the number for 21 January 1983.

Chapter Nine
(pp.156–183)

1. From a 1917 prayer written on the fly-leaf of Andrei Bloom's Bible presented to him in 1931 by Father Georgii Shumkin.
2. Metropolitan Anthony of Sourozh, oral communication.
3. Nicholas Coleridge in *The Tatler* for April 1981.

4. Metropolitan Anthony of Sourozh, first letter to Bishop Vasilii (Rodzyanko), undated. Copy in MASF Archive. Also a follow-up letter of 21 March 1984, indicating that the situation was more confused than he had thought, and that he could not in the circumstance continue as spiritual director from afar but would always read and answer letters. However, in the circumstances his advice was to retire to a monastery in America and live "in prayer and study, in silence and away from all other concerns, the life of a monk". Rodzianko, Anthony's junior by a year, elected to take early retirement.
5. Metropolitan Anthony of Sourozh, letter of 18 November 1999 to Merylin Pfeffer.
6. See, for instance, his insistence to the British-Soviet Friendship Society that the service at Milton Keynes which they had invited him to celebrate to mark the millennium of Christianity in Russia in 1988 should be politics-free and, in general, his very cautious approach to the media on the subject of *glasnost'* – the new "transparency", which appeared to him infinitely fragile.
7. Metropolitan Anthony, New Year's sermon for 1988, originally in English in *Sourozh*, No.3, 1988, pp.1-3, published in Russian translation in the Paris newspaper *Russkaya Mysl'*.
8. There is an excellent article on the state of the Orthodox Church in this period by A. Filonenko, translated by Jonathan Sutton for *Religion, State and Society*, Vol.27, No.1, 1999, originally a paper for a conference arranged by Keston College at the Leeds Centre for Russian "Reflections on the Laity – a Focus for Christian dialogue between East and West", 30 June-3 July 1988. In Russian the article appeared many years later in *Alpha et Omega*, No.34, 2002, pp.349-63.
9. Metropolitan Anthony of Sourozh, letter of 26 November 1990 to Jay Wilson-Rudd, who was to give a talk about him and had written to ask how *Perestroika* and changes in the Eastern Bloc had affected his relationship with Russia and the Church there. For Anthony's preaching on the subject of learning to be free in Russia in English translation see Chapters 12, "Freedom and Spiritual Obedience", and 13, "Pastoral Concern for Spiritual Life" of *Encounter*.
10. Metropolitan Anthony of Sourozh, letter to Metropolitan Pitirim of 12 August 1988. Copy in MASF Archive.
11. See, for example, the interview with Metropolitan Anthony, "V Londone my molimsia o Rossii" in *Komsomol'skaia Pravda*, 30 July 1991, in which he stresses the stringency of British immigration laws and the poverty of the Diocese of Sourozh, emphasising also his own personal ethos of poverty which enabled him to live, as the shocked interviewer commented, on "less than the basic wage of a hospital porter".
12. Metropolitan Anthony of Sourozh, letter to Mr Whitehouse of 9 July 1987. Copy in MASF Archive.
13. See letter from Malcolm Rushton of the Universal Church of Christ the King of 6 July 1988 and Metropolitan Anthony's reply of the same date. Copies in MASF Archive.
14. See correspondence between Metropolitan Anthony of Sourozh and John Salter of AECA, letters of 16 October and 6 November 1987. The reception was held the following year on the Feast of St Seraphim of Sarov, 8 October 1988.
15. See note 9 for English versions of these talks.

16. Peter Scorer, a report on his and his wife Irina's attendance at the Bishops' *Sobor* in Moscow on the occasion of the 400th anniversary of the Moscow Patriarchate, 7-16 October 1989. Typescript in MASF Archive.
17. Ekaterina Morozova, "O vstrechakh s mitropolitom surozhskim Antoniem (1973-1990 gody)", "Obshchina xxi veka", *Pravoslavnoe obozrenie*, 16 No.3 (40), 2004, pp.5-7. The talk itself, filled out with extracts from previous talks, was published in the journal *Chrysostom*, No.1, 1992, and in English as Chapter 3 of the book *Encounter*, pp.37-69.
18. Metropolitan Anthony of Sourozh, "Obrashchenie k pastve", 8 January 1989. See Chapter Eight.
19. Metropolitan Anthony of Sourozh, "Obrashchenie k dukhovenstvu i k chlenam Eparkhial'nogo sobraniia i vsem veruiushchim Surozhskoi eparkhii avgusta 1999". In Russian in MASF Archive, my translation.
20. See Metropolitan Anthony's letter to Patriarch Pimen of 9 January 1988 broaching the subject and subsequent persistent reminders. Copies in the MASF Archive.
21. See note 19.
22. Copies of the text of this proposal and of Ilarion's hand-written letter of support are available in the MASF Archive.
23. Cf. Anthony's positive assessment of the electoral process and of the elected candidate, Aleksii II, in the *Journal of the Moscow Patriarchate*, No.10, 1990.
24. Cf. A.I. Shmaina-Velikanova, "Obraz Apostola Pavla v propovedi Vladyki Antoniia", Biblical-Theological Institute of St Andrew the Apostle's evening on the occasion of Metropolitan Anthony of Sourozh's 40 years ministry as Bishop in the House-Museum of Marina Tsvetaeva, Moscow, on 25 February 1998.
25. Metropolitan Anthony of Sourozh, "O sluzhenii patriarkha" from the section "Propovedy na rukopolozhenie", *Pastyrstvo*, "Novye mekhi", Minsk, 2005, pp.269-70. Here in Russian, my translation.
26. Metropolitan Anthony of Sourozh, letter of September 1991 to Boris Nikolaevich Eltsin. Copy in MASF Archive.
27. Metropolitan Anthony of Sourozh, letter of 21 October 1990 to Patriarch Aleksii II. Copy in MASF Archive.
28. Metropolitan Anthony of Sourozh, letter of 5 June 1992 to Patriarch Aleksii II. Copy in MASF Archive. See also on this subject the copy of Anthony's long interview with Natalia Babasian (London, June 1993) in the MASF Archive in which the Metropolitan lays responsibility for defections to Roman Catholic and Protestant missionaries at the door of the Orthodox Church for failing to provide proper instruction in the Orthodox faith to the influx of Russians returning to the Mother Church after the dissolution of the Soviet Union.
29. Evgenii Borisovich Pasternak, oral communication, imparted with all sympathy for Bishop Basil.
30. Metropolitan Anthony of Sourozh, letter of 6 January 1994 to Patriarch Aleksii II. Copy in MASF Archive.
31. See also Metropolitan Anthony of Sourozh, letter to Archbishop Mark of Berlin and Germany of 2 March 1994. Further on the subject of reconciliation with the Russian Orthodox Church abroad, see Victor Pokrovsky's interview with Metropolitan Anthony, "Otnosheniia s zarubezhnoi Tserkoviu stali miagche", *Nezavisimaia gazeta*, 17 June 1992.

32. Metropolitan Anthony of Sourozh, letter of 6 January 1994 to Patriarch Aleksii II.
33. Metropolitan Anthony of Sourozh, letter of 31 January 1997 to Patriarch Aleksii II.
34. Metropolitan Anthony of Sourozh to Patriarch Aleksii II. The copy in the MASF Archive is dated only by year: 1998. There is a rather rough English translation or summary of content but the version quoted here is directly translated from the Russian, as are all the other letters to Patriarch Aleksii II, by the author.
35. Metropolitan Anthony of Sourozh, letter of 19 July 1998 to the Oxford parish on the occasion of the twentieth anniversary of the consecration of the church.
36. See the anonymous obituary for Sergei Averintsev in *Knizhnoe obozrenie*, 1 March 2006.
37. Metropolitan Anthony of Sourozh, letter of 15 August 1998 to Patriarch Aleksii II. There is no record of a reply in the archive but the "bitter" letter caused no rupture in the relationship.
38. Irina von Schlippe, paper read at the September 2013 International Conference on the heritage of Metropolitan Anthony of Sourozh in Moscow.
39. Metropolitan Anthony of Sourozh, letter of 6 July 1999 to Patriarch Aleksii II.
40. Metropolitan Anthony of Sourozh, letter of 25 October 1999 to Metropolitan Vladimir.
41. Fedor Vasiliuk, "On stoit kak by riadom s pervoistochnikom", *Russkaia mysl'*, no.4327, 20-26 July 2000.
42. Aleksandr Ogorodnikov at the 2013 International Conference in memory of Metropolitan Anthony of Sourozh, organised by MASF in Moscow, September 2013.
43. Valentina Matveeva, *O mitropolite Surozhskom Antonii, sbornik materialov k 10-letiiu so dnia prestavleniia*, Sourozhskaia eparkhia, London, 2013, originally online, mitras, my translation. "Vstrecha" was the first of a series of excellent films. The book she mentions was Tatiana Maidanovich's 1972 Paris publication in Russian circulated in *samizdat*.
44. Sergei Averintsev, "Po tu storonu 'traditsionalizma' i 'liberalizma'", *Kontinent*, No.1 (87), 1996. Reprinted in *O mitropolite Surozhskom Antonii* (2013), p.23. In this article, Averintsev, like Matveeva, pays tribute to the role of the Maidanovich sisters. Subsequently, Metropolitan Anthony enlarged on his reply. In Russia, he said, people are asking for guidelines to make choices: "I was approached by a Russian intellectual, a very learned man: 'Vladyka, can you tell me how I should make choices today, decide things for myself? I have never been taught how to do that.' I answered: 'If I tell you it will be another set of rules for you to learn by rote. You have to learn for yourself. The fashion for living to order is over, it is time to learn to live according to the voice of conscience. In reality, we don't need the Ten Commandments or the Gospel to know that if I do this or that I will be contemptible.' To develop this awareness in everybody: that's where, as I see it, 'creative morality' begins." Pavel ASS, "Nikogo nel'zia nasil'no vesti po svoiei doroge", *Obshchaia gazeta*, 6-13 November 1996.
45. See, for instance, the very lively accounts by Father Vladimir Timakov and Ekaterina Morozova in the memorial number of the newspaper *Obshchina* 16 No.3 (40).

46. Sergei Averintsev, "Ogon' ostaetsia ognem", *Zvezda*, 1991, No.1, pp.120-21.
47. A. Kyrlezhev, "Mistik v miru", *Kontinent*, 2005, No.117. Reprinted in *O Mitropolite surozhskom Antonii* (2013), pp.69-70.
48. Sergei Averintsev, "Ogon' ostaetsia ognem", *Zvezda*, 1991, No.1, pp.120-21.
49. Aleksandr Kyrlezhev, "K 80-letiu mitropolita Surozhskogo Antoniia. Mitropolit Antonii, zaezhii pravoslavnyi missioner v Rossii", *Kontinent*, 1994, No.82, pp.229-36.
50. Aleksandr Kyrlezhev, in the journal *Itogi*, 20 August 1996, pp.67-9.
51. Ol'ga Sedakova, "Propoved' dlia vzroslykh", *Russkaia mysl'*, 26 November-2 December 1998, No.42, 47.
52. Iurii Vilensky, "The Life and Fate of Anthony of Sourozh the Physician Andrei Bloom", *Doktor*, 2002, No.4, pp.88-90. Cf. also Metropolitan Anthony of Sourozh, interview with Michael Epstein in London in April 1989 in *Encounter*, pp.22-3.
53. Nikolai Balashev, "Diocesan Summer Camp in Wales: the impressions of a pilgrim from Russia", Diocesan Newsheet *Sobornii listok*, No.268, December 1993. On a personal note, I shall never forget the buzz created by my daughter Irina, a product of these same summer camps, when asked at one of the International Metropolitan Anthony Conferences at the Dom russkogo zarubezhiia in Moscow how we should speak to our children. "As we would to our contemporaries – tell them the truth," she offered. The audience looked genuinely startled, but one of the organisers who knew the Sourozh diocese exclaimed: "That's Anthony's school for you!" See also A. Filonenko, "Russkaia Pravoslavnaia Tserkov' v Velikobritanii XX veka: Miriane i otkrytost' miru", *Al'fa et Omega*, 2002, No.34, pp.349-63.
54. See "Points from Correspondence" in *Shepherd, an Orthodox Christian Pastoral Magazine*, Vol. IX, No.11, August 1989, which states the editors have received the script of a lecture in French by Metropolitan Anthony of Sourozh published in *Contacts* with a "theological comment" by an anonymous priest of the Greek Archdiocese of Thyateira (in London). The preamble expresses respect and liking for the Russian Metropolitan but speaks of "aberrant practises in insufficiently overseen small communities of the Diocese of Sourozh" and expresses some dismay at the Metropolitan's known support for serious discussion of the ordination of women in the Orthodox Church. The main thrust of the criticism, however, is against Anthony's opinion that, at the "Lama sabbachthani?" moment on the Cross, Christ identified not only with our physical humanity but with our loss of God (which equates with atheism). This, he says, is Nestorianism, i.e. the assertion that Christ was of two separate natures and so capable of losing His divinity at this or any other moment, whereas Orthodoxy holds the two natures to be mingled without confusion or separation. The writer also feels that Anthony is wrong to suggest sinners and non-believers are not necessarily the "enemies of God", whereas patristic teaching suggests all men after the Fall are His enemies. The "theological comment", interpreted as a "scathing attack" by some friends and supporters (see for instance Father Alexis of the St Edward Brotherhood's letter of the same year in the MASF Archive), did not cause any rift with the Greek Church in England, nor did Anthony reply specifically to the critique in print.

55. See, for instance, Priest Aleksii Ostaev, "Ne uvlekaetes' ucheniem mitropolita Antoniia (Bliuma)", *Russkii vestnik*, No.2-3, 1995. Father Aleksii, whose point of departure is a talk given by Metropolitan Anthony to students of the Theological Academy, claims his defence of reason and good works is "satanic doctrine" and appears to regret the censorship: "Nowadays, when numberless little books with Christian titles are circulating in our society with satanic teachings" such views are, he implies, particularly dangerous. One can be saved ONLY through faith in Jesus Christ: heretics and Muslims, however "good", cannot "receive salvation".
56. See Ieromonakh Ilarion (Al'feev), introduction to publication by Metropolitan Anthony of Sourozh in the collection *Pravoslavnoe bogoslovie na rubezhe stoletii: sbornik statei*, M, Krutitskoe Podvori'e, 1999, pp.255-382. Also the same author's "Pravoslavnoe svidetel'stvo. K 50-letiiu sluzheniia v sviashchenom sane Mitropolita Surozhskogo Antoniia", *Tserkov' i vremia, nauchno–bogoslovskii i tserkovno-obshchestvennyi zhurnal*, 1988, No.3 (6).
57. See internet publications "Mitropolit Antonii (Bloom) opravdyvaet vozmozhnost' abortov": http://antimodern.ru/abort-sourozh/.

   In fact, Anthony was in most cases firmly opposed to "killing children in the womb", but he did not consider that stillborn or aborted children were "deprived of eternal life". On the contrary, his opposition to abortion was founded on the conviction that the foetus, from the moment the sperm fertilises the egg, *is* an immortal soul. However, he was unwilling to lay down the law about the correct or incorrect Christian attitude to the ever-increasing possibilities of medical science and was prepared to argue and evaluate individual cases on merit, seeking always, as he put it, "the mind of Christ" rather than establishing a set of hard and fast rules.
58. This and all the above quotations are from speeches made at the services and reception for the fortieth anniversary of Anthony's consecration as Bishop in the *Sobornyi listok*, No.315, January 1998.
59. Igumen Ioann (Ekonomtsev), opening speech at the meeting of the Russian Orthodox University of 29 October 1997. Stenogram report in the MASF Archive. A later meeting at the House Museum of Marina Tsvetaieva on 25 February 1998 brought together an even wider diapason of speakers, from the scholar Anna Il'inichna Shmaina-Velikanova to the poet Olga Sedakova, from the psychiatrist Fedor Efimovich Vasiliuk to the theatrical critic B.N. Liubimov.
60. *Ibid.*
61. Metropolitan Anthony of Sourozh, answer to a letter to Bishops of the Orthodox Church written by participants in the Third Orthodox Youth Festival organised by Syndesmos in 1988.

Chapter 10
(pp.184-198)

1. See Chris Parish, interview with Metropolitan Anthony: "What is enlightenment?": http://silouanthompson.net/2008/11/such-people-we-have-never-seen/.
2. Metropolitan Anthony of Sourozh, "Certain categories of our existence in creation", address given to the Moscow Theological Academy on 1 December

1966, first published in Russian in the journal *Tserkov' i vremia*, 1991, No.2. Quoted here as translated by Tatiana Wolff, *Encounter*, p.83.
3. *Ibid.*, p.84.
4. Protoierei Aleksandr Stepanov, "Anglisskoe pravoslavie na russkoi pochve" ("English Orthodoxy from Russian soil"), interview with Irina and Vladimir von Schlippe originally broadcast from the radio station "Grad Petrov", quoted here from *O mitropolite Surozhskom Antonii* (2013), pp.113-35.
5. Gillian Crow, *This Holy Man*, pp.227-8.
6. Metropolitan Anthony of Sourozh, *On the Light that Shineth in Darkness*, Fond dukhovnogo naslediia Mitropolita Antoniia Surozhskogo, Moscow, 2012, p.64. This book is also available in Russian, translated by E.I. Sadovnikova and edited by E. and T. Maidanovitch with a commentary by A.I. Shmaina-Velikanova, as *Uverennost' v veshchakh nevidimikh. Poslednye besedy*, Moscow, 2012.
7. *Ibid.*, p.3.
8. *Ibid.*, p.23.
9. *Ibid.*, p.25.
10. *Ibid.*, p.42.
11. *Ibid.*, p.55. Metropolitan Anthony sourced this solution to the "problem" of the Fall to St Irinaeus of Lyons via Olivier Clément.
12. *Ibid.*, p.57.
13. *Ibid.*, p.58.
14. *Ibid.*, p.74.
15. *Ibid.*, p.75.
16. *Ibid.*, p.78.
17. *Ibid.*, pp.92-4.
18. *Ibid.*, p.90.
19. *Ibid.*, p.91.
20. *Ibid.*, p.100.
21. *Ibid.*, p.111.
22. *Ibid.*, p.120.
23. *Ibid.*, p.129.
24. *Ibid.*, p.147.
25. *Ibid.*, p.151.
26. *Ibid.*, p.156.
27. *Ibid.*, p.157.
28. For disparate Orthodox views on this controversy, see clips from *Nezavisimaia gazeta* and *Sourozh, Orthodox News*, on the internet under general title "European reactions to events in the Diocese of Sourozh".
29. See Gillian Crow, *This Holy Man*, p.229. Also announcement by Metropolitan Anthony after Liturgy on Sunday 2 February 2002.
30. *Ibid.*, p.230. For a description of the ceremony of consecration, conducted by Patriarch Aleksii in person, see http://www.pravoslavie.ru/news/020114/02.htm for 26 January 2002.
31. Irina von Schlippe, speaking at the Fourth International Conference in Memory of Metropolitan Anthony of Sourozh in Moscow, September 2013.
32. See address by Bishop Hilarion of Kerch at the Extraordinary Meeting of the Sourozh Diocese, 25 May 2002.

33. Bishop Ilarion of Podol'sk in *Nezavisimaia gazeta* No.8 for 21 August 2002. Anthony, Metropolitan of Sourozh, "Otkrytoe pis'mo Episkopu Podol'skomu Ilarionu (Alfeevu)", *Nezavismaia gazeta*, No.6, 21 August 2002.
34. Gillian Crow, *This Holy Man*, p.231. Also Metropolitan Anthony of Sourozh, address to London Parish of 12 December 2002: https://www.youtube.com/watch?feature=player_embedded&v=iAlVtZqhOq0.
35. Protopriest John Lee, "Ot mira k liubvi ('From peace to love')", *Tserkov_–bogochelovecheskoe obshchestvo*, materialy Tret'ei mezhdunarodnoi Konferentsii, 23-25 sentiabria 2011, Moscow, 2013, p.18.
36. Deacon Peter Scorer, oral contribution from the floor, Fourth International Conference on Anthony Metropolitan of Sourozh at the Dom russkogo zarubezhia in Moscow, September 2013. This particular Easter is touchingly described in Gillian Crow's *This Holy Man*, p.237.
37. Protopriest John Lee, "Vmesto predisloviia" ("instead of a foreword"), *Trudy* II, "Praktika", Moscow, 2007, p.14.
38. *Ibid.*
39. Father Michael Fortounatto, "On the tenth anniversary of the death of Metropolitan Anthony of Sourozh (4 August 2003): Personal memories", 18 October 2013. Originally in French at a memorial evening in Paris. Trans. by Deacon Peter Scorer and read out by him at the London Memorial Conference, October 2013. When Father Michael mentions six European languages he is, presumably, counting Church Slavonic and Latin. It may be, however, that Father Michael was thinking of the passage in "Without Notes" in which the Metropolitan said:

> I was made to speak Russian and French from childhood. I spoke in Russian to my father, in French to my grandmother, and in both to my mother.... Then I spoke German. I had been taught as a small child how to pronounce German correctly, and this has helped me a great deal and still does.... I can read in Spanish; Italian is no problem. Dutch is easy because it is very like German of the twelfth and thirteenth centuries. When I am mentally exhausted, I read German poetry of that period as a form of relaxation.

See *Encounter*, p.224, note 44.

Glossary of Proper Names

Abbott, Eric Symes (1906-1983). Ed. Nottingham High School and Jesus College, Cambridge. Chaplain then Dean of King's College, London, 1932-55. Warden of Keble College, Oxford, 1956-60. Dean of Westminster 1959-74.

Afanasii, Archimandrite (Nechaev, Anatolii Ivanovich) (1886-1943). Ed. Theological Seminary of Penza; worked on railway and as voluntary teacher. Emigrated to Finland in 1923, worked for the Salvation Army and became novice at Monastery of Valaam. In 1925 seconded to Paris, monk 1926, priest 1927. Served in various Russian churches in France under **Metropolitan Evlogii**, but, in 1931, opted to remain with the Moscow Patriarchate. Dean of Russian parishes of the Moscow Patriarchate in France 1933-43. Interrogated by the Gestapo in 1942. Spiritual director from 1933 to Andrei Bloom whom he professed monk under the name of Anthony in 1943.

Aleksii (Mensbrugghe, Albert Emil'evich van der) (1899-1980). Ed. Jesuit Gymnasium in Ghent, the Seminary of St Nicholas and the College of St Benedict in the Monastery of St Andrew in Bruges. Roman Catholic priest 1925. Received into the Russian Orthodox Church in 1928. Pastor to the Romanian Church in London. Inspector in the Orthodox Theological Institute, Vicar Bishop of Meudon 1960, Bishop of Philadelphia, Vicar of the Diocese of New York 1970-71.

Aleksii II (Ridiger, Aleksei Mikhailovich) (1929-2008). Ed. Leningrad Theological Seminary, Leningrad Theological Academy. Priest 1950, Bishop of Tallin 1961. Worked in the Moscow Patriarchate 1964, Archbishop 1964, Metropolitan 1968, served as a permanent member of the Holy Synod. In charge of the Leningrad and Novgorod Diocese and simultaneously of the Tallin Diocese. Patriarch of Moscow and all Russia 1990-2008.

Aleksii I (Simansky, Sergei Vladimirovich) (1877-1970). Ed. Lazarev Institute of Oriental Languages and the Nikolayev Lycée, Moscow University, and Moscow Theological Academy. Priest 1903, Bishop 1913, Archbishop 1929, Metropolitan of Novgorod 1932 and of Leningrad 1933. Twice arrested in the 1920s and banished for three years to Semipalatinsk. Patriarch of Moscow and All Russia 1945-70.

Ambartsumov, Evgenii (1917-1969). Son of the martyred Archpriest St Vladimir Ambartsumov. Archpriest, Vicar of the St Vladimir Cathedral, Leningrad, 1950-60 and 1967-69.

Anatolii (Kuznetsov, Evgenii Vlasovich) (b. 1930). Ed. Moscow Theological Seminary (graduated 1950) and Academy. Deacon 1954, priest 1956, Bishop of Vilensk and Litovsk 1972-74. Representative of the Moscow Patriarchate to the Patriarchate of Antioch and All the East 1979; Bishop of Ufa. Appointed Suffragan Bishop to Metropolitan Anthony of Sourozh, with the title "of Kerch", then Archbishop in 1993. At present serves in London and in Manchester.

Antonii, Metropolitan (Khrapovitsky, Aleksei Pavlovich) (1863-1936). Ed. St Petersburg Gymnasium and Theological Academy of St Petersburg; priest-monk 1885. Retired from his position as Archbishop of Kharkov and Akhtyr by the provisional government, although his election as a representative of the monastics to the All-Russian Local Council of 1917-18 was followed by appointment as Metropolitan. Arrested by Petliura in Kiev, was exiled with **Archbishop Evlogii (Georgievsky)** to a Uniate monastery in Galicia. Emigrated to Constantinople and became Chairman of the VTsU 1920. At Karlovy Sremtsy in Serbia in 1921, he chaired the first conference of the Russian Church abroad and acted as senior hierarch of this so-called Synodal Church. The cause of their split with Moscow was political rather than theological or canonical, but persisted until long after Antonii's death in 1936 and, indeed, until many years after the break-up of the Soviet Union.

Anthony (Mel'nikov) (1924-1986). Ed. Moscow Theological Academy, graduated 1950, Metropolitan 1975-78, Metropolitan of Leningrad 1978-96.

Athenagoros II (Kokkinakis) (1912-1979). Dean of Holy Cross Theological School in Boston. Archbishop of Diocese of Thyateira and Great Britain from 1963 (enthroned 1964). In 1967 hosted first visit by an Ecumenical Patriarch to England. Established *The Orthodox Herald*, diocesan journal, and worked towards a contemporary understanding of liturgical practice in the Greek Orthodox Church.

Averintsev, Sergei Sergeevich (1937-2004). Ed. Moscow University. Russian Byzantologist, encyclopaedist and essayist, fellow of several international academies and cultural societies. Study of the ancient and mediaeval world led him to seek baptism into the Orthodox Church during *Perestroika*, when he became one of Moscow's most popular publicists and speakers. In 1989, elected from the Academy of Sciences, of which he was by then a candidate member, to the Congress of People's Deputies. Author of many studies on patristics and Russian and European literature from the eighteenth century to modern times, he also made new translations of many psalms, the Book of Job and the Synoptic Gospels.

Baccolini, Gregorio (secular name Sergio) (1913-1997). Priest, Vicar of the Orthodox Church in Torino 1964-79. Brought up a Roman Catholic, Baccolini was at one stage close to Mussolini's Fascist Youth. Joined the Moscow Patriarchal Church after the war and had difficulty with the French authorities, first because of his "fascist" past and later because of suspected ties with Moscow. Eventually joined a non-canonical branch of the troubled Orthodox Church in Italy.

Baird-Smith, Robin (b. 1946). Ed. Winchester, Royal Academy of Music, Trinity College, Cambridge. Still active as publisher in 2004. Employee of Darton, Longman and Todd 1968-71 and Editorial Director 1971-78. Moved to Collins 1978-81; Editorial Director of Constable publishing house 1981-85; Director of *The Tablet* from 1999. Member of Analytical Psychology Club.

Basil (Osborne), Bishop. *See* Osborne.

Behr, Tatiana ("Tatisha") (née Zakharova) (1917-2006). Ed. Paris. Family background intensely musical. She was a pillar of the Orthodox Church in London and friend from youth of Metropolitan Anthony.

Behr-Sigel, Elizabeth ("Lizelotte") (1907-2005). French Orthodox theologian. Ed. Independent Protestant Theological Faculty in Paris. Devoted a doctoral dissertation to the Russian theologian Archimandrite Fedor Bukharev. Towards the end of the 1920s influenced by **Pavel Evdokimov, Vladimir Lossky**, and the **brothers Kovalevsky** and was received into the Orthodox Church in 1932. Together with **Father Lev Gillet** was one of the founding members of the francophone parish in which Andrei Bloom served from 1936. Member of the Fellowship of St Alban and St Sergius. Lectured at the St Sergius Theological Institute, the Higher Ecumenical School in Paris and the Tantour Ecumenical Institute in Jerusalem. Author of a book in French on "The Ministry of Women in the Orthodox Church" (1987) with an introduction by Metropolitan Anthony, a book (with Kallistos Ware) on "The Ordination of Women in the Orthodox Church" (2000) and a life of Lev Gillet (English translation by Helen Wright, 1999).

Bel'sky (Iudin-Bel'sky, Mikhail Andreevich) (1884-1963). Ed. the Alexander Military Academy in Moscow (graduated 1904). Served to rank of colonel as professional soldier. In World War One fought with Tsarist then Volunteer Army, was captured by the Poles and emigrated to Germany in 1920. Settled in France in 1924 and, vexed by disunity among the Orthodox, became an Eastern Rite Catholic in 1927 and attended lectures at the Roman Catholic Theological Institute in Paris, but returned to the Russian Orthodox Church under the jurisdiction of the Moscow Patriarchate in 1931. Priest 1933; served as Vicar of the francophone parish of Ste Geneviève and the Mother of God, Joy of all who Sorrow 1934-63; mitred archpriest 1954. Imprisoned by the Gestapo for helping Jews August 1942-April 1943; member of the governing body of the fellowship of Russian Resistance in France 1946.

Berdiaev, Nikolai Aleksandrovich (1874-1948). Ed. privately and at the military Cadets Corp, read first Natural Sciences then Law at Kiev University. Expelled for involvement with Social Democrats 1898, exiled to the Vologda region for three years in 1900. Studied Idealist Philosophy in Heidelberg 1903-1904. Lived in St Petersburg 1904-1905 where, with **S. Bulgakov**, he collaborated with the Merezhkovskys as editor of their journal *Novii Put'* ("The New Way"), which they renamed *Voprosy zhizni* ("Questions of Life"). As the 1905 Revolution subsided, both he and the founders of the "New Religious Consciousness" felt it expedient to spend some time in Paris, where the association cooled. On his return to Moscow, Berdiaev chaired the **Vladimir Solov'ev** Religious Philosophical Society and contributed to the 1909 collection *Vekhi* ("Milestones"). As author, was concerned to redefine the Russian intelligentsia's mission, which he saw as being to reconcile a modern, questioning Christian philosophy with traditional

Russian Orthodox spiritual piety. These problems he continued to foreground in books such as *The Russian Idea* (title of a 1941 work on "Fundamental problems of Russian thought in the nineteenth and early twentieth century"), *The Kingdom of the Spirit and the Realm of Caesar* (1949), and *The Existential Dialectic between the Divine and the Human* (1952). During the 1917 Revolution and thereafter was involved in Russian intellectual life as founder of the Free Philosophical Association for the promotion of "spiritual culture" ("*Volphil*"), President of the Moscow Writers' Union and, in 1922, Professor at Moscow University, in which year he was deported to Berlin where he founded, with the support of the YMCA, an Academy of Religious Philosophy. His friend **Lev Shestov** was instrumental in an invitation to take up residence in Clamart, Paris, where from 1925 to 1946 he edited the journal *Put'* (*La Voie*).

Beriozova, Svetlana (1932-1998). In 1940 her family emigrated to the USA where she studied classical ballet under her father. Joined Grand Ballet de Monte Carlo 1947, joined Sadler's Wells 1950. From 1955 prima ballerina. Retired in 1975.

Bernanos, Georges (1888-1948). Ed. Paris 1906-13. French novelist and essayist whose subject is the Dostoyevskian "God fights the Devil for the soul of man". His *Journal d'un curé de campagne* ("Diary of a country-priest") was often cited by Metropolitan Anthony.

Binns, John (b. 1951). Ed. St John's College, Cambridge, 1969-73, in the Orthodox Theological Faculty in Belgrade on a student exchange (1974), at the College of the Resurrection, Mirfield 1974-76 and then as part-time post-graduate student for PhD at King's College, London. Present post: Vicar of Great St Mary's, the University Church, Cambridge, as from 1994. Other positions at various times: Chair of the Fellowship of St Alban and St Sergius; Founding Director of the Institute of Orthodox Studies, Cambridge; Chair of Partners for Change in Ethiopia. Books include *Ascetics and Ambassadors for Christ* (OUP, 1994) and *Introduction to the Orthodox Christian Church* (CUP, 2002).

Bloom, Boris Eduardovich (1884-1937). Ed. at home where he was tutored in Latin, Greek and French, read Mathematics at Moscow University, then studied Oriental Languages at the diplomatic school of the Foreign Ministry. Entered the diplomatic service and was serving as Secretary to the Consul-General **N.A. Scriabin** in Erzerum when he met and married Scriabin's daughter **Ksenia Nikolaevna**. One son, Andrei (in religion Anthony), b. 1914. Soon after the beginning of World War One Bloom was appointed one of the Russian consuls, then Consul-in-Chief, in Persia. In the emigration, he sought to expiate what he felt as the responsibility of the educated classes for the Russian Revolution by a solitary life of physical labour (he only took clerking jobs after his health gave way), silence and prayer. He and Ksenia Nikolaevna divorced, though neither remarried, and he remained a distinct presence and influence in the life of his son.

Bolshakov, Sergei Nikolaevich (1901-1990). Ed. technical school in Russia. Emigrated via the Balkans, member of the Brotherhood of St Vladimir, proceeded to England where he studied Philosophy and defended his doctoral thesis in 1946; he wrote in English on Khomiakov and Russian mystic spirituality. Was an active supporter of the ecumenical movement.

Borisov, Aleksandr Il'ich (b. 1937). Ed. Moscow University, deacon 1970 then priest in one of the Moscow churches. In the early 1990s was elected Deputy to the Moscow City Council. Later served as Dean of the newly opened Church of Saints Cosmas and Damian and he served as President of the Russian Bible Society. A supporter of the use of modern Russian in church services; see also **Georgii Kochetkov.**

Borovoi, Vitalii Mikhailovich (1916-2008). Ed. Polish elementary school then Orthodox Seminary in Vilnius and from 1936 to 1939 at the Theological Faculty of the University of Warsaw. In 1941 became a reader in a country church. From March 1942 worked as diocesan secretary to Archbishop Filofei (Narko) of Mogilev, a post he resumed after a brief period (1942-43) during the German occupation. In 1944, he evaded evacuation to Germany by going underground in Minsk until the liberation. He was arrested by SMERSH but released at the intervention of Archbishop Vasilii (Ratmirov), to whom he had handed over the affairs of the evacuated diocese, on condition he was ordained priest (1944). In the same year he was appointed Vicar of the Cathedral of St Peter and St Paul in Gomel. Helped organise the Minsk Theological Seminary at the Monastery of Zhirzovitsk, while studying as an external student of the Leningrad Theological Academy, from which he graduated in 1953 with the degree of Candidate in Theology; doctorate in 1962, in which year he was also a delegate to the Second Vatican Council. From 1997, consultant to the Department of Foreign Relations of the Moscow Patriarchate. He helped pave the way for the entry of the Patriarchate into the World Council of Churches and, from 1962 for the next thirteen years served as their representative with this body in Geneva. Vicar of the Patriarchal Cathedral in Elokhov 1973-78, and 1984 "Honorary Vicar" of the Church of the Resurrection in Briusov pereulok in Moscow.

Bourdeaux, Michael (b. 1934). Founder of the Keston Institute, since 2007 under the care of the Keston Centre for Religion, Politics, and Society at Baylor University, Texas. Michael Bourdeaux, an ordained priest, has made a study of religious persecution under communism since the late 1950s.

Bouteneff, Vera Sergeevna (neé Troubetskaia) (b. 1926). Grew up among fellow Russian émigrés in Paris, in a climate of Orthodox theological renaissance. Moving to the USA in the 1950s, she maintained a deep involvement in the life of the Church and in the translation of Russian Orthodox literature.

Brodsky, Iosif Aleksandrovich (1940-1996). Ed. various schools in Leningrad, after which he scraped a living on the fringes of Soviet literature, which left him open to a sentence of five years forced labour for "parasitism" (being wilfully unemployed). In 1964 influential friends obtained his release and permission to return to Leningrad but the two books of poetry he then produced were published in the United States, not Russia, and, in 1972, he was exiled. A friend and disciple of Anna Akhmatova, an admirer of Osip Mandel'shtam and the English poets Donne, Eliot and Auden, he was also inspired by the classics of Ancient Greece, Rome and Renaissance Europe. Resident in the United States from 1972, he wrote some later poetry in English, received the Nobel Prize for Literature in 1987 and served as US Poet Laureate from 1991-92.

Brown, Janet (née Bell) (b. 1950). Ed. Trinity College, Dublin, and Imperial College, London; MSc 1973, PhD 1978. Known especially for her work on the history of nineteenth-century biology, she taught at the Wellcome Trust Centre for the History of Medicine, University College, London, before returning to Harvard, where she is currently Aramont Professor of the History of Science.

Bulgakov, Mikhail Afanasievich (1891-1940). Ed. school in Kiev and Faculty of Medicine at Kiev University. Practised briefly as a doctor in the provinces and in the army. After unsuccessful attempt to emigrate, he made a name for himself in the new Soviet literature. A novel, several plays and short stories depict, with great affection yet with a satirical edge which owes much to a perfect sense of timing, the "Whites" in their doomed struggle against the "Reds", as well as some of the absurdities of communist planning and Utopian attempts to manipulate science and/or society. Bulgakov trod a knife-edge between popularity, particularly at the box office, and ideological subversion. *Master and Margarita*, a highly controversial retelling of the Crucifixion against a background of Mephistophelian high-jinks in Soviet Moscow, was published posthumously but still during the Soviet period in 1966-67, and was an international sensation at the time.

Bulgakov, Sergei Nikolaevich, in religion Father Sergii (1871-1944). Ed. the Orel Theological Seminary, the Eletsk Gymnasium, Moscow University, and Berlin University (1988-89), and was awarded a Master's from Moscow University in 1901, after which he taught Political Economy in Kiev, and made the acquaintance of Nikolai Berdiaev, with whom he co-operated on the important compendium *Problemy Idealizma* ("Problems of Idealism"). They moved to St Petersburg in 1904 and co-edited the journals *Novyi Put'* ("The New Way") and *Voprosy zhizni* ("Questions of Life"). Back in Moscow, they co-operated on a second compendium *Vekhi* ("Milestones") in 1909. Was active in the **Vladimir Solov'ev** Religious Philosophical Society and the publishing firm Put', completed doctoral thesis on "The Philosophy of Economics" in 1912, served on the All-Russian Church Council in 1917 and Patriarch Tikhon's Higher Church Council 1917-18. A priest from 1918, he taught Political Economy and Theology at the University of Sympheropol' and served as Assistant Vicar at the Yalta Cathedral 1920-22; in 1922 was deported. In Prague (1923-25), he was attached to the Russian Church of St Nicholas, took part in the second council of the RSKhD and became founding member and spiritual guide to the Brotherhood of St Sophia. Founding member and first Dean of the Theological Institute of St Sergius (1925-44) in Paris. Mitred Archpriest in 1943 and doctor *honoris causa* in theology at the St Sergius Institute. His many books propounding his controversial Sophianic view of Christianity were translated into various languages.

Camus, Albert (1913-1960). Ed. high school in Algeria. French novelist, dramatist and thinker, whose doctrine of "the absurd" was influential on and expressive of the post-war existentialist mindset. Active in the Resistance, Camus, in his *Lettres à un ami allemand* (1944) and many later works, shows how his early, uncompromising moral nihilism metamorphosed into an agnostic and questioning reassertion of human dignity.

Chaliapin, Feodor. *See* Shaliapin.

Chartres, Richard John Carew (b. 1947). Ed. Hertford Grammar School; Trinity College, Cambridge; Cuddesdon and Lincoln Theological Colleges. Ordained deacon 1973 and priest 1974. Bishop of Stepney 1992 and London 1995. Responsible for relations between the Church of England and the Orthodox Churches; was present at the funeral of **Patriarch Aleksii II** and enthronement in Moscow of Kirill I.

Clément, Olivier (1921-2009). Ed. University of Montpellier. Was active in the French Resistance during the occupation. Influenced by Kierkegaard, Newman, **Lev Shestov** and by Hindu philosophy, he was drawn to Orthodoxy by **Vladimir Lossky**'s *Mystic Theology of the Orthodox Church*, **Berdiaev**'s *Philosophy of the Free Spirit* and the novels of Dostoevsky. In 1955 was accepted in the Orthodox Church, became a Professor of the St Sergius Theological Institute where he taught Moral Theology for thirty-five years, was doctor *honoris causa* of the Universities of Louvain, Bucharest and the Sacred Heart in Connecticut, editor of the Orthodox francophone journal *Contacts*, and president of the Society of Believing Writers of France.

Coggan, Donald Frederick (1909-2000). Ed. Merchant Taylor's School and St John's College, Cambridge. Took double first in Oriental Languages and served as Treasurer and Vice President of the Cambridge inter-collegiate Christian Union. University lecturer at Manchester 1931-34, ordained 1935, Professor for New Testament at Wycliffe College in Toronto 1937-44 and Principal of London College of Divinity 1944-56. Bishop of Bradford 1956 and, from 1961, of York. As Archbishop of Canterbury 1974-80 supported the ordination of women. Helped supply Russian children with the Bible.

Coleridge, Nicholas (b. 1957) Ed. Eton College and Trinity College, Cambridge. 1979-82 was associate editor of *The Tatler*, wrote for *Daily* and Friday *Telegraph*, *The Spectator, Financial Times, Evening Standard, Harpers & Queen*. In 1982 received prize for British Press Awards Young Journalist of the Year. President of Condé Nast.

Combes, Raoul (1883-1964). One of Andrei Bloom's lecturers at the Sorbonne.

Crow, Gillian (née Hood) (b. 1943). Ed. Swansea University, graduated with a degree in Latin in 1965 and married in the same year. Worked in local government and civil service. Became Orthodox in 1983 and Secretary to the Diocese of Sourozh in 1990. Represented Diocese then the Exarchate Deanery on CTE and CTB from their inception. Author of books *Grains of Salt and Rays of Light* (1994) and *This Holy Man* (2005); edited and introduced *Metropolitan Anthony of Sourozh: Essential Writings* (Orbis, "Modern Spiritual Masters", 2010).

Curie, Maurice (1888-1975). French physicist, specialist in fluorescence, photoluminescence and radiology. Nephew of Pierre Curie. He worked with Marie Curie 1913-14 in the Curie Laboratory Rue Cuvier; Professor of Physics at the Sorbonne, the Institute of Physics, Chemistry and Biology.

Denis (Dionisii) (Chambault, Lucien) (1899-1963). Half-French, half-English. Ed. Anglican school. In Paris worked as journalist writing on art for *Le P'tit Parisien* and the *Daily Mail*. In 1920 met I.C. Winnaert, and was consecrated priest of his

Catholic-Evangelical church in 1925. In 1936 the Moscow Patriarchate accepted Winnaert and his flock with permission to keep to their own ritual and the Gregorian calendar and Chambault was received into the Orthodox Church by **Mikhail Bel'sky** and consecrated deacon then priest by **Metropolitan Elevferii** in that same year. On death of Winnaert, Chambault became Vicar of his western Orthodox community. The job, however, was unpaid and he continued to work as a journalist. Having evacuated with his newspaper to Bordeaux, he decided to return to his duties to his flock under the occupation. At this time the Russian Patriarchal Church was cut off from contact with its bishops and was under the authority of the Dean of the Council Priest-monk Stephen (Svetozarov). Chambault was elected to succeed him but, because he did not speak Russian, chose to rank rather as his first representative. In 1944 he was professed monk under the name of Dionisii and chose to live as an Orthodox monk according to the rule of St Benedict. In 1948 Denis attended the Commission on "The Ecumenical Movement and the Orthodox Church" in Moscow. Appointed Archimandrite, he was discussed as a possible candidate for the exarchate, but was excluded – again for lack of knowledge of Russian. He visited the USSR in 1956 and 1960; after Archbishop Anthony's appointment in 1963 he became Chairman of the Synod of the Exarchate.

Ekonomtsev, Ioann (b. 1939). Ordained deacon, then priest in 1986, and took monastic vows with the name Ioann in 1989. Archimandrite since 2002. Rector of the Russian Orthodox University (retired).

Elchaninov, Aleksandr (1881-1934). Ed. Tiflis Gimnazium, where he was friend and classmate to **Pavel Florensky** and V.F. Ern, and the Historico-Philological Faculty of St Petersburg University. Secretary to Moscow Religious Philosophical Society 1905, studied for one year at Moscow Theological Academy. Teacher at then director of the Levandov Gimnazium, Tiflis. Emigrated to France, taught school in Nice, member of RSKhD and Brotherhood of St Sophia (1924), consecrated deacon then priest in 1926 under **Metropolitan Evlogii** and served in the Russian Cathedral at Nice until 1934, then in Alexander Nevsky Cathedral in Paris until his death. Elchaninov's notebooks were published after his death and became a classic of devotional literature.

Elevferii (Bogoiavlensky, Dmitrii Iakovlevich) (1870-1940). Ed. Kursk Theological Seminary. Worked as teacher in a parish school and parish priest. On death of his wife entered the St Petersburg Theological Academy (1890-94) and became a monk. He worked in various administrative capacities in religious education, then as Vicar and ruling Bishop of the Diocese of Litovsk, Archbishop of Vilensk and Litovsk from 1921. Imprisoned in a Roman Catholic monastery 1922-23, he was exiled from Poland and settled in Kovno, Lithuania; Metropolitan in 1928 and Head of the West European parishes of the Russian Patriarchate in 1931, in which capacity he visited the Soviet Union in 1933, and parishes of the Moscow Patriarchate in Europe until the onset of war in 1939.

Eliot, Thomas Stearns (1888-1965). Ed. Smith Academy and Harvard, the Sorbonne and Merton College, Oxford. Author of *The Wasteland, Four Quartets* and other long poems, several books of verse and poetic dramas, including *Murder in the Cathedral, The Family Reunion* and *The Cocktail Party*. Editor and founder of the literary magazine *Criterion* (1922-39). His work interested Metropolitan Anthony for its awareness of the desolation of the human condition and religious content. Eliot described himself as an "Anglo-Catholic".

Elizaveta, Mother (Medvedeva) (dates unknown). Superior of a small ROCOR convent of six Arab nuns who had followed her from Jerusalem to set up a community in London. Mother Elizaveta was an independently minded woman of spiritual stature who was a great support to **Timothy (later Kallistos) Ware** at a time when both ROCOR and Greek authorities were discouraging him from becoming Orthodox.

Ellison, Gerald (1910-1992). Ed. Westminster School, New College, Oxford. Studied for ordination at Westcott House, Cambridge, ordained 1936. Consecrated Bishop of Willesden 1950. Became Bishop of Chester 1955 and, 1972-81, Bishop of London.

Eltsin, Boris Nikolaevich (1931-2007). First President of the Russian Federation 1991-99.

Eschliman, Nikolai (1929-1985). Became famous together with **Gleb Yakunin** in 1965 as a signatory to an open letter challenging **Patriarch Aleksii I** to encourage the clergy in opposing repressive measures against the Church. While forbidden to celebrate or serve as pastor to his flock for this challenge to Patriarchal authority, he suffered a personal drama, divorced and remarried, which automatically debarred him from reinstatement to the priesthood.

Eusebio, Dom (Pace) (d. 1996). Brought up a Roman Catholic, he joined first the Moscow Patriarchal Church then a non-canonical off-shoot of the Orthodox Church in Italy. After the former suspended him from his position as Abbot, he took up residence in Genoa where he lived in retirement until his death.

Evdokimov, Pavel Nikolaevich (c. 1900-1970). Ed. Cadet Corps, entered Kiev Theological Institute but volunteered to serve with the White Army in the South and emigrated via Constantinople in 1920. In 1923 settled in Paris where he became First Secretary of the RSKhD and graduated from the St Sergius Theological Institute in 1928; he defended a doctoral thesis at the Philological Faculty of the University of Aix-en-Provence in 1942, worked in the Resistance 1943-44 and managed an ecumenical students' hostel in Sèvres 1947-62, then in Massey near Paris 1962-68. Member of Higher Ecumenical Institute in Boiset near Lausanne and founding member of Syndesmos 1953. Taught Moral Theology at St Sergius Institute 1953-59, as professor from 1959-70. Wrote prolifically in French on Orthodox theology, art and literature, introducing Jungian insights into some of his books, notably on the sacrament of marriage.

Evlogii, Metropolitan (Georgevsky, Vasilii Mikhailovich) (1868-1946). Ed. Belevskoe dukhovnoe uchilishche, Theological Seminary of Tula and Moscow Theological Academy. Worked as civil servant and teacher before taking holy orders in 1895. Served in various educational institutions and as Vicar, then Bishop and Archbishop in several Russian dioceses and as member of Second and Third State Dumas before the war. Member of the Holy Synod (1911-12), of the All-Russian Church Council 1917-18, and of the Ukrainian Council in 1918, when he was arrested and exiled by Petliura to a Uniate monastery in Galicia. On his release, emigrated 1920 via Constantinople to Yugoslavia, where, in 1926, he was appointed Archbishop in charge of Russian parishes in Western Europe by **Patriarch Tikhon** and moved to Berlin. Metropolitan from 1922 and member of the Archiepiscopal Synod abroad 1922-26. In Paris 1923 he founded the Theological Institute of St Sergius in 1925 and served as First Rector 1925-46. Broke with the Archiepiscopal Synod in 1926. They forbade him to celebrate 1927 but he was supported by the majority of his flock in Paris and, the following year, was confirmed by the patriarchal *locum tenens* **Sergii Starogorodsky** as ruling Russian Orthodox hierarch in Western Europe. Relieved of this post for implied criticism of Soviet anti-religious policies in 1930, he was accepted under the jurisdiction of the Ecumenical Patriarchate. Reconciled liturgically with the Synodal Church (ROCOR) in 1934 but continued to serve under Constantinople until shortly before his death, when he (personally, but without letters of release from Constantinople) rejoined the Moscow Patriarchate.

Fedotov, Georgii Petrovich (1886-1951). Ed. Voronezh Gymnasium and St Petersburg, where he was briefly arrested for revolutionary activity and left to continue his studies abroad for two years (1906-1908). On his return to St Petersburg as a pupil of I. Grevs was briefly involved with the Mystic Anarchist movement about the journal *Fakely* ("Torches"). During World War One he embraced traditional Christianity. From 1920-22 lectured on Mediaeval History at the University of Saratov, then joined the Theological Institute of St Petersburg which was closed down in 1923. Emigrated to Berlin in 1924 then Paris in 1925, where at the St Sergius Theological Institute he taught the Lives of Saints, Latin and the History of the Eastern Church (1926-39). He contributed to **Berdiaev**'s *Put'*, and in 1932 founded, with F. Stepun and **I. Fondaminsky**, the journal *Novyi grad* ("A New City"). Under **Metropolitan Evlogii**, he was active in the life of the Church and in the "Pravoslavnoe delo" society from 1937. In 1931, YMCA Press published his *magnum opus, The Saints of Ancient Russia*. During the war he evacuated to the USA. From 1943-47 worked as Professor of the Theological Seminary of St Vladimir and the Theological Institute from 1947 to 1951, and lectured on the history of Russian Christianity at Harvard. His books in English include *The Russian Religious Mind* in two volumes (1946) and *A Treasury of Russian Spirituality* (1948). He was also one of the founders of the émigré journal *Novyi Zhurnal* ("The New Review").

Fennel, Marina Nikolaevna (née Lopoukhine) (b. 1925). Born in Harbin but educated in Paris; married Dr John Fennel of Oxford University, a specialist in Mediaeval Russia.

Fernandez. *See* Scriabina, Ol'ga Il'inichna.

Fisher, Geoffrey Francis (Baron Fisher of Lambeth) (1887-1972). Ed. Marlborough and Exeter College, Oxford. Ordained 1913. Headmaster of Repton School 1914. Consecrated Bishop of Chester 1939. As Archbishop of Canterbury (1945-61) he was the first head of the Anglican Church to visit the Pope when he went to Rome to meet John XXIII in 1960.

Florensky, Pavel Aleksandrovich (1882-1937). Ed. Tiflis Gimnazium, the Physico-Mathematical Faculty of Moscow University and the Moscow Theological

Academy. Florensky's *magnum opus*, *The Pillar and Foundation of Truth*, is a book about the Christian Church perceived through the eyes of a twentieth-century scientist and aesthete. He was a close friend of **Aleksandr Elchaninov** and, in the years between the revolutions, of **S. Bulgakov**. He taught at the Moscow Theological Academy from 1908 and as priest from 1911 – until its liquidation by the Soviet government. From 1911-17 he edited their journal *Bogoslovskii Vestnik* ("The Theological Herald"). In 1917 served as Learned Secretary to the Commission for the Preservation of Art and Antiquities at the St Sergius Trinity Monastery and taught Physics and Maths at the local school, the beginning of an enforced shift towards work in Applied Physics, which probably ensured he was not exiled with other religious thinkers in 1922. Lectured on pictorial space in art at the Moscow Higher Artistic and Technical Studios (VKHUTEMAS) 1922-24. In 1927 he was exiled to Nizhnii Novgorod for three months but allowed to return at the intercession of Ekaterina Peshkova and to continue work on the *Soviet Technological Encyclopaedia*. In 1933 he was re-arrested and spent the rest of his life in various prison camps. He was shot in 1937 (rehabilitated 1958). Much of Florensky's later work was only published posthumously, beginning with the influential *Reversed Perspective* (1967).

Florovsky, Georgii Vasilevich (1893-1979). Ed. Classical Gimnazium and Historico-Philological Faculty of University of Odessa, he continued as *Privatdozent* until 1919, emigrated in 1920, worked as publisher's editor in Sophia, and was active in the Eurasian movement, with which he broke decisively in 1928; in 1921 moved to Prague where he married in 1922, defended a doctoral dissertation on A. Herz's philosophy of history in 1923 and was retained as *Privatdozent* at Prague University 1923-26, where he was Secretary to the Russian Religious Philosophical Society, member of the Brotherhood of St Sophia and active in the RSKhD. Lecturer 1926, then Professor of Patristics at St Sergius Theological Institute 1939. Consecrated deacon and priest in 1932 by **Metropolitan Evlogii**, protopriest 1936, took part in First International Conference of Orthodox Theologians in Athens in 1938, then took up position as priest and reader in Belgrade. From 1940 he occupied various posts attached to the Russian Exarchate of the Ecumenical Patriarchate in Prague; returned to France via Switzerland at the end of 1945 and resumed his work as Professor of St Sergius Institute until 1948, when he left for North America, where, under the jurisdiction of the North American Russian Metropolia, he served as Professor of the St Vladimir Theological Institute in New York 1948-55 (Dean from 1950-55), as a member of the executive committee of the World Council of Churches 1948-61 and the Union Seminary attached to the University of Columbia in New York. From 1955, Professor of Dogmatic Theology at the Greek Theological Institute of the Holy Cross in Boston, lecturer on the History of Eastern Christendom at Harvard 1956-64 and then at Princeton University. Metropolitan Anthony admired his works on patristics and the history of the Orthodox Church.

Fondaminsky (pseudonym Bunakov), Ilia Isidorovich (1880-1942). Ed. Kreiman private Gimnazium and at the Universities of Berlin and Heidelberg. Joined the Socialist Revolutionary Party while studying abroad and, in 1907, became a full member of its Moscow Committee. Was imprisoned but escaped from Russia to France where he joined the terrorist wing of the SRs, and contributed to the newspapers *Novosti* ("News") and *Za rubezhom* ("Abroad") and the journal *Prizyv* ("Mobilisation"). In 1917, he returned to Moscow and was elected to the All-Russian Congress of Soviets of Workers' and Peasants' deputies and appointed Commissar to the Black Sea fleet for the provisional government. He spoke for the right SRs at a meeting of the Constituent Assembly in January 1918, went underground after the dissolution of the Assembly and continued illegal work for the party. Emigrated to Paris in 1919. Editor, later publisher of *Sovremennye Zapiski* ("Contemporary Notes"). From 1932-39, together with F. Stepun and **Georgii Fedotov**, published the religious-philosophical journal *Novyi grad* ("A New City"), the ethos of which was not so much political as broadly sociological and humanitarian. Worked voluntarily in the RSKhD and joined **Mother Maria**'s Russkoe delo ("Russian Enterprise"). Interned by the Nazis during the occupation, Fondaminsky finally converted to the Orthodox Church, was active in cultural work among his fellow prisoners, turning down a chance to escape from the prison hospital, and was deported, eventually, to Auschwitz. Together with Mother Maria and **Dmitrii Klepinin**, he was canonised in 2004.

Fortounatto, Marianna Mikhailovna (b. 1929). Daughter of **M.I. Theokritoff**. Wife of **Michael Fortounatto**. Icon painter and pupil of **L.A. Ouspensky**. Taught icon-painting in the Diocese of Sourozh.

Fortounatto, Michael Vsevolodovich (b. 1931). Higher ed. St Sergius Theological Institute, Paris. Moved to England in 1962. From 1965 served as choir-master in Cathedral of the Dormition, London, where in 1969 he was ordained priest. Specialist in theory and history of Church chants. Retired 2004. Founder of the Russian Christian Movement in Great Britain and, for many years, active in the Orthodox summer camps for younger children.

Fostiropoulos, Alexander (b. 1952). Ed. in his native Greece, was ordained priest of the Russian Orthodox Church by Metropolitan Anthony in 1985. Followed **Bishop Basil** as Protopriest of the Deanery of Great Britain and Ireland of the Archdiocese of Orthodox Parishes in the Russian Tradition in Western Europe within the Ecumenical Patriarchate in 2004, having previously served in the Cathedral of the Dormition since 1962, and as Orthodox Chaplain of the University of London.

Fostiropoulos, Patricia (date of birth unknown). Icon painter, wife of **Father Alexander Fostiropoulos**.

Frank, Semen Liudwigovich (1877-1950). Higher ed. Faculty of Law, Moscow University. Exiled in 1899 for propagating Marxism. Completed education in Heidelberg and Munich. In 1900 produced an academic study of Marx's "Theory of Values" but rejected many of his tenets. Co-operated with **Berdiaev** and **Bulgakov** on the seminal collections of essays *Problemy idealizma* ("Problems of idealism") (1902) and *Vekhi* ("Milestones") (1909), and edited political weeklies *Poliarnaia zvezda* ("Polar Star") and *Svoboda Kul'tury* ("Freedom of Culture"). In 1912 converted to Christianity under the influence of the works of Vladimir Solov'ev, whose wide tolerance made him feel that he could do so without betraying the Judaism of his people. Lecturer at St Petersburg University 1912-15. He then spent a year in Berlin where he published *The Object of Cognition*. In 1917 became Dean of the Faculty of History and Philosophy at Saratov. On his return to Moscow four years later he was active in *Volphil* (see **Berdiaev**), was elected member of the Institute of Philosophy of the University of Moscow and published two new books. Deported 1922; with **Lossky, Berdiaev** and Karsavin contributed to the collection *Problems of Religious Consciousness* and *La Voie* and published prolifically between 1924 and 1930 with YMCA Press. From 1931 to 1937 lectured in German on the History of Russian Thought and Literature at the University of Berlin. Forbidden to continue teaching by the Nazi government, left Berlin for Paris where, in 1939, he published *The Inaccessible: An Ontological Introduction to the Philosophy of Religion*, before the occupation forced him into hiding. He found refuge in London in 1945, where he and his family became members of the parish of the Moscow Patriarchate.

Frank, Tatyana Sergeevna (née Barseva) (1886-1984). Wife, originally pupil, of S.L. Frank.

Garret, Anna Helena Ertel (née Duddington) (1913-1997). Ed. Kingsley School, Belsize Park and the Courtauld Institute, London University. Church warden of the London Cathedral of the Dormition and All Saints from 1974 until shortly before her death.

Gellhorn, Martha (1908-1998). Ed. John Burroughs School St Louis and Bryn Mawr College, Philadelphia. American writer and journalist. Reported on Great Depression in 1930s and on World War Two. Post-war, worked for *Atlantic Monthly*. Lived in London with husband T.S. Matthews, manager of *Time Magazine*, 1954-63. They were divorced in 1963 but she continued to live in the UK. Her stormy wartime marriage with Ernest Hemingway was the subject of a film.

Genofeva, Sister (Lavrova, Vera Aleksandrovna) (dates unknown). Orthodox nun, spiritual daughter of **Afanasii (Nechaev)**. Returned to Russia and eventually died in a convent there.

Gibbes, Nicholas (Charles Sydney) (1876-1963). Tutor to the children of Tsar Nicholas II in Ekaterinburg. Ordained priest of the Orthodox Church in 1934. Founded the first Orthodox church in Oxford in St Bartholomew's Chapel in Cowley Road, Oxford, a fourteenth-century building put at their disposal by the Bishop of Oxford. From 1949 acquired his own St Nicholas House where he consecrated a chapel dedicated to the saint.

Gillet, Lev (Louis) (1893-1980). Ed. at schools and university in Grenoble then at the Sorbonne, Paris. Spent most of World War One in German prisoner-of-war camps. Evacuated to Geneva in 1917, he spent two years in the city studying Psychology, translating Freud's *The Interpretation of Dreams* (1899) and researching the possibilities of Christian psychoanalysis. In 1920 entered the Benedictine Abbey of St Maurice de Cherveaux as a postulant, spent the next four years between the Benedictine House in Farnborough and Rome, where he became involved with the Eastern Rite Catholics. Instead of taking final vows as a Benedictine, joined the Uniate Metropolitan Szeptychy in L'vov, where he took final vows and was ordained priest-monk in 1925. In January 1928 the publication of the papal encyclical *Mortalium animos* put an end to his hopes of reconciliation with rather than conversion of the Orthodox to Roman Catholicism, and he was received as co-celebrant of the Orthodox Liturgy with **Father Sergii Bulgakov** by **Metropolitan Evlogii** "without abjuration". He saw this move not as a "conversion" but rather as a return to Christian roots. He served with the French-speaking Orthodox parish in Paris (Vicar 1928-36 and thereafter "spiritual father"), as prison chaplain for Orthodox detainees from 1932 and as chaplain to the homes for indigent Russians run by **Mother Maria (Skobtsova)** 1935-38, but embarked on an idiosyncratic course inspired by the kenotic ideal of monasticism "in the world", and spent more time in London, where the war cut him off from contact with Russian Orthodoxy in France. Acting as Chaplain to the Fellowship of St Alban and St Sergius and residing at their headquarters in St Basil's House, he spent his working days in the British Museum writing under the pseudonym "A Monk of the Eastern Church", and earning his living from 1949, when he was replaced as Chaplain by the newly consecrated Anthony (Bloom), as Secretary to the Spalding Trust.

Gogoleff, Mikhail (b. 1949). Archpriest. Spells his name in French fashion as Gogoleff. Born in the emigration of Russian Orthodox parentage. Ordained deacon in Poland and served in parallel with his regular job with a Western oil company with interests in Russia, in the Metochion of the Trinity St Sergius Monastery as proto-deacon. In 2000 he retired from the oil business and Metropolitan Anthony, whom he had first met in 1988 or 1987, co-opted him as a priest to help with the influx of Russians. Served for some time in Dublin and founded the parish of Ss Peter and Paul there. As Dean of West Midlands is in charge of the Birmingham, Bristol and Portsmouth Sourozh parishes.

Gorbachev, Mikhail Sergeevich (b. 1931). General Secretary of the Communist Party of the Soviet Union 1955-90, and President 1990-91. Recipient of Nobel Peace Prize 1990. After 1991 retired into social and cultural life.

Gregorie, Raymond (1875-1942). Professor at the Sorbonne. One of Andrei Bloom's science teachers.

Grishin, Vadim (d. 1987). Priest who accompanied Metropolitan Anthony on one of his visits to Russia.

Gorodetskaia, Nadezhda Danilovna (wrote as Nadejda Gorodetsky) (1901-1965). Ed. Gatchina and Poltava. Emigrated 1919 via Yugoslavia and arrived in France in 1924, where she contributed to a number of émigré journals and published novels in French and Russian. A stormy youth, failed marriage and difficult liaison preceded her meeting with **Father Lev Gillet**, under whose influence she became an active and devoted Orthodox Christian; with the son of Charles Péguy and Vsevolod de Voght, she founded the Franco-Russian Studio, which served as a meeting place for intellectuals of both cultures. Studied in Birmingham 1934-35, but remained on the board of **Berdiaev**'s *La Voie* (*Put'*) until 1940. Together with **Gillet** and **Zernov** she lectured regularly at the Fellowship of St Albans and St Sergius and founded a St Macrina Centre in Birmingham. At Oxford she defended her Master's thesis in 1938 and her doctoral thesis in 1944, after which, in 1945, she took up a lectureship at Liverpool University, and Chair in Russian Studies 1956-68. Her best-known works, *The Humiliated Christ in Modern Russian Thought* (1938) and *St Tikhon Zadonsky, Inspirer of Dostoevsky* (1951) investigate the symbiosis between Orthodoxy and Russian literature.

Hackel, Sergei (1931-2005). Ed. Bloxham School and Lincoln College, Oxford, graduated 1952 and worked for ten years as a school teacher. Ordained deacon in the Russian Cathedral of the Dormition and All Saints in London in 1958 and priest in 1965. Lecturer in Russian Literature then Reader at the University of Sussex (1964-88). Author of books on Aleksandr Blok and The Twelve and **Mother Maria (Skobtsova)**. Editor of religious broadcasting on the BBC Russian Service 1984-2005. Chairman of St Gregory's Foundation 1995-2005.

Harrison, George (1943-2001). Guitarist. Interested in the Hare Krishna movement and admirer of Indian music and culture. Worked with The Beatles until 1970, then on his own and with other groups, contributing much to Live Aid and to relief for Bangladesh.

Havelacque, A. (1880-1939). University Professor at the Sorbonne, one of Andrei Bloom's teachers.

Hayward, Derek (1923-2014). Ed. Stowe School and Sandhurst. Served with distinction in World War Two, then entered the family business for several years before embarking upon a course of Theology at Trinity College, Cambridge. Ordained in 1952. From 1974 served as Archdeacon of Middlesex and Diocesan Secretary to **Gerald Ellison**, Bishop of London, in which capacity he was regarded as an astute business manager as well as a distinguished cleric. Retired on New Year's Eve 1993 to Bath, where he continued to serve as Chairman of the SCM Press until 1998 and of St Luke's Hospital for Clergy until 2001. Trustee of the Bath Preservation Trust from 1996 to 2007.

Heenan, John Carmel (1905-1975). Ed. St Ignatius College in Stamford Hill, Ushaw College, Durham, and the Venerable English College in Rome. Ordained priest 1930, served as pastor in Brentwood until 1947, Superior of the Catholic Missionary Society of England and Wales and Bishop of Leeds 1951, Archbishop of Westminster 1963-75, Cardinal 1965, holding the parallel post of Cardinal Priest of S. Silvestro in Capite.

Hodgins, Michael (1912-1998). Ed. Wellington College and Ripon College Cuddesdon. Ordained 1939. From 1946 to 1976 Archdeacon of Hackney; Secretary to the London Diocesan Fund 1951-71.

Huddleston, Ernest Urban Trevor (1913-1998). Ed. Lancing College, Christchurch College, Oxford, Wells Theological College. Took vows in Community of Resurrection in 1941. In 1943 joined CR mission station in Johannesburg, South Africa, as Head of Mission, where he served until 1956. Active in anti-apartheid movement. Published his book *Naught for your Comfort* in 1956. He was appointed Master of Novices in the Mirfield Community for that year, then, in 1958, Prior of the Order's London Priory. In 1960 he was consecrated Bishop of Masasi (Tanzania), then Bishop of Stepney, then Mauritius and, finally, Archbishop of the Province of the Indian Ocean in 1978. He retired in 1981 and, in 1998, was appointed Knight Commander of the Order of St George.

Iakov (Akkersdijk) (1914-1991). Ed. Jesuit School. Novice in a Roman Catholic Benedictine monastery in Steenbrugge, Belgium; joined the Orthodox Church in 1940 and became a monk in 1948, hiero-monk 1954 and consecrated Bishop in

1965. In 1972 was received at his own request from ROCOR into the Moscow Patriarchal Church together with his flock and made ruling Bishop of the Netherlands diocese of the West European Exarchate of the Russian Orthodox with the title "of The Hague and the Netherlands". Archbishop 1979, retired 1988.

Iakovos (Virvos) (1901-1978). *Locum tenens* of London Diocese of Thyateira after the death of Athenagorus I (Kavvados) in 1962. Iakovos continued to serve as Metropolitan in the diocese until his retirement to Greece a few years before his death.

Ilarion (Alfeyev, Grigorii Valer'evich) (b. 1966). Ed. Moscow State Tchaikovsky Conservatoire. In 1987 was received as monk and consecrated priest. Graduated from the Moscow Theological Seminary as extra-mural student in 1987 and, in 1991, from the Moscow Theological Academy; was sent to Oxford University where under **Bishop Kallistos of Diokleia** he wrote and defended a doctoral thesis. From 1995 to 2000 worked in the Moscow Patriarchate's Department of Foreign Relations. In January 2002 consecrated Bishop of Kerch and sent to serve as Vicar Bishop in the Diocese of Sourozh. Appointed chief representative of the Moscow Patriarchate at Brussels with the title Bishop of Podol'sk 17 July 2002.

Il'in, Vladimir Nikolaevich (d. 1974). Ed. University of Kiev, faculties of Mathematics and Physics, Philosophy, History and Philology, and the Kishinev Conservatoire where he studied composition. Emigrated to Constantinople, where he lectured on Philosophy at various venues, including pastoral courses. In 1919 moved to Berlin, where he taught Logic and Philosophy and continued his studies at the Protestant Theological Faculty, then on to Paris, where he contributed to various Eurasian publications and taught Liturgical Studies, Psychology, Mediaeval History and Apologetics at the St Sergius Theological Institute 1921-41. Active member of the RSKhD. After the war Il'in passed under the jurisdiction of the Moscow Patriarchate and was expelled from the St Sergius Institute. From 1946 he attended the Church of the Three Holy Hierarchs and lectured at the Institute of St Denis. Wrote on religious and philosophical themes and composed symphonies, operas and songs.

Ioann (Snychev, Ivan) (1927-1995). September 1948 became a lay brother under the guidance of Bishop Manuil Lemeshevsky of Orenburg, who ordained him deacon in 1946 and priest in 1948. Entered the Saratov seminary in September 1948, and from 1951 to 1955 studied at the Leningrad Theological Academy. In October 1956 – by now a teacher of Homiletics at the Minsk seminary – he took monastic vows, later becoming an abbot with the rank of Archimandrite. In 1957 Bishop Manuil, freed from exile and appointed to the Cheboksary diocese, summoned Ioann to join him and they collaborated on gathering material on Church history. In 1959 Ioann returned briefly to teach in the Saratov seminary, before returning to parish work, but his church was closed during Khrushchev's anti-religious crusade of 1959-64. Bishop of Syzran 1965, then of Kuibyshev. Metropolitan of Leningrad 1990-95.

James, William (1842-1910). Ed. Harvard University, with frequent trips to Europe, James was an accomplished linguist of cosmopolitan culture and was influential throughout Europe, including Russia, where his work was translated from the 1890s onwards. *A Pluralistic Universe* (1908), the book that influenced Metropolitan Anthony's confessor **Afanasii (Nechaev)**, was a published version of his Hibert Lectures, and postulated the ability of the individual to experience and relate to the macrocosm of religious belief and all the variety of being beyond their apparent scope in time and space. It was translated into Russian by V. Osipov and O. Rumer in 1911 as *Vselennaia s pliuralisticheskoi tochki zreniia*.

Kallistos, Metropolitan (Ware, Timothy) (b. 1934). Ed. Westminster School; Magdalen College, Oxford. Raised in the Anglican Church, he became Orthodox in 1958, after which he travelled extensively in Greece and spent much time at the Monastery of St John the Theologian, Patmos. Ordained priest 1966 and tonsured monk with the name of Kallistos. From 1966 was Spalding Lecturer at the University of Oxford in Eastern Orthodox Studies. In 1882 consecrated Bishop of Diokleia, which subsequently became a Metropolitan diocese, but continued to work until retirement in 2001 as Spalding Lecturer and Fellow of Pembroke College, Oxford, and parish priest of the Oxford Greek Orthodox community. Publications include *The Orthodox Church* (1963, many subsequent revised editions), *The Orthodox Way* (1979) and translation of the *Philokalia* and Orthodox services (the Lenten Triodon with **Mother Maria**).

Katherine, Sister (as Anglican Benedictine Dame Mary Thomas) (1910-1988). Entered the Benedictine Anglican order in 1938 with the name of Mary Thomas and was Novice Mistress when Lydia Gysi (the future **Mother Maria**) entered the convent as an Orthodox novice to follow the Anglican Benedictine training. In 1971 she obtained a release from her vows as a Benedictine to be received as a nun into the Orthodox faith and to join Mother Maria at her own monastery at Filgrave, then at the Monastery of the Assumption, Mulgrave. In co-operation with Sister, later **Mother Thekla**, she translated Orthodox services into English and published a book of devotional verse: *Songs of the Servant of God*.

Korchinska, Maria (1895-1979). Ed. Moscow Conservatoire (piano and harp, 1903-11), and won the first Gold Medal awarded to a harpist. In 1919 became Professor of Harp at the Conservatoire and also Principal Harpist of the Bolshoi Orchestra. Founding member of Persimfans, the famous "orchestra without a conductor". In 1924 left Russia for Great Britain, where she founded the UK Harp Association and had a successful career as a soloist and ensemble player. She was the first harpist to play at the Glyndebourne Festival, was a founding member of the Wigmore Ensemble and was the first British judge at the Israeli Harp competition.

Kaznovetsky, Anatolii (1926-1995). Ed. Moscow Theological Academy where he served as Assistant Inspector. In 1972 appointed Rector of St Alexander Nevsky Cathedral in Alexandria, Egypt. From 1973 to 1975 he served as Patriarchal Representative in New York and from 1975 to 1978 as Vicar of the Church of the Holy Martyr John the Soldier in Moscow.

Khrushchev, Nikita Sergeevich (1894-1971). General Secretary of the Communist Party of the Soviet Union and undisputed ruler after "secret speech" denouncing Stalin in 1956. Succeeded by Leonid Brezhnev in 1964.

Kiprian (Zernov, Mikhail) (1911-1987). Ordained deacon 10 August 1944 and on 12 August priest of the Church of the Holy Trinity in the village of Natashino, near Moscow. In 1948 was appointed Rector of the Church of All Who Sorrow in Ordynka, Moscow, with the rank of archpriest. In 1963 he became Archbishop of Berlin and Central Europe.

Kirillova, Irina Arsen'evna (b. 1931). Ed. Lycée Français de Londres; Kensington High School; Lady Margaret Hall, Oxford. Lecturer in Russian Language and Literature and Fellow of Newnham College at the University of Cambridge. Retired 1998 as Fellow Emerita. From 2000, member of the governing board of the Orthodox Research Institute in Cambridge. Longstanding member and later Chairwoman of the Sourozh Diocesan Council and Assembly from 1999 to 2003. A special gift for simultaneous interpreting led to her accompany the royal family on a visit to Russia, for which and for other services as interpreter, she was awarded an MBE in the mid-1990s. Author of *The Image of Christ in Dostoevsky's Work* (in Russian, 2010), and *Vstrechi* ("Meetings with remarkable Russians in Russia and in the Emigration") (2012).

Klepinin, Dmitrii Andreevich (1904-1944). Ed. Odessa and, after emigrating via Constantinople through Serbia, at the St Sergius Theological Institute until 1929; then, for one year, in the New York Protestant Theological Seminary. Under the jurisdiction of **Metropolitan Evlogii** served as psalmist 1930-37, when he was consecrated deacon, then priest. Active in the RSKhD. Served as vicar in provinces 1938-39, at a Russian Orthodox Church in Paris and as spiritual director in the "Pravoslavnoe delo" society. Arrested by the Gestapo in 1943 and sent to Buchenwald then Dora, where he died of illness and undernourishment. Canonised 2004.

Kochetkov, Georgii (b. 1950). Priest. At variance with his superiors in the Moscow Patriarchate on the question of celebrating in modern Russian, but enjoys firm support from his own flock.

Konovalov, Sergei Aleksandrovich (1899-1982). Ed. Katkov Lycée in Moscow and (after emigrating with his parents in 1918) at Exeter College, University of Oxford, where he read Economics and Politics. Returned to Oxford and obtained a B.Litt 1925-27. Served as Professor of Russian Language and Literature and Head of the Russian Department at Birmingham University 1929-45, where he organised the Birmingham Bureau of Research on Russian Economic Conditions which published monthly papers until 1940. At the same time he lectured part-time on Slavonic Studies at Oxford and at the London School of Slavonic Studies. Headed the New Russian Department in the Faculty of Modern and Mediaeval Languages at the University of Oxford 1945-67. In 1950 founded the Oxford Slavonic Papers. His contributions were mainly on Russian history. Fellow Emeritus of New College, Oxford, from 1968.

Korenchevsky, Vladimir Georgievich (1880-1959). Ed. Military-Medical School. Worked in a hospital in Harbin at a time of plague during the Russo-Japanese war. From 1909 worked as *Privatdozent* in the Faculty of General and Experimental Medicine at Moscow University. Emigrated in 1919. In London he organised a Russian Academic Group and served as *starosta* to the Russian Patriarchal Church from the mid-1950s.

Kornilii (Fristedt, Dmitrii Nikolaevich) (1902-1982). Ed. The Galich Realschule and Moscow Boundaries Institute, banished to Finland in 1927, graduated from the Orthodox seminary at Knopio and went on to the St Sergius Theological Institute in Paris in 1938, but returned to Finland for the duration of the war. After the war he completed his studies in Paris. Monk from 1957 and priest of the parish of the Three Holy Hierarchs in 1958. He served as assistant to Bishop Anthony in London 1959-60 and, from 1960 to 1982, under **Vasilii (Krivoshein)** at the Church of St Nicholas in Brussels, where he was raised to Archimandrite in 1964.

Kovalevsky, Evgraf Egrafovich (at one time Bishop Ioann) (1905-1970). Brother of **Maksim** and **Petr Kovalevsky**, emigrated with family in 1920. Finished school in Paris and graduated from the Philological Faculty of the University of Paris and the St Sergius Theological Institute in 1928. Founding member of the Brotherhood of St Photius (1925). Psalmist for the francophone parish of Ste Geneviève 1928-31. Adhered to the Moscow Patriarchate in 1931 and took holy orders as deacon, then priest in 1937. Served as Assistant Vicar of the Ste Geneviève and Joy of all who Sorrow Church, then as Vicar of the French parish of St Irineaus in Paris 1938-70. Mobilised by French army 1939-40. Prisoner of war 1940-44. A founder of the French Orthodox Institute of St Denis in 1944 but excluded from Moscow Patriarchate clergy for attempting to found an "independent French Orthodox Church" and for various infringements of ecclesiastical discipline in 1953. Accepted as a priest of the Russian parishes under the Constantinople Patriarchate in 1954 but banned from serving in the same year. Admitted by ROCOR in 1960. Became a monk in 1964, Bishop of St Denis, Vicar of the West European Diocese and Head of parishes celebrating according to the Western rite in France in 1964. However, he left ROCOR of his own volition in 1966 and was stripped of his rank and excluded from their Church by a Bishops' Council of 1967, after which he became head of the break-away French Catholic Orthodox Church, styling himself Bishop Ioann.

Kovalevsky, Maksim Evgrafovich (1903-1988). Ed. Pages' Corps Saint Petersburg, emigrated in 1920 to South of France via Constantinople then to Paris where he read Mathematics at the University of Paris; worked for an insurance company. Consecrated deacon in 1921 by **Metropolitan Evlogii**. Founding member of the Brotherhoods of St Alexander Nevsky (1921) and of St Photius (1925). Served in his brother **Evgraf**'s (Bishop Ioann's) "French Catholic-Orthodox Church".

Kovalevsky, Petr Evgrafovich (1901-1978). Brother of **Maksim** and **Evgraf Kovalevsky**. Ed. St Petersburg Gimnaziia and Philological Faculty of the University of Paris. Emigrated 1920, consecrated deacon 1921, founding member of the Brotherhoods of St Alexander Nevsky (1921), the Holy Trinity (1924) and St Photius (1925-31). Taught Russian literature at the Russian Lycée in Paris (1926-41). Followed **Metropolitan Evlogii** under the jurisdiction of the Ecumenical Patriarch in 1931, taught Latin in the St Sergius Theological Institute 1925-50 and became Professor of the French Orthodox Institute of **St Denis** 1945, Dean in 1965. Influential and prolific writer, publicist and diarist.

Krivoshein, Vsevolod. *See* Vasilii.

Krug, Georgii Ivanovich (in religion the monk and icon painter Grigorii) (1908-1969). Ed. Russian Gymnasium Revel, and Applied Arts School in Tallin (graduated 1921), then in private "Pallas" Arts School in Tartu (1928). Left for Paris in 1931 where he studied under Nataliia Goncharova, Fedorov and Joanne Reitlinger until 1932, began painting icons and joined the society "Icon". In 1931 he chose the jurisdiction of the Moscow Patriarchate and became a member of the parish of the Three Holy Hierarchs, whose church he helped to furnish with religious paintings. Became a monk in 1948 and entered the brotherhood at Mesnil-Saint-Denis near Rambouillet, where he remained until his death.

Kuroedov, Vladimir Alekseevich (1966-1994). Ed. Nizhny Novgorod Pedagogical Institute. In the late 1950s became scientific editor of the newspaper *Soviet Russia*. Chairman of the Department for Religious Affairs of the Council of Ministers of the USSR 1965-84.

Kyrlezhev, Aleksandr Ivanovich (b. 1957). Russian historian of the Church, scholar and publicist. Member of the editorial board of *Bogoslovskie Trudy* ("Theological Studies"). Consultant of the Synodal Theological Commission of the Russian Orthodox Church.

Lampert, Evgenii Il'ich (1914-2004). Although his father was of Belgian origin, Lampert, whose mother was Russian, was brought up in Piatigorsk until his parents emigrated in 1922. Ed. Strasbourg University and, under **Sergii Bulgakov**, at the St Sergius Theological Institute in Paris, where he also acted as secretary to **Nikolai Berdiaev**. On the eve of World War Two he moved to England to continue his studies in Oxford. In 1965 he was invited to lecture at Keele University where he founded a Chair of Russian Language and Literature in 1968, and served as Professor until 1976. Retired in 1983 and moved to London, then Greece.

Laski, Marghanita (1915-1988). Ed. Lady Bon House School, St Paul's Girls' School, Hammersmith, and Somerville College, Oxford. An avowed atheist, she was a prolific lexicographer and journalist and served 1980-84 as Chair of the Literary Department of the Arts Council. As a broadcaster, she was popular on panel shows such as *What's My Line?*, *The Brains Trust* and *Any Questions?* Wrote and/or edited twenty-four books and plays.

Lee, John (1938-2014). Ed. Roman Catholic Seminary in the USA but felt it was not God's will that he be ordained, and trained as a male nurse and midwife. Moved to London and was ordained in the Orthodox Church by Metropolitan Anthony ("God may have changed his mind"). From 2004 Vicar of the Cathedral of the Dormition in London but followed **Bishop Basil (Osborne)** and other colleagues to the jurisdiction of the Ecumenical Patriarchate and continued to serve in the Deanery congregation at St Andrew's, Holborn.

Lewis, Clive Staples (1898-1963). Ed. Malvern School and University College, Oxford, from 1925 to 1954 a Fellow of Magdalen College, from 1954 Professor of Medieval and Renaissance English at Cambridge University. Wrote literary criticism, religious and ethical books, often presenting his ideas in lively imaginative form (e.g. *The Screwtape Letters*, 1962), as science fiction or through *The Chronicles of Narnia* for children. See also his autobiography, *Surprised by Joy* (1955).

Lossky, Nikolai Onufrevich (1870-1965). Expelled from his Russian gymnasium for "socialist and atheist propaganda" and had to seek a university education abroad in Switzerland (University of Bern) and Algeria, but returned to St Petersburg in 1889 where he succeeded in graduating from the Physio-Mathematical and Historio-Philological faculties of St Petersburg University. Doctor of Philosophy (1907), he taught at the Bestuzhev Courses for young women and co-founded a periodical, *New Ideas in Philosophy*. From 1919-21 lectured at the "People's University". Exiled from Russia with his family in 1922. He lectured at Prague University and wrote for various émigré periodicals. Moved to Paris in 1942 and then to the USA where he lectured on Philosophy in the Russian Theological Academy in New York 1947-50, after which he relocated to Los Angeles. Lossky's gift for setting out religious-philosophical ideas in a literary context ensures his *History of Russian Philosophy* (1951) remains a classic exposition of the subject for the non-Russian reader.

Lossky, Nikolai Vladimorovich (1929-2013). Son of the theologian **Vladimir Lossky** and grandson of the philosopher **Nikolai Onufrievich Lossky**. Friend of Metropolitan Anthony of Sourozh. Priest of the parish of the Mother of God, Joy of all who Sorrow and Ste Geneviève in Paris. Author of books on liturgical music and on the ecumenical movement. Professor of Church History at the St Sergius Orthodox Theological Institute in Paris and protopriest.

Lossky, Veronica Konstantinovna (b. 1921). Granddaughter of the priest Mikhail Bel'sky, sung in the choir of the Church of the Mother of God, Joy of all who Sorrow and Ste Geneviève in Paris. Doctor and Professor at the Sorbonne University in Paris. Teacher and writer on Russian literature and the place of women in the Orthodox Church. Married to **Father Nikolai Lossky.**

Lossky, Vladimir Nikolaevich (1903-1958). Son of the philosopher **Nikolai Onufrevich Lossky**, ed. Historico-Philological Faculty of University of Petrograd, 1920-22. When still an undergraduate, he was exiled from Soviet Union with his parents. He moved from Prague to Paris in 1924 where he completed his historico-philological studies in 1927. From 1925 a member of the Brotherhood of St Photius. He remained with the Moscow Patriarchate in 1931 and became a founding member of the parish of the Three Holy Hierarchs. In 1939 was mobilised into the French army and worked with the French Resistance during the occupation. 1944 to 1953 Professor of Dogmatic Theology in the Orthodox French Institute of St Denis, served on the editorial board of the journal *Zhivoi Bog* ("The Living God") 1945-48 and taught dogmatic and comparative theology at the Moscow Patriarchal Exarchate's pastoral courses 1944-53. From 1947 to 1957 participated regularly in the annual Orthodox-Anglican conferences arranged by the Society of St Alban and St Sergius and was one of the first members of the Moscow Patriarchal Exarchate to visit the Mother Church in Russia in 1956. As teacher, author and "senior friend" he contributed much to the formation of Anthony of Sourozh's understanding of theology.

Luka (Voino-Iasenetsky, Valentin) (1877-1961). Saint and Archbishop of the Russian Orthodox Church. Studied medicine and became a practising doctor. Took holy orders in 1921, and became a monk on the death of his wife in 1923. As secretly consecrated Bishop of Tashkent, he suffered a period of imprisonment and exile in the 1930s. Archbishop of Simferopol and Crimea from 1946, canonised 2000.

Maidanovich, Elena L'vovna (b. 1942). Ed. Russian Lycée Paris and school in Alma Ata. Active for many years with her sister **Tatiana** in recording, typing out and translating Metropolitan Anthony's talks and sermons. President of the Russian branch of the Metropolitan Anthony of Sourozh Foundation in Moscow. Retired 2015.

Maidanovich, Tatiana L'vovna (1935-2013). Ed. Russian Lycée in Paris. Returned with her family to Russia after the war. Worked during the middle 1960s to 1974 as interpreter and translator in the Moscow Patriarchate. Returned to Paris and restored her French citizenship in 1974. Worked for the Russian Patriarchal Church in Paris, then in London. With her sister **Elena** was active in recording, transcribing and translating Metropolitan Anthony's talks and sermons. Edited and raised the finance for his first two books published in Russian.

Makarios (Mouskos, Michail Christodoulos) (1913-1977). Admitted to Kykkos Monastery as a novice aged thirteen in 1926, he was sent to the Pancyprian Gymnasium in Nicosia where he completed his secondary education in 1936. During World War Two studied Theology at University of Athens, graduating in 1942. Became a priest but spent some years at Boston University, Massachusetts, on a World Council of Churches scholarship for further study. Here, he was consecrated Bishop of Kition under the name of Makarios and returned to Cyprus, where he became an active supporter of Enosis (Union with Greece). In 1950 he was chosen Bishop of Cyprus and, *de officio*, Ethnarch or leader of the Greek community of the island. By 1955 his political activity had brought him into conflict with the British government. Although Makarios subsequently denied involvement with EOKA, the violent resistance movement led by George Grivas, his support for self-determination led to his exile by the British in 1956 to the Seychelles, where he remained for a year, then returned to Athens (still forbidden from Cyprus) in 1957 and continued to work towards Enosis. In 1959 a compromise agreement was reached which envisaged cohabitation of Turks and Greeks as part of the Commonwealth. In 1959, Makarios returned to Nicosia and was elected president of the Greek part of the island, adopted a moderate stance and became a member of NAM (the Non-Aligned Movement). In 1974 he was toppled by a coup, Turkey invaded the island, the Regime of the Colonels in Greece imploded, the island was divided and Makarios, who had, ironically, turned to London for help, was able to return to Cyprus as President of the Greek territory.

Maria, Mother (Gysi, Lydia) (1912-1977). Ed. primary school, then gymnasium in Basle, from which she graduated *cum laude* in 1932. Brought up in the Methodist Church, the first Russian Orthodox influences in her life came while she was studying nursing, reading Dostoevsky and, in 1935, first met **Father Dmitrii Klepinin**. Left Zurich in 1936, to work in the American Hospital in Neuilly, Paris. On 7 June 1937 she was received into the Orthodox Church at **Mother Maria (Skobtsova)**'s Russian hostel on Rue Lourmel by **Father Lev Gillet**. In 1938 returned to Basle and, in 1942, joined the Red Cross, who assigned her to care for expectant mothers (Spanish and Jewish) near a concentration camp in the south of France. In 1943 she returned to

Switzerland and matriculated in Hebrew and Greek in order to study Theology and Philosophy at Basle University (1944-50), where she was profoundly influenced by the Platonist Hermann Gaus, who directed her doctoral thesis on the Cambridge Platonists. In 1949 she stayed at the Fellowship of St Alban's and St Sergius while studying Cudworth in the British Museum, where she felt increasingly drawn to the monastic way. Under the direction of Father Anthony, she entered the Anglican Benedictine Community at St Mary's Abbey, West Malling, already clothed as an Orthodox postulant but not yet professed, to follow the normal training of a novice. Bishop Anthony professed her as the nun Maria in 1958 before a mixed Orthodox and Anglican congregation and celebrated the Liturgy at the Abbey the following day. In 1965 she was joined by Marina Sharf (**Mother Thekla**) and they formed a small Orthodox enclave within the Anglican monastery. In 1970 they were joined by **Sister Katherine** and, seeing their future in a "non-national" jurisdiction, went under the Ecumenical Patriarchate. Mother Maria officially became Abbess in 1973. In 1974 they moved north to Robin Hood's Bay. Mother Maria, already ill with secondary cancer, was clothed in the Angelic Habit of the Great Schema. ". . . it seems a funny time to die," she wrote to a friend, "just at the outset of a new foundation. But heavenly thoughts are not earthly thoughts, and this is a supreme joy."

Maria, Mother (née Pilenko, Elizaveta Iur'evna, by first husband Kuzmina-Karavaeva, by second Skobtsova) (1891-1945). Ed. School in Yalta, then private gymnasium in St Petersburg and Philosophical Department of the Bestuzhev Courses. Married social revolutionary lawyer D.V. Kuzmin-Karavaev in 1910, attended the gatherings at Viacheslav Ivanov's Tower, and was on friendly terms with Aleksandr Blok who dedicated to her the 1907 poem "When you stand in my path" and advised her on her poetry (first book published 1912). Retired to live on the family estate in Crimea and was briefly Mayor of Anape during the civil war. After imprisonment by the White forces, she emigrated via Tiflis and Constantinople to Serbia (1920) and on to Paris, after her second marriage to D.E. Skobtsov in 1923. Worked as secretary to the RSKhD movement, was granted a Church divorce and made a nun by **Metropolitan Evlogii** in 1932. Founded the society Pravoslavnoe delo ("Orthodox Action") together with **G.P. Fedotov, I.I. Fondaminsky** and T.F. P'ianov in 1935, a hostel with church for indigent Russians in the Rue Lourmel, Paris, in 1936, and a canteen for the out-of-work and a convalescent home at Noisy-le-Grand. Arrested with her son and the priest **Dmitrii Klepinin** for hiding and succouring persecuted Jews and died in the gas chamber of Ravensbrück in 1943. Canonised in 2004, together with her son, the priest Dmitrii Klepinin and Ilia Fondaminsky, who also perished in the camps.

Mark (Arndt, Michael) (b. 1941). Ed. school in Frankfurt am Main and Frankfurt University, where he studied Slavic languages and literature. Converted to Orthodox Christianity while at university and went on to study Theology in Belgrade in 1973, graduating in 1979. In 1975 he became a monk and was ordained hiero-deacon and priest. In 1980 he was consecrated Bishop of Munich and southern Germany where from 1993-97 he headed the dialogue between the German-based ROCOR diocese to which he belonged and the Moscow Patriarchate. In 2000 he became President of the Committee on the Unity of the Russian Church and from 2003 President of the Commission for Talks with the Russian Patriarchate.

Matveeva, Valentina Ivanovna (b. 1934). Ed. Philological Faculty, University of Leningrad (graduated 1957) and Higher Courses for film directors. Specialised in documentaries and directed a remarkable series of films on Metropolitan Anthony of Sourozh.

Maxwell, Robert (Hoch, Ján Ludvík Hyman Binyamin) (1923-1991). Colourful tycoon who became a British citizen after the war. MP for Buckingham 1964-70. Proprietor of the Mirror Group and the Oxford publishing firm Pergamon Press. Rumoured to have had a long-standing connection with Mossad.

Medtner, Nikolai (1880-1951). A pupil of Taneev, Medtner established a reputation as composer and pianist on tour in Europe 1900-1902. Emigrated from the Soviet Union in 1921, settled in France, then later in England.

Men', Aleksandr Vladimirovich (1935-1990). Ed. Leningrad Theological Seminary, having been expelled from school owing to his religious beliefs. Ordained deacon 1958 and priest in 1960. In 1965 he completed his studies at the Leningrad Theological Academy. He wrote many books and, when attitudes became more tolerant towards the Church in the late 1980s, hosted a television programme on religion, founded the Open Orthodox University, and was one of the founders of the Russian Bible Society and *The World of the Bible* journal, while based in a country parish not far from the Trinity St Sergius Monastery in Novaia Derevnya. On the way from his home to catch the local train to his church he was attacked and murdered by a man wielding an axe. The assailant has never been identified.

Meshcherskaia, Princess Antoinette (née de Gogenek de Bois) (1908-1980). Widow of Princess Vera Kirillovna Meshcherskaia's third son Nikita, killed in 1942 in World War Two; she took over from her mother-in-law (who died in 1949) the care of the "Russian House" for old and indigent émigrés in Sainte-Geneviève-de-Bois, became Chairman of the Council of the Russian Cemetery there from 1953 and received the title of Honorary Director of the Russian House in the year of her death.

Meyendorf, John (Ivan Feofilovich) (1926-1992). Ed. the St Sergius Theological Institute in Paris, where, as a child, he had served as a bell-ringer and hypodeacon under **Metropolitan Evlogii**. Went on to Historico-Philological Faculty of the Sorbonne and defended a thesis on St Gregory Palamas at their School of Practical Theology. Ordained deacon, then priest in 1959, protopriest from 1964. Corresponding member of the British Academy (1977), honorary doctor of the University of Notre Dame (Indiana, USA), of the Theological Institute of the Episcopal Church in New York and of the St Petersburg Theological Academy. Was Secretary of Sindesmos, of which he was one of the original organisers, 1954-64. He was one of the architects of autocephaly for the American Orthodox Church, president of their Department of Foreign Relations, member of the Metropolitan Council, editor of the newspaper *The Orthodox Church*, and Dean of St Vladimir's Seminary in 1984. His expertise in patrology, the hesychast tradition and the pre-Chalcedonian Church was acknowledged worldwide and his works widely translated.

Moberly, Elizabeth (b. 1949). Anglo-Dutch Orthodox theologian. Research psychologist. Poet. Ed. Oxford, DPhil 1977. Research Psychologist Cambridge. Leverhulme Fellowship 1981-83. Books include *Suffering, Innocent and Guilty*

(1978), *The Psychology of Self and Other* (1985). Resident in the USA 1987-2003, where she lectured at various venues including St. Vladimir's Seminary (NY) and St Tikhon's (PA).

Moisevitch, Benno (usually spelled Moiseiwitsch) (1890-1963). Ed. The Odessa Music Academy and Vienna. British citizen from 1937. CBE 1946 for concert performances as pianist during the war. Friend of **Nikolai Medtner**.

Nikodim (Rotov, Boris Georgievich) (1929-1978). Served 1956-59 in the Russian Theological Mission in Jerusalem. Chairman of the Department of Foreign Relations 1960-1972 and, in 1975, elected one of the presidents of the World Council of Churches, Nikodim was a controversial figure who was criticised for overtly towing the party line abroad, but also for favouring the Roman Catholic Church, which impressed him by its authority. Metropolitan Anthony got on with him well enough and, far from resenting Nikodim's appointment to replace him as Exarch to Western Europe in 1974, remained well-disposed towards him and insisted on attending his funeral in Moscow in 1976.

Nikolai (Eremin, Stefan Pavlovich) (1892-1985). Evacuated with the White Army via Greece and Bulgaria where he worked as a coal-miner and studied at the Faculty of Pastoral Theology. At Prague University graduated from Faculty of Law and in Paris from the St Sergius Theological Institute. Deacon 1940 and priest 1942, served as Inspector, Librarian and Lecturer in Canon Law and Slavonic at the St Sergius Institute, became a monk in 1945 and, after **Metropolitan Evlogii**'s death, joined the jurisdiction of the Moscow Patriarchate and served in the parish of the Three Holy Hierarchs from 1946 as Assistant Vicar, Vicar, Archimandrite, Chairman of the Council of the West European Exarchate of the Moscow Patriarchate (1949-53), Bishop of Clichy entrusted with the care of Moscow Patriarchate parishes in Western Europe in 1953, Archbishop and Exarch 1954, Metropolitan of Korsun 1960. Retired in 1963 and lived in Villemoisson, as prior of a monastic community attached to the Church of St Sergius and St German of Valaam, until the late 1970s. Founder and spiritual guide of the Brotherhood of St John the Forerunner (1965-88).

Nikolai (Iarusevich, Boris Dorofeevich) (1892-1961). Ed. St Petersburg Gymnasium and St Petersburg Theological Academy. From 1915 he taught in the St Petersburg Theological Seminary. Appointed Vicar of the Cathedral of Peterhof in 1918 and, in 1919, of the Alexander Nevsky Lavra. In 1922 he was consecrated Bishop of Peterhof and Vicar of the Diocese of Petrograd. In 1927 he signed **Metropolitan Sergii (Starogorodsky)**'s declaration of loyalty to the Soviet government and became a member of the Provisional Patriarchal Holy Synod. Archbishop from 1935; from 1936 to 1940 in charge of the Diocese of Novgorod and Pskov. 1940 was appointed Archbishop of Volyn, Exarch to the Ukraine and Belorussia and in 1941 Metropolitan of Galich. In 1942-43 stood in for Metropolitan Sergii, who had been evacuated from Moscow and, at the Bishop's Council of 1943, was one of those who elected Sergii Patriarch. From then on he was a permanent member of the Holy Synod and, in 1944, was appointed Metropolitan of Krutitsy and Kolomna, head of the Diocese of Moscow. Nikolai was the chosen go-between between the Church and Stalin and suffered intensely both in his own mind and from general mistrust and opprobium for his acceptance of this invidious role.

Obolensky, Dmitrii (1918-2002). Ed. Trinity College, Cambridge, of which he subsequently became a Fellow. Professor of Russian and Balkan History at Oxford University 1961 until retirement. Editor of bilingual *Penguin Book of Russian Verse* – still unrivalled of its kind – first published in 1962. Author of *The Byzantine Commonwealth* (1971). Influential from the beginning in the BBC Russian Service. Vice President of the British Academy 1983-85. Knighted in 1984. An active member of the Russian Orthodox Church, he attended the Moscow Millennial Church Council in 1988 as a lay delegate.

Osborne, Alfred Herbert, Bishop Basil (b. 1938). Ed. University of Cincinnati, where he was awarded a doctorate in Classical Studies in 1969, having been introduced to the Orthodox Church by Father Michael Gelsinger in 1957. He moved to continue studies towards a doctorate in Oxford, where he was ordained deacon by Archbishop Anthony of Sourozh in 1969 and priest 1973. After the death of his wife Rachel in 1991, was consecrated Bishop and served as a Suffragan of the Diocese of Sourozh, then as acting successor to Metropolitan Anthony with the title Bishop of Sergievo until 2006, when he sought release from the Moscow Patriarchate and passed under the omophorion of the Patriarch of Constantinople. The move was officially recognised by Moscow the following year, 2007, and he continued to serve as Assistant Bishop under Archbishop Gabriel of Comana within the Ecumenical Patriarchate's Arch-diocese of Parishes of the Russian Tradition in Western Europe in the Episcopal Vicariate of Great Britain and Ireland, which, after his retirement in 2009 at the age of seventy-one, became a deanery. In 2010 he was laicised at his own request and released from his vows. A distinguished scholar, he edited the diocesan journal *Sourozh* from 1980 and headed the commission for the translation of liturgical texts into English.

Ostapov, Daniil Andreevich (1894-1975). Personal secretary and *keleinik* to **Patriarch Aleksii I (Simansky)**; Deputy Chairman of the Economics Department of the Moscow Patriarchate in the 1950s and 1960s.

Ouspensky, Leonid Aleksandrovich (1902-1987). Ed. Gymnasium of Zadonsk, fought in the civil war in the Red Cavalry 1918-20, was captured by the White Army and sentenced to death but reprieved and emigrated with the Volunteer Army to Constantinople from where he made his way to Bulgaria (1920), where he worked as a miner until, in 1926, he moved to Paris and worked in a car factory while studying at art school (graduated 1929). Member of the Brotherhood of St Photius 1930, one of the founders of the Moscow Patriarchate's Church of the Three Holy Hierarchs in 1931 which, with **Grigorii Krug**, he furnished with religious paintings. During the war he was dispatched to forced labour in Germany but escaped and joined the Union of Soviet Patriots in France (1945-47). Taught icon painting at the French Orthodox Institute of St Denis 1944-53, Professor of the Theology of the Icon at the Pastoral Course of the Exarchate of the Moscow Patriarchate 1953-58, was invited to lecture at the Moscow Theological Academy 1969. His first book *The Meaning of Icons* (1952) written in collaboration with **V.N. Lossky** was a treasured possession of Metropolitan Anthony's.

Payne, Richard (b. 1938). As editor of the Paulist Press, he conceived the idea for a 130-volume series, "The Classics of Western Spirituality", and later, for other publishers, of "Classics of the World", "Eastern Spirituality", and an *Encyclopaedia of the Religious Quest*. In 1991 founded, with his son Stephen, Arcadia Films, a Roman Catholic grassroots film and television production company.

Philaret (Denisenko, Mikhail Antonovich) (b. 1929). Ed. Odessa Seminary and Moscow Theological Academy. Took Monastic vows under name of Philaret in 1950 and was ordained hierodeacon in same year, priest in 1951. In 1957 he was appointed Inspector of Kiev Theological Seminary with the rank of Hegumen and Rector, with the rank of Archimandrite, in 1958. He represented the Russian Orthodox Church in Alexandria and, in 1962, was consecrated Bishop of Vienna and Austria. In 1964 returned to Moscow as Bishop of Dmitrov and Rector of the Moscow Theological Academy and Seminary. In 1966 was appointed Archbishop, then Metropolitan of Kiev where he opposed the Ukrainian Greek Catholic and the Ukrainian Autocephalous Churches. By 1980, was effectively in charge of the Ukrainian Exarchate of the Russian Orthodox Church in Kiev where he served in St Volodymir's Cathedral. After Ukraine split from Russia in 1990, the Moscow Patriarchate recognised Philaret as independent and self-governing Metropolitan of Kyiv. In 1991 a *Sobor* of Ukrainian bishops unilaterally declared autocephaly and appointed Philaret their primate. In 1992, however, he was recalled to Moscow and asked to resign for the sake of peace in the Church. This he did at the time but afterwards claimed the resignation had been made under pressure and rescinded it. After a period of confusion, Philaret was re-established as leader of the movement towards autocephaly.

Philaret (Vakhromeev) (b. 1935). Archbishop, Exarch to Central Europe. Later Metropolitan of Minsk and Belorussia, Exarch of the Moscow Patriarch in Western Europe 1978-84. Retired 2013.

Picot, Gaston (1878-1961). Surgeon attached to the Faculty of Medicine at the Sorbonne, whose operational technique was the subject of Andrei Bloom's doctoral thesis.

Pimen (Izvekov, Sergei Mikhailovich) (1910-1990). Ed. primary school. In 1925, aged fifteen, became a monk in the Moscow Monastery of the Presentation and served as conductor of various church choirs; priest in 1932. As hieromonk he served as pastor, purser and teacher until 1952, eventually attaining the rank of Prior (Namestnik) in the Pskovo-Pechery Monastery and subsequently at the Monastery of St Sergius and the Holy Trinity at Zagorsk. In 1957 became Bishop of the Baltic, then of Dmitrov, and Vicar of the Diocese of Moscow. From 1960 he was manager of the Moscow Patriarchate as Archbishop of Tula. In 1961 became Metropolitan of Leningrad and, in 1963, of Krutitsy and Kolomna and close co-operator with **Patriarch Aleksii I (Simansky)**, after whose death he was elected Patriarch 1971-90.

Pitirim (Nechaev, Konstantin Petrovich) (1926-2003). Ed. Moscow Theological Seminary and from 1951 by the Moscow Theological Academy, where he presented his doctoral thesis on Simeon the New Theologian. He was ordained deacon in 1952, priest in 1956, Bishop of Volokolamsk in 1963, Archbishop in 1971, and was appointed Metropolitan of Volokolamsk and Yuryev in 1986. Editor of the *Journal* *of the Moscow Patriarchate.*

Pitirim (Sviridov) (1888-1963). Ed. St John the Theologian Church school in Kozlovsky district and the Saratov Theological Seminary, graduating in 1913. Bishop and member of the Holy Synod of the Russian Orthodox Church. Bishop of Minsk and Belorussia 1947-59. Metropolitan of Leningrad and Ladoga 1959-60 and of Krutitsy and Kolomna until his death.

Pivovarov, Boris (b. 1950). Ed. from 1967 at the Odessa Theological Seminary. In 1971 he entered the Moscow Theological Academy and, in 1989, achieved the degree of Master of Theology. Protopriest, Chairman of the Department of Education in Novosibirsk.

Platon (Rozhdestvensky, Porfirii Fedorovich) (1861-1934). Ed. Kursk Theological Seminary. Consecrated priest in 1887 and served for four years in a rural parish in Kursk province. In 1891 entered the Kiev Theological Seminary after the death of his wife, became a monk 1894. Graduated from the Academy in 1895 and continued to work there until 1902 when, having attained the rank of Rector, he was enthroned as Bishop of Chigirinsk, Vicar of the Diocese of Kiev, but continued as Rector and Superior of the Kiev Fraternal Monastery, until 1907 when elected to the Second State Duma. In 1907 he became Archbishop of Alaska and North America. Recalled to serve in the Holy Synod in 1909; Archbishop of Kishinev and Khotin 1914; Archbishop of Kartalin and Kakhetin 1915, Exarch in Georgia and member of the Holy Synod. Member of the 1917-1918 Local Council, he was made Metropolitan of Tiflis and Baku, and Exarch in the Caucasus in 1917. In 1918 appointed Metropolitan of Kherson and Odessa. Emigrated to America in 1920. In 1923 his appointment as governing Metropolitan of North America and Canada was confirmed by **Patriarch Tikhon**. His subsequent dismissal by the Moscow Patriarchate in 1924 led eventually in 1933 to his declaring the American Church autonomous. He was forbidden to celebrate but the ban was posthumously lifted in 1946, when the Moscow Patriarchate recognised the self-declared autocephaly of the American Orthodox Church.

Platt, Stephen (b. 1972). Ed. Old Swinford Hospital and Pembroke College, Cambridge. Brought up in the Roman Catholic Church but was attracted to Orthodoxy as a boy under influence of Greek friends, holidays in Greece and Father Barnabus, who became his spiritual father and received him into the Orthodox Church at the age of sixteen. Studied Theology at Oxford University under **Bishop Kallistos of Diocleia (Timothy Ware)**. Met and married (in 1992) Anya Asarkan, an Orthodox Russian woman who helps him run the children's camps for the Diocese of Sourozh and who introduced him to that diocese of which, with Bishop Kallistos's blessing, he became a member. Ordained deacon in 1996, priest in 2001. Remained with the Moscow Patriarchal Diocese as Co-Vicar of the Oxford Orthodox community with Metropolitan Kallistos (Ware) after 2006. Priest of the Russian Orthodox parish of the Annunciation, Oxford, 2003-2006. Rector of the Russian Orthodox parish of St Nicholas, Oxford, from 2006. General Secretary of the Fellowship of St Alban and St Sergius since 1996.

Potter, Alford Philip (1921-2015). Ed. in the West Indies but attended a conference in Oslo as representative of Jamaica Student Christian Movement and served as a member of the Methodist Missionary Society in London. Moved to work in WCC's Youth Department in Geneva in 1954 and served as third General Secretary of the WCC 1972-84.

Powell, Enoch (1912-1998). Ed. Norton Grammar School for Boys then King Edward's School, Birmingham, and Trinity College, Cambridge. Gained a double-starred first in Latin and Greek and stayed on as research fellow. Professor of Greek at University of Sydney, 1937. Served in the war, in intelligence, and added Portuguese and Russian to the Urdu and German he had acquired at and after university. Demobilised with the rank of Brigadier and an OBE. Conservative MP and Minister of Health 1960-63, his career in politics was marred by the controversial "Rivers of Blood" speech in 1968 and by the uncertainties of his political affiliations.

Putin, Vladimir (b. 1952). Elected President of the Russian Federation after **Boris Eltsin** 2000-2008 and, after serving 2008-2012 as Prime Minister, was re-elected President for a further, ongoing term.

Ramsden, Benedict (b. 1938). Ed. Keble College, Oxford. First attended an Orthodox service in the Oxford house-church of **Archimandrite Nicholas Gibbes**. Under the instruction of Father Kirill (Taylor) he was received into the Orthodox Church. His wife independently became Orthodox shortly thereafter and, because they lived far from an Orthodox church, they designated one room as a chapel and began, with their children and later houseguests, to say Vespers at home. They attracted "needy" people, and, unofficially, their home became the centre of what was to become the Community of St Anthony and St Elias for the mentally ill. Father Benedict was ordained deacon in 1971 and priest in 1973 and moved to Devon, where the community is now managed by his son. In the course of his service as priest, Father Benedict established parishes in Builth Wells, Truro and Newton Abbot and now oversees the "Deanery" of South-West England for the Diocese of Sourozh.

Ramsey, Arthur Michael (1904-1988). Ed. Repton School and Magdalene College, Cambridge. Ordained 1928. Served as Canon in Durham Cathedral and Professor of Theology at Durham University. From 1950 was Regius Professor of Divinity at Cambridge and, after consecration, served as Bishop of Durham and Archbishop of York before his appointment as Archbishop of Canterbury 1961-74. He did much to further ecumenical relations between his own communion and the Roman Catholic and Orthodox Churches.

Ratlevy, Francis Edmé Marie (1879-1941). Professor at the Sorbonne. One of Andrei Bloom's teachers.

Reverdin, Claude E. (1921-2006). Studied Theology in Geneva and Basle. Minister of the Swiss Reformed Church in Endell Street, London, 1944-60. After 1960, took office at the Eaux-vives Centre and at the St Pierre Cathedral in Geneva. Author of *L'Eglise Suisse de Londres (1762-1897)* (1952) and, with Roselle Pauletti and others, of *La mort restituée: l'expérience médicale et humaine des hospices* (1982), a book that reflects an interest in palliative care originating from his years of service in London.

Rodzianko, Vladimir. *See* Vasilii.

Sadovnikova, Elena Iurevna (b. 1960). Immunologist, candidate in Biological

Studies. Spent years in London where she became a member of the Parish Council of the Diocese of Sourozh and, later, did much research in newspaper archives, Lambeth Palace and various medical institutes on Metropolitan Anthony of Sourozh. Active member of the FMAS; President from 2015.

Sartre, Jean-Paul Charles Aymard (1905-1980). Ed. Ecole Normale Supérieure and Universities of Berlin and (under Heidegger) Freiburg (1932-34). Briefly (1940-41) prisoner of war. Freed in Paris, where he took up teaching and served in the Resistance. After the war, gave up teaching to devote himself to writing and editing his review *Les Temps Modernes*, the extremely influential organ of French existentialism.

Satterthwaite, John Richard (1925-2014). Ordained deacon 1950, priest 1951. Consecrated bishop 1970. Served as Assistant General Secretary to the Church of England Council on Foreign Relations 1955-59, General Secretary 1959-1970. Incumbent of London Guild Church St Dunstan in the West 1959-70, Suffragan Bishop of Fulham 1970-80, Bishop of Gibraltar in Europe 1980-93. Returned 1993 to the Diocese of Carlisle.

Schmemann, Alexander Dmitrievich (1921-1983). Ed. school in Paris from 1929 where he served as altar-boy then deacon in the Alexander Nevsky Cathedral. Higher ed. Historico-Philological Faculty of the University of Paris and the St Sergius Theological Institute. Consecrated priest 1946, served in a church in Clamart and as editor of the diocesan journal *Tserkovnyy vestnik* ("The Church Herald"). In 1951 he moved to America and joined the North American Russian Metropolia, serving as Docent of St Vladimir Theological Institute in New York. Doctor of Theology 1959, Professor in the Faculty of Liturgical Theology 1960-83 and Dean of the Institute 1962-83, Vice President of the RSKhD in America from 1963 to 1979 and visiting lecturer to various American universities and seminaries. He played an important part in talks with the Moscow Patriarchate which led to the recognition of autocephaly of the American Orthodox Church in 1970, and wrote influential books on Church history, liturgics and the spiritual life. First published in English were *For the Life of the World* (1964), *Ultimate Questions* (1965), *The World as Sacrament* (1965), *Great Lent* (1969), and *The Journals of Father Alexander Schmemann, 1973-1983* (2000).

Scorer, Irene (née Hoecke) (b. 1942). Wife of **Deacon Peter Scorer**.

Scorer, Peter (b. 1942). Ed. New College, Oxford, and St Vladimir's Seminary, New York. Ordained deacon by Metropolitan Anthony in 1973.

Scriabin, Aleksandr Nikolaevich (1871 NS-1915). Composer and luminary of the Russian Silver Age. Son of **Nikolai Aleksandrovich Scriabin** by his first marriage to concert pianist Liubov' Petrovna Shchetina (d. 1872). His Moscow home at 11 Vakhtangov Street gave hospitality to the Bloom family in 1914 before **Boris Eduardovich**'s posting to Persia. Metropolitan Anthony possessed several books about his illustrious uncle and was to keep up with his family during post-1960 visits to the Soviet Union. They are said to have shared the gift of "seeing" sounds as colours.

Scriabin, Nikolai Aleksandrovich (1849-1914). Ed. Moscow University. Entered the Imperial Diplomatic Service and served in Constantinople, Turkey and the

Balkans. Acted as Consul General in Erzerum, Turkey. Married (1) Liubov' Petrovna Shchetina, concert pianist and mother of composer **Aleksandr Nikolaevich**; (2) **Ol'ga Ilinichna Fernandez** (b. Trieste, 1863, d. London, 1967), by whom he had three sons and one daughter, **Ksenia**. The children were educated in Russia but spent much time abroad with their father. Nikolai Aleksandrovich retired in 1913 and took up residence in Lausanne, where his grandson Andrei Bloom was born the following year.

Scriabina, Ksenia Nikolaevna (1889-1958). Ed. Smolny Institute, St Petersburg. Was proficient in Russian, French, German and English. Married **Boris Eduardovich Bloom**. Son Andrei (Anthony in religion) born June 1914. Accompanied her husband to various postings as Russian Consul in Persia at the end of that year. In 1921, leaving Bloom to close down the Consulate, she embarked on an adventurous journey with her widowed mother and son via India to Europe, where they lived initially in Austria, then in France. She and Bloom divorced and she resumed her maiden name, under which she took French citizenship in 1936. After supporting mother and son throughout the latter's student years, she accompanied him to England in 1949, where she died of cancer, much loved and respected by his parishioners, in 1958.

Scriabina, Ol'ga Il'inichna (née Fernandez) (1863-1957). Grandmother of Andrei Bloom who lived with her daughter Ksenia as an inalienable part of the family after the death of her husband **Nikolai Aleksandrovich Scriabin** in 1914. Ol'ga Ilinichna was born native Italian within the bounds of the Austro-Hungarian Empire, spoke French with her husband but learned to read and speak Russian after her marriage at the age of seventeen, when she was also received into the Orthodox Church with the name Ol'ga.

Seraphim (Lukianov, Aleksandr Ivanovich) (1876-1959). Ed. Saratov Theological Seminary and Kazan Theological Academy. Took monastic vows in 1902, ordained priest in 1903. Worked in various theological seminaries until 1911. Consecrated Bishop of Serdobol' in 1914; Archbishop of the Diocese of Finland in 1920; took part in the 1917-1918 Local Council of the Russian Orthodox Church; opposed the autonomy of the Finnish Orthodox Church under the jurisdiction of the Ecumenical Patriarch; and was retired to Konevetz Monastery 1924-26. Exiled, he served briefly under **Evlogii** but changed to ROCOR from 1927-45, when he rejoined the Moscow Patriarchate and was appointed Exarch to Western Europe in Paris 1946-49. In 1954 he returned to the USSR and settled in the Gerbov Monastery.

Seraphim (Nikitin) (1905-1979). Ed. State Institute of Architecture and Leningrad Theological Academy. Bishop of Kursk 1962-71 and Metropolitan of Krutitsy and Kolomna 1971-77, when he retired.

Sergii (Larin, Sergei Ivanovich) (1908-1967). Ed. Second Petrograd Gymnasium, renamed 37th Soviet School, Second Grade, 1915-30, and Historical Faculty of Leningrad University. From 1925 served the Renewal Church as psalmist, deacon (1926) and priest (1930). In 1933 he divorced his wife and became a monk in the Tikhvinsky Monastery from whence he was appointed Vicar of the Church of St Peter and St Paul in the district of Leningrad and, in 1935, Acting Prior of the St Panteleimon Monastery in the city. In 1937 transferred to Moscow and was promoted to Archimandrite and Dean of the Renewal Churches there. Bishop of Zvenigorod in 1941 and, in 1942, took on the management of the Diocese of Moscow. In 1943, after his appointment as Bishop of Tashkent and Samarkand, repented of his attachment to the Renewal Church and rejoined the Russian Orthodox Church. After 1944, as Bishop, was put in charge of a succession of dioceses in south Russia, then in Belarus. In 1961 he was awarded the degree of Candidate of Theology for a thesis on the Renewal Schism and appointed Archbishop of Perm and Solikamsk. The following year he was made Archbishop of Berlin and Central Europe, Exarch to Central Europe. From 1964 to 1965 he served as Archbishop of Yaroslav and Rostov and, in 1964, was temporarily charged with the administration of the Vologda diocese, from which he was retired for health reasons the following year.

Sergii (Shevich, Kirill Georgievich) (1903-1987). Ed. Oxford University, worked for a time in a Paris bank, active member of RSKhD and contributor to *Le Messager*. Parishioner of the Church of the Three Holy Hierarchs, member of the political group Mladorossi for which he was interned by the French at the beginning of World War Two (1939-41), but released and received as a monk 1944 and hieromonk the following year. Served as Vicar of the Trinity Church in Vanves near Paris, then as Prior of the Skete of the Holy Spirit in Mesnil-Saint-Denis near Versailles 1948-87, and member of the Diocesan Council of the West European Exarchate of the Moscow Patriarchate 1949-58.

Sergii (Starogorodsky, Ivan Nikolaevich) (1866-1944). Ed. Arzamasskoe dukhovnoe uchilishche; Nizhegorod Theological Seminary; St Petersburg Theological Academy. Orthodox missionary in Japan 1890-93 and 1897-99. Taught and served as Inspector, then Rector of the Theological Academy of St Petersburg 1893-94 and 1899-1905. Chaired the pioneering Religious-Philosophical Meetings in St Petersburg 1901-1903. From 1905 to 1907 Bishop, then Archbishop (1907), of the Diocese of Finland. Member of the Holy Synod from 1911. Elevated to Metropolitan 1917; served as senior hierarch of the Diocese of Vladimir 1917-22 and on the Local Council of 1917-1918. A brief flirtation with the Renewal movement ended in full reconciliation with **Patriarch Tikhon** and the Orthodox Church. From 1924 was in charge of the Nizhegorod diocese, where he was twice arrested for anti-Soviet activity. After the arrest of Metropolitan Petr, *locum tenens* of the office of Patriarch, Sergii took over this function with Petr's blessing and throughout 1926-27 negotiated recognition for the right to exist of a temporary Patriarchal Holy Synod and the return of a number of bishops from internal exile in return for a declaration of loyalty to the Soviet State, which entrained disassociation with ROCOR. In 1930 he reluctantly dismissed Patriarch Tikhon's appointee as Head of the Russian Parishes in Western Europe, **Evlogii**, who was replaced by **Elevferii** in December of that year. In 1934 appointed Metropolitan of Moscow and Kolomna and, in 1937, became official *locum tenens*. In recognition of his patriotic stance after the invasion of Russia (the Church contributed 300 million roubles and many treasures to the Soviet war effort) he was, after two years in the evacuation in Klianovsk, elected Patriarch at the Bishop's Council of 1943 in Moscow, where he died the following year.

Shaliapin, Fedor Ivanovich (1873-1938). Largely self-taught, Shaliapin made his name in the mid-1890s in Mamontov's private opera at Abramtsevo, then sung in the opera houses of Moscow and St Petersburg, performing the great bass roles in Russian opera with remarkable dramatic ability. Diaghilev's "Russian Seasons" in Paris, which began with opera in 1901, brought him world fame and from then on he made frequent guest appearances in Europe and North America. During World War One and the civil war he carried on performing in Russia, often under very difficult circumstances, but emigrated in 1921. From 1922 to 1925 he toured America, then settled in Europe, continuing to perform, as far as age and health permitted, until his death on the eve of World War Two. His last performance was at the Monte-Carlo Opera in 1937.

Shariatmadari, Mohammad Kazem (1905-1986). A Shiite of Azerbaijani provenance; Grand Ayatollah of Iran. In 1963 he prevented the Shah from executing Ayatollah Khomeini. A liberal who considered the clergy should remain aloof from politics, he consistently spoke out for moderation in spite of having been instrumental in toppling the Shah and the recall of Khomeini from France, and died under house arrest, having suffered considerable violence and persecution from the regime he had helped to set up.

Shestov, Lev (pseudonym for Lev (Cheguda Leib) Isaakovich Shvartzman) (1866-1938). Ed. Mathematical Faculty, then Faculty of Law at Moscow University and for a further year (1889) in Kiev. Lived from 1895 to 1914 for much of the time in Austria, Germany, France and Switzerland. 1914-18, in Moscow, he was an active member of the Moscow Psychological Society; moved back to Kiev in 1918 and lectured in Greek Philosophy at the People's Institute and the Tauride University. Leading member of the Free Philosophical Association in Petrograd. From 1920 lived in Paris where he was Professor of Literature at the University of Paris from 1922 to 1936 and taught at the Institute of Slavic Studies. He was friendly with E. Husserl and corresponded with M. Heidegger, Martin Buber and L. Lévy-Bruhl. A temperamental opponent of rationalism in philosophy, Shestov based his "philosophy of tragedy" on the works of Dostoevsky and Nietzsche, Kierkegaard and Pascal. Comparing and contrasting Greek philosophical enquiry with Old Testament personal revelation, Shestov set up a dichotomy between Athens and Jerusalem which resonated in the thought of his Russian contemporaries, writers and theologians. He was also close to the existentialist school popular with French contemporaries. An associate of the Silver Age thinkers grouped about Diaghilev's "World of Art", the Merezhkovskys' *New Way* and **Berdiaev**'s *Questions of Life* from the early twentieth century, Shestov advocated an apotheosis of free will which has much in common with the views of Berdiaev, with whom he co-operated on the journal *Put'*.

Shmaina-Velikanova, Anna Il'inichna (b. 1955). Docent of the Centre for the Study of Religion, RGGU, and Doctor of Culturology. Specialist in Hebrew and Judaic Studies, Biblical scholar and translator, historian of early Christianity and Judaism. Grew up in a family of distinguished Jewish origin who had converted to Christianity. They left Russia under pressure from the security organs in the 1970s and emigrated to Israel but moved to France, where Anna's father was ordained priest. He served in Paris and in Jerusalem. They returned to Russia after the collapse of the Soviet Union.

Shumkin, Georgii (1894-1965). Ed. Technical School and Pavlov Military

Academy (graduated 1915), served in World War One. Joined the White Army, emigrated to Czechoslovakia and studied at Prague University, then at the St Sergius Institute in Paris. Consecrated deacon under **Metropolitan Evlogii (Georgievsky)** in 1923, priest in 1927. Served as vicar of various French parishes under Evlogii and, after his death in 1946, the Moscow Patriarchate. Active in the ACER movement from early days in Prague, he acted as spiritual guide to the RSKhD summer camps from 1932 to 1940 and helped persecuted Jews during the occupation. Retired with the rank of mitred archpriest in 1954. He lived for the next ten years in the elderly persons' home at Sainte-Geneviève-de-Bois.

Saint Silouan (Antonov, Semen Ivanovich) (1866-1938). Served as conscript in Russian army then, after four years in the novitiate, became a monk in the Russian Monastery of St Panteleimon on Mount Athos in 1896, schema monk from 1911. His teaching and some account of his life is preserved for us in a book by his disciple **Sophronii**. Silouan taught constant prayer "for the world", keeping "his mind in the hell of repentance" for the sake of sinners, those who suffer, those who have lost their faith in an ever more secular world. It was, he said, "to shed blood" . . . yet as a man he was approachable, simple and serene. Canonised in 1988.

Silouan (Strizhkov) (1911-1995). Became a monk under the influence of **St Silouan** the Athonite. Joined **Father Sophronii**'s community in Sainte-Geneviève-de-Bois during the 1940s to 1950s but did not follow him to England, continuing as priest to the old people's home at Sainte-Geneviève-de-Bois. Hegumen from 1958.

Solzhenitsyn, Aleksandr Isaevich (1918-2008). Ed. Physico-Mathematical Faculty of Kislovodsk University, from which he graduated in 1941, having pursued in parallel a correspondence course with the Moscow Institute of History, Philosophy and Literature, for which, ironically, he had been awarded a state grant. During the war he obtained a commission and served to the rank of captain before he was arrested on active service and sentenced to eight years in the camps. He remained in exile until 1956. Rehabilitated in 1957, Solzhenitsyn kept a low profile teaching Mathematics and Physics until 1962, but the publication of his "One Day in the Life of Ivan Denisovich" in Tvardovsky's *Novy Mir* ("The New World") brought him international renown and fermented new trouble with the authorities. "Ivan Denisovich" was a Russian Everyman and his "day" ran its course in a prison camp, in which he quite clearly should not, even on Marxist reasoning, have been incarcerated in the first place. Further short stories and a play were published in the Soviet Union during the 1960s but the more explicitly analytic novels, *Cancer Ward* (1968) and *In the First Circle* (1968), depicted critically thinking individuals and failed to pass the censor. Their circulation in *samizdat* and publication in *tamizdat* (abroad), together with rumours of the compendium of "camp folklore" *The Gulag Archipelago*, and with ventures into publicistic writing such as the "Lenten letter" to the Patriarch, led to a virulent campaign against Solzhenitsyn in the press, his expulsion from the Writers' Union and, eventually, to his arrest and exile in 1974. In the USA, where he eventually took up residence, his historical novels had comparatively little resonance; the moralistic, religious and somewhat nationalistic standpoint of the series was not appreciated in the West. He returned to Russia in triumph after the fall of the Soviet Union, devoted much of the money brought him by worldwide fame to helping ex-prisoners and to cultural projects, and instituted a vigorous campaign to inspire probity in the public sector on film, television and with his pen.

Sophronii (Sakharov, Sergei Semenovich) (1896-1993). Ed. Moscow school. Served in World War One as a junior officer, twice arrested by Cheka in Moscow 1918, emigrated through Italy and Germany to Paris (1921) where he worked as an artist and exhibited (1922-24), studied a preliminary year at the St Sergius Theological Institute in 1925 but entered the monastery of St Panteleimon on Mount Athos later that year. He became a monk in 1927, and was the spiritual son of St Silouan whose life and sayings he was afterwards to record in the book *Starets Silouan* (1948). Having taken the Great Schema in 1935 and gone into retreat as a hermit on Karcola in 1938, he served as priest-monk and spiritual guide at the Greek Monastery of St Paul on Mount Athos until 1942 and was a member of the Trinity Skete (1943-47) when he left Athos for France and began to study in the fourth year at the St Sergius Institute, but was expelled because he belonged to the Moscow Patriarchate. He settled in Sainte-Geneviève-de-Bois and served as Assistant Vicar at the Church of St Nicholas at the old people's home there (1947-56), was raised to Archimandrite in 1954, and, in 1956, founded a monastic community on a nearby farm. In 1956 he moved to Tolleshunt Knights, Maldon, where he founded the Stavropigial monastery St John the Forerunner, initially under Bishop Anthony of Sergievo, then as a daughter house of the Monastery of St Paul on Mount Athos under the Ecumenical Patriarch. Sophronii served as Abbot of this foundation until 1974, then as spiritual guide 1974-93.

Sophronitskaia, Elena Aleksandrovna (née Scriabina) (1900-1990). Wife of the pianist Vladimir Sophronitsky and Metropolitan Anthony's first cousin.

Sophronitskaia, Roxana Vladimirovna (called Ksana, married name Cogan) (b. 1937). Daughter of **E.A. Sophronitskaia**, niece of Metropolitan Anthony. Now lives in the United States.

Spieler, Vsevolod (1902-1984). During the Civil War served in the White Army and emigrated to Bulgaria, where he was ordained in 1934 and served in Razardchik and Sofia until 1950, when he returned to the Soviet Union and became Vicar of the Church of St Nicholas on Kuznetsy. Reverence for the hierarchy of the Church kept his highly critical attitude to Patriarchal conformism discreet and low-key, but he was nevertheless deeply respected for his percipient independence of mind.

Stalin, Joseph (Dzhugashvili, Iosif Vissarionovich) (1879-1953). Secretary-General of the Central Committee of the Communist (Bolshevik) Party from 1922-53 and supreme ruler of the Soviet Union until his death.

Statov, Pavel (d. 1982). Russian priest who spent some time under the auspices of the Moscow Patriarchate in France.

Thekla, Mother (Sharf, Marina) (1918-2011). Ed. at the City of London's Girls' School and Girton College, Cambridge, where she read Part I of the English Tripos and Russian for Part II in Modern Languages. She worked in RAF intelligence 1941-46, then in the Ministry of Education before taking up a teaching career at Kettering High School in 1952 where she became Head of English. When possible she attended the Russian Orthodox Cathedral of the Dormition and All Saints in

London, where she met and decided to join Sister Lydia, later **Mother Maria (Gysi)**. At St Mary's Abbey, West Malling, she was clothed as an Orthodox postulant by Archbishop Anthony of Sourozh in 1965. In 1966, Mother Maria became Abbess of her own Orthodox convent at Filgrove and they were joined by **Sister Katherine**. In 1971 they obtained an amicable transfer to the Greek Orthodox Church under Archbishop Athanagoros, who professed her nun with the name Thekla. In 1975 the little convent sought greater solitude and, after a homeless year in Bede's House, Robin Hood's Bay, acquired and adapted an old farmhouse with some land somewhat to the north and inland, within sight of Whitby Abbey, which from 1975 to 2005 became the Monastery of the Assumption. Mother Thekla succeeded **Mother Maria** as Abbess after her death. With Sister Katherine, she initiated the monastery's publishing projects, translated a number of Orthodox services, and wrote the words for John Tavener's oratorio *St Mary of Egypt*. It was a great sorrow that the monastery was not blessed with continuity and it was dissolved, the little graveyard for Mother Maria and Sister Katherine desanctified, and their remains transferred after Thekla retired to the care of the Anglican Sisterhood in Whitby, in whose graveyard of the Holy Paraclete they are all three buried.

Theokritoff, Mikhail Ioannovich (1888-1969). Ed. Penza Theological Seminary, psalmist in Moscow 1910-20, emigrated to Germany in 1920, psalmist in Berlin 1921-24 and of the Church of St Elizabeth in Wiesbaden 1924-34. Came to London in 1946 and, from that time, served with his brother **Father Vladimir** as conductor of the choir and psalmist until his death.

Theokritoff, Vladimir Ioannovich (1881-1950). Ed. Theological Seminary of Penza, psalmist in the Diocese of Penza 1902-1904 then singer in the Choir of the Metropolitan of St Petersburg; taught at the Alexander Nevsky Church school then sent to serve as psalmist abroad in Po, Biaritz and, eventually, from 1908 to 1911, in the Embassy Church in London. From 1911 to 1914 he was psalmist at the Alexander Nevsky Cathedral in Paris, then deacon back in London until 1939, when he was consecrated priest of the parish of the Dormition and St Phillip, of which he served as vicar from 1940 to 1950. Promoted to archpriest in 1944. After **Evlogii**'s death he chose the jurisdiction of the Moscow Patriarchate and was succeeded by Father Anthony.

Saint Tikhon (Belavin, Vasilii Ivanovich) (1865-1925). Ed. The Toropets Theological School and the Theological Seminary in Pskov. Graduated from the St Petersburg Theological Academy in 1888. For ten years he worked in education and was consecrated Bishop of Liublin in 1897, from 1898 to 1907 was ruling Bishop of Aleut and Alaska (from 1900 the Aleut and North American Diocese). On his return to Russia served as Archbishop in the Diocese of Yaroslav and Litovsk. In 1917 was Metropolitan of Moscow and in November that year chosen from three candidates by lot at the Local Council as Patriarch of Moscow and all Russia – the first since Peter the Great abolished the Patriarchate after the death of Patriarch Adrian in 1700, establishing the Holy Synod as governing body of the Orthodox Church in Russia from 1721 to 1917. In May 1922 Tikhon was arraigned before the court for opposing the confiscation of Church property by the State. In the following year a council of the Renewal Church stripped him of his office and even of his status as monk. He refused to acknowledge the validity of their pronouncements and remained under house arrest in the Don Monastery until June 1923. On his release, he did his utmost to strengthen the position of those in the Church who had remained loyal to the newly re-established Patriarchate and pursued a difficult policy of opposing the Renewal movement, the more favoured of the two factions at the time, and avoiding provoking the State into openly crushing his own followers. In the long term, Tikhon's firmness of purpose outlasted the rather hesitant and divided efforts of the Renewal Church to establish a modernised Orthodoxy which could continue in collaboration with a communist state, but he himself died in great anxiety as to the future. Tikhon was canonised by the Church in exile and later by the Moscow Patriarchate.

Timofeev, Vasilii Gavrilovich (1878-1952). Ed. Odessa Theological Seminary and St Petersburg Theological Academy (graduated 1902). He was appointed to the choir of the London Embassy Church of the Dormition in 1903 and served as psalmist then deacon then priest from 1923, Assistant Vicar 1926, Archpriest 1925 and Vicar from 1926 to 1929, when he broke with **Metropolitan Evlogii** and joined ROCOR, who entrusted him with a parish in Paris. However, he returned to the Moscow Patriarchate in 1945 and from 1946 to 1949 served as Archpriest on the council of their West European Exarchate. In 1949, together with the parishioners of Znamenskaia Church, he transferred once more, this time to the jurisdiction of the Ecumenical Patriarchate.

Tito (Broz, Josip) (1892-1980). First President of the Yugoslav Federation from 1945. Politically, after an acrimonious split with **Stalin**, he became the first Secretary-General of the Non-Aligned Movement (NAM), working with Jawaharlal Nehru of India, Nasser of Egypt and Sukarno of Indonesia.

Turintsev, Aleksandr Aleksandrovich (1896-1984). Ed. Vladimir Gimnazium, emigrated in 1919, to Prague 1922 and Paris 1927. Graduated from the Faculty of Law at Prague University in 1927, the Paris School of Higher Social Sciences and the St Sergius Theological Institute in 1931. Consecrated deacon 1948 and priest 1949, Assistant Vicar at the Three Holy Hierarchs 1949-53, and Secretary to the Diocesan Council 1950. Temporarily relieved Anthony to minister to the London parish on various occasions beginning from 1950; Archpriest and Vicar of the parish of the Three Holy Hierarchs 1964-84.

Ustinov, Peter (1921-2004). Ed. Westminster School. English, born to Russian émigrés, Ustinov spoke a number of languages fluently and was much appreciated as an urbane, witty and eminently civilised raconteur. He received many media awards and was knighted. Served as Chancellor of Durham University, President of the World Federalist Movement (1991-2004) and did sterling work for UNESCO's Save the Children. His journalistic diary of current events and his biography *Dear Me* (1977) are classic commentaries on the vagaries of the twentieth-century world.

Utenkov, Evgenii Georgevich (1926-2010). Artist. Member of Moscow Union of Artists. *See also* **Utenkova, E.P.** He and his wife were prominent among those who hosted unofficial gatherings to meet Metropolitan Anthony in their flat.

Utenkova, Ekaterina Petrovna (née Morozova) (b. 1935). Teacher at the Russian Economics Academy. One daughter, Elena Evgenevna Utenkova-Tichonova, artist and teacher at the Academy of Applied Arts, Moscow, Member of Moscow Union of Artists. See also **Utenkov, E.G.**

Vasilii (Krivoshein, Vsevolod Aleksandrovich) (1900-1985). Ed. Historico-Philological Faculty of the University of Petrograd then of Moscow University (1917-18), fought in the White Army during the civil war, graduated from Philological Faculty of Paris University in 1921, attended lectures on Philosophy at the University of Munich 1922-23, entered the Monastery of St Panteleimon on Mount Athos as a novice in 1925, professed monk 1927, member of the Council of his monastery 1937-47, which he also represented in the Kinot 1938-47. In 1947 was arrested by Greeks on a false charge of co-operation with the German occupiers and had to leave Athos. Not welcome in France because of the arrest, he went from Athens to Oxford in 1951 where he was ordained priest and served in the house-church of St Nicholas under **Nicholas Gibbes** and Father Anthony 1951-59. While at Oxford he contributed to a theological dictionary of the language of the Greek fathers published by the university. In 1956 he accepted the invitation to the Soviet Union refused by Father Anthony as a delegate from the Moscow Patriarchate's West European Exarchate, was made Archimandrite in 1957 and, briefly, Vicar of the new Church of the Annunciation in Oxford in 1959. Later that year, however, he was consecrated second Suffragan Bishop to the Patriarchal Exarch in Western Europe with the title Bishop of Volokolamsk and from November moved to Paris. From 1960 he was Bishop then Archbishop of Brussels and Belgium, which became his home, although he continued a frequent visitor to France as editor of the *Vestnik russkogo zapadno-evropeiskogo patriarshego Ekzarkhata*. He represented the Russian Patriarchal Church at various conferences, particularly between Anglicans and Orthodox, in the 1960s and 1970s. Much respected for his academic work, particularly his *magnum opus* on St Simeon the New Theologian (1980), he was awarded a doctorate of Theology at Leningrad Theological Academy in 1964. He visited the USA twice in 1969 and 1970 and Russia some twenty times.

Vasilii (Osborne). *See* Alfred Herbert Osborne.

Vasilii (Rodzianko, Vladimir Aleksandrovich) (1915-1999). Ed. Theological Faculty of Belgrade in 1937, received a grant for further study in Theological College in London 1937-39, lectured in educational institutes in Novy Sad 1939-41, in which year he was consecrated deacon, then priest by Serbian Patriarch Gavriel. In 1949, he was arrested for "religious propaganda" by the Serbian communists and sentenced to eight years forced labour but, at the intercession of the Archbishop of Canterbury, was released and exiled to France, then appointed as Vicar of the Serbian Patriarchal Church in London (1951-79). He was active from the beginning in the BBC Russian language broadcasting programmes. Widowed, he was consecrated monk in 1979 by Metropolitan Anthony of Sourozh, his spiritual director, left for the USA and was accepted as priest, then Bishop (1980-84) of the Autocephalous Orthodox Church of America. Retired 1984.

Vasiliuk, Fedor Efimovich (b. 1953). Doctor of Psychology, Dean of Faculty of Psychological Consultation of the Moscow City Psychological-Pedagogical

University.

Veniamin (Fedchenkov, Ivan Afanasevich) (1880-1961). Ed. Tambovsk Theological Seminary and St Petersburg Theological Academy where he remained attached to the Chair of Biblical History 1907-1908. Priest-monk 1907; representative of the Tver province at the All-Russian Local Council 1917-18. In 1919 enthroned as Bishop of Sympheropol and evacuated with the White Army to Constantinople in 1920; from 1925 in Paris, where he joined, under **Metropolitan Evlogii**, the St Sergius Theological Institute and served with a break in Yugoslavia from 1927 to 1929, until, in 1931, he remained with the Moscow Patriarchate and founded the parish of the Three Holy Hierarchs in Paris, where he lived in great poverty as Archbishop until 1933. Exarch to the Moscow Patriarchate in the Diocese of North America 1933-47, promoted to Metropolitan in 1939. In 1945 he visited Moscow to take part in the Local Council of the Russian Orthodox Church and, in 1947, returned to the Soviet Union for good, where he served in Riga, Rostov and Saratov until after his retirement in 1958 to the Kievo-Pechersky Monastery until his death in 1961.

Vilensky, Iurii Grigor'evich (b. 1938). Psychiatric doctor, writer and historian of medicine. Specialised for many years in researching the life and works of **M.A. Bulgakov**, from the medical point of view.

Visser 't Hooft, William Arnold (1900-1985). Ed. University of London where his doctoral dissertation was approved in 1928. From 1929 edited *The Student World*, a quarterly published in Geneva by the World Student Christian Federation; was active in German resistance to Nazism. In 1938 became First Secretary-General of the WCC until retirement in 1966; Honorary Chairman from 1968. Fifteen honorary degrees and fifteen books in various languages.

Vitalii (Ustinov, Rostislav Petrovich) (1910-2006). Emigrated with his parents via Constantinople to Serbia (1920), where he attended the Crimean Cadet Corps in Bela Tserkov 1921-23, then journeyed on to Paris and Cannes where he finished his schooling and did military service in the French army. Took a job with an English firm in Yugoslavia but entered the St Sergius Theological Academy in 1937 and then the Monastery of St Job in Ladomirovo in 1938 under the jurisdiction of the Synodal Church. Tonsured monk in 1946 and consecrated priest-monk in the same year. He evacuated to Bratislav in 1944, then fled via Berlin to Hamburg when the city was occupied by Soviet troops. In the displaced persons camp at Fischbeck 1945-46, he strenuously opposed forced repatriation to Soviet Russia. From 1946 he was Vicar of the Church of the Dormition and St Philip in London for the Synodal Church in Great Britain (1946-53), editor of the journal *Pravoslavnoe obozrenie* ("Orthodox Review") 1947-51, Bishop of Montevideo and Vicar of the Diocese of Brazil from 1951, then from 1956 of the Diocese of Western Canada, where he founded a community and printing house first near Edmonton then in Mansonville near Montreal. Bishop of Montreal and Canada 1968; senior hierarch of the Synodal Church and Metropolitan in charge of the East American and Canadian Diocese 1986. Retired in 2001 but split with his diocese that same year to become head of ROCOR, where he remained firmly opposed to reunion with the

Moscow Patriarchate. He lived out his days in the Hermitage of the Transfiguration, Mansonville, Canada.

Vladimir (Sabodan) (1935-2014). Ed. at school in Odessa and at the Leningrad Theological Seminary. In 1965 he completed the postgraduate course at the Moscow Theological Academy, was appointed Rector of the Odessa Theological Seminary and elevated to the rank of Archimandrite. In 1966 he was appointed Deputy Head of the Russian Orthodox Ecclesiastical Mission in Jerusalem, Metropolitan of Rostov and Novocherkask 1982, Exarch of the Moscow Patriarchate in Western Europe 1984-88, Metropolitan of Kiev and Ukraine 1992.

Vladimir (Tikhonitsky, Viacheslav Mikhailovich) (1873-1959). Ed. Theological Seminary of Viatsk and Theological Academy of Kazan, from which he graduated in 1898, having been received as a monk the previous year. Consecrated Bishop of Belostok in 1907 and served on the All-Russian Church Council in Moscow 1917-18. Appointed Archbishop to Belostok, now part of Poland, by **Archbishop Tikhon** in 1923. He was put under house arrest by the Polish government 1923-24 for refusing to acknowledge the self-declared autocephaly of the Polish Orthodox Church, then exiled to Prague. He made his way to Paris and **Metropolitan Evlogii (Georgievsky)** appointed him Archbishop of Nice. Together with Evlogii he went under the jurisdiction of the Ecumenical Patriarch in 1931, managing parishes in the South of France, Italy, Switzerland and North Africa. 1945-46 he replaced Evlogii, who was ill, in charge of the Exarchate of Churches of the Russian Tradition under the Ecumenical Patriarch, as Exarch from 1947. Served as Rector of the St Sergius Theological Institute 1946-48. As Honorary Rector of the Theological Academy he remained a key figure in Church politics until his death.

von Schlippe, Irina Yanovna (née Chymanovsky) (b. 1936). Moved from Poland to Berlin with her family during the war at the age of six. After the war, made her way to France, having lived for some time in Morocco, then, from 1961, took up residence in England where she worked as teacher and interpreter, and for the Russian service of the BBC. Member of the Parish Council of the Cathedral of the Dormition and All Saints, London, and later, of the Sourozh Diocesan Council. During the early 1990s she became a founding member and organiser of the St Gregory Charitable Foundation in St Petersburg, where her husband **Vladimir Borisovich von Schlippe** worked as a nuclear physicist from 1996. She was "exceptionally fortunate" in her spiritual advisers "due to fate throwing me back and forth". They included, besides and before Metropolitan Anthony, Father (later Bishop) John Shakhovskoi, Father Alexander Kiselev, Father Adrian (later Archbishop Andrei) Rymarenko, Father (later Archbishop) Mitrofan Znosko-Borovsky, and **Father Vasilii Zenkovsky**.

von Schlippe, Vladimir Borisovich (b. 1931). Ed. primary school in Germany, where he was born to a family of émigré aviation engineers. In 1946 the family were deported together with key workers of the "Junkers" factory to the Soviet Union, to the town now known as Dubna, where he completed his schooling and, after working for a year at the local aviation factory, entered the Kuibyshev Industrial Institute and switched in his second year to the Physics Faculty of the Gorky University. At the end of 1953 he returned to Berlin, then to Frankfurt where he continued to specialise in Physics. From 1963 to 1996 taught Physics and directed research at the

University of London. In 1997 accepted an invitation to the Petersburg Institute of Nuclear Physics, where he worked until 2011, lecturing at the St Petersburg and Moscow State Universities.

Vysheslavtsev, Boris Petrovich (1878-1954). Ed. school in Moscow and Faculty of Law at Moscow University, from which he graduated in 1899. Doctor of Law 1908, he obtained a grant to study abroad (Berlin, Heidelberg, Rome, Paris). In Marburg in 1914 he prepared a thesis on "Fichte's Ethics", the success of which won him a professorship at Moscow University where he lectured on the History of Political Doctrines. With **Berdiaev**, founded the Free Philosophical Academy (*Volphil*) and was deported in 1922. He continued to co-operate on a number of projects with Berdiaev in Berlin and Paris, where 1927-43 he lectured in the Department of Moral Theology at the St Sergius Institute. A popular visiting lecturer, he was invited to various countries in Europe, often to lecture on Orthodoxy in an ecumenical context, and took an active part in Franco-Russian intellectual life. His *magnum opus, The Ethics of Transfigured Eros: Problems of Law and Grace*, was an eloquent apologia for Christian morality, combining knowledge of modern psychology (he was a friend and translator of Karl Jung) with patrology. A vigorous supporter of **Sergii Bulgakov** in the dispute over the cult of Sophia, Vysheslavtsev became estranged from Berdiaev and the editors of the YMCA Press. An increasingly passionate nationalistic anti-communism led him to identify with pro-Nazi elements in the emigration. In 1943 he quit Paris for neutral Switzerland, where he lived until his death from tuberculosis in 1954.

Waddams, Herbert Montague (1911-1972). Ed. Choral scholar of King's College, Cambridge. Studied History at the University of Lund and Theology at Cuddlestone College. Ordained deacon 1935, priest 1936. General-Secretary of the Church of England Council of Foreign Relations 1945-59. Author of a number of books including *Communism and the Churches* (1950) and *Meeting the Orthodox Churches* (1964).

Weil, Simone (1909-1943). Studied Philosophy but chose to work in the factory and on the land as a kind of existential ascesis. During the war she served with the Free French.

Williams, Charles Walter Stansby (1886-1945). Ed. St Alban's School, Hertfordshire, and University College, London, but did not take his degree owing to lack of funds. From 1908 worked at OUP as Proofreading Assistant, then Editor, in which capacity he edited the works of Søren Kierkegaard. After evacuating to Oxford with OUP in 1938, he became a valued member of the Inkling Society and a close associate of **C.S. Lewis**. Metropolitan Anthony frequently quoted from his books.

Williams, Rowan (b. 1950). Ed. Dynevor College and University of Cambridge. Ordained deacon 1977, priest 1978. Taught Theology at Cambridge University then, from 1984, held the Lady Margaret Chair of Divinity at Oxford and served as residentiary Canon of Christ Church. Doctor of Divinity 1989; FBA 1990. Bishop of Monmouth and Archbishop of Wales 1991/2. Writer of scholarly studies and poetry; wrote his DPhil thesis on **Vladimir Lossky**. Patron of Fellowship of St Alban and St Sergius. Conversant with the Welsh language, English, Spanish,

German, Russian, Hebrew, Syriac, Latin, and Ancient and modern Greek. Present positions: Master of Magdalene College, Cambridge, and Chancellor of the University of South Wales.

Yakunin, Gleb Pavlovich (1934-2014). Ed. Biological Faculty at University of Irkutsk. Baptised in the late 1950s by **Father Aleksandr Men'** and studied in the Moscow Theological Seminary 1959-62, when he was ordained priest. One of the signatories, together with **Nikolai Eschliman,** of the *samizdat* published an open letter to **Patriarch Aleksii I,** challenging the Church to speak out in defence of human rights. Both signatories were forbidden to celebrate. Yakunin became an active dissident, member of the Christian Committee for the Defence of Believers in the USSR. In 1980 he was arrested for anti-Soviet activity and sent to the forced labour camp "Perm 37" until 1987. During *glasnost'* he was re-instated as a priest, rehabilitated in 1991 and elected to the Supreme Soviet. Here he acted as member of a commission to investigate KGB files and was again forbidden to celebrate, then ex-communicated, for publishing compromising material on the Orthodox senior hierarchy. He devoted himself to full-time party politics, founding the Democratic Alliance "Choice of Russia" and, in 1995, the "Committee for Defence of Freedom of Conscience". In 1996 he was elected member of the Russian parliament from the "Democratic Russia" party.

Yeltsin. *See* Eltsin.

Zenkovsky, Vasilii Vasilievich (1881-1962). Ed. Gymnasium in Kiev, studied in Physico-Mathematical Faculty of Kiev University from 1900 and, in 1904, transferred to the Historico-Philological Faculty, where he was retained to teach Philosophy from 1909. Founding member of the Kiev Religious-Philosophical Society, Chairman from 1911. Awarded doctorate in 1915, Chair of Psychology 1916. Under Skoropadsky in 1918 was Minister of Cults and took part in the All-Ukrainian Church Council in May of that year. Emigrated via Odessa to Belgrade in 1920. Member of the St Seraphim circle from 1921, Life-Chairman of the RSKhD from 1923. In Prague from 1923 to 1926 served at Prague University in the Faculty of Experimental and Child Psychology and as director of the Russian Pedagogical Institute. After nine months in the USA studying Religious Education he settled in Paris at the invitation of the St Sergius Theological Institute, where he taught History of Russian Philosophy, Psychology and Apologetics (1926-62). At the beginning of the war he was interned for fourteen months by the French and, on his release, was consecrated deacon then priest by **Evlogii** in 1942, after which he served in various Paris churches as well as continuing at the St Sergius Institute where he acted as Dean 1944-48 and 1949-62, founding a theological course for women in 1950. His *History of Russian Philosophy* earned him a second doctorate in Ecclesiastical Studies. **Metropolitan Evlogii** had plans to enthrone him as Bishop and as successor, but he refused this high honour, preferring to serve on in various pedagogical and editorial capacities and as priest and spiritual father to his Russian flock in Paris.

Zernov, Nicholas (Nikolai Mikhailovich) (1898-1980). Ed. Polivanov Gymnasium, briefly studied in the Medical Faculty of Moscow University but joined the White Army and emigrated via Constantinople to Serbia, where he was active in the RSKhD, studied at the Theological Faculty of Belgrade University, joined the St Seraphim circle from 1923. In 1925 he moved to Paris where he was secretary to the RSKhD, founder-editor of their journal *Le Messager* (*Vestnik RSKhD*) 1925-29, undertook research in Oxford 1930-32 and finally settled in London in 1934; British citizen from 1936. Served as Secretary to the Fellowship of St Alban and St Sergius 1934-47, founded St Basil's House in Ladbroke Grove in 1945, Professor of the History of Eastern Orthodoxy 1947-60 at the University of Oxford where he served from 1959 as Director of the House of St Gregory and St Macrina, Doctor *honoris causa* of Oxford University 1966.

Zernova, Militza Vladimirovna (née Lavrova) (1899-1994). Founder of the Pushkin Club 1953. Active member of the Fellowship of St Albans and St Sergius. A pillar of the Orthodox parish in Oxford, she was also a stalwart friend to Metropolitan Anthony, although they did not always see eye to eye on questions of Church policy.

Index of Proper Names

Abbott, Eric Symes, 90
Afanasii vi, 17, 18, 19, 23, 24, 25, 26, 28, 30, 31, 32, 35, 36, 37, 38, 44, 50, 59, 107, 202, 203, 204
Aleksii (Mensbrugghe) 87, 94, 95, 98
Aleksii II (Ridiger) 106, 166, 167, 172, 174, 181, 221, 224, 225, 229
Aleksii I (Simansky) 43, 50, 80, 92, 96, 97, 99, 106, 107, 110, 118, 119, 128, 204, 205, 213
Ambartsumov, Evgenii 79
Anatolii 164, 165, 169, 171, 181, 187, 192, 193, 194
Antonii (Khrapovitsky) 201
Anthony (Mel'nikov) 107, 109, 212
Athenagoros II 95, 96, 109, 112, 214
Averintsev, Sergei Sergeevich 14, 173, 176, 177, 178, 201, 208, 209, 225, 226

Baccolini, Gregorio 95
Baird-Smith, Robin 131
Basil, Bishop, see Alfred Herbert Osborne
Behr, Tatiana 20, 65, 76, 111, 118, 202, 225
Behr-Sigel, Elizabeth 148, 149, 150, 203, 222

Bel'sky, Mikhail, 28, 31, 70, 71, 207
Berdiaev, Nikolai Aleksandrovich 41, 42
Beriozova, Svetlana 63
Bernanos, Georges 152
Binns, John 218
Bloom, Boris Eduardovich 1, 2, 3, 5, 6, 9, 12, 18, 23, 32, 42, 57, 229
Bolshakov, Sergei Nikolaevich 47
Borisov, Aleksandr Il'ich 170
Borovoi, Vitalii Mikhailovich 92, 98, 99, 105, 208, 210
Bourdeaux, Michael 213, 218
Bouteneff, Vera Sergeevna 20
Brodsky, Iosif Aleksandrovich 178
Brown, Janet 135, 220
Bulgakov, Mikhail Afanasievich 151
Bulgakov, Sergei Nikolaevich 13, 29, 30, 31, 41, 42, 189
Camus, Albert 13, 152
Chaliapin, Feodor, see Shaliapin
Chambault, Lucien, see Denis

Chartres, Richard John Carew 182
Clément, Olivier, 100, 110, 126, 202, 204, 211, 213, 228
Coggan, Donald Frederick 126, 136, 138, 220, 221
Coleridge, Nicholas 157, 223
Combes, Raoul 37
Crow, Gillian 108, 113, 151, 186, 190, 194, 199, 213, 214, 217, 222, 228, 229
Curie, Maurice 23

Denis (Dionisii) 70, 72, 85, 98, 100, 101, 207

Ekonomtsev, Ioann 182, 209, 227
Elchaninov, Aleksandr 30
Elevferii 16, 91
Eliot, T.S. 152, 222
Elizaveta, Mother 76
Ellison, Gerald 220
Eltsin, Boris Nikolaevich 167, 174, 224
Eschliman, Nikolai 104, 106, 212
Eusebio, Dom 95, 211
Evdokimov, Pavel Nikolaevich 28, 30, 149
Evlogii 16, 25, 28, 29, 89, 94, 105, 109, 201, 202, 207, 209, 219

Fedotov, Georgii Petrovich 41
Fennel, Marina Nikolaevna 21, 37, 202, 204
Fernandez, *see* Ol'ga Il'inichna Scriabina
Fisher, Geoffrey Francis 70
Florensky, Pavel Aleksandrovich 139
Florovsky, Georgii Vasilevich vi, 31, 41, 43
Fondaminsky, Ilia Isidorovich 35
Fortounatto, Marianna Mikhailovna 47, 111, 125
Fortounatto, Michael Vsevolodovich 47, 110, 111, 116, 125, 179, 181, 197, 229
Fostiropoulos, Alexander 111, 192
Fostiropoulos, Patricia 111
Frank, Semen Liudwigovich 41, 48, 60
Frank, Tatyana Sergeevna 62

Garret, Anna Helena Ertel 20, 118, 128, 165, 202, 213
Gellhorn, Martha 135, 220
Genofeva, Sister 24, 203
Gibbes, Nicholas 47, 70
Gillet, Lev 28, 29, 30, 31, 41, 42, 45, 46, 57, 61, 70, 71, 203
Gogoleff, Mikhail 187
Gorbachev, Mikhail Sergeevich 160
Gregorie, Raymond 37
Grishin, Vadim 211
Gorodetskaia, Nadezhda Danilovna 28, 47

Hackel, Sergei 23, 72, 88, 110, 128, 152, 180, 203
Harrison, George 114
Havelacque, A. 37
Hayward, Derek 137, 220

Heenan, John Carmel 90
Hodgins, Michael 58, 59, 205
Huddleston, Ernest Urban Trevor 132

Iakov (Akkersdijk) 110
Iakovos (Virvos) 70, 207
Ilarion 165, 174, 180, 192, 193, 194, 224, 229
Il'in, Vladimir Nikolaevich 41
Ioann 103

James, William 24, 25
Johnson, Frank, 73-4, 222

Kallistos 148, 207
Katherine, Sister 50
Korchinska, Maria 63
Kaznovetsky, Anatolii 210, 211, 212
Khrushchev, Nikita Sergeevich 89, 245
Kiprian 92
Kirillova, Irina Arsen'evna 47, 118, 131, 151, 162
Klepinin, Dmitrii Andreevich 35
Kochetkov, Georgii 170
Konovalov, Sergei Aleksandrovich 47
Korenchevsky, Vladimir Georgievich 62, 116
Kornilii 88, 93, 94, 100, 101, 211
Kovalevsky, Evgraf Egrafovich 16, 28, 29
Kovalevsky, Maksim Evgrafovich 16, 28, 29, 203
Kovalevsky, Petr Evgrafovich 16, 29
Krivoshein, Vsevolod, *see* Vasilii
Krug, Georgii Ivanovich 17
Kuroedov, Vladimir Alekseevich 99, 104, 106
Kyrlezhev, Aleksandr Ivanovich 177, 178, 179, 226
Lampert, Evgenii Il'ich 47
Laski, Marghanita ix, x, 114
Lee, John 111, 118, 165, 179, 186, 195, 229
Lewis, C.S. 152
Lossky, Nikolai Onufrevich 35, 41
Lossky, Nikolai Vladimorovich 20, 30, 35, 37, 39, 41, 54, 100, 109, 204, 211, 213
Lossky, Veronica Konstantinovna 35, 36, 40, 54, 204
Lossky, Vladimir Nikolaevich 28, 31, 35, 41, 42, 43, 46, 72, 100
Luka, St 179

Maidanovich, Elena L'vovna xiii, xiv, 182, 202, 207, 209, 217
Maidanovich, Tatiana L'vovna xiii, xiv, 79, 128, 185, 199, 209, 222, 225
Makarios 55
Maria, Mother (Gysi) 50
Maria, Mother (Skobtsova) 30, 31, 35, 152, 203
Mark (Arndt) 170, 196, 225
Matveeva, Valentina Ivanovna 225
Maxwell, Robert 161
Medtner, Nikolai 61
Men', Aleksandr Vladimirovich 4
Meshcherskaia, Princess Antoinette 94
Meyendorf, John 180
Moberly, Elizabeth 174-5
Moisevitch, Benno 63

Nikodim 83, 85, 86, 87, 90, 92, 93, 94, 95, 98, 99, 100,

Index of Proper Names

103, 106, 143, 208, 210, 211, 217
Nikolai (Eremin) 49, 50, 56, 57, 59, 62, 63, 65, 66, 68, 69, 70, 71, 72, 77, 81, 84, 85, 86, 87, 98, 199, 205, 206, 207, 208, 209, 210
Nikolai (Iarusevich) 66, 74

Obolensky, Dmitrii 213
Osborne, Alfred Herbert 110, 124, 168, 169, 171, 181, 192, 193, 194, 195, 196, 197, 225
Ostapov, Daniil Andreevich 98, 99
Ouspensky, Leonid Aleksandrovich 16, 17, 31

Payne, Richard 130, 131, 219
Philaret (Denisenko) 168
Philaret (Vakhromeev) 143
Picot, Gaston 37
Pimen 102, 104, 106, 110, 118, 119, 157, 165, 224
Pitirim (Nechaev) 161, 223
Pitirim (Sviridov) 59
Pivovarov, Boris 165, 166
Platon 201
Platt, Stephen 174
Potter, Alford Philip 90
Powell, Enoch 130
Putin, Vladimir 196

Ramsden, Benedict 110, 213
Ramsey, Arthur Michael 87, 89, 92, 99, 105, 126, 134
Ratlevy, Francis Edmé Marie 37
Reverdin, Claude E. 64
Rodzianko, Vladimir, *see* Vasilii

Sadovnikova, Elena Iurevna xiii, 215, 228
Sartre, Jean-Paul 152
Satterthwaite, John Richard 84, 213
Schmemann, Alexander Dmitrievich viii, 174, 180
Scorer, Irene 224
Scorer, Peter vii, 76, 164, 179, 195, 198, 208, 224, 229
Scriabin, Aleksandr Nikolaevich x, 2, 22, 79
Scriabin, Nikolai Aleksandrovich 1, 2, 7, 22
Scriabina, Ksenia Nikolaevna vii, 2, 3, 4, 6, 8, 9, 10, 11, 12, 13, 18, 20, 27, 32, 33, 34, 35, 38, 40, 45, 53, 55, 65, 66, 67, 79, 88, 106, 198, 200, 204, 206, 229
Scriabina, Ol'ga Il'inichna vii, 2, 3, 6, 10, 18, 20, 33, 34, 35, 40, 53, 65, 67, 106, 115, 126, 196, 198, 229
Seraphim (Lukianov) 43, 46, 47, 48, 49, 204, 205
Seraphim (Nikitin) 119, 217
Sergii (Larin) 83, 84, 103, 210
Sergii (Shevich) 68, 84, 85, 94
Sergii (Starogorodsky) 16, 102, 107, 170, 201
Shaliapin, Fedor Ivanovich 51, 107
Shariatmadari, Mohammad Kazem 157
Shestov, Lev 41
Shmaina-Velikanova, Anna Il'inichna 224, 227, 228
Shumkin, Georgii vii, 11, 12, 15, 70, 94, 200, 202, 223
Silouan, St 19, 97

Silouan (Strizhkov) 94
Snycher, Ivan, *see* Ioann
Solzhenitsyn, Aleksandr Isaevich 118, 119, 143, 217, 218, 220, 221
Sophronii 63, 73, 76, 77, 95, 96, 109, 181, 208, 211
Sophronitskaia, Elena Aleksandrovna 79
Sophronitskaia, Roxana Vladimirovna 79
Spieler, Vsevolod 103, 106, 212
Stalin, Joseph 36, 52, 53, 82, 101, 119
Statov, Pavel 94

Thekla, Mother 50, 213
Theokritoff, Mikhail Ioannovich 47
Theokritoff, Vladimir Ioannovich 46, 47, 56, 118
Tikhon, St 172, 201
Timofeev, Vasilii Gavrilovich 46
Tito 56
Turintsev, Aleksandr Aleksandrovich 50, 65, 84, 85, 212

Ustinov, Peter 157
Utenkov, Evgenii Georgevich 80
Utenkova, Ekaterina Petrovna 80

Vasilii (Krivoshein) 70, 81, 85, 87, 93, 98, 100, 105, 209, 210, 211, 223
Vasilii (Osborne), *see* Alfred Herbert Osborne
Vasilii (Rodzianko) 57, 70, 89, 90, 91, 92, 94, 158, 210
Vasiliuk, Fedor Efimovich 174, 225, 227

Veniamin 16, 17, 88
Vilensky, Iurii Grigor'evich 179, 226
Visser 't Hooft, William Arnold 92
Vitalii 51, 170
Vladimir (Sabodan) 105
Vladimir (Tikhonitsky) 81
von Schlippe, Irina Yanovna 118, 185, 194, 217, 225, 228, 229

von Schlippe, Vladimir Borisovich 185, 228
Vysheslavtsev, Boris Petrovich 41

Waddams, Herbert Montague 57, 58, 61, 64, 70, 205, 206
Ware, Timothy, *see* Kallistos
Weil, Simone 152
Williams, Charles Walter Stansby 152

Williams, Rowan 196, 198

Yakunin, Gleb Pavlovich 104, 106, 212
Yeltsin, *see* Eltsin

Zenkovsky, Vasilii Vasilievich 41
Zernov, Nicholas 28, 41, 47, 109, 209, 213
Zernova, Militza Vladimirovna 28, 47, 162, 165

You may also be interested in

The Mystical Theology of the Eastern Church

Vladimir Lossky

Paperback ISBN: 978 0 227 67919 7
PDF ISBN: 978 0 227 90509 8
ePub ISBN: 978 0 227 90508 1

Lossky's great work on Eastern Orthodoxy covers the whole range of its spirituality and theology. Combining careful theology with the warmth of the deep personal devotion of the author, The Mystical Theology of the Eastern Church is the best introduction to Orthodox teaching and theology available. It provides a reliable and informative presentation of the theological spirit of the Eastern Church.

His account makes clear the profound theological differences underlying the practices of the East and West, and yet it is also an important contribution to ecumenism and to the life of Christian devotion. It brings together subjects that are more usually separated, asserting that there is no true mysticism that is not firmly rooted in theology, and no true theology that is not experienced, and therefore mystical. The tradition of the Eastern Church is presented as a mystical theology with doctrine and experience mutually conditioning each other.

You may also be interested in

Gazing on God
Trinity, Church and Salvation in Orthodox Thought and Iconography
Andreas Andreopoulos

Paperback ISBN: 978 0 227 17446 3
PDF ISBN: 978 0 227 90249 3
ePub ISBN: 978 0 227 90250 9

Gazing on God is an exposition of Orthodox theology viewed through the lens of the experience of the faithful. This new theological approach encourages a critical and constructive dialogue across denominational, historical and cultural divides.

We are led through an exhibition of icons, which are seen not only as objects of history and beauty, but also as tools to aid our understanding of theological thought. In this journey we discover that we need to change our expectations, and therefore admit that terms like 'understand' or 'know' are too limited when faced with the concept of the mystery of God. We may never be able to gaze on God completely, and grasp this mystery in its fullness. However, the theology of experience will help us on our journey and we may see that God is gazing on us instead.

Gazing on God breaks away from the typical boundaries of introductory theological and iconological works and is essential reading for scholars interested in Eastern Christian theology, but also for anyone interested in Christian spirituality.

You may also be interested in

Divine Essence and Divine Energies

Ecumenical Reflections on the Presence of God in Eastern Orthodoxy

Edited by
C. Athanasopoulos and C. Schneider

Paperback ISBN: 978 0 227 17386 2
PDF ISBN: 978 0 227 90012 3
ePub ISBN: 978 0 227 90008 6

The result of a colloquium organised by the Institute for Orthodox Christian Studies (Cambridge, UK), *Divine Essence and Divine Energies* offers a rich repository of diverse opinion about the distinction between essence and energy in Orthodox Christianity – a doctrine which lies at the heart of the often fraught fault line between East and West, and which, in this book, inspires a lively dialogue between the contributors.

The contents of the book revolve around several key questions: In what way were the Aristotelian concepts of ousia and energeia used by the Church Fathers, and to what extent were their meanings modified in the light of the Christological and Trinitarian doctrines? What are the differences and similarities between the notions of divine presence and participation in seminal Christian writings, and what is the relationship between the essence-energy distinction and Western ideas of divine presence?

A valuable addition to the dialogue between Eastern and Western Christianity, this book will be of great interest to any reader seeking a rigorously academic insight into the wealth of scholarly opinion about the essence-energy distinction.

You may also be interested in

The One and the Three
Nature, Person and Triadic Monarchy in the Greek and Irish Patristic Tradition
Chrysostom Koutloumousianos

Paperback ISBN: 978 0 227 17514 9
PDF ISBN: 978 0 227 90417 6
ePub ISBN: 978 0 227 90419 0

The One and the Three explores parallels between Byzantine and early Irish monastic traditions, finding in both a markedly trinitarian theology founded on God's contemplation and ascetic experience. Chrysostom Koutloumousianos refutes modern theological theses that affect ecclesiology, and contrasts current schools of theological thought with patristic theology and anthropology, in order to approach the meaning and reality of unity and otherness within the Triadic Monad and the cosmos. He explores such topics as the connection between nature and person, the esoteric dimension of the Self, the relation and dialectic of impersonal institutions and personal charisma, and perennial monastic virtues as ways to unity in diversity.

"*Fr Chrysostom offers here a rich and penetrating analysis of the ways in which the mysteries of the Trinity and Incarnation intersect with ecclesial life. This is a work of great learning and profound reflection, which will merits deep study and careful attention.*"
John Behr, Dean and Professor of Patristics, St Vladimir's Orthodox Theological Seminary, New York

You may also be interested in

Purification of Memory
A Study of Orthodox Theologians from a Catholic Perspective
Ambrose Mong

Paperback ISBN: 978 0 227 17513 2
PDF ISBN: 978 0 227 90414 5
ePub ISBN: 978 0 227 90416 9

Although its various bodies boast at least 300 million members, the Eastern Orthodox Church is widely perceived among those of other denominations as an exotic branch of the faith, shrouded in mysticism and a misunderstanding exacerbated by the longstanding Eastern-Western split. In *Purification of Memory*, Ambrose Mong casts light on the true nature of Orthodox theology, illuminating the thinking of eight distinguished modern Orthodox theologians who have made important contributions on topics as ecclesiology, ecumenism, Christology, and Mariology. Approaching the work of John Meyendorff, Nicholas Afanasiev, John Zizioulas, Georges Florovsky, Sergius Bulgakov, Vladimir Lossky, Nicolas Berdyaev, and Jaroslav Pelikan from an ecumenical standpoint, Mong deftly draws comparisons with the theology of their Roman Catholic counterparts to reveal points on which the two traditions have much more in common than either side will always admit.

The author interweaves these comparisons with a fascinating exposition of the history of the schism between the Eastern and Western Churches to demonstrate decisively their shared heritage which could, and should, serve as a basis for reunification.

Available now with more excellent titles in Paperback, Hardback, PDF and ePub formats from James Clarke & Co

www.jamesclarke.co